Learning from

Wonderful Lives

Lessons from the study of well-being
brought to life by the personal stories
of some much admired individuals

Dr N.V.K. Baylis

This first edition is published by

Cambridge Well-Being Books Ltd, Cambridge, England.

Published by Cambridge Well-Being Books Ltd
6 Pearce Close, Newnham in Cambridge, England, CB3 9LY.

www.CambridgeWellBeingBooks.com

ISBN: 0-9550503-0-8   First Edition.   160,000 words.

Printed by The Burlington Press, Cambridge, who worked on this project with outstanding passion and professionalism. Visit www.Burlingtonpress.co.uk

All paper used in the making of this book has been produced from sources respecting the natural environment.

Typeset with consummate care and consideration by Carolyn Griffiths and Donna Pedley of Textype Typsetters, Cambridge. Email textype@btconnect.com

The dust-jacket's beautiful landscape is from the painting, *Blaze of Glory*, that is the original work of the acclaimed contemporary English artist, Lawrence Coulson. I am grateful for his permission to reproduce his art. Visit www.halcyongallery.com

For advice on book-jacket artwork creation, thanks to the expertise of Dale Tomlinson.

Website design and technical support by the multi-talented www.ClaudeSchneider.com

I apologise for any accidental hurt or offence caused to any individual or organisation mentioned within this book, by any inaccuracies or misprints or omissions it may contain. I have tried my best to benevolently and correctly represent individuals and the current level of scientific understanding about well-being, and to work from reliable sources.

I pledge ten percent of my income from this book to 'The Wonderful Lives Benevolent Fund' that will foster well-being in a charitable way far beyond these pages.
Please visit www.NickBaylis.com to find out more.

At Cambridge University, Dr Nick Baylis is a Well-Being Scientist studying the hows and whys of wonderful lives, looking for the most reliable routes to happiness, good health, a sense of accomplishment, and lasting companionship. Nick also enjoys working as a coach and psychologist with individuals of all ages. This is his first book.

www.NickBaylis.com

Table of Contents

* * *

I've designed the following chapters
to be enjoyed in whatever order
you may choose to read them.

* * *

PART ONE

Partnering-Up with Good People

Why our loving friends and soul-mates are so important. How to prioritise our partnerships. The essentials of finding and fostering a special relationship.

Finding a profound sense of purpose in life. Following our heart and being stronger than the disapproval. Feeling happier with who we are and playing to our signature strengths. Age isn't important if we keep flexible in our thinking.

Respecting our instincts and subliminal signals. Making the most of our eye-contact and voice, our clothes and cooking, our dancing and sensuality. Taking it slowly. Paying heed to our intuitions and sixth sense.

How mentoring can make all the difference in working or personal life. How to use Socratic Questioning and gentle teaching to bring out the best in someone. The essentials of raising happy youngsters. The rich rewards of voluntary work.

PART TWO

Becoming an Expert
in Our Favourite Pursuits

We don't need special gifts nor star genes to become really good at
something, but we do need lots of practice, heart-felt passion, loving
support, and insider know-how. Here are some inspiring lives, past
and present, to show us the way.

Focusing precisely on what we really want to learn. Enriching our
training environment. The essential skills for rapid improvement.
The importance of enjoying it. Being clear about our priorities in
life.

Whether it's college exams or professional diplomas, business presentations or sporting performances, the same key principles apply.
Likewise for coping well on social occasions and big dates, or with
interviews and negotiations. Here's how to feel comfortable and in
control. Perfection is the enemy not only of high performance but of
happiness. Optimism and exuberance are far more helpful than fear.
Learning self-hypnosis can be a powerful ally. Don't let success sink
us.

Not realising how we, too, can get really good at something . . . and
not turning off that flickering tv.

PART THREE

Helping Mind and Body
to Thrive and Flourish

The fundamental importance of sufficient sleep, broad daylight, physical activity, and smart nutrition. How to beat dieting and feel good inside our body. Finding out about the many ways to be beautiful.

Changing even our smallest routines can open up the routes to profound progress. How to break unhelpful habits and build rewarding ones. Harness our anger and frustration so they carry us forward. Defuse our rage and fear. How to use psychological time-travel to motivate ourselves.

Doing is far more enjoyable than owning. Have we got the right ratio between work and recuperation? Preventing exhaustion and burn-out by creating balance and variety. Making the most of time-off and time-out. Relaxation techniques and the restorative powers of singing, humour, and the natural environment.

How to take swift and effective action against physical and psychological troubles, including innovative ways to tackle depression, anxiety, phobia, shyness and emotional trauma, as well as migraines, digestive disorders and premenstrual syndrome. Let's consider alternative approaches, not least the remarkable capacity of Clinical Hypnosis to help a whole range of ills, from back-aches to skin complaints, from chronic fatigue to sleep disturbance, and from fertility problems to pregnancy pains.

PART FOUR

Choosing and Changing
our Journeys and Life Directions

Some Final Pages and a Starting Place

Further Information

PREFACE

Wonderful Lives

The extraordinary research findings about the hows and whys of life going well, are illustrated in this book by the voices of some remarkable people.

A wonderful life doesn't mean a life that's trouble-free or without fault or flaw. It means it's wonderful that the person is still smiling and going strong after all they've been through. And that's not to say these ships won't see high seas and storms in the future, or appear to sink beneath the waves for a while. But for now, at time of writing, they look like ships in full sail.

It was through wanting to understand how such individuals managed to cope so well, that I embarked upon this exploration. I'm hoping these personalities represent a rich mixture of women and men in all walks of life, and I chose these particular individuals because they so memorably illustrate what the best science is beginning to discover about well-being. Their unique experiences may not *prove* a point, because one example or even 50 can't do that, but they can certainly demonstrate it.

It's their lasting happiness and accomplishments that are the focus of my attention, and their fame is only relevant because it means their lives have been recorded in biographies and interviews, and in that sense are open to study by all of us.

Some of the names you'll recognise fondly, others not; but be prepared for some surprises because their personal stories go well beyond their public faces.

It's heartening to know that if we look among the most inspiring people in our own everyday lives . . . perhaps our closest friends and family . . . we can see these very same principles at work; and we can better appreciate how and when their outstanding qualities came about. I am reminded of the words on a stained glass window in The Queen's University, Belfast:

"Their deeds are written not on stone, but on the hearts of men."

The heart has its reasons
of which reason does not know

Blaise Pascal
1623–1662

Nick's Introduction

What's this book all about?

The Royal Society

The Study of Wonderful Lives

Who am I?

And for whom did I write this book?

How do we know it will work?

* * *

What's this book all about?

Each week for quite some time now, I've been writing a column on *The Science of Happiness* for *The Times* newspaper's *Saturday Magazine*. It's been a privilege to share with a million British readers, my passion to understand how lives progress. But I've always wanted to explain how those seemingly individual ideas fit into the bigger picture of what I call *'the study of wonderful lives'*. So I set out to recount the findings from my past ten years of research, writing and teaching at Cambridge University.

By 'wonderful lives', I mean lives that are happy and healthy, helpful and good-hearted – in ways that are profound and enduring not superficial or fleeting. I mean leading a life that is not only good for you and me, but also good for the people for whom we care, and among whom we live and work. Being the sort of person who's a pleasure to have around, and who makes a wonderful difference to whatever they're part of.

Our setting out to see what we can make of ourselves is by no means a selfish pursuit, because if we're happier in what we do, our high spirits will benefit everyone around us. Likewise, if we continue to develop, we become ever more capable of doing good.

What's more, far from being a luxury or self-indulgence, positive emotions such as happiness are a powerful ally in the prevention and remedy of physical and psychological problems, as well as better enabling us to thrive and flourish in all arenas of our life. Putting happiness at the top of our to-do list makes pretty good sense.

This isn't just wishful thinking, either. Happier people really do suffer less illness and lead much longer and more productive lifetimes. And we're not talking fractions here. A study of 180 nuns revealed that despite the Sisters leading remarkably similar lives, the ones who wrote the happiest self-reports when age 22, went on to live a full nine years longer than their less positive companions.

That's not to say we should anaesthetise our painful feelings, because feeling miserable is most often a healthy response, simply Nature's way of telling us to make important improvements. The trouble is, we don't always know how to generate wholesome, sustainable happiness, and sometimes our default response is to reach for a quick-fix in one form or another. So here's our chance to cultivate our home-grown, evergreen, deeply rooted happiness, without the hangovers. All the evidence suggests that how well we play the hand we're dealt, can make all the difference to how life feels; but willingness isn't enough, practical know-how is definitely needed.

To this end, I take inspiration from the first-rate research work that is now being done to understand the workings of enjoyable lives. For instance, the 2002 Nobel Laureate, Daniel Kahneman of Princeton University, now devotes himself to the science of well-being. The professor ended a captivating lecture in Washington D.C. by declaring "Happiness *is* a skill" – which I was more than pleased to hear, because it's on account of *happiness being a skill*, that we can learn it, we can practice it, and we can improve it.

It's been about two thousand four hundred years since Aristotle began pondering such things, and yet you and I are still wrestling with it. And by my reckoning we always will be, because life isn't about looking for final answers, it's about learning to be satisfied with things getting better, clearer, simpler – it's about you and I being pleased with a sense of progress and of evolution on a personal scale. What's more, I think two and a half millennia pretty much qualifies the determined investigation of wonderful lives as a truly classical Odyssey, so let's enjoy the journey.

The Royal Society

The Royal Society in London was founded in 1660 and is arguably the world's leading team of scientists. At last count, it had 67 living Nobel Prize Winners in its Fellowship. So you can imagine how delighted I was when back in November 2003, The Royal Society invited my two Cambridge University colleagues and I to host its first ever conference on *The Science of Well-Being* – the systematic study of lives going well.

Men and women came from some of the finest research institutions across Britain, Canada and Australia, as well as France, Italy,

Spain, Germany and the USA. These people were professors of science who don't just theorise about life, they systematically test their ideas in the real world. For three whole days, I listened hard and scribbled fast. It's not that we think there's a right way to live, or some sure-fire formula for success, it's just that some particular attitudes, skills and experiences do undoubtedly increase the likelihood of things working out rather well. What was so remarkable about this conference was that many of these individuals had never met before, and were little aware of each other's work. Bringing them together in the same room meant we could begin to build an holistic understanding of well-being that embraced all of life's essential elements.

And in this book, I've tried to achieve the very same thing: weaving together the newest ideas on life going well: a healthy mind, a healthy body, and a sense of love and meaning.

This new science of well-being has arrived not a moment too soon, because in the aftermath of the Second World War, psychology very rightly poured itself into healing the injured. And this has all been to good ends, as many psychological illnesses are now curable or at least treatable. But 60 years on, we now realise that we can learn a great deal from looking not just at people running into problems, but at people who've found paths forward. This is based on the simple principle that if we learn what works, perhaps we can spread the word.

In our 21st century world, where the demands upon every individual are accelerating faster than ever before, we're clearly in need of some helpful new approaches.

The Study of Wonderful Lives

The Study of Wonderful Lives and The Science of Well-Being are one and the same subject. As a Well-Being Scientist, I'm endeavouring to look at the world in at least two ways.

First, I try to see *the bigger picture* of what can help our all-round well-being, and this means taking into account the major arenas of our life, such as our body, brain, relationships and working world, as well as our man-made environments and the natural landscapes.

Second, I try to appreciate the relationship of the different parts in that bigger picture, which means that if we make changes to one part of our life, it will require us to readjust the other parts if we're to keep things in balance and make lasting progress. Thinking and behaving holistically like this brings great benefits. If we support our efforts in one arena of life, with simultaneous adjustments in several others, the progress in the first arena will be all the greater for it. It's the very same principle that allows the effects of one vitamin to be enhanced if it can work in synergy with all the other vitamins. This is why such integrated and all-round thinking can make major and lasting improvements. (Continued overleaf . . .)

The power of such a united approach very probably explains why Nobel Prizes so often go to those who cross-over from one discipline to another: by taking one set of ideas into a whole new subject, they can see things with fresh eyes ... and they can make unexpected connections.

This all serves to remind us that it's not only a scientific approach we need for the study of well-being. The surveys and experiments aren't enough. We also need the know-how and insights from the creative arts and humanities and every discipline that can explore and portray how positively human life can be led ... because living life is an infinitely interwoven process.

In respect of this, The Study of Wonderful Lives comprises at least eight contributing areas of exploration, as shown in the pie-chart on the previous page. Together, these make for a better understanding of lives that are happy and healthy, helpful and good-hearted.

Who am I?

What my Mum would have said:
"Nicholas was a chubby baby, but very little trouble." With some prompting, Mum might have added "I'm hoping he'll get a proper job soon, and have lots of children."

The sort of thing my friends of many years would add:
"By some unfortunate oversight at St. Albans Boys School, the classical subjects of *happiness*, *women*, *money*, *speaking*, and *life-in-general* got left off the curriculum. Either that or we were bunking-off class when the teacher finally got around to them one Friday afternoon. In the years that followed, those teeny-weeny gaps in our understanding of the world caused us all a few problems, and Nick was no exception. From the age of 10 upwards, he had a stutter so bad that sometimes he couldn't even say his own name, and his first university threw him out for failing his exams. By the time he was 25, he was a hopelessly incompetent waiter causing havoc with

bowls of soup and the cake-trolley in unsuspecting restaurants."

What my Curriculum Vitae says:
I was a volunteer teaching Creative Writing in the high-security surroundings of Feltham Young Offender Prison, when it dawned
upon me how much we knew about lives that ran aground, but how
little we knew about lives that went well. So I set up a charitable
mentoring project called *Trail-Blazers* to help the young guys find
jobs upon their release, and then I turned all my attentions to
studying lives that flourish. I earned my Ph.D. from Cambridge
University exploring that very same subject and straight away
started a not-for-profit research project to better understand *How
to Achieve Your Goals in Life, and How to Enjoy the Journey.* With
support from the likes of Reuters and Nike, I interviewed 200 of the
most accomplished individuals of their generation in many walks of
life. Since then, here at Cambridge, I've helped my colleagues create
the newly emerging field we call The Science of Well-Being.

And for whom did I write this book?

This book is meant for all of us who want to know how good life can
feel, both for ourselves and those we care for. It's meant for any brave
soul willing to change the way they do things day to day.

Perhaps the true measure of oneself is the way we've chosen
to square up to life – the journeys we've thought were worthwhile
and the people we've gathered around us as travelling companions.
We should also bear in mind the particular challenges we've had to
overcome.

It doesn't matter what age we are or where we're starting out
from, the same principles and approaches still apply. No period in
our life is simply a rehearsal for any other, and every stage is equally
valuable. What's more, no period in our life is predetermined to be
happier than any other, despite everything our parents probably told
us about our school and college days.

I'm assuming that as well as learning from your own mistakes, you'd like to learn from other people's. Even better, you'd like to learn from anyone who has made life look easy and enjoyable. *What exactly was it they were doing so well?* And it was this very thought that prompted this book's study of 50 remarkable personalities. Many strategies for dealing with life don't ever get written down, they get passed on by word-of-mouth or by good example. This can mean that if we're not lucky enough to have particular experiences or people in our lives, we can miss out on some key lessons.

That's why the new study of wonderful lives can prove so helpful. But these suggestions are only meant as general principles, not specific rules or the only way to do things. It's an opportunity to compare notes. Each idea is simply a tool you can adjust to fit your own circumstances.

How do we know it will work?

It may not. All we can do is increase the likelihood of things going well.

This book is built on the understanding that learning to live happily is a skill, just like swimming. And like swimming, it can go from being about sheer survival, to being highly pleasurable, all depending on our level of competence.

The skills, strategies, route-plans and philosophies that I'm about to present are drawn from the world's most extraordinary research, some of which has followed hundreds of accomplished individuals for sixty years or more. Let's see what such lives can teach us. The spirit of this approach is captured by the words of Sir Isaac Newton who, in a letter to a friend in 1725, wrote: "If I have seen further, it is by standing on the shoulders of giants."

So it is that I've gathered the most promising ideas and distilled them down to fit within these pages. I've filled my pockets with them, like they were maps and a compass, cake and hot chocolate, and I've set off on the trail. By reading on from here, you and I become companions on the journey.

* * *

Making the Most of This Book:
Some Guiding Principles

The following principles . . . strategies or approaches . . . whatever we care to call them, have shown themselves time and again to be guiding lights in all of the wonderful lives I've studied these past ten years.

That's not to say they're the only principles that can help good things happen, but they seem a fine place to start. Their aim is to help us live with happiness in our heart and a satisfying sense of progress.

What follows below is how these principles can also guide us in making the most of this book, because they unite and bind its chapters.

Partner-Up

Partner-up whenever possible . . . for the companionship that halves the troubles, doubles the joys, and improves the journey. *(This is the opposite of isolating ourselves.)*

Partnering-up is by far the best way to make enjoyable and

satisfying progress. We are far happier and far more productive when we team-up with the right person, rather than travelling alone. So let's be thinking of the special souls with whom to share encouragement, compare notes, and confide in.

Our companion hasn't got to be a best friend, just someone we have a good feeling about. In any case, we will need to spread the load between two or more individuals, a different friend for each endeavour. Who could we team-up with for which activity? Who would we be well-suited to working with on which particular mission?

It takes guts to ask if someone is interested, but it's a small price to pay for the likely benefits of hooking up. To hell with the taboos and embarrassment. Self-help is not the best way forward; partnering-up is.

Invest in Real Life

Invest in real life . . . so as to deepen our intimate relationships with the people, skills and places that mean the most to us. *(It's quite the opposite of running from problems and resorting to the quick-fixes and superficial experiences which can compromise our most valued relationships.)*

Let's not simply dream about all the good things we'd wish to do with our everyday lives, or watch them on the telly. Let's take a pad and paper and work out some step by step plans to how we're going to make things happen. There's no daydream that can beat the pleasure of living things for real.

And let's bear in mind that anyone trying to sell us 'instant happiness' is little more than a drugs-dealer. Happiness worth having is the warm glow that comes from investing ourselves in the world around us, come what may. It cannot be passively consumed, or gulped down like a sugary drink. Happiness must be created by our own ingenuity.

Enjoy the Journey

Enjoy the journey . . . because a good journey is a worthy goal in itself. *(It's quite the opposite of spoiling the journey for the sake of the destination.)*

We always do a better job of things when we're enjoying ourselves, largely because good feelings lead to positive actions. Start with a chapter that takes your fancy and plunge in. I've designed things to work this way. All you'll need is a mug of hot chocolate and your favourite pen to cross-out what you don't like, and highlight what you do. This is *your* book now, not mine, and it's meant to keep you company on buses and beaches and at bedtime.

Take it slowly. Improving how our life feels isn't selfish, it's vital. It helps us get on so much better with the world around us. So let's not make it a rush or a race. There's no competition in life with anyone but ourselves: How well can we live it? Let's listen to our heartbeat, our positive, creative passions, and wonder what they might be telling us about how to proceed. I'm hoping you'll play to your signature strengths . . . your distinctive set of skills that bring you the most pleasure. Why not see this book as a rough map, and let happiness be both your compass and your timekeeper. Go at a pace and by a path that puts a smile on your face.

Learn to Thrive in the Face of Adversity

Learn to thrive in the face of adversity . . . by using our pains to drive our passions. *(This is quite the opposite of trying to anaesthetise our painful feelings.)*

Life is beautiful and difficult in equal measure, and the wonder comes from how well we cope with it. Our skills and strategies for coping will determine whether we are ground down by the problems which everyday life will throw at us, or whether we are able to channel the painful feelings to carry us forward. What will be our alternative goals and routes so we don't get blocked? How can we become ever more versatile and inventive, and learn to duck and weave? How can we occasionally step back and see the bigger picture of how we could be living in six months time?

It seems to me that life entails countless problems and tragedies, joys and treasures, for each and every one of us. From time to time, it's frightening stuff; and all we can do is try not to let the fear paralyse us; at least not for very long. And if The Study of Wonderful Lives had a theme tune, *Singing in the Rain* would be a prime contender. We could all do with knowing just a little more about how to keep our spirits up – how to dance, whistle and sing no matter the frequent showers.

Explore and Experiment

Explore and experiment with how we think and behave so as to find more satisfying ways to lead our life. *(It's quite the opposite of being passive, rigid or blinkered.)*

This book is not trying to be an A to Z of all we know about how life works, nor a 16-step guide to perfection. It's aiming to inspire action and provide some tools to get us started. Some of the ideas you'll have come across before, others not. We need to foster our spirit of exploration and find out what works for us in our particular situation at this time in our life. We could try a new course of action for a couple of weeks, then review and revise it in the light of our road-test. We then put this revised version into practice for another two weeks, and carry on like this in pursuit of meaningful progress. In this, we need to be more than open-minded (that's too passive), we need to be adventure-minded. In exploring our true passions, it helps to be playful, questioning, versatile in our thinking, and quick to innovate.

Harmonise our Mind and Body, our Conscious and Sub-Conscious

By co-ordinating all of our internal resources like this, we greatly increase our power to progress. *(This gentle, harmonious approach is quite the opposite of us trying to bully our body and emotions.)*

Having our mind and body work well together is vital to

feeling at home inside of ourselves. It requires us to appreciate how our body can express and heal our thoughts and emotions, for instance through dance or dynamic physical activity. Likewise, our mind can learn to heal our body, perhaps through developing our capacity for self-hypnosis. So real and active is this relationship that it's likely that more than half of the problems that take us to our doctor are 'psychosomatic illnesses', which means very real physical symptoms that are unconsciously caused by our psychological unhappiness or stress. The bottom line is, if our mind is not happy, it will express this through our body, in the same way our body lets our mind know if it's in pain. Put another way, psychosomatic symptoms occur when our psychological distress takes bodily form. The good news is, Mother Nature meant our body to care for our brain, and vice versa, and an appreciation of this benevolent relationship can help make our psychosomatic distress-signals a far less common occurrence.

(I explain a lot more about this vital subject in the chapter called *Nick's Special Topic* which is the last chapter of my book.)

Our all-round well-being and progress in life will also benefit greatly from helping our conscious and sub-conscious goals and strategies work hand in hand. Once again, learning and developing the skill of self-hypnosis is just one means by which to achieve such a happy alliance, as is being sensitive and responsive to our essential drives and heart-felt passions . . . channeling these productively rather than bottling them up. Our sub-conscious is a store-house of all the habits and assumptions acquired from our previous experiences in life, kept in a part of our mind that is ordinarily out of reach of our self-awareness. It's the tug of war that can sometimes occur, between our present-day conscious wishes and our out-dated sub-conscious fears, that accounts for why it can be so difficult to bring about lasting change in ourselves. But once we fully recognise this relationship, we can begin to unify both parts of our mind and help them pull happily in the same direction.

Make Connections

Make connections . . . by seeing the bigger picture, and how every one thing is joined to every other. *(It's quite the opposite of tunnel vision, or treating our life as a collection of barely related parts.)*

Let's appreciate the seamless canvas that underlies the bigger picture: the threads and pathways that connect one part of our life with another.

Between how we treat ourselves and how other people treat us.

Between how well we work and how well we recuperate.

Between how we use our body and how our mind feels.

If we can see the inter-connectedness, then we're far more likely to be considerate of what effects our thoughts and actions will have on our wider lives and the world around us. We'll be better able to promote harmony.

We can make connections between our present day and our future three months hence, simply by conjuring vivid images in our mind's eye to show ourselves progressing. These images, if positive and achievable, help give our sub-conscious mind something to aim for.

The Study of Wonderful Lives is, by its very nature, a cross-border approach to living, keen to include new possibilities and fresh liaisons. After all, the mind and body, the arts and sciences, may stand apart in academic and professional training, but in our real life they walk hand in hand at all times. So, just for example, we could turn to any page of this book, and then, without losing our place, to a page in a quite different chapter. How could we connect the ideas on either page so as to create a new possibility in how we approach things? What bridges can we build? Because the better we become at seeing the possible connections, then the more versatile we will be in our thinking, the stronger our problem solving, and the more pleasure we'll find in everyday things.

When it comes to how we lead our lives, the whole is far greater than the sum of the parts. All-round well-being requires us not only to *appreciate* the rich relationships interwoven in the world around us, *but to create them.*

* * *

I dedicate this book
to my much loved friends and family
who mean all the world to me,
and to wonderful lives
wherever we might find them.

Learning from
Wonderful Lives

PART ONE

Partnering-Up
with Good People

Companionship comes First

Teaming-up is the number one route to happiness

Happiness is a game better enjoyed when there are two or more play-ers, and the breadth and depth of our personal relationships are crucial to our well-being. If we have a small handful of soul mates and confi-dants, neighbourly neighbours and supportive co-workers, we are far less likely to experience sadness, loneliness, low self-respect, and problems with eating and sleeping. In fact, good companionship is so beneficial to health, that it's difficult to say which is riskier: smoking 20 cigarettes a day, or *not* belonging to any teams, clubs or societies that allow us to brush shoulders and share life with other good souls.

These research findings come from Professor Bob Putnam, the former head of Harvard's JFK School of Government. He analysed 500,000 intimately detailed interviews which revealed how people lived their lives day to day. In so doing, Professor Putnam has popu-larised the term 'Social Capital' by which he means all the mutual support, trust, and good-will networks we have accumulated in our social bank account by dint of our personal relationships and community involvement.

And Professor Putnam is not alone in prizing such things so highly. The Harvard Study of Adult Development analysed 824 American lifetimes as they unfolded over 60 years. One major conclusion was this: that our ability to 'take others inside of us' by learning from their strengths and by caring for ourselves as they would care for us, is a key skill common to all the most healthy, accomplished and satisfying lives. Such individuals decorated their rooms with photographs of loved and loving people, and filled their diaries with sociable activities, notably ones that didn't centre around alcohol. The message of those lifetimes was clear: no matter our age, it is vital that we cultivate a strong and richly varied social network. And no matter whether we count ourselves outgoing or introverted, we should boldly join groups in which we can eventually feel welcome and valued. It's poignant that the veteran BBC wildlife scientist, David Attenborough, observes that "No amount of wildlife can make up for human company."

Let the pain of loneliness prompt intimacy

Loneliness tells us so much about the human spirit, it should be no surprise that the sorrow of enforced isolation is a key theme in classical tales from *Robinson Crusoe* to *Cinderella*, from the *Count of Monte Cristo* to *Bridget Jones's Diary*.

Firstly, loneliness reminds us of nature's insistence that we make progress in our relationship with the world around us. After all, loneliness is our hunger not simply for company, but for closeness, for something deeply shared. What's more, this intimacy we crave requires not just knowing but also understanding and caring, and this can be for the place we call home or the skills of our vocation, just as much as for another living creature. Seen this way, rather than fearing or resenting the pain of loneliness, we might regard it as a benevolent feeling, and a reminder to us that pain is not in itself a bad thing. On the contrary, nature has helpfully endowed us with two systems for motivation: the pains which repel us, and the pleasures which attract us. So when it comes to loneliness, nature punishes us for being too detached, and rewards us for getting to know things better. (We might also ponder how those rare individuals who have too little sensitivity to pain and the fear that foreshadows it, are usually dead before they're even 30.)

Let's be cautious, then, of anything that dulls or masks our various pains lest we reduce the sense of purpose they can muster. It is by refusing to run from the pain of fear, that we overcome our phobias; and it is only by suffering through exercises after an injury, that we restore our strength and flexibility. Rather than them being stop or go signals or even signposts, our emotions, both pleasurable and painful, are better viewed as forms of energy, energy that it's up to us to channel into activities that complement our well-being rather than compromise it. For instance, to meet the challenge of our loneliness, we could engage our attention with a fully involving task. Equally, an excellent film will take us so deeply into its world that we'll care about the characters and all that's at stake. Likewise, we rarely feel lonely when walking in the countryside because of the connection to our natural world, just as being alone with the peace and tranquillity of an historical place can elicit a strong sense of empathy with the lives that were once lived there.

The very notion that it's a good thing to deepen our worldly relationships, reflects yet another fundamental aspect of our human nature, because happiness itself can touch us on quite different levels. At the most superficial, if we passively consume a pleasure such as food or a glass of wine, it might quench an appetite but the effect is fleeting. By comparison, if we actively invest our mental or physical abilities as we do when working happily at something or reading a good book, this is deeply satisfying and can leave us glowing for days after. But the most profound happiness of all, is the closeness we call love for a person or place or vocation, and these intimate relationships can imbue our whole lifetime with purpose and meaning. Let's use our loneliness to inspire such loves.

Loving friends

My father recently gave me *All Quiet On The Western Front*, the story of a First World War German soldier and his comrades serving in the trenches of Northern Europe. I told myself I'd save reading it for a holiday treat, but thankfully I glanced at the opening pages and, after a long evening in front of a log fire, I'd finished it. The book's heart-rending insights persuaded me to reconsider the nature of our loving friendships. I realised how it's all too easy to take our closest companions for granted and to squeeze them around the pressing demands of our everyday life. But this laissez-faire attitude is quite unwarranted given their extraordinary role in our physical and psychological well-being. A loving friendship halves the troubles and doubles the joys and by doing so makes life's journey all the more enjoyable. That much we know already; but let's also appreciate that there are dimensions of our personality that would not blossom half so well, if at all, without the catalyst of the right relationships. For this reason, our best friends help create who we are, and our growth and progression is reflected in who we let go, who we deepen our roots with, and who we reach out to embrace. As with so many facets of life, a rich variety is a very healthy thing, whether in terms of our thoughts, nutrition, or exercise, and likewise it should be no surprise if our dearest companions are quite different from each other.

Eleanor Roosevelt, who was a U.S. First Lady and the key architect of the Universal Declaration of Human Rights, observes another key feature of the strong personal friendship: "Human relationships, like life itself, can never remain static. They grow or they diminish. But, in either case, they change. Our emotional interests, our intellectual pursuits, our personal preoccupations, all change. So do those of our friends. So the relationship that binds us together must change, too."

What distinguishes these rare individuals as so important, is that they feel our pains and pleasures, our setbacks and triumphs, as if they were their own. For this reason they will encourage us in our best endeavours, and haul us up if they think we're letting ourselves down. Their level of empathy is matched by their level of intimacy with how we think. After all, in the company of a true friend, we dare to think aloud without the need to edit ourselves. These privileged insights enable our ally to question the very process of our thoughts and to suggest better ways of approaching things. This presents a crucial opportunity, but only a kindred spirit will take it. It is because they think we're worth it, a true confidante will dare to risk our irritable indignation, when less caring friends would shy away. But the health of our relationship is reflected not in how hotly we argue, but in how well we make up afterwards. Best friends may bruise each other, but they are loathe to bear a grudge.

What a good friend isn't, is simply a conspirator who lets us moan on about things. They know that simply acting as a sandbag to soak up our fury or despair is doing us no favours. What they want instead, is to know what positive measures we're going to take to improve a situation. After all, blowing our top over something as a means of letting off steam has no evidence to recommend it. What we need is someone to help us see the different perspectives and remedial possibilities.

In respect of all the trouble they take with us, we could encourage these priceless individuals in their own hopes and passions, and we could challenge their inhibiting thoughts and behaviours. Our actions will work better than words, so we could make more time for shared activities. We could also introduce our friends to each other in the hope of creating some unexpected partnerships. At the very least, let's be sure our closest companions have an honoured place on our list of priorities.

We know loving relationships are life's priority, so what can go wrong?

Very often we've got into unhelpful habits as we've grown up, and our natural sense of priorities has got itself out of order.

And how did that happen?

Well . . . happiness is not the reason for living prioritised by *all* parents; sometimes, a parent can put all the emphasis on *achievement*. With the best of intentions, they drive their girls and boys towards educational and professional accolades, because they themselves were brought up to believe that ever-increasing income and status are the surest routes to finally feeling that all is well with life.

Such mums and dads can accidentally make their love and approval conditional upon their children achieving the appointed goals and standards. Rather than encouragement and praise for progress in all its forms, any unapproved interests or abilities are either neglected or squashed so as to maximise the parental agenda. There is no malice in this, only misunderstanding, but one legacy of the 'quid pro quo' relationship is yet another generation of adults who feel worthless if they stop bringing home the A-grades in one form or another. This in turn leads to the climate of loneliness in which singletons and married couples struggle to compete with the lure of overwrought career goals – their own and their partner's.

Such a climate dominates modern-day living, but hope is at hand:

By studying the development of several hundred lives, we can observe that once an individual has even modest means by which to live, additional money and status don't have the happiness-procuring powers with which we credit them. In fact, it is happiness itself that increases the likelihood of sustainable high-achievement, not the other way around. Moreover, in my own interview research as part of my YoungLives research program, star individuals who have known longstanding career success have invariably been at pains to point out to aspiring youngsters that it's the closeness with friends and family which is far and away their greatest source of life-satisfaction. Here's what two highly impressive and publicly accomplished women have to say about this:

Cathy Freeman is the indigenous Australian who won the Olympic 400 metre gold medal in 2000. "I don't want to be rich, not at all. I don't want to be a celebrity, either. As long as my family and loved ones are there, I'm happy. I think I have my priorities straight. I have always been family-orientated. My family has always come first. I have always found security and comfort in their arms." In this spirit, Cathy declined the opportunity to participate in the 2004 Olympics.

Oprah Winfrey is America's leading talk-show host and media entrepreneur: "Experience, and not just a little heartache, has taught me money buys convenience and conveniences. But life's true meaning is about the time you can spend comfortably with your mate – and with yourself."

Their claims are supported by a host of studies illustrating how even the most dramatic increases in income or job-status bring only temporary improvements in our happiness, whereas a loving marriage fosters lasting ones. But surely such research only helps confirm what our own experience tells us. After all, what is more comforting in the face of adversity than dear friendship? New York State Senator and former First Lady, Hillary Rodham Clinton, has this to say about one of the hardest times in her own life. "It made me feel better to have friends around who had known me forever, who had seen me pregnant and sick and happy and sad and could understand what I was going through."

And in the very same way, when something really wonderful happens, the first thing we want to do is share it. U.S. women's soccer captain, Mia Hamm, put it beautifully: "The reason why I play is to see the smiles on my friends' faces and the tears in their eyes and see how hard they embrace."

Although we may consciously agree with much of the above, on a sub-conscious level where our deepest beliefs and strategies are stored, we can still harbour our parent's agenda. Like so many souls before us, we may not have received sufficient love and support for vital aspects of our lives, and we're attempting to take away the pain of our emotional hunger by extra work or whatever else we can find to overdose on. Pop singer, Madonna, said of losing her beloved mother when she was only five years old: "This left me with a certain kind of loneliness and an incredible longing for something . . . If I hadn't had that emptiness, I wouldn't have been so driven".

If we wish to restore happiness to its rightful place of paramount importance, for our own sake and that of our loved ones, we must not allow our career targets to jeopardise the bonds of our closest relationships, either by keeping us apart, or by diluting our time together through worry and exhaustion. Let's beware of having an 'alibi boyfriend or girlfriend', that person we tell ourselves we're dating though we'd be hard pressed to prove it. Such long-distance or time-limited partnerships can too easily be a flag of convenience that allows both sides to soldier on with parallel but separate paths. Veteran agony aunt and social campaigner, Claire Rayner, has a warning on just that point: "Togetherness is everything in a relationship. It takes a very special sort of couple to survive prolonged separation." Similarly, the BBC's veteran broadcaster, Terry Wogan puts his loved ones first: "Family's the most – the only – important thing. That's the way I feel about marriage to Helen after 38 years. You can take risks in work, but not in your personal life."

We should treat ourselves and the other person far better than second best. So let's beware of isolating ourselves with our over-zealous goals, stringing together one overwhelming mission after another, as we march to the subliminal drum of our childhood training. In short, let's beware the 'mermaid calling' of wealth, beauty, status and fame. There is good evidence that these do not bring even a fraction of the lasting happiness we presume they might.

From my own experience

At 18 years of age, I set off late in September to begin my time at Exeter University deep in the South West corner of England. It dawned upon me that Exeter had once been a Roman place, and this cheered me a little as I stood in nervous expectation in the cold and shadow of Paddington train station waiting to go there. Good place to complete my education, I thought. After all, it was the Romans who invented orgies and Latin vocab tests, which in every other respect were so regrettably unconnected. They were also a long way from home, which made them rather sad and huggable old Romans.

To pass the time, I imagined myself to be an undercover Secret Agent on active service in the field. Maybe I'd never even make it to Exeter because the mission that day would go badly wrong, and I'd be taken down in a hail of enemy bullets just like my favourite outlaws, Butch Cassidy and The Sundance Kid. No matter, because sewn into the lining of my blazer, the police would find my identity papers bearing the winged dagger of the Special Forces, and a crumpled photo of me and some gorgeous foreign girl perched on a Harley Davidson.

So that's what I'd *really* been doing on the French exchange last summer! My secret life would be a pretty big surprise to everyone who thought they knew me. Now they'd see. To the trumpeting of bands of The Grendier Guards, my laurel-covered coffin would be borne through the London streets towards the Cemotaph, as hordes of tearful young women struggled with their grief to sing Abide With Me. And in his address to the mourners, the Archbishop would tell them all about the young lieutenant in British Intelligence who had lived "an extraordinary existence quite unimagined by even his closest chums".

I could picture it all so clearly, and though it's probably not done to sing at your own funeral, I didn't want the hymn to taper off, so with tears in my eyes I led the last line "In life . . . as in death, O Lord . . . a-bide with me!"

My old school would probably erect a marble statue . . . me in the full-monty wearing nothing but an enigmatic smile and leaning nonchalantly on a javelin . . . with a willy that breaks off in a hard frost to create that truly classical look.

But as I stood there young and scared on Paddington station, I wasn't so sure of my glory anymore. Oh yes, I wanted to be terribly unexpected and pimpernellian, didn't I. But I wasn't so much 'scarlet' – the colour of captains and aristocrats – as 'beige', the colour of waterbiscuits and kitchen worktops. And if I died unexpectedly, most likely by choking on a mint, I knew that Mum would find that photo she always showed to friends. I'm ten years old in purple trousers and an orange tank-top and sitting on a camel at London zoo. Mum said it showed off my curls.

And then it struck me how after 18 years on Planet Earth, I'd wound up all alone. No one waving me off, and no one waiting to greet me at the other end. No one to whom I could say "You shouldn't have worried . . . of course I'd be okay." And in that moment I was weary to my bones of being so alone. I wanted the privilege of caring for someone else more than I cared about me. And in that moment I envied every grinning pair of faces across an airport arrival lounge, every soppy hugging couple on that station platform. I could have cried then in the humility of my own unimportance. I remembered being four years old and crying on my father's lap because my brother had stolen my bowl of coloured jelly. But Chrisy was welcome now to all the jelly I was owed, if only these things could change.

Let's share enjoyable journeys

Studies have shows that children who believe that money or popularity will make them happy are very likely suffering from some level of depression as a result of these unfruitful objectives. By contrast, those who believe that happiness results from personal development through close relationships with others, tend to be far happier. The reason is, that their core beliefs determine which life-goals they set themselves, and that's when the trouble really starts. The same goes for adults. It's all too easy to say to ourselves: "Once I'm earning this amount, or driving that car, or have so and so qualification, then surely I'll be happy". The critical flaw in such thinking, is that we forget to ask ourselves whether the journey is going to be enjoyable. Then we close all our other interests down so as to divert all our energies towards those material goals. We exclude new people and we cancel old friends, because our timetable is all about getting the job done. Happiness gets put on hold. We become mesmerised by winning or by owning. Alas, the very nature of modern media tends only to show us outcomes rather than the journeys which precede them. We see the prize, the final product, the glory moment, all the highly visible stuff. But that's simply a misunderstanding of how life works in terms of happiness and health. The fact is, that by teaming up and being happy we *increase* our chance of success in our working life. Golf champion, Tiger Woods says "No matter how tough we think we are, we can't do it alone. You always need support. And I have a wonderful family, a great girl, and great friends."

Oprah Winfrey would agree: "Nobody gets through this life alone. Everybody needs somebody to show them a way out, or a way up. Everybody does."

Mia Hamm also supports the point: "Soccer is not an individual sport. I don't score all the goals, and the ones I do score are usually the product of a team effort. I don't keep the ball out of the back of the net at the other end of the field. I don't plan our game tactics. I don't wash out training gear (*Okay, sometimes I do*), and I don't make our airline reservations. I am a member of the team, and I rely on the team. I defer to it and sacrifice for it, because the team, not the individual, is the ultimate champion."

So let's remember: enjoying the journey because of the people we share it with, is an end in itself. A victory in its own right.

Finding someone special (whether for friendship or romance)

A whole combination of factors has meant that meeting new people with whom we can develop a friendship can be dishearteningly difficult. Months and years can go by being on one's own but always open for love. Some of the trouble seems to be that people are working longer hours, are going to fewer social clubs for their leisure activities, (not least because of tv and other such passive distractions), and we tend to commute quite a way from home, so there's just less time and opportunity for the informal brushing of shoulders from which can spark a friendship. A self-punishing lifestyle can lead us to chasing jobs around the country and working over-long hours. Worse still, we might even turn down invitations by would-be partners because their affections threaten to topple the rigid hierarchy of our overblown ambitions.

But the truth is that our partner doesn't care whether we're a star or not . . . not if the price of being so is that we're less interested in them and the relationship we're sharing. This isn't selfishness, this is good sense. The most powerfully healthy instinct in life, (once we're breathing in the arms of the midwife), is to team up, and if anything gets in the way of that instinct, like bloated ambition, then it's a hindrance not a help. Once striving for success gets in the way of striving for partnership, it stops being healthy and starts being ugly.

Partnering up doesn't mean we don't need to know how to be self-reliant, because half the fun of being in a team is having something to bring to the table, some skills and know-how and being able to take the helm in times of trouble or when the other person needs a rest. Skills are meant for sharing and will feel all the better when we do.

So if this all sounds spot on, where do we start?

The best way to win someone's love is to love them, and by that I mean care for their well-being whole-heartedly, and share adventures with each other in doing so. We want to make an irreplaceable difference to people's lives, and sharing daily life with them is a good starting place. But sometimes finding a kindred spirit to get started with can be hard going. And it's not an individual problem, it's just that the usual ways of partnering up have become accidental casualties of the high-tech, highly mobile, over-urgent modern age. There was a time when one's friends and family would keep their eyes open for suitable romantic partners, but that system no longer operates effectively. The old ways have broken down, and nothing's grown up to replace them.

This unhelpful climate of accidental isolation has very naturally led to a great interest in the means by which to foster opportunities to meet new people. I think the best method is to consider what clubs and societies offer an activity that we not only would thoroughly enjoy for its own sake, but has the crucial added benefit of attracting the sort of potential partners we'd like to meet. The great advantages of joining such evening classes, weekend courses or holiday adventures, are as follows:

- We can see other individuals busying themselves in something rather than posturing and preening.
- Face to face we're open to all the soft, subliminal signals emanating from the other person, and this gives us a chance to consider whether our personalities and chemistries are a good fit or not.
- No matter the outcome in terms of teaming up with someone, we're learning something valuable and keeping our spirit open to new things. This might be Tai Chi, film appreciation, creative writing, pony trekking, hill walking, or art history. In fact, it's nothing less than exciting to think of all the places our search might take us.

Claire Rayner as a young nurse met her life-long husband at the local drama club. And acclaimed gardener, Alan Titchmarsh, had some similar good fortune happen to him that all began with him getting invited by a female neighbour to join his local Amateur Operatic Society for musicals and the like. "She said they were short of men and did I want to join? The prospect of getting out of the house one night a week and doing something different swung the balance. What had I got to lose? As things turned out, I did like it, mainly because everyone was so laid back . . . so pleasant . . . I was bowled over by the good-natured sociability of it all."

It was at another Operatic Society that Alan would meet his future wife, Alison, to whom he has been married for 30 years. He says he joined up as a means of making new friends when he moved down south to Kew Gardens.

Thriving Partnerships

Successful life-partnerships are the single richest source of happiness. Countless surveys have consistently shown that a good marriage produces some of the very happiest people who, on average, are noticeably happier than those who have not yet married, and heaps happier than the divorced or separated. Those findings are supported by world-respected Social Scientist, Robert Putnam of Harvard University, who also observes that in the pursuit of greater happiness, getting married is a far more potent strategy than acquiring extra money. And it's not just happiness we gain; our good spirits help protect and nurture our mental and physical health, so working everyday at maintaining and improving our partnership, is a routine even smarter than our daily work out.

With all this good to be gained, what does the best research flag as the essential principles for a fruitful and enduring partnership between two adults?

Thousands of couples who've profoundly enjoyed several decades together, invariably describe each other as their very best friend, and such profound friendship has certain distinguishing qualities. Above all else, *it's a union of equals,* and though they might not share every role, they nonetheless regard each other's activities as equivalently important to the welfare of the team. In short, their different needs and resources are a good fit and dovetail into one another very nicely, allowing the two halves to make a well-rounded whole far greater than the sum of the parts.

The evidence suggests that we can foster such a friendship of mutual enjoyment, reliance, and respect through sharing enjoyable activities in which to grow and progress together, whether those activities be gardening, drama, sport, travelling or child-rearing. Such shared adventure is the crucible in which are born all of our loving companionships, and under no circumstances should work nor the host of worldly demands be given priority over those relationship-building activities. *Not even child-rearing*, because the children of *married* couples are likely to do better by all and every measure of well-being than those children growing up under any other parental arrangement, so it is for their sakes as much as ours that the health and happiness of parental partnership should never be jeopardised.

Preventing break-ups and maintaining a good relationship with our partner . . . for richer, for poorer, in sickness and in health . . . takes a lot of dedication and effort. Fabulous comedian, Dawn French, says "I'm conscious all the time that you've got to work very hard at marriage. I think everyone has to – I can't imagine how people survive otherwise."

And Terry Wogan has this to say about his wife of 40 years: "When Helen and I married, that was *It*. There was going to be no turning back, no running away, and if things didn't work out, we knew that we had to stick with them until they did."

Former US President Bill Clinton and his wife, Hillary, also sought outside help to save their marriage. "The first thing we had to do is just get through the days," says Bill. "We had to let some time pass and Hillary had to decide whether she wanted to stay married to me. And then when she decided she was willing to try, that's when we agreed that we would work together – we'd take a day a week. And we did. A whole day a week every week for a year. Maybe a little more. And did counseling. And we did it together. We did it individually. We did family work. It was hard and interesting and I would say to people who have invested a lot of time in a relationship, that before they give up on it, it's well worth trying . . . First thing you learn is that any relationship that was once good, that is grounded in love but is in trouble, then one big reason is because you let it get on automatic. People begin to take each other for granted."

And here's another key thought to ponder. Eighty percent of couples who split-up, do so because they stop thinking and behaving like a 'we' and retreat again into unhelpful and self-protective 'me' strategies. Two such individuals who are not working sufficiently as one entity will only wind up feeling lonely inside of their marriage. Having an affair with a third party may be the eventual consequence of this loneliness, but it's very rarely the root cause.

To prevent ourselves drawing apart like this, we can actively seek to deepen our sense of shared purpose. This ever-increasing intimacy requires us to develop our capacity not only to love another, but to let ourselves be loved; and it's this latter skill which most often needs some practice. Our existing capacity to trust our partner to love us well enough, will reflect our previous relationships all the way back to how our own parents or primary care-givers treated us. Fortunately, the human spirit has a wonderful ability to mature throughout a lifetime, and we can take heart from the example of Claire Rayner, who says: "After years of conviction that I would never marry and inflict on another person the misery I had seen in my own childhood, and particularly the misery of children caught in the crossfire of a marriage, I went and married." Claire and her husband have now been very happily married for 57 years and raised three children.

Endeavouring to understand the makings of a successful marriage

Emeritus Professor John Gottman of the University of Washington in Seattle, has now studied several hundred married couples. He films them interacting as they spend the weekend in a apartment, and keeps in touch with them for several years then after. Gottman concludes that it's not *whether* we argue but rather *how* we argue which is crucially important, and that the partners who stay happily married all deal with their disagreements in a quite distinctive way:

- When embarking upon a disagreement, they avoid using a harsh start-up. "I'm wondering how we could better help each other do so and so", is a lot more inviting than beginning with "Why do you *always* have to . . . ?"
- They recognise just how emotionally and physically distressing arguments can be, so they soothe themselves and their partner by speaking slowly and gently, body relaxed. It's when we feel flooded with emotion that we're in danger of turning-off and tuning-out.
- They don't criticise the whole person, but instead they raise a specific complaint. So rather than beginning "You *always*... you *never*", instead they'll try "It hurts my feelings when sometimes you say . . ."
- In the course of the disagreement, they offer lots of little repair attempts for their own wrong-doings, perhaps by poking fun at themselves, or simply offering to make a cup of something soothing.

An important caveat to these rules of thumb emerges from research at Germany's Max Plank Institute of Human Development, which has noted how folks who've been happily married many years are extremely good at adjusting their level of involvement in a potential argument, and this skill allows their partner to ventilate a worry or gripe without things escalating. In other words, while one person lets off steam, the other person wisely shuts up. Less experienced couples tend to go head to head indiscriminately and insist on unpacking every comment or problem.

And here's another useful way to go about things: in our own mind and the other person's, we would do very well to downplay their shortcomings, and build upon their strengths. If there's a falling out, a wrong doing, or an irritation, we should make it *our* job to get over it without a fuss or a sulk. The only stuff to make a big deal about is the good stuff. Let's fan the embers of fondness and admiration by finding specific incidents of our partner's strengths. In fact, research by Dr Shelly Gable at UCLA says that how we share our successes is very important to a healthy relationship. Is our partner jealous, uninterested, or delighted? If we're sufficiently involved with the other person's life, we'll feel really delighted when things work out for them, and we'll be sure to show it.

Meanwhile, Professor Gottman proposes that just five hours per week of extra investment in the marriage relationship can make all the difference. His underpinning message is never to miss an opportunity to engage positively with your partner through affectionate gestures, cuddles, compliments, taking a genuine interest, and sharing at least one romantic date per week. Reason being that *one* special factor can over-ride all your shortcomings, and that factor is simply to let your partner know on a daily basis that your loving partnership is the one thing you treasure above all else. Inspirational chef, Jamie Oliver, seems to have swallowed the guidebook when it comes to his wife Juliette: "I leave her little notes when I leave her asleep. And I speak to her ten times a day on the phone to make sure she is alright. When I get home, I tell her I love her."

To foster such profound and focused commitment, I'm glad to say that certain approaches come up time and again in the studies of successful partnerships. We should never stop learning about our partner's most significant hopes, daydreams, fears and pains, and their most formative episodes and relationships. It's a wonderful thing for a soul to feel so thoroughly shared, understood and loved, all at once. Claire Rayner has been married to her first love, Des, since 1957, and she agrees. "The closer you are and the more you know each other, the more there is to know and the more interesting it is. That's why when we're apart for a day – I may be working in another town or he may be spending a day at the galleries instead of painting at home – we phone each other two or three times. There's too much to tell each other to wait until the evening."

What's more, with such privileged insights into our loved one, we are better able to nurture their ambitions, and to trust that our own essential self will likewise be fostered. Indeed, it's through helping each other to thrive and flourish, that we'll grow even closer together. Using *our* abilities to help others realise *theirs*, and being able to accept for ourselves the same all embracing care, is the quality that seems time and again to characterise those who lead the happiest and healthiest lives, so we shouldn't be surprised to find this at the very heart of a great partnership.

* * *

Planning for Progress

• How could you make more time for shared activities with your loved ones?

• How could you be a better friend to those you love?

• Where would you go to increase the likelihood of meeting new friends?

* * *

Developing our Passions in Life

Paying respect to our passions

Few pursuits are more helpful to our happiness in life than finding and feeding at least one passion – for an activity, a person or a place that thrills us, and about which we're hungry to know more. The feeling from a passion goes well beyond pleasure, it's a calling from deep inside of us; and though we might not be very good at expressing it yet, if we treat our passion properly, we soon will be. What matters is that we acknowledge our feelings and act upon them wisely.

Gertrude Elion was the American scientist who pioneered the use of chemotherapy against childhood leukaemia and was awarded The Nobel Prize for Medicine in 1988. She said "The most important advice is to choose the field that makes you happiest. There is nothing better than loving your work . . . I've been very fortunate that my work led to useful drugs for a variety of serious illnesses. The thrill of seeing people get well who might otherwise have died . . . cannot be described in words."

This sentiment is reflected in the words of Country and Western legend, Emmylou Harris: "So much of who I am and the way I express myself and how I see the world is wrapped up in music, that I can't imagine who I would be without it."

And as a newly qualified lawyer in her mid-twenties, Hillary Clinton had felt the very same way about changing her whole life so as to be with young Bill, though he was not yet her husband. "I chose to follow my heart instead of my head. I was moving to Arkansas . . . a place where I'd never lived and had no friends or family. But my heart told me I was going in the right direction."

While we may not choose to *marry* one of our passions, or to make a particular activity our means of earning a living, at the very least we definitely need to incorporate that source of positive energy very deeply into our lives. How we treat our passions is all about respecting the instinctive gut feeling of 'it-just-feels-right'. It's this owning up to our callings, and giving them full rein, that makes our living honest and satisfying.

Following our heart –
not fame, nor fashion, nor fortune

"There are no road maps, no instruction manuals. Passion is your guide," declares Anita Roddick, founder of The Body Shop. Such sentiments echo a theme that I have heard time and again these past ten years while reading about or interviewing highly inspiring individuals in their respective fields. They, each and every one, testified that to chase wealth or popularity was to miss the point of life. Particularly memorable was my interview with General Sir Peter de la Billiere, who had won two Military Crosses for outstanding courage before he was even 25, and went on to serve in and command for many years the SAS, Britain's most famous Special Forces regiment. As he reflected on a fifty year career of leadership, the General convinced me of the paramount importance of following your heart into whatever made you happy. Reason being, that no matter what else happens, if you've enjoyed the experience, you will have had the lion's share of what any endeavour has to offer.

Whether the enterprise is a success by any other yardstick is, by comparison, of much less importance. Money and recognition become insignificant beside the sheer pleasure of doing what your heart does best.

When Gertrude Elion was asked if the Nobel Prize was the pinnacle of her career, she said, "Of course not!" and explained that if you worked all your life simply for an award and didn't get it, your life would have been wasted . . . whereas hers could never be wasted, because her real reward was the pleasure of living what she called *the inventive life*.

Leading talk-show host, Oprah Winfrey, would say the same of her own extraordinary career. "Success wasn't the goal. The process was. I wanted to do good work."

Thankfully, psychological studies are now also quite clear on the priority of passion: if we chase the goals of financial success, social recognition or someone else's approval, we'll not be nearly as happy or healthy as if we do what's truly satisfying to us in the here and now. If our journey feels right, we'll be much the better for it.

Respecting our true callings rather than trying to please others

If our attempts to please others by our actions lead us to neglect our true values and strengths, we can pull ourselves badly off course and thereby jeapordise our own well-being. This thought is strongly related to the proposition that shyness and showing-off are two sides of the same coin, both reflecting an over-anxiety about what other people might think of us. While the shy person adopts the strategy of keeping out of the limelight, the show-off thinks they have to shine in it. On a similar theme, I'd like to suggest that when we're so eager to please that we don't care what it costs our heart and soul, we're making a similar strategic error, no matter this be the product of our conscious or sub-conscious mind.

The person we're trying to please might well be a much loved parent, alive or passed away, and our behaviour will most likely be workaholic as we strive to measure up to some impossible yardstick.

Whatever form it takes, there are few if any lives that haven't experienced such an episode in which we were dutifully doing what someone else wanted, rather than what would have felt right, and we made ourselves unhappy and ill by our misjudged appeasement. One manifestation of what I'm describing was termed 'the disease to please' by American psychotherapist, Dr Harriet Braiker, who shrewdly discerned the self-defeating fear of confrontation that was driving some people's smiling subservience to everyone else's wishes. But in my experience, our motivation to please can equally be the fear of being ignored or rejected, so we set out to do whatever we think might make the other person love us, or at least win their nod of approval. Yet someone's approval or pride in our achievements are not true signs of their caring, not if they disregard our essential make-up. Genuine, selfless love only wants us to be happy and to progress, and the best way that each of us can do that is to help our skills, experiences and passions work harmoniously.

When we're respectful of ourselves like this, it's as if we're hitting a ball with just the right place on the racquet. That 'sweet spot' reflects the idiosyncratic mix of strengths that are born of both our joys and our adversities, and we play at our best when we're true to them. Doing so is all about recognising the intrinsic value of fostering our own profound happiness on account of it being the most fertile source of positive energy, productivity, open-mindedness, physical health and goodwill. If we appreciate that happiness can be not only a product of positive actions but also their initiator, we can appreciate that our lasting happiness is not to be sacrificed for someone else's selfish, aggressive, or misguided demands upon us. Giving of oneself to bring joy to another is one of life's great pleasures, but such actions should nourish the giver just as much as it benefits the recipient. This would explain why The Harvard Study of Adult Development found that personally satisfying altruism was one of the hallmarks of the most healthy, happy and accomplished lives. However, such altruism should not be confused with the urge to self-sacrifice that comes from a shortage of self-worth masquerading as generosity to others. If we wish to be a force for good, we must be good to ourselves first of all. The more we can recognise and respect our own centre and sources of well-being, the more we will respect those of the people around us.

Being stronger than the disapproval

Eleanor Roosevelt, who was the single most important driving force that brought about the Universal Declaration of Human Rights in 1948, was in no doubt about the need to resist disapproval. "Do what you feel in your heart to be right – for you'll be criticized anyway. You'll be damned if you do, and damned if you don't."

Oprah Winfrey speaks with equal conviction: "Every single bit of pain I have experienced in my life was a result of me worrying about what another person was thinking of me."

So we shouldn't expect or seek approval from our peers, elders or anyone else. The test of our passion is whether it's strong enough to resist all those who mock us, or dismiss us, or forbid us out of hand. *As long as we're not trespassing on other people's lives, our life is ours to lead.*

It wasn't all green fairways for Tiger Woods, but he stood firm: "I always got made fun of. They'd say, 'Golf is a wussy sport' . . . and I got teased a lot. They may have been criticizing me for what they perceived the sport to be, but I was playing something that I loved. No one could take that away from me . . . One of the things that my parents have taught me is never listen to other people's expectations. You should live your own life and live up to your own expectations, and those are the only things I really care about."

Once again, Nobel Laureate Gertrude Elion has something rousing to say on this subject: "Nobody took me seriously. They wondered why in the world I wanted to be a chemist when no women were doing that. It took seven years of various jobs, including a year in graduate school and two years of high school teaching before the shortage of men in civilian jobs gave me the opportunity to prove myself. But after that, I never looked back." In later life, Gertrude was famous for cheering-on students in her lectures. "Don't let others discourage you or tell you that you can't do it . . . keep your eye on the goal. And in the words of at least one admiral, 'Damn the torpedoes, full speed ahead!'"

In that spirit, when real-life Horse Whisperer, Monty Roberts, was forbidden by his bullying father to pursue his gentle and non-aggressive 'Join-Up' method of working with young or traumatised horses, Monty pursued his passion in his own time, and started his own training ranch just as soon as he could.

So let's not for one moment expect or demand that anyone encourage us unreservedly. Even those who love us and want what's right for us, cannot always see into our hearts and know all the subtle and complex union of experiences, abilities and hopes that create and fuel our calling. We may for quite some time have to journey on alone until it becomes clear to those closest to us that we really mean business.

The transforming role of a supportive person

"Sometimes one person can be all you need, and that was the case with my mother. She managed to be two parents and a best friend packed into one 5-foot 3-inch person, although it wasn't easy."

So says Lance Armstrong who recovered from cancer to win the Tour de France cycle race an incredible six times at the last count.

Though Anita Roddick was just ten when her father died, she recalls that "From day one, I was taught that I had a bold spirit and could create a world that allowed that spirit to flourish."

And Hillary Rodham Clinton declares "I was lucky to have parents who never tried to mould me into any category or career. They simply encouraged me to excel and be happy."

These three voices prompt me to remark that I know of not one single example where someone has achieved creative heights without having at least one powerful source of deeply supportive love ... a supportive relationship whether in childhood or later years, that has served as a catalyst to their flourishing. With this in mind, it would make very good sense to seek out encouraging souls with whom to realise our dreams. I ponder, too, just how much potential to do good each of us has within us, simply by caring for someone enough to support them in their passions.

Being happy with who we are

Now we've considered the fundamental importance of respecting our passions, let's dare to take stock of where we are at the moment:

How happy are you with the person you've become?

How at home are you with whom you see in the mirror when you step out the bath?

And, if you spent 48 hours in your own company without chores or distractions, how good would it feel?

Mark Twain wrote that "a man cannot be comfortable without his own approval", and we certainly have the capacity to be our own worst enemy. For instance, we might try to compensate for the loss of our own goodwill by performing all sorts of stunts to be popular with others. This child-like strategy won't prevent us from becoming angry or fearful or frustrated, and we'll probably try to escape those feelings with alcohol or fantasy or over-work. We might lie to ourselves, let ourselves down, and be self-critical. Feeling insecure like this, we're prone to play catch-up with some perfect image of who we should be by now, or perhaps we'll give in altogether. We might also punish ourselves by withholding pleasures or by the self-sabotage of some high-risk behaviours that are bound to bring us down, sooner or later. (Driving too fast, spending too much, binge eating, or some other self-destructive addiction.) There are countless disguises for under-valuing ourselves, but the bottom line is we're our own cruellest critic.

But that voice whinging in our ears isn't ours. It's just our imitation of a key figure from our past . . . perhaps a parent, a sibling, or a partner . . . someone who year in and year out let it be known that we didn't match up to *their* requirements . . . impossible requirements, of course, born of their own frustrations, fears and pain. The trouble is, their poisonous legacy can lead us into civil war with ourselves. What's more, this internal campaign of demoralisation will scare-off the folks around us who'll wonder what we know about ourselves that's so darn terrible. With her typical insight, Eleanor Roosevelt wrote "Friendship with oneself is all-important, because without it one cannot be friends with anyone else in the world." Indigenous Australian, Cathy Freeman, who lit the cauldron and won a gold medal in the 400m at the 2000 Sydney Olympics, makes a similar point. "It's really important to surround yourself with people you want to be like and to always remember to keep things in perspective by having a healthy sense of humor and a healthy sense of self. These things all stem from loving yourself and believing in yourself because all these others things will fall into place around that."

If we find ourselves under-valuing our own self-worth, let's conjure the example of someone we know who's been blessed with a background of profoundly loving support. Such an individual will very likely stride through life with a smile on their face, head held high, happy in the knowledge that they're treasured and respected. Far from leading to slothful complacency, all the evidence is that feeling pleased with oneself and feeling glad to be alive are far more likely to foster a fruitful relationship with the world about us. This reminds us how true happiness is a highly fertile emotion that produces a stream of helpful thoughts and actions. So here's a key thought: could we begin to practice some of the very same qualities which radiate from those confident souls I've just described, or that make our dearest friends such a pleasure to be with? Based on those criteria, my bet is our 'things-to-do' list would contain at least the following:

Happiness

- Focus on using our passions and special strengths to make a real difference in the lives of those we care for.
- Set out to explore the world about us and beyond ourselves, and leave behind our self-obsessions.
- Remember that encouragement and reward reap far better results than criticism and punishment. (That goes for how we treat ourselves just as much as other people).
- Be honest about ourselves, no matter how unpalatable. Dare to air life's important stuff and act boldly upon it. Let nothing be taboo or not spoken about.

- Start keeping our promises to ourselves, by making only small, manageable ones.
- Keep our spirits up *without* resorting to the quick-fixes that only land us in trouble. (For instance, the spending sprees and consumer binges.) Humour works wonders here, as does the company of friends.
- Invest in our future well-being, like we gladly invest our time and caring in those we deem well worth it. Aim to treat ourselves just as helpfully as those we love.

With the above list in mind, why not go walkabout? That might mean all day in the countryside, or it might mean a long weekend. No phones, no books, just our own thoughts and feelings for company. Being so completely alone like this is a chance to have a chat with ourselves, take stock, and see what's needed.

In the last few years of her tragically short life, Princess Diana had found peace by telling herself "I am going to own myself now and be true to myself. I no longer want to live someone else's idea of what I should be." And how close this thought seems to what Oprah Winfrey says about writing her own autobiography: "As I peeled away the layers of my life, I realised that all my craziness, all my pain, all my difficulties, stemmed from me not valuing myself."

Playing to our special strengths

Here's a thought to put some spring in your step: why not let this year be a personal 'renaissance', a reawakening, of all your signature strengths – those half-dozen activities, mental or physical, that you so thoroughly enjoy that it feels like your spirit is flying.

Consider for a moment that modern film classic, *American Beauty*, and the observation by its lead character, Lester Burnham, that "Both my wife and daughter think I'm this gigantic loser. And they're right. I have lost something. I'm not exactly sure what it is, but I know I didn't always feel this sedated. But you know what? It's never too late to get it back."

That kind of talk gets the big thumbs-up from 21st Century

psychology, because all the best evidence suggests that to increase our net yield of happiness and accomplishment, we should be setting aside what we're bad at, and investing the bulk of our energies in what we do best. We should get back in touch with what really brings us joy. You will note, however, that the undiluted pursuit of our heart-felt prowess is not the guiding strategy under which the great majority of individuals and organisations presently operate. Since 1970, the Gallup Organisation has interviewed two million top per-formers in 60 countries about 'how and when they best work'. It seems that as few as 20% of employees in large organisations said they got to play to their distinctive abilities each day. People felt their true potential was being wasted. Apparently, this problem affects Eastern cultures such as Japan and China as much as the Western ones of Europe and America; and even in the best companies, only 50% of employees said they got to use their strengths each day. These figures are troubling, not least because this special strengths factor very significantly reflects itself in rates of staff-turnover, sick-days, accidents, productivity, and customer-satisfaction. Nonetheless, large companies carelessly do the staffing-equivalent of making motor-racing legend Michael Schumacher drive a milk-float.

One explanation for this state of affairs seems to be as follows. There's been this presumption by parents, educators and managers alike, that strengths will automatically flourish in the absence of negatives. But the fact is that strengths need specialist nourishment if they're to thrive, in the same way that our genetic potential, let's say for athletics, language or musical creativity, will only bloom if exposed to sufficiently fostering environments.

Spotting the things we're good at, and weaving them together
Harvard's most eminent Educational Psychologist, Professor Howard Gardner, has made a career out of studying high-achievement and concludes that we would all greatly benefit from paying less atten-tion to our weaknesses, and giving more respect to the unique collection of our strengths, idiosyncrasies and experiences. One way of doing this is to tailor-make our tasks and working environments to better suit our abilities.

It was Howard Gardner who more than 20 years ago outraged the psychological establishment by rejecting the accepted wisdom that there was just one sort of intelligence responsible for how well we did absolutely everything. Gardner challenged that single IQ notion with his Theory of Multiple-Intelligences, which identified not one but eight quite separate human dimensions of ability. His theory very neatly explains why our friend might be the Cary Grant of social situations, but is a complete plonker when it comes to computers.

All of us have a mixture of these eight foundation strengths mixed within us, but sometimes one stands out. That said, like a Boy Scout trying to light a fire, it seems likely that we need at least two sticks to rub together if our skills are to create sparks and catch alight. For instance, I reckon all of the individuals below have at least one other well-developed quality supporting their front-running strength:

- *Linguistic ability:* talk-show host, Oprah Winfrey, and computer-language wizard, Bill Gates.
- *Logical:* Nobel Scientist, Marie Curie, and Nobel Physicist, Richard Feynman.
- *Musical:* Soprano, Dame Kiri Te Kanawa, and country and western singer, Emmylou Harris.
- *Bodily:* 2004 Olympic gold medalist, Kelly Holmes, and former French soccer captain, Zinedine Zidane.
- *Inter-Personal (good with people):* agony aunt, Claire Rayner, and Special Forces General, Sir Peter de la Billiere.
- *Intra-personal (good at using your own feelings):* comedienne, Dawn French, and children's novelist, Joanne K. Rowling.
- *Spatial: (able to picture three dimensional space)* Physicist, Albert Einstein, and NASA shuttle commander, Eileen Collins.
- *Naturalist abilities (closeness with Nature):* tv gardener, Alan Titchmarsh, and horse trainer, Monty Roberts.

It can be helpful to consider into which categories fall our own strongest abilities, and what implications this has for how we should develop our passions. The good news is that our present levels of the eight intelligences are not set in stone. We can develop any one of them if we apply the approaches that I detail in Part Two of this book, *Becoming an Expert in our Favourite Pursuits.*

In addition to his work on Multiple-Intelligences, one of Professor Gardner's more recent studies suggests it is crucial that we appreciate which of the following four skills best suits our particular personality and the way our brain works:

- *Mastering a well-established field:* exemplified by Speaker of the House of Commons, Dame Betty Boothroyd; and golf champion, Tiger Woods.
- *Creating a whole new approach:* Body Shop CEO, Anita Roddick; and Founder of the modern Hospice movement, Dame Cicely Saunders.
- *Profoundly influencing others:* Nobel Peace Laureate and former President of South Africa, Nelson Mandela; and U.S. Secretary of State, Madeleine Albright.
- *Introspecting and then communicating our inner feelings:* best-selling author, Bill Bryson; and Oscar winning actress, Julia Roberts.

Professor Gardner believes that if we don't realise that we've not got a well-developed creative mind, or are not good at introspecting, we risk considerably disadvantaging ourselves by investing in activities or professions that are likely to be unrewarding for us. Once again, it would be very helpful if we can identify our special strengths and the particular combination in which they are mixed within us.

Focusing on our strengths

Once alerted to this Darwinian notion that we search out a niche to suit us in life, and then mine it for all it's worth, we can spot the good examples all around us. Computer pioneer, Bill Gates, is already a convert to playing to our strengths: "Maintaining focus is a key to success. You should understand your circle of competence, the things that you're good at, and spend your time and energy there."

Of course, any time spent on irrelevant pursuits is a waste of potential practice time. Take soccer player, David Beckham, for example. Age 12, he was probably trying to learn which verbs take *avoir* and which take *être*, while just across the English channel the soon-to-be French soccer captain, Zinedine Zidane, was already bunking off school to practice his body swerves and ball control 24-7 in the Marseille backstreets. And Zinedine never lost his head-start from all those thousands of extra practice hours. Still, it is to David Beckam's enormous credit that he very graciously acknowledged Zidane as "the greatest player in the world".

And it can be no coincidence that this approach of focusing on what we do best is all rather akin to what economists know as The Pareto Principle. This states that no matter the field of endeavour, roughly 80% of the rewards will result from just 20% of the activities, and we should therefore identify what's so characteristic about that ever-so-fruitful one fifth, so as to better invest in it. And this principle is even reflected in our interpersonal relationships, because we don't love someone for what they're not, we cherish them for what they are, their distinctly positive attributes, and we forgive them their foibles accordingly.

It's no accident, either, that the most effective approaches to psychotherapy very deliberately build on a client's existing strengths and accomplishments, rather than churning over past mishaps and misfortunes.

All that said, we can still do something strategic about the worst of our weaknesses. The consensus is that we should work on any life-inhibiting frailties just enough so they don't sink us, and then team-up with someone who has the compensating expertise to give covering-fire to our short-comings. For instance, if we're a bit shy, then team up with an extrovert; if we're highly creative but don't relish details, go 50-50 with someone who does. All the great partnerships are based on this principle:

Bill Gates focused on software design, and left the business-side to Steve Ballmer.

Elton John wrote the music and left the lyrics to Bernie Taupin.

Sundance did the shooting, and left the thinking to Butch.

And that's what's doubly good about having a passion for something: it's an extremely attractive quality. It seems to broadcast our good psychological health to those around us and can help forge our partnerships with other special people who also have passions of a similar or complementary nature.

Our age doesn't matter

Passion can strike us at any age. The U.S. Olympic women's soccer captain, Mia Hamm, was entranced with playing football just as soon as she could toddle; and Luciano Pavarotti was barely six when he declared opera singing to be his life's goal. Tour de France champion, Lance Armstrong, was also an early starter, doing several hours daily training by the age of 12 and winning adult triathlon races by 15. Likewise, Madonna and Julia Roberts both knew by their early teens that they wanted to perform professionally, whereas BBC's Head of News, Kate Adie, didn't realise that she was quite so curious about other people's worlds until she visited Germany and Sweden as a university student. That's all but twenty years ahead of U.S. Secretary of State, Madeleine Albright who didn't take a permanent full-time paying job until she was 39. But her story fabulously illustrates one of the defining features of a true passion: *it takes all of our resources from our life hitherto, and channels them into our new activity.* Madeleine had preceded her extraordinary political career with being a mother, a charity fund-raiser, and writing her PhD in history. By the time she took on the world of formal work, she had a wide range of life-skills extremely well-honed.

And just for good measure, here follows the typically courageous, clear and insightful admission by Eleanor Roosevelt. "My chief objective as a girl, was to do my duty. This had been drilled into me as far back as I could remember. Not my duty as I saw it, but my duty as laid down for me by other people. It never occurred to me to revolt. Anyhow, my own overwhelming need in those days was to be approved of, to be loved, and I did whatever was required of me, hoping it would bring me nearer to the approval and love I so much wanted.

"As a young woman, my sense of duty remained as strict and rigid as it had been when I was a girl, but it had changed its focus. My husband and my children became the center of my life and their needs were my new duty. I am afraid now that I approached this new obligation much as I had my childhood duties. I was still timid, still afraid of doing something wrong, of making mistakes, of not living up to the standards required by my mother-in-law, of failing to do what was expected of me.

It was not until my middle age that I had the courage to develop interests of my own, outside of my duties of my family. Franklin's illness finally made me stand on my own feet in regard to my husband's life, my own life and my children's training. The alternative would have been to become a completely colorless echo of my husband and mother-in-law and be torn between them. I might have stayed a weak character forever."

Where to look

If inspiration doesn't step up to greet us, we have to go looking for our passions, or even create them. The following steps can help:

- Ask all and sundry around us, this very direct question: "What do you most love to do, and why?"
- Then personally experience as many promising activities as possible, rather than hearing them second-hand.
- Look for clues in our childhood and teenage interests that may have been neglected as schoolwork or other responsibilities took over.
- Look for clues in the subjects that never fail to grab our attention when we stumble across them.
- Whatever we fantasise about for the sheer joy of it, might be a good indicator; or even the cheering thoughts we use to lull ourselves to sleep at night.

Let's also ask ourselves for whom, for what and for where would it feel well worth turning off the television, keeping fit, and staying sober?

For whom, for what and for where does our heart beat fastest, and our face make the biggest smile?

Appreciating it's a process

Helpful though the above strategies will be, it's well to be aware that identifying one's passion is unlikely to be a single moment of enlightenment, but rather more of a process, a cumulative and drawn out discovery over months or many years. For Steven Spielberg at age 12, it didn't take long. "I knew after my third or fourth little 8mm epic, that this was going to be a career, not just a hobby."

For NASA Astronaut and shuttle commander, Eileen Collins, her revelation came even earlier. "I remember reading an article called *'Should We Spend Money on the Space Program or Not?'* I could not understand why anybody would say 'no'. It was obvious to me as a nine year old that we needed to learn about space. I was more fascinated with what we *didn't* know rather than what we did. That was when I started learning about the astronauts and their backgrounds, and figuring out what you needed to do to become one. From that point on, I was always very interested in space."

But for British gardening guru, Alan Titchmarsh, the process was rather more gradual and unconscious. "I blame it all on my mother. If she hadn't whisked us out of the house for a walk almost every day, then I'd never have noticed nature. As it was, I grew up with an insatiable curiosity about anything that crawled, flew, swam or grew. I don't remember the moment it started; it has always been there."

And the words of anti-apartheid activist and former President of South Africa, Nelson Mandela, illustrate how even well into adulthood our calling might still be gathering strength. "I had no epiphany, no singular revelation, no moment of truth, but a steady accumulation of a thousand slights, a thousand indignities and a thousand un-remembered moments that produced in me an anger, a rebelliousness, a desire to fight the system that imprisoned my people. There was no particular day on which I said, 'Henceforth I will devote myself to the liberation of my people'; instead, I simply found myself doing so, and could not do otherwise."

Zeroing In . . . or opening out

A fine example of this focusing very clearly on what motivates us, is
Steven Spielberg's attitude to his early career. He had absolutely no
intention of working his way up through the movie-making hierar-
chies of assistant coffee-maker onwards. The only thing that interested
Steven was directing, and on his very first professional picture,
age 17, that's exactly what he did. That said, we shouldn't lose sight
of the fact that 'directing' was a role young Steven had been practising since he was still in short trousers, so he'd already done a good
deal of ground work.

But let's not be disheartened if we have more than one strong
passion. I'm reminded of how Alan Titchmarsh loved not only
gardening but also performing in amateur operatics. No accident,
then, that he ended up as British television's best-loved gardening
personality. He had taken his two passions and, over a number of
years, woven them seemlessly together.

Fuelling our passions

We need rocket fuel to get our callings off the ground, and this is
where our emotions come in. Our anger, our fear, our hope, our
shame, and our sheer joy, they all need to be channelled into constructive action. Rather than suppress these emotions (perhaps by
consuming too much alcohol and television), or squander their
energy (perhaps on fantasies or a string of superficial experiences), it
will prove far more satisfying and rewarding if we channel that emotional energy towards helpfully developing our real life calling. The
greater our emotion, the more likely our progress. It's our emotional
energy . . . whether it be drawn from positive or negative experiences . . . that will enable us to overcome our embarrassment about
asking questions or asking for help. And it's our emotional energy
that will stop us giving up when the going gets tough, and will
instead urge us to be versatile and duck and weave around the
inevitable problems and set-backs.

The older sister of indigenous Australian runner Cathy
Freeman suffered from celebral palsy and died from a sudden

asthma attack when Cathy was just 16 years old. "A defining moment was when I saw my sister's casket lowered into the ground. I was in so much pain but I gained so much strength and I think that made me determined to make the most of who I was and what I had. I just believe so much that people do take strength out of great loss, despair or pain. I took that energy and all of the passion and it fed my soul and gave my heart strength. I live my life in honour of Anne-Marie and I always will."

It's worth noting, however, that there's not one jot of convincing evidence that we need to be filled with a rage for revenge, nor sail close to insanity, in order to achieve extraordinary things in life. Madeleine Albright was inspired by the deeply positive memory of a wise and loving father. And for Nobel Laureate, Richard Feynman, love was more important than science; but it just so happened that, as well as loving people, he also loved physics.

Keeping our passions flexible

Our passion mustn't become obsessive nor self-destructive, whereby we allow our focused enthusiasm to accidentally isolate us from others, or lead us to neglect vital sides of our life. We need to balance the passion with some other activities which recuperate us, and so allow our pursuit to provide a lifetime of nourishing enjoyment. Golf champion, Tiger Woods, would heartily agree. "Golf is my job, it's one thing in my life, but not the only thing. The key to life is moderation. When I have free time, I love fishing and just hanging out with my friends."

All we should require of our passions is that they pay their way in terms of satisfaction and joy. If the passion is wearing off, the sooner we own up the better, and let our heart tell us where to head next. But in this, as in all things in life, it's up to us to conjure the things that will make it work. What's missing from the way we're doing it? What special ingredients could we helpfully add? A new ally, a fresh setting, an alternative approach? Our inventiveness will pay off.

Our passions will naturally evolve and metamorphose, and very often in unexpected ways. Allowing our life to progress organically like this, to let our joys and happiness guide us and let our spirit respond to unforeseen opportunities, is a recurrent theme throughout my research findings. We do ourselves a disservice if we think that there is only one route forward, or only one destination worth achieving. Our passion needs a strong theme, but it doesn't need an exact form.

Madeleine Albright puts similar thoughts very nicely. "I have often said that women's lives come in segments, dictated in part by biology. I have also said that this is actually an advantage because it allows women to explore different paths. It is important, however, to have some guiding star."

Lance Armstrong's breath-taking response to testicular cancer epitomises this sense of making the best of whatever life throws at us. "I had a new sense of purpose . . . I no longer felt that it was my role in life to be a cyclist. Maybe my role was to be a cancer survivor."

On this same vital theme, three times World Heavy Weight Boxing Champion and now a UN Messenger of Peace, Muhammad Ali, writes, "Each time I thought I had achieved my life's purpose, I discovered it was only another step in my journey. I thought boxing would help me be that public 'Black role model' who was missing while *I* was growing up. I thought my purpose was to be that hero who showed children that Black is beautiful. I thought my purpose was to be that champion who showed White people they couldn't treat Blacks like second-class citizens. I learned that all of these accomplishments were important, but even *more* important, I gained a platform that allowed me to carry out my real mission, which has been to encourage all people to respect each other and to live in peace."

Making it a mission

Explaining her motivations that led her eventually to the 1988 Nobel Prize for medicine, Gertrude Elion tells how "I was very close to my grandfather . . . I watched him die of cancer in the hospital. And that made a terrific impression on me. I decided that nobody should suffer that much. That was the turning point. It was as though the signal was there: *this is the disease you're going to have to work against.*" Years later, Gertrude said, "When we began to see the results of our efforts in the form of new drugs . . . our feeling of reward was immeasurable. What greater joy can you have than to know what an impact your work has had on people's lives?"

Compare her words with the experience of horse-trainer Monty Roberts, whose childhood was darkened by physical violence. "My father was a cruel and frightening man," and when as a young boy Monty first demonstrated his non-aggressive 'join up' method of winning a horse's confidence, his father tried to beat 'the evil' out of him. "He raised the stall-chain and brought it down hard, again and again, on my thighs and buttocks. . . I was left in a pitiful, grieving state." By the age of 12, Monty had received 71 broken bones, all inflicted at the hands of his father. Monty Robert's triumph was to revenge himself on the violence that was used against him, by investing his own lifetime's work to raising horses and young people without any recourse to fear or threat. By doing so, he had broken the cycle of violence.

And now let's consider Dr Viktor Frankl, the Viennese psychiatrist who survived the Holocaust death camps largely by setting himself the task of using the experience to improve his understanding of human resilience. From the outset, he promised himself that if he survived, he would teach about his observations. In post-war Europe, he did exactly that, developing an approach to therapy based upon helping people find meaning and purpose in their lives. Dr Frankl quotes Nietzsche: "He who has a *why* to live for, can bear almost any *how.*" That's to say, living with a sense of meaning, with a sense of purpose, gives us extraordinary strength. In respect of which, the writings of Dr Frankl urge us to seek not a *less* demanding life, but quite the contrary, a *more* challenging one that deserves our deepest resources and heart-felt passions. It is by rising to challenges that we forget ourselves, be it tending a garden, nurturing a person, or building a business. The journey, the doing, should be the end in itself, because the rewarding feelings will come from the route we've taken, the spirit in which we walk it, and the companionship upon the road. Simply by reaching outwards we can find our meaning, through feeling part of something greater than ourselves, something well beyond the boundaries of our own body and thoughts.

On which note, here are some more thoughts from Eleanor Roosevelt: "Do not stop thinking of life as an adventure. You have no security unless you can live bravely, excitingly, imaginatively; unless you can choose a challenge instead of a competence. And there is another requirement for happiness: that is the feeling that you are, in some way, *useful*. Usefulness, whatever form it may take, is the price we should pay for the air we breathe and the food we eat and the privilege of being alive. And it is its own reward, as well, for it is the beginning of happiness."

Such thoughts brings us back, I hope, to love: that sense of vocation to invest ourselves in someone or something we deem just as important, or more so, than oneself. In the last scene of *Casablanca*, it is for love of a person and belief in a cause that Bogart plays all his aces – and *we* would do no less, if inspired by such a strength of feeling.

From my own experience

I grew up thinking my role in life was to resist my passions rather than develop them.

I thought it was clever, and a lot less trouble, to do what other people wanted of me. It wasn't until I was 20, that it dawned upon me that even good people could be rather careless or mistaken in what they advised for me, so I gradually began to ignore them.

Trouble is, I'd been burying my passions and faking my interests for so many years, that I found it impossible to own up to what my heart really wanted.

This feeling was made worse because I'd gone from a school of 600 boys in which everyone knew my name, to a university of 5,000 people. It seemed to me that in one stroke, I'd become absolutely invisible. Just another student among thousands. It didn't seem to matter what I did with my days, because no one would notice anyway. My confidence spiralled downwards and in sheer despair at a meaningless future, I simply stopped trying.

When I left university four years later with no sense of direction and a third class degree, I suffered that classic confusion caused by superficial appetites and physical instincts masquerading as 'missions in life'. All I seemed to want for myself was a long career involving palm trees, cold beer, and gorgeous Brazilian women playing beach volleyball. I didn't realise that such things were not my authentic vocations and had no power at all to bring lasting satisfaction.

It would have helped at this time had I taken a weekend off and gone walkabout to think things through, because there were clues aplenty in my childhood and teenage years to a whole host of passions, any one of which I could still have pursued very happily. I would have loved to become a Pilot, or a Film-Maker, or an Accident and Emergency Medical Doctor. Quite un-connected on the face of it, but each inspired sufficient excitement in me that I could have fuelled any one of those flames and made it my lifetime's career.

But I didn't take the time to explore those feelings, and I didn't dare share them with anyone who might be in a position to help. I thought I was too late and would look too stupid for all my wrong directions and not having spoken up years before. That was a big mistake, because at age 23, with a calling for planes, big screen movies, and emergency medicine . . . just as long as these involved working in teams of good people . . . what did I actually end up doing?

Creative Writing, that's what.

I embarked on a novel . . . sitting at home and lonely all day long, desperately hoping the phone would ring, and too scared to walk into town because people might think I was an unemployed drifter. Which I was, of course.

Thus followed three unhappy years with the pain of loneliness and a lack of progress and my heart calling loudly to me to make a major change, to stop and think again. But I still ignored that inner voice and held on to that balloon that was taking me upwards, too afraid to conjure the time and courage to own up to my mistakes and put things right. I didn't realise that the very moment I set out on a truly happy path of my own choosing, all the wrong roads would suddenly seem like the perfect preparation for my new life. Happiness heals us.

Finally, I was saved by a dear friend who left London to go to university out in the provinces. We teamed-up to move into a house together, and in all the confusion, I let my heart-felt hopes get the better of me. I started enjoying things again, meeting new people . . . many from overseas . . . and became curious about the possibilities in the world around me. Little by little I got my confidence back, and one day while supervising a knitting class in a local primary school, (. . . it's a long story . . .) I stared out the window and quite simply asked myself "What would I most like to do in life?"

I felt I had nothing much to lose by asking myself such a really big question, and the reply from inside me all but knocked me over it was so strong and immediate. *I wanted to be a psychologist . . . but one who looks at how lives go well . . . not at how lives go wrong.* I knew lives could be beautiful because I'd been bumping into some real corkers that year, and I thought that studying them would be beautiful, too. I realised now why I'd always read the half-page obituaries in the newspapers, and wondered what had shaped and driven the personality and lifetime summed-up there on the page. From that moment on, my road forward could be as rough and tumble as it liked, but I was sure to enjoy the journey.

* * *

Planning for Progress

- How would your life feel different if you more openly pursued your heart-felt passions?

- What could you do to help a loved one develop their passions?

- What's the relationship between your heart-felt passions, and the most important people in your life?

* * *

A Special Sense
of Rapport

Rapport is a special level of intimacy characterised by an instinctive, intuitive relationship . . . a closeness and trust, and a natural and easy communication that goes well beyond words. Rapport embraces how we speak, the clothes we wear, and our eye contact. It's about cooking together and dancing together, our sensuality and our sixth sense. Rapport is an elusive quality, but I try to explore a little of what it's about in this following chapter.

The gentle partnership

"My greatest accomplishment was learning to be gentle. Without that, I would have accomplished nothing," writes Monty Roberts, the American who has spent a lifetime training horses, fostering 47 youngsters, and having three of his own children with Pat, his wife of 50 years. His life story is all the more remarkable because by the age of 12, Monty had sustained 71 broken bones at the hands of his cold and brutal father who used threats and acts of violence to extract compliance.

Disillusioned by the world of adult humans, Monty as a child found comfort and love among horses. And then as a teenager, he gained extraordinary insights into animal rapport by spending days out on the high desert ranges of Nevada studying wild herds through binoculars. By his caring observation of these powerful but profoundly social creatures, Monty Roberts did not simply transcend the bullying he'd endured as a youngster, he created its very opposite: the active application of gentleness to achieve what he calls 'Join-Up', which is a willing partnership between man and horse built upon trust and mutual benefit. He has clearly demonstrated through his success with young horses and young people, that gentleness reaps far greater rewards than the harshness of an abusive or coercive atmosphere.

One autumn evening, I watched enthralled as Monty Roberts worked with the frightened and troubled horses who their owners had brought to be helped by his methods. I recognised in his rapport-building the very same principles and skills that I have witnessed as most effective in human psychology. For example, when trying to foster a partnership with someone, we can in our enthusiasm push too hard, which only leaves the other person feeling bullied by our insistence and they pull away. By offering our warm invitation and then gently and patiently withdrawing, we send the signal that any decision to develop the hoped-for relationship is the other person's free choice, and this in itself provides a strong foundation for partnering-up. If our initial offer is met with reluctance, rather than use our determination to push harder, we do better to look for an alternative way to bond. In all of this, it is vital that we respect the values and goals important to the other person, and the language and rules of engagement they're willing to accept. This considerate approach is further helped by keeping our own breathing and heart-rate calm so as not to radiate any sense of urgency or agitation which could be misperceived as a threat. In short, we should channel our determination not into greater outward pressure, but into greater control of ourselves. Likewise, rather than chasing, we should seek to make a sufficiently attractive offer, and then back-off so that the other party can feel they have full ownership of the next move.

Whether we're inspiring others to learn, or we're doing business, offering romance or negotiating peace, it is by being gentle, by self-calming, and by seeking to understand the language and values of the other person, that we are most likely to foster a helpful rapport. It is by gently inviting Join-Up that we salute the human spirit's need for self-respect and pride as well as for acceptance and love.

Sending signals that we're comfortable with ourselves

If we want a rapport with someone else, it can only help to first of all put ourselves at ease. Being and seeming comfortable with ourselves can be about the speed at which we walk, our body posture, our eye contact, and our readiness to smile. It's about taking time to feel at home inside our own skin.

My YoungLives research in 2000 suggested that some of the most endearing personal qualities someone can possess are happiness and self-confidence, caring for others, and a passion for life. With this in mind, it should be no surprise that it's our voice, eyes and smiles which provide the most enduring physical attractions to those around us, not least because these features so effectively convey our personalities and our approach to life. Other parts of our body are, by comparison, far less important than we give them credit for. There's many a top fashion model who has none of the likeability of those individuals whose faces might be far less symmetrical, but who nonetheless radiate a heart-felt courage and warmth which win us over. In my younger years, I thought the physical body dictated who was attractive, but it became increasingly obvious to me that it was the spirit and personality who inhabited them that was the true source of their seductive power. Which is why I whole-heartedly agree with Anita Roddick: "Passion is the most important element of communication."

Eye to eye
Our being able to look long and deep into someone's eyes, tells us a lot about how we feel about them, and how we feel about ourselves. If we find eye contact difficult, if we shy away from doing so and

catch someone's gaze only fleetingly, then this is telling us something we need to listen to and understand.

Do we lack confidence and liking in ourselves?

Is it something about the other person that puts us off?

Or is it just possible that we're falling in love?

In any event, we should do something about it. It's worth taking stock of just whose eyes we're willing and happy to meet face on. Being around people who are wrong for us, who don't bring out our best sides, is something we do well to be aware of and to put right.

It is because of the importance of our eye contact and smiles, that we should try to communicate face to face whenever possible, since e-mails, texts and even phonecalls leave too much room for misunderstanding. Simply making time to be with someone, time in which to converse patiently with each other, already communicates a great deal of good will. And the most rounded and satisfying mode of communication is through shared activities, as actions speak louder than words.

In your own words
What does our voice say about our personality and the sort of conversation we want to have? Are we uncertain or confident . . . hurried or calm?

A voice can be as attractive as any face, body or movement, and many of us can quickly recognise the voice of the biggest film stars from a previous generation: the shlurred speech of Humphrey Bogart, the slight hesitation of James Stewart, and the musical intonation of Cary Grant and Katherine Hepburn. These days, film star voices are far less distinctive, largely I think because of the emphasis on action in the movies rather than character, and this shift in focus takes away the need for their lines to be spoken in such a distinctive way.

It's worth pondering upon, because what we say can mean far more to our listener if we adjust our speed, intonation, and vocabulary. But speech is such an automatic activity, that unless we single out a particular phonecall or conversation when we're trying to do things differently, then our voice will stay the same. So what sort of things could we work on:

- We could halve the speed and glide the words together. Speaking more slowly not only calms us down, but it sounds more self-assured.
- We could let our emotions carve out the tone with which we say the different words, so a melody comes through.
- We could use pauses both within a sentence and between them . . . not just for breath, but for emphasis . . . either to make a point, or to give ourselves time to think of one.
- We could move our body as we speak, which helps free-up the voice.

We certainly wouldn't be the first to consider improving upon such an automatic, unconscious feature of ourselves. Katie Couric, the lady who became leading anchor on US tv's CNN, was initially banned from the airwaves by the corporation's president on account of her high-pitched, squeaky voice. She took voice classes to correct this. Likewise, Lady Margaret Thatcher was taught to lower the pitch of what she herself described as her "rather shrill voice", while Academy Award winning Actress, Julia Roberts, has never had formal acting training, but she did see a voice coach to help her change her accent.

Clothing matters
Evolution has made us social animals, and we naturally use our choice of clothes to broadcast messages about ourselves. Since we are each comprised of several different identities depending on who we're with and what we're doing, it doesn't seem extravagant to have an outfit for all our personality dimensions. On which point it's worth remembering that the characteristic thoughts, feelings and

behaviours that comprise our personality are constantly evolving, which begs the question 'Does our present wardrobe reflect our progress, or are we wearing a personality from the distant past?'

Such questions deserve our consideration because our clothing automatically communicates something to those around us, and all we can choose is to what extent we actively craft the message. This is quite an opportunity because how well we get on with the world depends not only on how we view life, but how life views us, and some part of that impression will be shaped by our appearance. In respect of which, it's not sufficient for us to be a voyeur, we also need to be an actor.

But before this all becomes a burden, let's not forget that pleasure can serve as a fuel for good things, and that learning to turn a chore into something cheerful is a life-transforming skill on account of its power to energise. Dressing-up should always be a pleasure, and it's a good time to remember how our clothes not only express our emotions but also support them. What's more, we can use clothes as a catalyst for pushing the present boundaries of our personality, which is by no means 'faking it' just as long as what we're wearing reflects some side of us that we already possess or would like to cultivate. All the better if our new look displays some inner calling that we've never fully explored.

If this approach to our appearance seems rather deliberate, I think bothering to communicate well with the world around us is always smart, and so someone making that effort is always admirable. We might even use this experimentation to achieve a better balance, so if we need to look buttoned-down in our professional capacity, we could introduce some flamboyance into our personal attire. These alternative get-ups can make our time off-duty all the more refreshing. Come Monday, we can throw ourselves back into our business suit without feeling as if the pinstripes are prison bars.

I don't by any means want to suggest our self-expression should require any great expenditure. A coloured neckerchief, a proudly polished pair of shoes, or a lapel-badge might be all it takes to indicate some important part of us. It's the passion behind it, not the price tag, which makes the message valuable. But if we are off to the stores for some seasonal clothing, it will undoubtedly help if we take some time to put ourselves in a positive mood before we hit the highstreet. Some optimism and good spirits will help us be more confident in our choice of colour, cloth and cut, and more willing to experiment and express ourselves. Rather than be at the whim of this season's shop window, we will fashion a look to suit ourselves, and happiness is never out of style.

Cooking a meal together . . . and eating it slowly

Cooking a meal with someone is even better than cooking it for them. Celebrity chef Jamie Oliver was brought up in a country pub and says "My family upbringing really taught me the importance of food in bringing people together", and goes on to say that "A good meal can be a wonderful thing. It can repair feuds, seal firm friendships, and spark wonderful romances."

For my part, I've been slow to learn all of this, and have to confess that there's little in the way of food I haven't tried to microwave. In my first 25 years of life, eating was something that you were just aiming to get to the end of, and it was a revelation to begin to see the pleasure in taking one's time . . . to appreciate that, as with just about everything else in life, *the process* was so much more important than the ending place . . . that a good journey was in itself a good result, and that the finishing point was just the last fraction of the journey, and not the be all and end all I'd mistaken it for.

Making a good impression

My teens and twenties were characterised by a host of misunderstandings about life, but notable among them was the following: I thought that building a relationship was all about impressing the other person. In fact, this strategy motivated most of my activities. For instance, the main reason I would have considered learning a musical instrument was not to express myself, but rather to impress others. I imagined how women's eyes would mist over with tearful admiration as I sang guitar ballads while we sat in front of the fire. The truth was that I much preferred the piano, but didn't figure I could quite so easily get a girlfriend into my bedroom by asking her to give me a hand up the stairs with a Steinway.

On reflection, I would have been better off inviting the girl to go dancing. Dance brings more joy than just about any other leisure activity, with no negative side-effects. All forms of partner and solo dancing are a wonderfully positive expression of our intimate self, and are very healthy for it. So if in doubt, let's dance . . . cheek to cheek.

Coming to our senses . . . *Slowly*

It would seem that close and personal contact with the people and world around us isn't only very pleasant, it may be vital. Dr Charles Spence, an experimental psychologist at Oxford University, is investigating the possibility that many of us may unwittingly be suffering a mild form of sensory deprivation because we're over-fed with visual stimulation from rapid-fire television images and barely changing computer screens. Not only are we trapped for hours in such sight-centred environments, but many of us spend 90% of our daily life inside, shut away from the richness of the outdoor natural elements.

Dr Spence suggests we redesign our homes, workplaces and machines using an approach more considerate of our full range of senses, by combining mood-enhancing music, touch-friendly surfaces, and pleasing aromas. For instance, experiments have long shown that peppermint can improve concentration, lemon can raise our feelings of energy, and lavender relaxes. By way of contrast, it is thought that stress and high blood pressure can be caused by insufficient stimulation of our need to touch and be touched. This possibility may well be related to a finding from The Harvard Study of Adult Development that observed how men who had played physical contact sports such as American football and wrestling while at college, went on to have healthier, happier lives and more successful careers. It's just possible that this success in later life may have something to do with their well-practiced confidence and rapport in interacting at close quarters with other chaps. After all, we homo sapiens are highly social creatures, so our thriving on physical touch with our fellow humans would be a natural characteristic of our whole evolution. There could, however, be a host of other explanations for this finding, but Dr Spence's take-away message from his own work is that a full and balanced range of sensory stimulation is a fundamental biological need that we should feed far more often.

Helen Keller, the American writer who was deaf and blind since infancy, wrote poignantly, "I sometime wonder if the hand is not more sensitive to the beauties of sculpture than the eye. I know that I can feel the heart-throbs of the Ancient Greeks in their marble gods and goddesses."

With all of this in mind, I'd like to advocate a very particular approach to nourishing our senses. It requires an often unappreciated ingredient that will considerably improve almost any positive experience. This Agent X is called '*doing it slowly*'. By simply taking sufficient time, we allow our senses to savour more information. When did we last stroll somewhere and pause and ponder the world around us, rather than power-walking our way to some destination seemingly more important? How slowly can we eat, speak or breathe, yet not lose their essential fluidity? If this idea appeals, rather than telling ourselves to slow-down, like the voice of an anxious mum, we'll respond better if we encourage ourselves to 'turn on the slow motion', because trying actively to do something is usually far easier than trying not to.

Doing things slowly isn't right for every occasion, of course, just as there are times to nip in the shower and times to take a leisurely bath, but it's crucial to have slow in our repertoire. An added bonus is that taking an automatic skill and doing it in slow motion, the way we speak for instance, renders the activity more accessible to our conscious mind and so presents an opportunity to recraft even deeply-ingrained habits.

Seeing strength in going slowly, hopefully reminds us that the science of well-being strongly supports the philosophy that far more happiness and satisfaction can be found in savouring a good journey while we're actually on route, rather than compromising our travels for the sake of some final destination. On this point, it's interesting that elite athletes often recount how, if they allow themselves to be distracted from the job-in-hand by imagining the moment of their impending victory, that's when the game can suddenly slip away. So we all do well to cherish the here and now. But taking our time doesn't have to mean finishing late. It can mean planning to cover less ground so as to increase the quality of the experience. And let's remember: the object of bringing slowness to our senses like this, is that even though we eat less, say less, do less, it will mean so much more.

Sensuality

My research in the arena of romance, is still underway . . . as the women of Cambridge will be only too happy to testify with hoots of knowing laughter. Hence, this is one of the shorter sections of the book, as I wish only to convey three lessons I've personally learned:

- One year as an undergraduate, I sent out a whole pile of Valentines written on graph paper, in an attempt to bring some order to what I felt to be the 'irregularities' of romance. This wasn't a successful strategy, and I don't recommend it.

- When it comes to teaming up with the right partner, *timing* can be very important. For example, I used to have an absolutely gorgeous Danish au-pair . . . the only snag being that I was six at the time.

- Reading aloud is one of the loveliest things two individuals can do for each other in bed. *The Wind in the Willows* is a fine place to start, or Oscar Wilde's *The Happy Prince*.

Paying heed to our intuitions

Oprah Winfrey rose from the severe problems of her childhood to become one of America's wealthiest women, an Oscar-nominated actress for *The Color Purple*, and the host of one of the world's best known talk shows. She explains "I am guided by a higher calling. It's not so much a voice, as a feeling. If it doesn't feel right to me, I don't do it . . . I never took a business course. I run this company based on instinct. I'm an instinct player, an instinct actor – and I use it to guide me in the business. *Gut* is what got me where I am today".

So has science got anything to say about our intuitions?
It's pronounced 'sigh', written 'psi', and is the term specialists use in preference to 'parapsychology'. Psi is the Greek letter that in mathematical equations denotes an unknown quantity. This makes it a particularly apt term to label the study of those unknown factors responsible for a whole range of unexplained interactions between our mind and our environment. The field of psi investigates the possible existence of extra-sensory perceptions such as telepathy (mind to mind communications), psychokinetic phenomena (the mind affecting matter), premonitions of the future, and also the sense that we're being stared at.

Undoubtedly fraudsters abound in such a pioneering and seductive field, but that shouldn't be a reason for dismissing the good science that does seem to exist.

Before we roll our eyes and mutter things like 'pscyhobabble and baloney!', let's consider the advantages of keeping a flexible and inquiring mind. The Study of Well-Being is all about how good life can get and how good we can get at living it. By my reckoning, this makes psi's systematic exploration of some unconventional means for rapport with our world, a highly relevant enterprise. But is it just wishful thinking that the human mind has such paranormal potential for enhanced communications?

In 1995, Jessica Utts, a professor of statistics at the University of California, was requested by both US Congress and the CIA to evaluate the statistical evidence for what was termed 'Psychic Functioning' (i.e. psi phenomena), based upon the previous two decades of US government research. The summary of the official report by Professor Utts read as follows: "Using the standards applied to any other area of science, it is concluded that psychic functioning has been well established. The statistical results of the studies examined are far beyond what is expected by chance." Professor Utts goes on to say that "Effects of similar magnitude . . . have been replicated at a number of laboratories across the world. Such consistency cannot be readily explained by claims of flaws or fraud."

Of course, this report did not go uncontested, and the arguments still rage.

For more than 16 years at Cambridge University, Professor Brian Josephson, a Nobel prize-winning physicist, has led his Mind-Matter Unification Project. He caused considerable controversy in 2001 when he wrote that quantum theory (which explores the world of energy particles that are smaller than atoms) "may lead to an explanation of processes still not understood within conventional science, such as telepathy."

Controversies aside, it's an intriguing suggestion that a fusion of physics and psychology may well be necessary to make headway in these uncharted territories. As Josephson says "I began to sense that conventional science is inadequate for situations where the mind is involved."

It seems that understanding psi phenomena may not only require the detection of presently unrecognised forms of energy, comparable perhaps to light, electricity or radiation, but there might also be unidentified extra-dimensions that link space and time via hitherto unidentified pathways down which energy and information are invisibly travelling. Rather like in those B-movies when the hooded phantom takes advantage of a set of secret doors and concealed passages so as to pull-off seemingly impossible feats.

On the theme of unidentified extra-dimensions, it's worth noting that in July 2004, Professor Stephen Hawking of Cambridge University argues that there are ten or eleven dimensions of time and space. So 'science fiction' may yet become 'science fact'.

Should this whole notion of parapsychology be hard to believe, let's just remember that Planet Earth circles a sun that's part of a galaxy of 100 million other suns burning brightly. What's more, there are some 100 million such galaxies in our universe, and this universe is being stretched outwards by something physicists call 'dark energy' that they are still some way from understanding. My point is, that real life, *by its nature*, is quite incredible.

Nonetheless, let's ask what level of evidence have pioneering 'psi' experiments hitherto provided, and with what implications for our everyday happiness. Could it be that our intuitions and goodwill have a greater potential than we presently credit them? In terms of well-being, any extrasensory methods for improving our interpersonal rapport and intuition are a welcome boon, but what's the evidence for the human mind having paranormal capacities?

Taking stock, we see that research into parapsychology is conducted at a range of leading universities around the world, including Adelaide, Cambridge, Edinburgh, Gothenburg, and Princeton. One of the most promising avenues is well illustrated by the classic telepathy experiment in which one person tries to mentally transmit one of four photographic images to a second, distant person. Nobel Laureate, Brian Josephson, strongly supports the claim of many experimenters that the seemingly isolated receiver can correctly name the image about one third of the time, rather than one quarter of the time as would be expected if the law of averages was the only dynamic at work here.

This level of effect is broadly comparable to the experimental evidence for 'the sense of being stared at', which usually involves someone in a sound-proofed room being observed intermittently through a video camera by someone in another part of the building. Findings from thousands of trials indicate the average recipient's 'special sense' to be circa 60% accurate, rather than the 50% that mere guessing would achieve. However, like being double-jointed, not everyone can do it. On the other hand, if participants have a close emotional bond, the strike-rate for both of the experiments above can be far higher. And, of course, laboratory conditions cannot readily imitate the real-world occasions when there might be a powerful incentive to communicate telepathically. It's logical to presume that a greater incentive would enlarge the effects, just as adrenaline enhances our physical capacities.

The psi phenomenon called premonition seems another promising arena. Professor Jessica Utts's 1995 official report to the U.S. Government read: "Precognition, in which the answer is known to no one until a future time, appears to work quite well. Recent experiments suggest that if there is a psychic sense then it works much like our other five senses, by detecting change. Given that physicists are currently grappling with an understanding of time, it may be that a psychic sense exists that scans the future for major change, much as our eyes scan the environment for visual change or our ears allow us to respond to sudden changes in sound."

The idea of at least some humans being able to scan the world around us with an as yet un-recognised energy, is hardly implausible. After all, dolphins, whales and bats send out high-frequency soundwaves that read their physical environment, and we humans have machines that imitate this principle to scan human bodies with ultrasound or to guide submarines with sonar.

By contrast to the above, the least persuasive findings are in the arena of telekinesis, meaning 'mind directly affecting matter' (other than our own bodies). At Princeton University, Professor Robert Jahn ran the School of Engineering and Applied Science for 15 years, and was founder of the famous PEAR laboratory. Professor Jahn has publicly stated that after 25 years work, "over tens of millions of trials, we have a very strong case that people's intentions can have a small but persistent effect on the results." That term 'small' translates as an un-startling *one* abnormal movement per *ten thousand* tiny movements of a high-precision instrument whose error rate would normally be one in a million. "We have observed very tiny but repeatable effects," affirms Professor Jahn.

Of course, there are physicists down the hall at Princeton who think it's all hogwash, but science has a colourful history of angry dismissal and then a grudging acceptance years later, only once the stick-in-the-muds have literally died away. For instance, in the field of medicine, when it was first suggested in the 1870s by the brilliant French research chemist, Dr Louis Pasteur, that infection and even deadly diseases were spread by invisible micro-organisms he called germs, the notion was for a long time ridiculed and rebuffed by the medical establishment in both France and England.

Taken all together, I presently believe it very likely that some of us, under certain conditions, have the ability to send and receive forms of energy in ways hitherto little charted by science; and I look forward to an era when more of us learn how to magnify, harness and channel these elusive abilities. Meanwhile, in terms of happiness, at least two thoughts occur to me.

First, we do ourselves a disservice if we ride roughshod over our gut feelings and intuitions to which we cannot always put clear thoughts or words. Let's not forget that other subtle forms of communication, such as art, music or smell, have great sway over us and for good effect.

Second, it's rather cheering to think that when we silently send our love to absent friends, we might not be the only one benefiting from our good will.

* * *

Planning for Progress

- What signals might you be sending, and are they what you really want to say?

- Where in your life could you be gentler so as to achieve a greater effect?

- With whom would you like to cook something up?

* * *

Helping Others

It's a cast iron fact of human psychology, that the higher our spirits, the more willing we are to help others. Far from being smug and self-possessed, happier individuals are far more likely to take an interest in the world around them, and be a source of good within it. All by itself this is a very good reason for why we need to keep ourselves chipper and cheerful. But what's even better is, that the very act of helping others out will itself contribute to our good feelings, which means everyone benefits.

Having and being a mentor

The GoodWork Project has to date interviewed more than one thousand working-world professionals, each of whom is widely regarded as quite outstanding by their peers. The essential question to these exceptionally high-achievers was this: How did they tackle the challenge of consistently producing work that is both of excellent quality yet also considerate of the well-being of the wider community. In essence, *what promotes 'honourable work'*?

This research is a joint research venture between leading psychologists at Harvard, Stanford and Chicago universities, and the
fields under investigation include genetics, journalism, business, law,
medicine, and education, i.e. wherever the pace of development and
market pressures might urge some form of corner-cutting. One of
the findings so far seems to be that a key ingredient for good work
to take place, *is good mentorship*. It's particularly noteworthy that
whereas the veteran professionals who were interviewed tended to
recount how their own apprenticeships had strongly benefited from
mentors and role-models, by stark contrast the relative newcomers
felt an unhelpful sense of loneliness and being left to get on with it.

So mentors are valuable people, that's for sure, but what makes
one?

At its best, mentorship is a one to one, non-parental relationship that allows the mentee to confide in someone who understands
something of that younger individual's wider life, as well as their
past experiences and aspirations for the future. To mentor, we don't
need to be wise, we need to be willing to care and to teach by our
own good example. For instance, American basketball star and
breast cancer survivor, Edna Campbell, says the following: "I don't
mind talking about it. Not at all. If what I say can benefit somebody
else, well then let it be known and let it be said. As long as I feel like
I can help someone, I have a purpose."

In the very same spirit, the veteran agony aunt and social campaigner, Claire Rayner, has said that by owning up to and sharing
her own pains from across her lifetime, she can be more help to
those around her than by giving the false impression she was always
a pillar of unshakeable strength and clear-mindedness.

In a mentoring relationship, rapport and mutual respect must
come first, because only then will the mentee be ready for a mixture
of thoughtful questioning and guidance on how they might go about
finding some answers to their own questions. And we should not
wait to be asked to mentor, because the very individuals who would
benefit most, are often too nervous to invite that relationship. The
Oscar-winning actor and Second World War bomber pilot, James
Stewart, said something touchingly sensitive on just this point. "I

think every living creature is capable of feeling left out, and I almost look at it as a duty for one creature to watch out for another."

Particularly telling are the results from my research on the YoungLives project. In 1999, I interviewed one to one and in small groups for an hour or more some of the most accomplished young men and women of their generation. I realised that two aspects of growing-up had far and away brought the most pain to these young people in their teens and mid-twenties. These were:

- their lack of self-confidence, i.e. the confidence to speak their mind, ask for help, declare their strongest hopes, fears and passions, or to step out from the crowd.
- the absence of a mentor with whom to freely broach life-topics of crucial interest to them.

So, as potential mentors, let's take heart in knowing that we could be providing a unique relationship in that young person's life that will prevent the profound loneliness that comes from being unable to confide in anyone. And mentors do get appreciated, often for a lifetime. Veteran BBC broadcaster, Terry Wogan, says this about his mentor, Denis Meehan: "Without him, I would now be a retired bank clerk. He heard and saw something in me that was not apparent to most. Throughout the all-too-brief years that I was privileged to know and work with him, he was never the less a great friend, adviser and advocate."

And here's another testimony to the value of mentorship. The indigenous Australian gold medal sprinter, Cathy Freeman, was in the early stages of her comeback after the Sydney 2000 Olympics. "I had always wanted to sit down and talk to Michael Johnson about how he coped with everything throughout his career. He was the greatest there had ever been – five Olympic gold medals and nine world titles – and I'd always been too shy to approach him. However, he'd been really enthusiastic when we'd seen each other in Manchester – he'd greeted me with a big hug – so I decided a couple of weeks later to ring him and ask for some help. *It was the best thing I could have done.* For ten days, I was like a sponge, soaking up all that Michael could offer. We went to dinner together, he came down and watched a few training sessions, and we had some very intense, open and honest conversations. It was like we'd known each other for years. *I had myself a mentor.* He agreed to play a part in my future and be on hand for any advice."

This close relationship between master craftsman and apprentice is a recipe for excellence. Nobel Physicist, Richard Feynman, underlines just this point: "The best teaching can be done only when there is a direct individual relationship between a student and a good teacher – a situation in which the student discusses the ideas, and thinks and talks about things."

Capturing the beauty of that one to one rapport, Claire Rayner tells how when she was a Nursing Sister, she had a superb consultant in paediatrics. "He taught me to listen to the silences. To what people don't tell you. He taught me to use my eyes. The way children would sit. The body language. He taught me all that."

Columbia University psychology professors, Charles Harrington and Susan Boardman, jointly interviewed for a full three hours, each one of 60 very high achieving mid-career professionals who had thrived despite the odds of their seemingly disadvantaged backgrounds. Three quarters of these individuals reported that mentors had been very important in their careers. This ratio prevails in all the research I've seen since; i.e. most people who are living life with flying colours can point to a mentor, often several mentors, even though there are some souls who make it through without. The former always enjoyed the experience, the latter are always regretful they didn't have someone guiding their enthusiasm.

So let's become a mentor to someone, because when we teach something we learn more about it ourselves, and the encouragement we give will reverberate within us. That's the beauty of a mentoring relationship – both parties thrive.

From mentors to role-models

In the absence of a suitable mentor, identifying a role-model in our everyday life can be a guiding beacon. In the late 1990s, Cambridge University's Dr Sarah Fitzharding explored the coping strategies of

80 very highly accomplished men and women in the UK and USA, all of whom were lesbian, gay or bisexual, and nearly all of whom had endured considerable adversity because of their sexual orientation. Towards the end of each interview, Dr Fitzharding asked "What one thing above all else would have made the greatest improvement to your experience of growing up?" More than half the participants gave fundamentally the same answer: *"The example close at hand of an adult who was gay and out, and thriving in their personal and professional life."*

As well as looking for role-models in our everyday life, we could also read the autobiographies of those people we most admire. This way, we can read in helpful detail how their progress in life was not over-night or unearned, as it can so often appear from afar, but was in fact a natural development of their determined practice, their passion, and their enduring positive relationships.

Eileen Collins, the former U.S. Air Force test pilot who became the first woman to command a NASA Space Shuttle, has told how her family were of modest means and couldn't pay for her flying lessons. So as a child and teenager, young Eileen found other ways to feed her enthusiasm for the ambition of one day becoming a pilot. "I began reading voraciously about famous pilots, from Amelia Earhart through to women airforce service pilots who played an important role in the Second World War. Their stories inspired me. I admired the courage of these women to go and fly in dangerous situations!"

In the same spirit, New York Senator and lawyer, Hillary Rodham Clinton, drew on the experience of a former First Lady to guide her in coping with that very same role. "I am a huge fan of Mrs Eleanor Roosevelt, and I have long collected portraits and mementos from her career. Seeing her calm, determined visage brought to mind some of her wise words . . . I often joked in my speeches that I had imaginary conversations with Mrs Roosevelt to solicit her advice on a range of subjects. It's actually a useful mental exercise to help analyse problems."

It's rather nice to know that even Albert Einstein had the portraits of Isaac Newton and Michael Faraday watching over him as he worked at his desk. It's a reminder that we all of us benefit from the inspiration of other people's lives which can help us embody in our own grand plans and day to day activities something of their winning spirit. It might also prompt us to give an autobiography to one of our loved ones as a way to support and encourage them in their passions.

Taking this thought one step further, my YoungLives research among the hundreds of highly accomplished individuals that I mentioned above, reminded me that one of our greatest natural resources is the goodness of people around us, and their willingness to help. I wonder if we couldn't do rather more in our universities and schools to promote a systematic and sensitive study of lives that go well. Some means by which to harvest and convey what is presently passed on by good luck rather than good planning. Because it's one thing to allow the emerging generation to determine their own path . . . that's only right and natural . . . but do we really want them to reinvent the wheel? Good schools have always appreciated the value of close-at-hand mentors and role-models; and what I would suggest is something to complement that: classes to sensitise students to the underlying dynamics that shape a life, so they can better appreciate the ones they see around them. Not that this can replace first-hand life experience, but it can help us make more sense of the rough and tumble when we're on route.

Why tv doesn't provide good role-models

In the absence of suitable mentors and role models, a young person will look around for whom so ever catches their eye. My Mum and Dad divorced when I was six, and it was about then that I accidentally adopted tv characters as my male role-models, since the adults in the weekly shows seemed a good deal happier that the ones I knew in the everyday life around me. From that time onwards, I aspired to be a rather confusing mixture of James T. Kirk of the *Star Ship Enterprise*, Errol Flynn in *Robin Hood*, and Bugs Bunny. But one thing was clear: everything would turn out alright in the end, just as it always did for the screen characters I so admired. And along the way, no sadness would go unseen, no kindness un-rewarded.

The trouble is, screen-fiction misses out too many of life's important details, and the battles and the beauties are always won within two hours. This all meant that my end goals were clear enough to me, embodied as they were by Cary Grant, Indiana Jones, and Hawkeye, but I lacked the detailed life-strategies and specific know-how to make even a first step in the right direction. I didn't want to grow up, I wanted to be shot down . . . in a Spitfire. Might even get to do a stint digging tunnels in Stalag Three . . . me and Steve McQueen wandering around with half a garden hidden in our trousers.

The net result of this accidental education by my tv heroes, was that my expectations of real life grew very inflated. Little did I realise that it would take more than three Cs in English, French and Economics to make me an ocean-going pirate. And it never dawned upon me to read autobiographies to see in more detail how other people had tried to live their lives. I was 19 and on my way to Wyoming when I finally stumbled across a book called *What Life Has Taught Me*, written by a retired Admiral. His advice had limited value, though, as it largely consisted of how to bring your gunboat into harbour in a heavy sea. Now that might have been a metaphor for all sorts of useful things, but it sailed well over my head. I was like a one-man Titanic . . . thinking that the white blob looming towards me was just bird-pooh on the windscreen.

Asking helpful questions

Some of the best friendships are forged in the crucible of tough times shared, but when we are the helper, we need to resist the urge to offer our ready-made answers or to bail the person out. In the long run, we play a far more valuable role if we can free-up their thinking by debating with them some new perspectives and creative routes forward. In all of this, the greatest skill on our part is to raise the sorts of questions which let our companion generate solutions for themselves, so they feel they really own them. This is the essence of Socratic questioning, and will nurture both their self-respect and their skill in coping; in which case, we would have done our friend a jolly good turn.

Here's a good example of how an unhelpful question can get an unhelpful answer. When researchers ask 'Are you satisfied with your job?' . . . a suspiciously high percentage of people claim 'yes!' But when asked 'Would you recommend your job to your son, daughter or a best friend?' . . . the numbers plummet.

The discrepancy seems to occur because we're reluctant to admit to ourselves, let alone a researcher, that we're unhappy in our work but haven't done anything about it. Makes us feel feeble, so we fib instead. For a question to be helpful, it needs to nip around such natural defenses, which is why asking a loved one, 'Are you happy?' won't prompt the same considered reply as 'What sorts of things would you like to improve in your life?' Their answer might be a wish for more companionship or variety or adventure, and such answers as these can readily lead on to our next question: 'What sort of activities would that require?' and then 'How could I help you right here and now to get the ball rolling?'

The trouble is, in our pressing desire for progress, we're rather too partial to short-cuts. This is self-defeating because short-cuts rather miss the point that most of the pleasure and goodness of life comes from experiencing the journey, not simply arriving. For instance, too much wine might catapult us into some imitation of happiness, but what have we learnt on route? For just the same reasons, helpful questioning needs to be a gradual, cumulative process that builds on the firm ground of a person's responses, step by step.

Helpful questions deserve helpful answers . . . or rather, helpful action. Because a helpful answer can be found in any action that begins to test out in the real world whether or not the first stage of our solution is going to make a positive difference. We need to investigate not just interrogate. We need to trial run it: 'If I do this, only that happens, so to improve things, I must try something else.'

Changing the way we do things is one of the most powerful mechanisms we have for changing how we think and feel. Just as lateral thinking prompts creative action, so our getting active in novel ways can foster novel thoughts. This is why confronting something we'd normally avoid will, if we stick it out with the help of a friend, scotch the fear once and for all.

Once again, 'process' is the name of the game, and rather than taking isolated pot-shots at a problem, we're better to seek a solution through a series of experiments that build brick by brick upon our findings. Whether it's making a career decision or improving a relationship, how things turn out will depend largely on the goodness of the route taken, so we should set out to explore on foot rather than trying to parachute ourselves in to the future. Instant solutions are in grave danger of depriving us of the learning curve of experience that is the real path forward. After all, we don't just want the diploma, we want the education that earned it.

When our process of inquiry leads on to open-minded investigation, we go from being a philosopher to being a scientist. "I have no special talents", said Albert Einstein, "I am only passionately curious" . . . and being curious about how we might progress our everyday life by asking helpful questions and testing out the answers, is a cornerstone of healthy living.

Gentle teaching

In the previous chapter on rapport, we can see how the lifetime's work of real-life 'Horse Whisperer' Monty Roberts has profound implications for the way individuals relate to each other. The gentleness that Monty advocates may not appear in the index of psychology books, but it's one of the foundations in all good and lasting relationships, and all good learning. A teacher or mentor can use gentleness to create a safe, enjoyable and supportive atmosphere and so foster the student's eager and willing self-motivation. Bullying is never the answer, and it's far better to provide sufficiently attractive routes forward that offer meaningful benefits for both sides. In other words, the mentor seeks to understand the learner; causes the learner to want to learn; and respects their choices and needs as regards what they learn and how. Monty Roberts has a memorable turn of phrase for his view of learning: "Knowledge needs to be pulled into the brain by the student, not pushed in by the teacher." In this he echoes an equally good metaphor written down by the Greek Philosopher, Plutarch, almost 2,000 years ago: "The mind is not a vessel to be filled, but a fire to be kindled." Which rather reminds us that life's most important challenges are time-honoured.

Principles based on the Monty Roberts methods were suggested to the Kingshurst Junior School in Birmingham by one of the school's teachers who then helped devise its everyday application. Mutually agreed contracts were drawn up to recognise and reward the children's achievements, but which also required a forfeit of privileges for un-met agreements (perhaps a breaktime being taken away because of too much litter). As far as the children were concerned, the active ingredients seemed to be the absence of threat or humiliation and the increased sense of empowerment: they could make pleasurable things happen by their own positive actions. Very importantly, the co-operation has to be willingly offered, with theself-evident benefits on offer to the child acting as fuel for their self-motivation. By these means, the children willingly became responsible for the consequences of their own actions. They had to accept ownership of their mistakes, but they also owned the rewards. On which point, making mistakes must be viewed as an essential part of learning, since hands-on learning with immediate feedback is the best way to acquire knowledge and skill. Hence the need for adults who are strong enough to be gentle and patient while the child learns by trial and error. Monty Roberts notes that if we're doing it right, multiple repetition is our greatest ally; if we're doing it wrong, multiple repetition is our greatest enemy. So it's very important to have good and immediate feedback on our performance. Seeing immediate results and seeing our ability to change those results by our actions, is not only guiding but it's also highly motivating.

This whole approach certainly worked for Kingshurst Junior School. Between 1998 and 2002, the school went from being earmarked for closure, to being awarded so called 'Beacon Status' as a model of good practice to other Junior Schools.

Helping children acquire a passion for life

Passion for life is the character trait I would most wish upon a child. That irrepressible enthusiasm: so eager to create and so excited to explore. The roots of such passion are comprised of two skills, and the first of these is the ability to create feelings of profound pleasure through healthy, positive means. As a primer to this, a child needs to discover that true happiness is not something that we can just wait around for, or purchase or consume. Rather it is a feeling we must generate through investing our skills, efforts and ingenuity, in the same way we learn to make friends. We can't turn it on like we turn on the tv, we have to stoke it up.

Such emotional craftsmanship can be directly nurtured by encouraging children in their happiness-making activities, no matter they join in a game or a voluntary project, or are kind and humourous and come up with good ideas. Can they dream-up schemes to make seemingly tedious chores more enjoyable? Can they earn pocket-money by doing what they love in such a way that the world rewards them for it? By rising to these challenges, children become resourceful in their play, rather than expecting adults to provide happiness on a plate. It is hands-on know-how more than well meaning words that will solidly improve a child's inventiveness and hence their self-confidence and standing among their peers. What's more, they will derive a life-long sense of security from being able to trust themselves to drum-up satisfying pursuits rather than resorting to pre-packaged thrills.

To increase a child's mastery of these mood-cheering skills will require practise for the sheer joy of progress, and they will readily seek guidance and coaching. Simply instructing children to 'have fun' won't do it. Let's heed the words of veteran BBC broadcaster Terry Wogan, "Children learn not from what you tell them, but from what they see at home, watching you." And the first woman to be Speaker of the House of Commons, Dame Betty Boothroyd, the only child of a Yorkshire textile worker and weaver, would readily vouch for the importance of the first-hand example set by a parent. "Having political ambitions was hard enough for a young woman in days when men dominated public life; I was considered doubly suspect because I was unmarried. But I grew up in a family whose convictions were set in granite, and I would not be beaten. The strength of my parents, who faced adversity with courage and dignity, flowed in my veins. They bore their hardships lightly and never wavered in their high standards. Their love and example were my bedrock."

Underpinning any apprenticeship in happiness needs to be a self-evident pledge from adult to child: '*I love you and because of this I will unceasingly help you progress in whatever positive directions joy takes you*'. For such a child, learning is a delight; and in times to come their increasing intimacy and appreciation of the people, skills and workings of the world around them will prove their greatest source of joy. These are the happiest, strongest children … the ones who are urged to develop themselves and make progress in their relationships with life, the ones who are absolutely and equally supported in these endeavours, no matter if they are faced with mistakes and setbacks or achievements and plain sailing. Those who love them do *not* withdraw support as a punishment for insufficient results or for passions that are disapproved of. Such reliable back-up from parents or mentors leaves the young individual free from any hunger for approval or liking, and free from any shame or despair at their own sense of coming up short in the eyes of the adults they most care for. With no need for any painful introspection as to their own imagined inadequacies, it is the world around them that becomes the focus of that child's attention, and they're not afraid to take it on.

Such a relationship couldn't be more different from accidentally communicating that '*I will love you but only if you progress in the ways that I prescribe*'. After all, true love is to want what's best for a child, to which end it is passion for life in general that we need to impart, not the specifics of whatever subjects most captivate *us*. Yes, it might be tempting to think I'd like my child to represent Britain some day in the distant future. But why not aim big? Why not endeavour to help her become exceedingly good at creating happiness, so that she will be welcomed, appreciated and rewarded in every aspect of her life. Her emotional acumen will at all ages allow her to be a deeply loved and loving person who plays special roles in the lives around her.

Children who thrive not just survive in the face of adversity

The other half of helping children acquire passion for life, is helping children learn not only to cope with but to prosper in the face of adversity. Without this skill, the pain of loss and rejection, setback and uncertainty, might otherwise sour their relationship with life.

Studies have repeatedly shown that youngsters surrounded by troubles are nonetheless likely to do extremely well if they have at least one close relationship with a caring and competent individual. This might be a family member, neighbour, teacher, coach, or school friend, but children can internalise their mentor's benevolence and so begin to view themselves as worthy of care and will treat themselves accordingly. (It's cheering to note that how much goes right for a child far better predicts their future than how much goes wrong. Positives will outweigh negatives.)

The formative years of Former First Lady and key instigator of The Universal Declaration of Human Rights in 1948, Eleanor Roosevelt, are a fine example of the above principle. "My mother died when I was six. After my father's death when I was eight years old, I did not have that sense of adequacy and of being cherished which he gave me until I met Mademoiselle Marie Souvestre when I was 15. As the headmistress of the school I went to in England, she exerted perhaps the greatest influence on my girlhood. I had lived in a family with some very beautiful aunts and two attractive uncles who looked upon me as a child to whom they were always kind but about whom there was certainly nothing to admire. I was conscious of their pity because my looks fell so far below the family standards and I had no special gifts of any kind to redeem my looks. Miss Souvestre, on the other hand, laid a great deal of stress on intellectual achievements, and there I felt I could hold my own. She took me travelling with her and evidently felt I was an adequate companion. That gave me a great sense of reassurance. For three years, I basked in her generous presence, and I think those three years did much to form my character and give me the confidence to go through some of the trials that awaited me when I returned to the United States.

Though I was to lose some of my self-confidence and ability to look after myself in the early days of my marriage, it came back to me later more easily because of these trips with Miss Souvestre."

With Eleanor's story in mind, let's keep our eyes open for the youngsters around us. Recent research suggests that as many as one in five adolescents will have an episode of depression by the end of high school. Despite this, approximately 70% of depressed children and adolescents *never* receive treatment because their plight isn't recognised. Depression in childhood is likely to reoccur in adulthood, so it's doubly important that all of us as parents, educators and mentors make it our good business to teach children the skills that will protect them against this preventable problem. (My chapter on 'Powerful New Approaches to Common Health Problems' offers a compact list of anti-depression strategies.)

A good mentor will naturally role-model some key coping skills, and the foundation for all of these is the central principle that though life might be frightening at times, we needn't freeze in the face of it. However, to make headway in spite of fortune's slings and arrows, requires that we duck and weave. We might, for instance, generate several attractive but possible goals, and several attractive but possible routes towards each and every one. By spreading our ambitions across multiple baskets like this, we're far less likely to be thwarted. Without such a strategy, when faced with emotional pain or fear, children are tempted to escape into quick-fixes or anaesthetising distractions such as too much television or fantasy, which serve only to inhibit their real-life progress. Of course, drumming up such an array of pathways forward in the face of adversity requires considerable skill and confidence. This is where a mentor can helpfully use Socratic questioning: "What are the various ways you could begin to make things better?" and might then go on to recount their own past problems, all the time illustrating a versatile range of positive responses: "What I did at the time was so and so, but I could just as well have . . . or alternatively . . . or perhaps even . . ."

Encouraging a child's sense of their own power to create meaningful improvements doesn't only protect them against depression and self-destructive behaviour. When life is proving difficult, a saving grace can be a child's growing sense of mastery in just one well-respected activity such as school work, dancing, musicianship, drama or sport. An added bonus from their burgeoning skill is the appreciation and respect of their peers. Once children can trust their own capacity to bounce back, they will be less reluctant to throw themselves into life for fear of having their feelings hurt. They can begin to view everyday opportunities as a win-win situation, because even when life dishes out the lemons, they can trust themselves to find a way of making lemonade – to find a silver lining no matter how dark the cloud.

A catalyst to such alchemy can often be found by encouraging children simply to explore the problem, rather than run from it. Their research might reveal, for instance, that golf champion Tiger Woods, actor Bruce Willis, comedian Rowan Atkinson, singer Carly Simon, composer Andrew Lloyd Webber, and Second World War prime minister Winston Churchill, are just a handful of the many accomplished individuals who suffered from a difficult stammer. The example of these lives provide unexpected proof that if we respond with some positive know-how, there's no problem that need be a show-stopper.

Unexpected allies

Help can come from the most unexpected quarters, because it's about kindred spirits rather than outside appearances. Perkins was a black cat by trade, who lived well beyond his 18th birthday, but he was many other things besides: peace negotiator, mentor, and minder. This last role came to light when I was about 9 and our two rabbits had a dozen babies. They almost drown in the spring rainstorm into which they'd been born, so my brother and I put them on a towel and warmed them on the kitchen radiator. Perkins Cat supervised the whole procedure letting them dry on one side and then turning them over as if he was grilling sausages. Not all survived their traumatic birth, but that summer, when an Alsatian dog got in the garden and headed for the rabbit pen with its young litter, murder in his eyes, old Perkins leapt out from the bushes and placed himself in harms way to defend his baby sausages. That dog didn't know what hit him when Perkins leapt on his back like a black mountain leopard. I witnessed the whole thing from a bedroom window, and since I had recently seen the war epic, *Where Eagles Dare*, I awarded Perkins the highest honour for courage under fire.

The whistling volunteer

No matter how downhearted I went into Feltham Young Offenders Prison, by the end of the day I was whistling. I can't entirely explain the psychology of what took place, but I'm not the least bit surprised to read the studies that consistently indicate that volunteering does a power of good for the person doing it. Whether I was teaching creative writing or road-testing my new *Trail-Blazers* mentoring project, volunteering seemed to elevate my happiness, physical health, and self-respect because I could see myself making a real difference in my own life as well as someone else's. *And this is exactly what the studies say it does.*

Former nurse and Britain's favourite agony aunt, 80 year old social campaigner, Claire Rayner, would agree. "The sense of warmth, relief and peace of mind that comes from making an effort on behalf of someone in need, is very rewarding." Golf champion, Tiger Woods, expresses similar feelings about working with his charitable foundation that inspires underprivileged youngsters. "We've affected so many kids in a positive way. It's more gratifying than anything else. I would much rather be remembered for that, for influencing kids, than winning the golf tournaments. Because I tell you what, the satisfaction you get from helping others far outweighs that." He goes on to say, "When I was young, my dad encouraged me to change the world . . . The lessons I've learned from him simply transcend the game. And the most important lesson I've ever learned from my father, is to share and care for others".

Senior citizens particularly benefit from using their interests and lifeskills in voluntary work, and not surprisingly they make highly effective helpers. Better still, a study led by Doug Oman at Berkeley University in California, studied more than 2,000 elderly individuals over four years, and found those who were strongly involved in volunteering had almost half the mortality rate of non-volunteers. This is only circumstantial evidence, but would be well-explained by the self-motivated stimulation of our physical, intellectual and social resources that voluntary work entails. Such findings would be wholly consistent with everything we know about living a healthier, happier life.

Young men and women in their teens and twenties also gain a great deal from involving themselves in some structured community action. It can be an impressive means by which to demonstrate what's important to them and the abilities they can bring to a job, particularly if they're not yet doing the paid work they really wish for. Not only that, but there's bags of unexpected learning to be had by putting ourselves in unfamiliar situations. For instance, in an average day in Feltham, I might find myself in long conversations with teenagers who'd robbed banks, with a Holy Friar, with women who'd single-handedly set up major charities (despite irritable resistance from the authorities), as well as a British Army general doing charitable work in his retirement. In addition to which there were half a dozen men and women prison officers, sometimes not much older than the young men in their care. What's nice about it is, *we all got on* . . . bound, perhaps, by the common purpose of making life in this high-security environment not just survivable but liveable and full of learning. I, for one, learnt in spadefuls because I was seeing such a wide variety of views on the world.

Choosing what to do

All told, then, the benefits of volunteering on a regular basis are wide-ranging and well-established, but there are still some caveats worth considering.

First off, we need to find something which speaks to our heart-felt interests. This can mean passing on the good that has made a difference in our own lives. Thus, the philanthropic activities of pioneering show-host and media entrepreneur, Oprah Winfrey, tend to centre on educating and empowering people. "Education is what liberated me. The ability to read saved my life. I would have been an entirely different person had I not been taught to read at an early age. My entire life experience, my ability to believe in myself, and even in my darkest moments of being sexually abused and being physically abused, I knew there was another way. I knew there was a way out. I knew there was another kind of life because I had read about it. I knew there were other places, and there was another way of being. It saved my life, so that's why I now focus my attention on trying to do the same thing for other people."

Indeed, some of the healthiest personalities are characterised by individuals taking revenge on their own painful past by engaging themselves in the sort of highly constructive charitable work which puts things right for the next generation. U.S. women's soccer star, Mia Hamm, is tireless in her work against bone-marrow disease since her brother Garrett died from complications related to anaemia. In 1999, she created the Mia Hamm Foundation, a non-profit national organization dedicated to raising funds and awareness for bone-marrow disease, as well as developing more opportunities for young women to participate in sports.

So in considering how and where we can volunteer, we should not be shy to consider what we personally hope to earn from the experience. Perhaps it's honing our skills, demonstrating our passions, or simply having the company of good souls; but to select our activities accordingly isn't being selfish, it's being sensible. Six times Tour de France winner and cancer survivor Lance Armstrong explains, "My encounters with other cancer fighters are often mis-construed: I don't stay involved with cancer just to help others. I do it to help myself . . . it gives me a sense of peace and perspective to talk to a fellow patient". After a disappointing time trial during the 2002 Tour de France, a family was waiting for Lance with their young son who had cancer. "I paused to chat with them on a grassy hillside, and as we spoke, as the sun was setting, the events of the day receded. What they couldn't know was that talking about cancer was like medicine for me. That night, talking with that little boy and his family put me back on my feet. Finally, I thanked them for com-ing and went inside to join the team for dinner. But I did so with a surer grasp of what's right and real in the world, and with a sense that there was always a larger community that I belonged to, from which I would always get help in a tough time."

At its best, helping others in need can give us a new sense of identity and purpose. Diana, the Princess of Wales, achieved this wonderfully. "I was very confused by which area I should go into. Then I found myself being more and more involved with people who were rejected by society. And I respected very much the honesty I found on that level with people I met, because in hospices, for instance, when people are dying, they're much more open and more vulnerable, and much more real than other people. And I appreciated that. I remember when I used to sit on hospital beds and hold people's hands ... And when I saw the reassurance that an action like that gave, I did it everywhere, and will always do that. I have found my role."

So it is that our foresight about what will feel most meaningful to us, will help us stick with things through thick and thin because the work can draw on a deep well of genuine enthusiasm. All the research evidence suggests that the more we gain from the activity, the longer we'll pursue it ... a principle of learning that applies across the board in life.

Choosing a suitable project is also about playing to our signature strengths – those enjoyable activities which bring out the best in us. Perhaps we're a whiz with figures or people or practical matters, but we should be careful not to move beyond our area of competence without adequate mentorship. My pleasure from those Feltham Prison days came from the in-depth conversations out on the prisoner wings, whereas I loathed the painstaking paperwork that went with running a charity. Administration simply was not one of my signature strengths, whereas others around me were consummate organisers.

We also need to be realistic about our own emotional resources, because planting trees with an environmental group is going to make very different demands on us than working with hospice patients who are so close to death. If we're feeling fragile, then we should start off with something manageable, perhaps a couple of hours per week assisting someone who knows the ropes. On the other hand, if we feel game for it, why not partner up with a friend to create our very own voluntary project, and then offer to run this under the umbrella of an already registered charity, and so minimise the admin duties. Either way, the benefits could be far reaching for all concerned.

Voluntary work has always done wonders for me, so I'm delighted to mention four of my favourite benevolent organisations:

The Prince's Trust offers practical solutions to help young people age 14 to 30 get their lives working. To do this, they always need trainers and mentors, which might mean you and me. Visit www.princestrust.org.uk or Freephone 0800-842-842.

Teach First trains and fast-tracks the most dynamic young graduates during at least two years of full-time teaching at some of the most challenging and rewarding inner-city secondary schools. During those two years, participants not only qualify as teachers, but also receive top-flight leadership training from Teach First, as well as one to one mentorship from senior individuals within leading companies. Participants can then decide either to continue with their teaching career, or to take their skills and confidence to pastures new. This mixture of a worthwhile challenge, supportive training, and freedom of choice, begins to explain why Teach First is consistently voted one of the very best graduate employers. Visit www.TeachFirst.org.uk

St Christopher's Hospice in East London is one of the flagships of the modern-day Hospice movement which cares for terminally-ill children and adults and offers support to their families and loved ones. The Hospice movement is always glad of volunteers for a host of valuable roles in more than 250 hospices throughout the UK. Visit www.stchristophers.org.uk or phone your local hospice and ask how you might help.

The Open University is one of the UK's best respected universities and offers supported distance learning to adults of all ages and backgrounds. Better still, very few of the courses have any entry requirements at all in terms of previous qualifications. There are 150,000 undergraduates studying for Certificates, Diplomas and Bachelor degrees, and 30,000 postgraduates doing Masters, PhDs and professional qualifications. Courses aren't free of charge, but many OU students are in full-time employment (and so study part-time), perhaps being sponsored by their employer. Many students live outside the UK, and that's not a problem. Visit www.open.ac.uk or telephone General Enquiries on 01908-653-231

Hollywood actor and film producer, Tom Cruise, recounts how his mother inspired helpfulness in her children. "One of the best Christmases as a kid was the time when we didn't buy anything. My mother came up with this idea to pick names out of a hat and for a month you had to do nice things for that person, every day leading up to Christmas. And you couldn't reveal who it was. I picked one of my sisters, so I would go into her room and make her bed while she was in the shower so I wouldn't get caught. It was fantastic. Then Christmas Day came and we each stood up and told each other who we were helping for the past month... My mother was very giving. We would go to nursing homes to help people. What is a life if you are not contributing to others and doing something to help someone?"

Having grown up with a mother who took such an attitude to life, it is not surprising that Tom Cruise, who suffered from dyslexia as a youngster, is now investing considerable time and money in a literacy project. "I don't want people to go through what I went through," Tom says. "I want kids to have the ability to read, to write, to understand what people are saying to them, and to be able to solve life's problems."

* * *

Planning for Progress

- Who could you mentor and who could mentor you?

- Is there a youngster you know who you could take under your wing?

- Is there a voluntary project you would find particularly satisfying?

* * *

PART TWO

Becoming an Expert in our Favourite Pursuits

Introduction to Part Two

Why Become an Expert?

In this part of the book, I'd like to explain how we can get really good at our favourite activities, whether that be our work, a hobby, or even parenting. But before I do, let's step back a pace and ask the big WHY.

Why bother to get really good at something in the first place?

The short answer is this:

Being good at something is far more enjoyable than being bad at it – which is true for at least six compelling reasons . . . and a seventh even better one.

1 It brings us profoundly satisfying feelings to get to know something really well, becoming intimate with all its dimensions,

whether that be a skill, a place, or a person. The greater our level of skill, the more rewarding will be the feelings from exercising that skill. We have naturally evolved to be that way.

2 We gain a wonderful sense of confidence in our future from knowing how to get good at something. It reassures us that things can and do progress, and that life gets better if we work at it.

3 Every other domain of our life will benefit from our expertise in a single arena. As golf champion Tiger Woods puts it: "I think golf is a microcosm of life, you learn so many different things. I've learned discipline, integrity and sportsmanship. Golf taught me how to concentrate for long periods of time and I was able to take that lesson into the classroom. Patience, accepting a tough situation, prioritizing – all of these things I learned from the game and was able to apply to school."

4 Aiming to become expert reliably teams us up with other like-minded souls just as passionate about life as ourselves. U.S. Olympic soccer captain, Mia Hamm, was moving around a lot as a child because her father was in the armed forces. She gladly acknowledges that her football skills helped her settle-in socially because every time she joined a new team, she immediately made new friends. In fact, that rapport with team-mates, practice-partners and coaches, is probably the single most important skill and experience that we gain from our training activities.

5 Being good at something establishes our individuality in a positive and attractive way. This thought strikes a chord with American rock musician and songwriter, Bruce Springsteen. "If my work's about anything, it's the search for identity, for personal recognition, for acceptance, for communion." What's more, there'll come a time when we're good enough to coach others, which is a source of even greater satisfaction and a sense of self-worth.

6 We're going to have to do something to make our way in life, so we can either get really good at something we'd dearly like to do, or we can let the working world randomly allocate us to wherever it wants. If we've got a skill, if we've something rare and valuable to offer, this might well give us the power to make some choices about what, where, and with whom we wind-up working.

7. If we don't get better and better … we'll get worse and worse.
This seventh reason to get good at something is on account of 'The
Matthew Effect', whereby an initial success in something tends to
lead to even greater success. On the other hand, if we are *unsuccessful*, we're likely to become even less so. In short, it seems that success or failure will grow like topsy whichever gets the upper-hand
first. The effect derives its name from a passage in *The Gospel of St.
Matthew, 25:29. "To everyone who has, will more be given, and he
will have abundance. But from him who has not, even what he has
will be taken away."*

Heavy stuff, but the effect seems to be true no matter what activity we look at. For instance, children who start-off reading well will
get better and better compared to their peers, because they will read
ever more broadly and quickly. The more words they learn, the easier
and more enjoyable it all becomes. On the other hand, it's very hard
for poor readers to catch up, because for them the spiral goes downwards. Due to The Matthew Effect, the gap between those who read
well and those who read poorly grows ever bigger rather than smaller.

The same principle applies in the working world. If someone
wants a job done, they tend to ask a busy and successful person, not
only because that person has acquired bags of experience and confidence and so ends up doing a better job, but that person also has a
booming business that brings lots of good contacts and a growing
reputation. So if we're hot property, we get hotter. But if we're finding
it hard to get work, we become even less employable because we're
out of practice, we're losing confidence, and we're short of contacts.

This phenomenon operates in every arena of life you care to
think of, and for institutions just as much as individuals. For example, leading companies and universities attract the best applicants
and so continue to top the charts even though the elite institutions
themselves may be no better at training their people.

That's The Matthew Effect: success snowballs, but so does
failure, so we need to get our spiral going in the right direction.

* * *

Facts and Fiction
about Becoming an Expert

The real roots of expertise

If ever you find yourself pondering wistfully those things you dearly wish you were really good at, you'll be interested to hear the following:

Just about any individual of average learning ability is quite capable of acquiring a professional level of expertise in virtually any field of endeavour, no matter whether this be with a musical instrument or foreign language, fiction writing or fine art, science or sport.

That's a wonderful thought . . . perhaps even unbelievable . . . so how do we know it's true?

Some of the best evidence is from the lifetime's work of my one-time tutor, Professor Michael Howe, who carefully analysed the routes to expertise of some of history's most eminent achievers, as well as modern-day athletes and musicians. After a whole career spent studying the development of exceptional abilities, Professor Howe declared he had found absolutely no evidence to support the widespread belief that we need some inborn head-start by way of special gifts or talented genes.

In support of this assertion, stands the work of two of America's most celebrated Educational Psychology professors: Harvard University's Howard Gardner, and Yale University's Robert Sternberg, who are world-leaders in the field of extraordinary achievement and expertise. They would agree that extremely high levels of skill must be learned in the course of life rather than inherited at birth; and what we commonly refer to as 'talents' are, in reality, 'skills-in-development'.

There appear to be *four* key ingredients which need to be in plentiful supply if we're to learn to excel in our chosen pursuits. These are:

- Lots of determined practice ... always aiming to improve, not just go through the motions. Practice is the single most important factor determining how good we get at something.
- A heart-felt, self-motivating passion to fuel those long hours of practice.
- Warm support and encouragement from someone deeply important to us.
- A rich learning environment comprised of practice buddies, coaches and role-models.

This chapter will look at each of these in turn.

The paramount importance of practice

Let's take for example, musical ability, which is commonly considered something you've either got or you haven't. And let's start by laying to rest the myth of 'perfect-pitch' (which is the ability to identify or strike a particular note without any guiding reference point). It may not have been *deliberately* learned by a young child, but that doesn't mean it was in-born. Think how, in our early years, we invisibly and unconsciously acquire many skills and habits. Add to this the fact that perfect-pitch can readily be learned simply through sufficient practice, and that accomplished musicians do not regard the skill as especially beneficial to top-level performance. In light of that accumulated evidence, perfect pitch now seems far less miraculous or important. So let's up the stakes. Let's consider Mozart.

It reliably requires 3,000 hours of determined practice to turn the everyday novice into an impressive amateur of county standard, no matter that be in salsa dancing, horse-riding, or speaking a foreign language; and music is no exception to this rule of thumb. In other words, getting really good at an instrument would require two hours per day, six days per week, for five years. By way of comparison, it requires on average a total of 10,000 hours to reach professional concert level. Yes, Mozart was a competent violinist by the age of six, but his father was a pre-eminent music teacher who made his three year old son practice several hours per day. Bearing in mind the 3,000 hours that little Amadeus must have notched-up by age 6, we should be more surprised if he *hadn't* become a prodigy.

Numerous studies have also confirmed that it takes at least *ten years* of full-time dedicated practice to become world-class in just about any domain. This is not to say that the quality of motivation or of training technique or of tutoring are not also vitally important; it's just that the number of practice hours which individuals recollect doing, will all by themselves accurately predict the heights to which they have soared – whether that be county, national, or international standard. For instance, by the time they're 21, music academy scholars with 10,000 hours under their belt become professional concert performers, whereas the ones who've clocked only 5,000 hours become teachers. 'Amount of practice' is the distinguishing factor.

Some past masters

Of course, there need to be opportunities for all this practice. Let's take for example the life of Charles Darwin. After a thoroughly privileged childhood happily engrossed in natural history and surrounded by excellent mentors, the 22 year old then had five years on HMS Beagle with bags of cabin-time to swot-up on his subject. Within two years of returning home, he had formed his theory for how 'natural selection' could explain evolution. Similarly, the teenage Albert Einstein grew up surrounded by an extended family whose daily working banter was steeped in the ideas of new science and technology. Appropriately, young Albert then went on to thoroughly enjoy three years assessing new inventions within the Swiss Patent Office, and subsequently wrote the four theoretical papers which, at age 25, would make his reputation as the greatest physicist of the 20th century.

The crucial role of the 'practice principle' is further born out by the master artist, Joseph Turner, who put his own accomplishments down to "dammed hard work", just as the painter Joshua Reynolds believed that the faculty to draw could only be acquired by "an infinite number of acts". It is a tragedy that we know too little of the life of William Shakespeare to ever fathom the source of the playwright's towering strengths.

Even stark poverty need be no hindrance to the principle that sheer practice combined with enriching opportunities can create exemplary skills. In early Victorian England, Michael Faraday made great contributions to the world's applications of electricity as a form of power, despite his leaving school at just 13 in 1804. This quite unremarkable schoolboy went straight into seven years apprenticeship as a bookbinder, a job which fortuitously exposed him to all the finest scientific books of his era. Better still, he could take full advantage of this because his devoutly religious parents had taught him to read so well. Faraday then became deeply influenced by an excellent self-help book called *The Improvement of the Mind* by Isaac Watts, and his kindly employer set up a mini laboratory to indulge the teenager's burgeoning interests.

In retrospect, then, we can see how the serendipity of several positive experiences combined to supply Faraday with a splendid education, and though none of this rules out the existence of innate gifts, at the very least it demonstrates that they need not be the key factor in someone's accomplishments. Taking yourself from beginner to big-shot can come from dedicated practice and a rich learning environment, no matter your gene pool.

It is through the study of so many wondrous lives that we can begin to appreciate how these acorns did not necessarily fall from a different oak tree from you and I, they simply fell into extremely fertile soil; and that the experiences that forge expert or even extraordinary achievements are merely further along the same road upon which lie far more ordinary accomplishments. It's no accident that *all* of the above giants of history strenuously denied that they ever possessed 'special thinking powers' of any kind, claiming instead that they were distinguished only by the sheer joy they took from their work.

Some modern day champions

The careful study of extraordinary abilities is only confirming what we can see in the everyday world around us once we've attuned ourselves to what's happening.

Yes, it's certainly striking that American Olympic soccer captain, Mia Hamm was invited to join the U.S. Women's Team in 1987 when she was just 15 years old. But Mia had been in love with the sport since she could first toddle, and all because her Marine pilot daddy had taken the family to Italy with his new tour of duty. In Italy, everyone was fanatical about the game. Hence, Mia and her slightly older sisters and brother played it in every spare moment. Dad became a great fan, too, and often took the whole family to live soccer matches. Though they all returned to the U.S. just a few years later, little Mia at age 5 was now all set to excel in the new surrounds of an unsuspecting Texas. Though her journey to expertise was a profoundly enjoyable one, it was not until Mia was 24, *after a full nineteen years of dedicated footballing*, that this petite but determined lady led her team to Olympic Gold. (She retired after the 2004 Athens Olympics, age 32, as part of the victorious gold-medal team.)

Lasting success is never overnight. Most likely it takes a decade or more of dedicated investment. American media entrepreneur, Oprah Winfrey, is now in her 50s and widely considered to be one of America's most highly paid and influential women. Yet, she came from a childhood of poverty and long-term abuse while living with her mother. But at age 14, the seemingly uncontrollable teenager was sent to live with her father who, in her own words, 'saved her life' by instilling in her self-discipline and determination and a love of books and learning. And when Oprah tells the story of her success as a media presenter, she also cites another crucial factor. For the first six years of her life, she was raised by her Grandmother who taught her to read, so that from the age of just three, young Oprah was frequently reading aloud to Baptist Church congregations. "I believe that my first Easter speech at the age of three and a half, was the beginning. And that every other speech, every other book I read, every other time I spoke in public, was a building block. So by the time I first sat down to audition in front of a television camera, and somebody said, 'Read this!' . . . what allowed me to read it so comfortably, and be so at ease with myself at that time, was the fact that I had been doing it for quite a while."

The teenage Oprah had excelled in public speaking and debate, and gone on to study for a speech communications and theatrical degree at Tennessee State University. In her second year, age just 19, she was already working as a news presenter for a local radio station. Her career progressed from there, but it wasn't until she was 30 that she was given her own Chicago-based show which made her a household name across the States. She observes wryly: "So the fact that we went on air with 'The Oprah Winfrey Show' in 1986 and people said, 'Oh, you are so comfortable in front of the camera; you can be yourself.' Well, it's because I've been 'being myself' since I was nineteen!"

Not so surprising then, that more than 20 years on, The Oprah Show is the gold standard for exploring in a public forum the possibilities of life-change.

We need a driving passion

Only intense self-motivation can generate the energy and spirit needed for extended periods of practice, and all of the above individuals without exception undertook their work with a ferocious passion for their subject and its applications. They said of themselves, and it was observed in them by others, that their capacity for fierce and sustained concentration was driven wholly by a rapacious curiosity and deep enjoyment. And this makes fine sense: if we're happy in our work, we'll readily put in the extra practice-time, and our increasing expertise will foster ever more profound pleasures, so that our skills and satisfaction spiral upwards together. NASA Astronaut and Shuttle Commander, Eileen Collins, would whole-heartedly agree. "If you enjoy what you are doing, you'll find it much easier to excel at your job."

Former boxing champion Muhammad Ali is onto something when he declares: "Champions aren't made in gyms. Champions are made from something they have deep inside them – a desire, a dream, a vision. They have to have last-minute stamina, they have to be a little faster, they have to have the skill and the will. But the will must be stronger than the skill."

This is why it's no good an ambitious, well-meaning parent pre-scribing what field they would dearly wish their child to excel in, because lasting passion . . . and the intensity of passion needed for enthusiastic practice . . . is by its very nature a product of our free will, our sense of having chosen something for ourselves. Such a pas-sion cannot be imposed upon us.

BBC veteran broadcaster Terry Wogan, himself the proud father of three grown-up children, has some thoughts on this point: "Often parents live through their children, expecting the children to achieve their ambitions, to succeed where they have failed. It is always a mistake. My children are not me . . . Hard as it is to grasp, our children may not want the same things as we do, may not be the same as us. Do the best you can, and let them be."

Warmth and encouragement from someone special to us

In the 1980s, Dr Lauren Sosniak studied 22 young Americans who were the leading concert pianists of their generation. In trying to work out how they'd done so well for themselves, she found some unexpected results. For instance, rather than coming from musical dynasties as we might have presumed, half of these pianists had parents who didn't play an instrument themselves. Nor did the young pianists show precocious early ability. Though they began at around 6 years of age just like all of their contemporaries, most of them weren't shining in competitions even in their early teens. It was sheer determination to succeed that helped them to keep going. Nor were their first teachers musical virtuosos. Their later teachers were certainly top musicians, but the distinguishing qualities of those early teachers as remembered by their pupils, were *warmth and encouragement*. The only finding that wasn't surprising is that the mums and dads were equally warm and encouraging, not only towards their children and their frequent and regular practice, but also towards the teachers themselves. For instance, a parent would frequently sit in on lessons to show their support. It's good to know that all of Sosniak's findings have been born out by recent research, with much larger numbers of musicians, across a wide range of instruments.

An excellent study by a leading educational psychologist, Professor Mihaly Csikszentmihalyi found that it helps to come from families that are both stimulating and supportive, and by that he means parents who not only help the youngster conjure up challenges, but then also support them in the process of achieving them.

Looking at other lives and other arenas of worldly success, it's the intense and enduring support of at least one caring person which helped give wings to the lives of each and every person named in the this book. For golf-champion Tiger Woods, and for former U.S. Secretary of State, Madeleine Albright, their loving fathers were key influences. For Tour de France champion, Lance Armstrong, and for movie-maker, Stephen Spielberg (and as we shall see below, for children's writer Joanne K. Rowling and entrepreneur Richard Branson), their mothers were the touchstone of loving inspiration.

But we can take heart if we have not found such support in our own parents. Oprah Winfrey has said, "For every one of us that succeeds, it's because there's somebody there to show you the way out. The light doesn't necessarily have to be in your family; for me, it was teachers and school". Likewise, for former American First Lady and key instigator of the Declaration of Human Rights, Eleanor Roosevelt, it was a teacher at the school she attended at age 15, "Whatever I have become since had its seed in those three years of contact with a liberal mind and strong personality."

And as for country singer Emmylou Harris, she met her mentor, Gram Parsons, in her late twenties. "I was struggling and no one was interested in what I was doing . . . I didn't really have a style . . . a focus. He had an extraordinary effect on me, and I will always love him."

We should take hope and inspiration from all the above stories, and invite a warm and encouraging mutually-supportive relationship with someone in the world around us. In fact, a handful of such relationships at any one time would be ideal, so as to spread the load and introduce a healthy variety of perspectives. We can, too, look to become that all important encouraging voice in the lives of the young people around us.

Create a rich learning environment

Our goal should be to put ourselves in a place where on a daily basis we're exposed to good quality new ideas and experiences. Those who have excelled have, at times by good fortune and at other times by good planning, managed to achieve this. Steven Spielberg had just such an out-going attitude, taking unpaid clerical jobs in film studios. "I visited every set I could, got to know people, observed techniques, and just generally absorbed the atmosphere."

Teaming up with a suitable coach

A coach can seriously speed up our learning, so any time and effort invested in finding the right trainer or supervisor who's a good match for us, is time well spent. Every task or activity has unwritten rules that make a big difference. We need to do some detective work to uncover the insider know-how, and a coach can guide us . . . or put us in contact with helpful people, books or ideas.

At catering college, the future 'naked chef' Jamie Oliver's ambition was to learn how to make really good bread and pasta so he went to work with the legendary Gennaro Contaldo. "I used to help him out by getting all his stuff out. I managed to start working with him in the middle of the night quite regularly. He has this brilliantly positive attitude to every single thing he does. He always wants it to taste perfect and he never tires of trying to improve things. I loved working with him and I learned so much about cooking. He was like my second father".

A good coach will play to our strengths and will go at the pace at which we're learning, not any faster or slower. We know if we've got a good coach if we progress; this will prove that the fit between us is right. Our strengths are playing to theirs and vice versa. One to one sessions, or classes with just three or four friends at tops, and we'll progress far faster than if we're in a larger class. If we club together, it becomes affordable, and in the long-run a much more cost-effective way to learn than having hours of half-baked sessions when we come home not really having learnt anything.

Practice partners
Our coach might only be there once per week, but if we have a range of practice partners we can train as often as we feel like it and so progress as fast as our passions will carry us. And let's not be embarrassed about our as yet inept performances but instead be determined to embrace every opportunity to practice with people more advanced then ourselves, because playing beyond their own present level is how every famous sports person honed their skills. As a boy, England soccer captain, David Beckham, went along to the training sessions of the local team his father played for. "I'd sit in the bar and watch the men training and then, towards the end of the session, they'd let me join in with the five-a-sides. The fact that I always seemed to be playing football with players who were bigger and stronger than me when I was young, I'm sure, helped me later on in my career."

The same hungry approach has helped Mia Hamm score her way all the way to the top of women's soccer. "All my life, I've challenged myself by competing with players older, bigger, more skillful, more experienced . . . in short, *better than me*. When I was six, my big brother, Garrett, ran circles around me. At ten, I joined an eleven-year-old-boys' team and, eventually, led them in scoring. Seven years later I found myself playing for the number-one college team in America after becoming the youngest player ever to suit up for the U.S. Women's National Team. *Was I that good?* No, but early on coaches detected a competitive fire in me and fed it by continually pitting me against superior opponents. Back then I wasn't sure I'd fit in; after all, I was shy and a bit intimidated by players I had idolized. But each day I attempted to play up to their level and earn their respect, and I was improving faster than I had ever dreamed possible."

Unexpected findings and exploding myths

Though all of the above is exceedingly good news, there's a whole host of myths and misunderstandings that can prevent such a rosy picture, and it's these we now move onto.

We wrongly presume that major improvements are impossible after a certain age

Fair enough, some things about us simply aren't designed to be changed, at least not easily. Height, for example, is very much inherited from mum and dad. Good nutrition will allow a young person to reach their genetically pre-determined height, but there is no known exercise we can practice to make us taller, and though exercise will thicken and strengthen our bones, it won't lengthen them.

Happily, many other organs, functions and characteristics of the human body are designed to be highly changeable. In the event of losing a kidney, the remaining kidney if in good health will grow by 70% within just a few weeks to deal with its new workload. In just the same way, our bodies will change their shape and weight in response to our daily activities and nutrition. Our brain can do much the same. Experienced London cab drivers have identifiable brain differences reflecting their well-developed skills for creating mental maps of their routes around the city. This ability to adapt is called 'brain plasticity', and rather reassuringly the brains of seventy year olds have been shown to develop in exactly the same way with intensive new learning; so it really is never too late.

Chess masters demonstrate how astonishingly adaptable our memories can be when they play several games at once . . . and just to make it interesting, they do it *blind-folded,* i.e. they have to hold all the present positions and possible moves of several games in their mind's eye. This party trick is just one of the perks of practicing to improve something for 8 hours per day for ten years. The body is also capable of more than we might realise. We might be able to do a handful of press-ups one after the other, or perhaps 20 if we're keen and practice from time to time. In which case, it's quite a shock to hear that the world record is *twenty-six thousand press-ups* in 24 hours, which translates as a press-up every three seconds of the night and day. Like learning to run a 26 mile marathon, the record holder has gradually built up to it. The onlooker can be forgiven for thinking such feats are a trick or a gift, but that's not being fair or accurate about the performer's true role in learning their astounding level of ability. The fact is, our emotions, body and brain are hungry for learning. We're all well designed to be extremely good at developing. Indeed, if we still doubt our ability to acquire daunting new skills, we should remember just how impossibly awkward driving a car felt when we first did it. But after 50 hours or so, the co-ordination of hands and feet became a subconscious, well-learnt response.

And if it's our emotional transformations which seem unlikely, we should also consider that by using a highly reliable therapeutic approach to phobias we can entirely lose our fear of spiders or heights or public speaking in less than half-a-dozen hours. We simply re-train our emotions to respond with calm rather than alarm. Similarly, if we spent just one year in a foreign country, immersing ourselves in the new language through our work and social life, we would comfortably become a very competent speaker. And just to make the point that we can readily develop *all three* of our emotional, physical and thinking skills, we could train in 'bomb-disposal' by doing a fourteen week course. The British Army take very regular, everyday recruits who, at the beginning of their training, rate themselves as extremely scared of the prospect of going any where near a bomb. Quite rightly, and who wouldn't be? Yet, by the end of training, these very same recruits rate themselves as bored and frustrated if they don't get called into action on a frequent basis, so confident are they in their new abilities.

What all of these learning experiences have in common is that to acquire a skill, no matter that skill be characterised by requirements that are physical, mental or emotional, all we need is sufficient self-motivation, sufficient practice, and sufficient know-how, all brought together in a rich learning environment.

What this all means for our everyday lives

The great legacy of all this research into acquiring expertise, is that no child nor adult of seemingly ordinary abilities need ever be discouraged from pursuing a longed-for career or extracurricular ambition because of a false belief that they lack some special gift for it. The scientific study of lives going well has shown how we can all help carve our own future. Our expert performance can be acquired through learning and is *not* reliant on our having some kind of inherited head-start by way of unusual levels of innate gifts, special talents or aptitudes ... call them what you will. Unless there are exceptional circumstances inhibiting us, (perhaps some permanent damage through accident or illness), we can each and every one of us comfortably become a consultant, an expert, indeed a highly skilled contender in whatever field we choose.

The compelling story of two modern-day high performers

What follows, are the detailed case-studies of two awe-inspiring life stories which equally well illustrate how determined practice and formative experiences over many years, combined with warm encouraging relationships, can pave the way to expertise and achievement. Let's look first at Joanne K. Rowling and then Richard Branson.

Joanne K. Rowling, creator and writer of the Harry Potter novels, was 30-something before her life-long apprenticeship as a reader and writer of stories was finally recognised. Though at first glance it might appear that it all happened in one stroke of good luck, it was not by magic that Joanne was good with the written word, nor was it wizardry that enabled her to tell a story. Joanne K. Rowling was in every sense *writing from experience*.

Joanne was brought up by committed and hard-working young parents who had no financial advantages nor writing acumen. Mum was a school laboratory assistant and dad was a factory worker. Very importantly, though, this was a close-knit loving family – warmly encouraging – with a home full of books. Her mum in particular was a super role-model for joy in life, a sense of humour, and a love of reading, all of which inspired the teenage Joanne to read Jane Austin's *Emma* more than a dozen times, and be equally fond of *Lord of the Rings*.

Throughout her childhood, teens and twenties, Joanne was happiest when in her internal, imaginative world and inventing stories; and at senior school, her skill in spinning tales full of intrigue and humour, gradually became her signature strength that won her friendship and popularity. However, at university, she shyly kept quiet about her yearnings to be a professional writer, and studied not English but *French* Literature & Language, though she never let go of her true ambition. So strong was this, that after graduation, the 22 year old spent three years temping, during which time she had a go at writing a couple of novels for adults. Though nothing came of these, how many other 25 year olds could claim they'd tried such a feat? And it was only now, after years of imagining and telling stories and taking seemingly false directions, that the idea for *Harry Potter* occurred to Joanne while on a long train journey.

But this was sadly timed, because in that same year her mother died tragically young at the age of 45, having been progressively disabled by multiple sclerosis. The loss hurt Joanne terribly, and soon afterwards she took off to work in Portugal as a teacher of English. Not even two years later, she had married a local man and was trying to have a child; yet, just a few months after giving birth, Joanne took her baby daughter and fled the country to escape her physically abusive young husband.

Setting up a home for herself in Edinburgh, Joanne now suffered the financial hardships and social humiliations that are heaped on a single mum relying on inadequate state benefits. But she was never one to give up. It took two years and some therapeutic counselling, but by then Joanne had earned herself a place on a one year, full-time course of Scottish Teacher Training. Despite finding it hard at first, by the end of that year and her graduation, she was much praised for her highly imaginative methods in the classroom. It was during that productive time that she sent off *Harry Potter and The Philosopher's Stone* to be read by an agent, and three revisions later, the book found a publisher. The £1,500 advance on royalties was hardly a fortune, but it was an encouraging start.

Those six years since her mother's death must have been a terribly hard journey for Joanne, but throughout all of this time she was writing notes and having her sister and closest friends read her work-in-progress, as she strived to improve it. Indeed, throughout her life, Joanne Rowling had showed great determination in continually developing the skills that were sure to make her a highly successful educator in one guise or another.

Now let's look at another life to see again the roots of success

Richard Branson was running his million pound Virgin Music business by the age of 24, and went on to create one of the world's best liked airlines, amassing a vast personal fortune along the way. Considering his autobiography, we can see how his up-bringing made it almost inevitable that he would be an entrepreneur of one sort or another, even if the extraordinary level of his success was quite unpredictable.

Despite being born in 1950 and thus part of the first generation of children exposed to tv, it's particularly noteworthy that his family never had a television in the house, and even the radio was rarely on because his parents were too busy doing things. His father was a gentle-mannered lawyer, but his mother was a dare-devil and inventive personality who made ends meet by running a one-person cottage industry making tissue boxes and wastepaper bins. She was a gung-ho woman who, during the war years, had rather wonderfully talked her way in to becoming a glider-pilot instructor with the RAF, and after de-mob went on to become a poster-girl airhostess for a new airline.

These two loving parents strove to develop a confident self-reliance in their children from a very early age, and expected them to put forward and debate their thoughts as equals among adults. Mum and Dad also instilled a cavalier disregard for petty rules and formality, but a deep respect for warm and considerate relationships, and the Virgin business has always endeavoured to reflect these traits. They also lent a shoulder to even his earliest enterprises as well as bags of encouragement.

Richard's mother's antics served as a fine role-model for entre-preneurial money-making, and barely into his teens, Richard was hooking-up with his best friend, Nik, to try their hand at some business schemes that ranged from growing Christmas trees to breeding budgerigars. When at age 15, Richard formed a national magazine called *The Student*, it was only part of a long line of bright ideas that hadn't quite come off, but had nonetheless given him a taste for business. Though it took three years to launch *The Student,* this idea did better than the others, and he left school at 17 to devote himself to it, once again teaming with his childhood friend, Nik. The magazine folded three years later, but the business savvy, media contacts, and even the counselling skills they'd honed on the phones of the magazine's Student Advisory Centre, all helped the two twenty-year-olds move immediately into their Virgin Records mail-order operation. This rapidly grew into a string of 20 record shops, and then their own recording label.

The fundamental rules apply ... as time goes by
The biographies of Joanne and Richard helpfully illustrate that once we know what to look for in a life-story, we can better identify and appreciate the firm foundations of an individual's longstanding success and happiness. Far from being a genetic inheritance from mum and dad, we can see that an individual's wonderful achieve-ments rely on skills that have been earned through a mixture of rich learning experiences and a lot of determined practice. Accomplished

individuals have invariably made earlier attempts at a breakthrough which haven't worked out, and even their so called 'turning-points' have taken years to cultivate. It has been sheer tenacity and a sense of calling whether it be for entrepreneurship or novel writing that has seen them through the setbacks and disappointments. We can see, too, that their ability to keep going has come *not* from inherited wealth, but rather from a loving family member or friend who has provided that all important warmth and encouragement to keep practicing, to bounce back, and to progress. Indeed, learning to team-up and accept help in a mutually rewarding relationship, has been as important a skill as any other.

* * *

Planning for Progress

- Who do you know in your everyday life who is exceptionally good at something? Modesty aside, how do they personally explain their route to developing that level of skill?

- What would you dearly like to be good at? What social skill? What physical activity? What professional expertise?

- How much effort would you be prepared to invest to achieve those goals? What are they worth to you?

- What could you do today to put yourself in a rich learning environment of kindred spirits and experienced coaches?

* * *

The Surest Routes
to Getting Really Good at
Something

So much happiness in life comes from a sense of self-propelled progress, no matter our starting point, and such progress requires us to develop our full range of skills – emotional, intellectual, social and physical. The Catch-22 is that 'learning to improve' is a skill in itself, in respect of which we need to acquire the know-how of learning.

In the previous chapter we saw how there are four essential foundations to becoming expert in our chosen field; but there are also a large handful of additional strategies which support these foundations and will make our journey to expertise all the more swift and enjoyable. Many of these have only been properly understood over the last few years.

As proof of the power of these technical insights into how to train our body and brain, we should note that human performances have improved so dramatically in recent times, that the determined amateurs of today would have comfortably won Olympic medals at The Games of 1908.

Let's also remind ourselves that there is considerable agreement among world-leading psychologists who specialise in the acquisition of expert performance skills. They say that for a person who is ordinarily healthy in brain and body there are no inborn limits to their potential. In short, the practice and processes that forge expert or even extraordinary achievements are merely further along the continuum upon which lie far more ordinary accomplishments. (For instance, it is nothing more miraculous than our total number of practice hours that is the strongest predictor of what level we attain in any field.) Though it's quite a responsibility to bear, the fact is there's rarely anything stopping us but ourselves. Just think how many first-timers teach their mind and body to run a marathon.

That said, packing away the tv isn't enough, and merely putting in the practise time in a slap-dash fashion, isn't enough either. It is crucial that we practise with a determination to improve, because if we just do things like we've always done them by simply going through the motions on automatic pilot, then our gains will be minimal despite many years of repetition. We do well to bear in mind that our brain is hard-wired with a ravenous appetite for learning whatever comes its way, whether or not those skills and associations are likely to be useful. In respect of this, if we're to get the best from our brain, we have to use our ingenuity to nourish ourselves with healthy experiences in a helpful form. Besides which, keeping mentally active through learning new skills is the best known defense against dementia and other brain-degenerative conditions.

And here's another encouraging thought when we embark upon learning something new, only to find a whole bunch of negative voices racing painfully through our mind. Perhaps the worst of these voices is the one saying "I wish I'd started this long ago, because I'll never catch up with everyone else." So it's rather reassuring to know that 95% of people reach a certain level of ability within the first 100 hours of doing something and barely improve after that unless they decide to make a special effort. The truth is, we're not one year or five years behind other practitioners, we're only 100 hours behind them. Catching up is easy . . . but we want to be sure to enjoy it.

Only learn what we want to learn

Before setting out, we should be very clear about how little we really need to learn to satisfy and quench our thirst for something . . . at least for the time being.

It is very unlikely we really want to learn the A to Z of everything. We want to know just as much as we need to know to really enjoy it. So it's helpful to ask ourselves what is at the very heart of our interest in something. Then we can go straight to that, rather than wade through 90% of what never really interested us in the first place.

For instance, there's rarely any need to learn the whole syllabus for an academic subject or a martial art or a musical instrument. We can reap most of the benefits we wish for simply by becoming good at one tiny but sufficient part of something – just a handful of well-practised, much-loved moves. Applying this principle, we could sample a little bit of every part of the syllabus, and then decide which parts best play to our strengths and passions. I may not want to become a Grade 8 pianist, I may be satisfied with learning half a dozen songs I can play and sing at the piano. Indeed, three songs would do me for the time being. Now to learn three songs might only require one weekend a piece . . . whereas Grade 8 piano would probably require around 100 times that investment. Likewise, 97% of karate moves are unlikely ever to be of use for self-defense. Better I learn to be highly proficient and quite automatic in the bare minimum to protect myself. And do I really want to know 100 Salsa dance moves . . . or would half a dozen well-rehearsed little numbers be quite sufficient?

The big idea, then, is to trim our goals as small as possible so that we aim to become just as good as we need to be at something in order to extract the maximum pleasure and rewards in return on our investment. This proposition pays respect to the scientific observation called the Pareto Principle which states that around 80% of the rewards result from just 20% of the activities, no matter the field of endeavour. Put in everyday terms, this means that . . .

- 20% of our exercise leads to 80% of the physical and psychological benefits.
- 20% of our spending leads to 80% of our pleasure.
- 20% of our work leads to 80% of our productivity.

If we want to use this law of nature to our advantage, we need to identify the active ingredient of that ever-so-fruitful 20% which is producing 80% of the rewards of an activity, in order that we can better invest in it. The Pareto Principle works for companies and nations just as much as for individuals: 20% of a company's products will bring in 80% of its income; just as 20% of a population will own 80% of a country's wealth.

When trying to allocate our time and energy in the most rewarding ways, it's worth considering how every hour we put into one activity, is an hour we are not investing in another. This is the so called 'opportunity cost' i.e. the lost opportunity incurred because we could have been doing something else. Every investment has an opportunity cost . . . which refers to the lost opportunity to invest our time and energy in some other activity. So, yes, I might like to earn my black belt in karate, but the 600 hours of practice that it might take me, could be better spread around three or four pleasures which would bring me, all told, a far greater sense of accumulated satisfaction. For instance, if I invested not 600 hours but just 120 hours in my karate to become highly proficient in a few useful moves, I could also learn to sing three songs (120 hours), earn my gliding wings (120 hours), explore yoga (120 hours), and do a weekly drama class (120 hours).

So, if we can prevent ourselves from becoming fixated by the need to gain a qualification, we can instead design our very own, tailor-made life-development program of extra-curricular activities . . . a portfolio of skills and experiences that will bring pleasure and prove invaluable no matter our direction.

Learn at our own pace
It's not just *vital* to learn at our own pace . . . we can *only* learn at our own pace, which is why learning in classes may at one time or

another have felt either difficult or near impossible. You, like me, will probably have ground to a painful halt while trying to learn a dance style or a martial art or a foreign language, because the instructor either bored us to tears by labouring the point of some piffling detail, or tore ahead leaving us feeling dazed and confused and unable to clearly learn even one small piece of information. Our brains and bodies were not designed to learn that way . . . in classes where one size and speed of learning is meant to fit all. Hence, we have to design our own learning.

Linking our learning

Looking for a moment at the bigger picture of our lives, we can use the wisdom of our hard-earned life experience from one arena to help us in another. We have transferable skills and insights. This is all to the good, because the more ways we can find to learn something, the better we'll become at it. Our brain likes to learn things from many different angles. From my own experience, improving as a well-being scientist is helped by my teaching it to students, by being a therapist, by writing about it, by attending weekend workshops in new techniques, and by enjoying relevant books and feature films . . . whether that be *Silence of The Lambs* or *Good Will Hunting*. I also discuss psychology every chance I get, and when I'm taking up a new activity, I wonder what it's telling me about the psychology of learning.

Likewise, when Hollywood actor Tom Cruise decided to take flying lessons while he was making *Top Gun*, his dyslexia made it difficult for him to understand the flight training manuals he had to read in order to get off the ground, so he worked around the problem. "When I was studying for my pilot's license, I kept a model airplane nearby as a reference, and some pictures of a cockpit in front of me so I could study the instruments. I would also go over to a shop where mechanics were working on planes."

Our own practice sessions can apply similar strategies. We can approach new challenges from different perspectives, for example by closing our eyes so as to better focus on the physical sensations of our swing or our song. And whatever we're doing, we need to keep some joie-de-vivre in our activities.

The idea of linking different parts of our life and experiences together to help us progress faster, is well illustrated by French soccer captain, Zinedine Zidane, the son of immigrants from Algeria, who talks poignantly about growing up in an impoverished neighbourhood of Marseille. "I was *lucky* to come from a difficult area. It teaches you not just about football but also life. There were lots of kids from different races and poor families. People had to struggle to get through the day. Music was important. Football was the easy part. This desire never to stop fighting is something else I learnt in the place where I grew up."

One of America's leading sociologists, Robert Putnam has said that 'teaming-up' . . . in other words "the breadth and depth of our personal relationships" . . . is our greatest single source of happiness. For my part, I suspect that our ability to make links between one area of our experience and another, is our greatest source of progress.

We need to learn with our head, heart and hands all at once

For openers, we need first-hand experience of doing things rather than to be shown or told, because it's the depth of our 'mental processing' which entirely determines how much we learn from a task. Hollywood actor James Stewart has this to say about the origins of his Oscar-winning abilities: "You learned your craft in the best way I know of learning how to act, and that's by acting!"

It's worth noting here that this emphasis on 'experiential learning' . . . on feeling ourselves actively doing rather than merely watching . . . can also apply to imaginal rehearsal, because when appraising a mental image, feeling or thought, it is a fact that our brain makes little distinction between a real-life event and a vivid imagination. Indeed, many of the same parts of our brain will fire-up when we practice deeply imagined rehearsals, just as much as they do in real ones, so immersing ourselves in imagining something is very much like living it, certainly for the purposes of learning.

The ideal learning scenario is when our hands-on progress minute by minute is being commented upon there and then in the form of immediate feedback. To this end, a coach might require their apprentice to think aloud as they try to solve a problem, in order that their thinking strategies can be guided in mid-flight.

Harvard psychologist, Professor Helen Langar, has shown that children learn far better when they're not just told the facts but are also asked to imagine what it must have been like being this or that historical person, and how might they have thought through the options open to them before a particular event. Madeleine Albright, America's first woman Secretary of State, took this highly involving approach with her students when she was a professor at Georgetown University in Washington, DC. "I taught classes on international affairs to women and men . . . I was a great believer in role-playing, so I had my students re-negotiate the Panama Canal Treaty and argue the merits of arms control from the perspective of senior government officials. Often I was able to provide them with newly declassified documents to help them bolster their arguments." It comes as no surprise that for four years in a row, Madeleine was voted best professor at the School of Foreign Service.

Let's appreciate, too, that we don't learn nearly as well from facts, as we learn from emotions. Twenty-five years on I can remember my reading J.D. Salinger's *Catcher in the Rye*, or Jane Austen's *Emma*, because I was there with those characters in my mind's eye. I was living their life alongside them. Compare this approach with how text books mistakenly try too often to teach us. I can't recall my text books because they told me a whole bunch of stuff in a way that I couldn't imagine. By contrast, my Latin classes were brought to life by appealing to all of my senses. With the help of excellent teachers, I was constantly whisked away in my mind's eye to Italian villas of 2,000 years ago . . . and the daily life of a centurion . . . the olive oils, the clay jars, the hot baths and long, exotic meals. Learning Latin was a delight because I was living the life in my imagination even as I sat there in a scruffy, winter classroom.

Such experiential learning and expert tuition all came together for 14-year-old Claire Rayner, who for many years was Britain's favourite agony aunt and is now a social campaigner in her 70s. She reminisces fondly about when she was training as a nurse in a London hospital after the Second World War. "What I was experiencing, of course, was classic apprenticeship. I learned the right way to do hands-on tasks under the direct supervision of persons who were themselves fully qualified and knew exactly what had to be done, and also knew the theoretical reasons for it being done in an particular way. These were told me as I carried out the tasks, and at the same time Sister encouraged those patients who were able to communicate to tell me why it felt better to have something done one way rather than another. That was the most educational thing of it all. Even more so than the nursing books that Sister lent me and made sure I read by quizzing me on them. It was in the wards, clinics and operating theatres, rather than in the lecture rooms, that my skills slowly and steadily developed until I was able to perform the most complex technical tasks without ever forgetting the underlying imperative of watching over and catering to my patients' comfort. I learned then to accept responsibility and, in due course, to teach as I had been taught."

Pushing beyond the skills plateau

I pointed out above how most of us go from beginner to intermediate standard in let's say our first hundred hours of determined and frequent practice (whether it be salsa dancing, car driving or tennis), and then after our progress tends to level off very dramatically until we're not increasing our skills level at all, we're simply treading water. If we want to take ourselves beyond that plateau towards advanced and even expert levels of performance, then we have to take special measures to ensure our continued progress.

To this end, I could not over-emphasise how important it is to push beyond our comfort zone by taking what we do at present and modifying it. For instance, a study of first-class ice skaters observed how the best among them spent considerable time attempting new moves and so incurring numerous mistakes, while their less accomplished peers more often repeated what they could already do well. The experience of French-Canadian singer, Celine Dion, nicely illustrates how pushing our limits can lead to an uncomfortable sense of loss of control, which is why so few folks care to do it. When she was around 18 years old, her manager decided to have her record an album in the United States. "And so, I enrolled in a language school for nine hours a day, five days a week, for two months. At times, it was a nightmare. I stopped understanding words in any human language at all. I started talking nonsense and all my ideas got mixed up. And then, all at once, everything became clear and intelligible."

Making mistakes is all part of the learning process, so we must-n't be afraid of messing up. The horse trainer and young people's learning specialist, Monty Roberts, reminds us that "Learning empirically, i.e. hands-on trial and error, is *essential* to achieving wisdom."

And rather than compare ourselves with our peers, let's compete against our own limitations. Luciano Pavorotti illustrates the resolve it took for him to become one of the best opera singers. "I was extremely competitive with myself, not so much with others. I concentrated on doing better than I had done the day before and stopped worrying about what other singers were doing . . . No matter how much success I have had, there has never been a time when I was not working on improving my singing."

It is vital, too, that our determination to reach the heights of our field are translated into a set of clear goals and measurable milestones. At a turning point in her life, Olympic runner Cathy Freeman was flying back home to Australia from the European racing circuit. "I grabbed a piece of scrap paper from my purse and wrote some objectives for the lead-up to the 1994 Commonwealth Games. '*My 400 personal best has to improve, more 300 and 400 sessions have to be done, and they have to be of good quality*'."

The trick is never to get complacent with our achievements. After dozens of Hollywood blockbusters Spielberg comments, "Every film is an experience. I'll be learning when I'm sixty years old."

And when our rate of progress is slowing down, we might need to make painful decisions about leaving cherished training environments and training buddies. In 2002, Britain's Olympic runner, Kelly Holmes, parted company from Dave Arnold, her coach since 1982, and moved to Johannesburg to train with a new coach, the American Margo Jennings, and with a new runner, the Mozambican Maria Mutola. Two years later, Kelly's move was rewarded with a pair of gold medals in the 2004 Olympics for the 800 and 1500 metres.

Time spent overseas also helped Dame Betty Boothroyd, who would go on to become the first woman Speaker in the House of Commons. She had contested two seats in Parliament without success, in 1957 and 1959, and so she decided to take herself over to join the election campaign for John F. Kennedy. Before flying out, Betty said to her critics, "When you get the chance of a lifetime, you don't ask questions. They can ask me to lick stamps or make the tea. I'll be quite happy, I shall be looking for pointers and ideas which I might be able to use in future campaigns." She concluded: "It was a formative experience that gave me a new outlook on the world and one I would not have missed for anything."

The need to strengthen the absolute focus of our concentration

Any 'intent to improve' requires concentration, and such high-level attention is very hard to achieve, all the more so in a distracting environment. Multi-tasking, of course, is the nemesis of concentration, which means if we're half-heartedly practising our salsa steps or golf swing while making a mental grocery list, we're severely reducing the benefits. It's notable that Charles Darwin and Sir Isaac Newton were both able to focus their attention not only for hours *but days* at a time, so as to work through a problem, to such an extent that they would need to take to their beds afterwards for several days of recuperation.

One classic study has shown that stroke patients trying to relearn physical skills while being chatted to by a cheery nurse, recovered far *slower* than a comparison group of patients who were simply encouraged to attend completely to the task. It's notable, too, that world-class novelists have almost invariably worked only in the mornings, just until their full concentration can no longer be maintained. Then they park their quill and spend the rest of the day recuperating in readiness for their next intense immersion.

Hearing about the power of concentration rather makes one ponder what it would take to immerse ourselves quite as deeply in improving the passionate pursuits and the intimate relationships that we most dearly prize.

The emotional aspects of learning: make it pleasurable

Positive emotions play a key role in learning well. As we have seen in the previous chapter, warmth and encouragement provide the richest and most reliable climate in which skills develop, and bearing testimony to this are the many virtuoso musicians of the highest standard who had parents who didn't even play a musical instrument, but these same parents nonetheless took a wholly positive interest in their child's practice and the relationship with the teacher, and who often sat in on lessons.

This prompts us to remember that joy in learning is self-motivating, so we should take care to associate practice with pleasure rather than pain.

Let's hear it from five-times Olympic rowing champion, Steve Redgrave: "I think the biggest advice is to enjoy it. If you don't enjoy something you won't put your best efforts into it. That is not to say that you will enjoy every training session, but the key is to look forward to it and not try to shy away from it."

We hear exactly the same from British Olympic double-gold champion, Kelly Holmes: "You need to train hard and be dedicated in what you're trying to achieve. But remember to enjoy what you do."

So let's not try to learn stuff while we're in a grump or a gloom. Good moods make hard tasks easier, and it will also mean that we will be embedding the good mood along with the memory. The idea being that when we recollect the scientific formula or whatever it is, we will get a little wave of positive emotion along with it, which will help us cope with the task we're engaged in.

Make it playful
And if pleasure is good for learning, play is even better. The top performers in every field have learnt to play with the possibilities... which can lead to breakthroughs... and also their playfulness allows them to practice for longer. For example, golf champion Tiger Woods is wise to this and explains, "I practiced quite a bit as a kid, but I always kept it fun." For instance, he would often pretend to be playing against one of his heroes. Tiger also likes to listen to R&B and hip-hop music when he practices. "I need music to keep the adrenaline pumping. I have my golf cart all maxed out, with the radio console and six speakers. I crank the music up pretty loud."

Six times winner of the Tour de France, Lance Armstrong and his team of eight fellow riders constantly used jokes to get them through their training schedule. "We encouraged good humour, because we believed it was an excellent painkiller. Laughter took away the suffering of training. Our jokes were profane and boyish and silly, but within the team, among nine people who knew and loved and trusted each other, mouthing off was an important part of every day, our ritual morale-builder. I'd say 'Give me a frickin' tricycle, and I'll kick some ass!'"

Celine Dion and her husband cum manager, René, are taking a similar approach. "Every day we need to take a dose of laughter. And on tour, René manages to find moments here and there when we can all be together. He believes that socializing is necessary and fun. It's a bond that strengthens us."

End every session on a high note
Nobel Prize-winning psychologist, Daniel Kahneman, and his colleagues have shown that two things almost entirely determine how pleasurable we rate an experience, whether it be a holiday or a training session:

a) How the experiences felt when it was at its peak (i.e. the best and worst).

b) How it felt when it ended.

It seems that this 'peak-end' rule of Kahneman's affects how we summarize the experience in our own mind, and then we rely on that summary later to remind ourselves of how the experience felt. The summary in turn influences our decisions about whether to have that experience again, whereas factors such as the proportion of pleasure to displeasure during the course of the experience, or the duration of such feelings, have almost no influence on our memory of it.

The moral of this intriguing peak-end phenomenon is that rather than pushing ourselves until we're sick to death of something, it's far better to be sure to end each of our training sessions or our day's work on a distinctly high note, finding something to cheer ourselves so that we'll want to come back for more.

The wisdom of knowing what to learn

Learning to get good at things isn't that difficult once we know how – but what really takes wisdom, is deciding what to learn. When I was doing my YoungLives research, star individuals who've known long-standing success at the top of their professions, were invariably at pains to point out to aspiring youngsters that it's the closeness with friends and family which has proved far and away their greatest source of life-satisfaction.

Hence, I conclude that it is only a matter of personal values as to whether the rewards of expertise are worth the potential sacrifices that may be required by solitary practice . . . I mean sacrifices in terms of the intimate personal relationships that make our lives so fulfilling. The real challenge is to pursue our passions without spoiling our life and the lives of those who love us.

* * *

Planning for Progress

- Thinking about the skilled activities you most want to develop, what level and range of skills would satisfy you at this stage?

- What steps could you take to optimise the learning process and environment?

- How are you going to keep the learning as enjoyable as possible?

* * *

Performing Well
while Under Pressure

Whether it's college exams or professional diplomas, business presentations or sporting performance, the very same principles will underpin our performing at our best. This also applies to coping well on social occasions and big dates, or with interviews and negotiations. We can quickly learn to feel sufficiently comfortable and in control, but like any other skill, we need to work at it, and do so in the right way.

Perfectionism is the enemy
of high performance and happiness

Nothing is more inhibiting of a pleasurable sense of progress than its arch-enemy, *perfectionism*. Perfectionism is a 'false ally' pretending that it's merely trying to do a decent job, while secretly it feeds the malign feeling that whatever we are, or have, or try to do, *just isn't good enough*.

Perfectionism can blight any dimension of life, and it's the master of disguise. It can cause the painfully shy and silent child, just as much as the one who speaks too fast for fear of wasting your time. It can produce the sullen, stagnant teenager scared to make mistakes, or the one who pretends to be cheerful and is all too eager to please. It's responsible for the student who does nothing at all, just as much as the one who earns straight A grades at the cost of their friendships. It might show itself in a slovenly appearance (scared to compete), or a look that's just too pristine and better suited to a display case.

Recognise any of those feelings or behaviours as familiar enemies? (Either in yourself or someone close to you?)

Such symptoms as these, or a dozen more besides, result in painfully slow progress or a full-blown paralysis . . . either that, or the sort of manic activity that ends in isolation, self-damage and exhaustion. No matter which, perfectionism cruelly scuppers our loves, our health and our happiness. Worse still, it can too easily infect all and any part of our life: how we shop (for instance, never being able to make a final decision, or overspending in an attempt to get *the best*), all the way through to how we regard our body, our choice of romantic partners, and our professional progress.

Perfectionism is so good at disguising itself that even *we* might not realise that the reason we've never done this or that is because it's very important to us and so we want it to be perfect . . . which means we daren't do it . . . *not yet*.

But hold on a moment: things can be very important to us . . . like the people we love . . . and yet they're not perfect. They're wonderful . . . gorgeous . . . absolutely lovely . . . but not perfect. That's because perfectionism is ugliness merely claiming to be beautiful.

There are other give-aways

A tell-tale sign of perfectionism is being enslaved to the goal rather than relishing the journey, so when a goal is reached we have the urge to set off immediately for some new objective, without barely a pause to savour the sense of achievement and what the journey has taught us. Even in play or sport or leisure, we are hoping to 'maximise'. What's more, we always take on too much because we are deeply irritated by others seeming too slow or slapdash. There's always a sense of time pressure and of a clock inside of us ticking, and we hurry on scared that the bell will go and a voice will shout "Stop what you're doing now, it's Judgement Day!" and then there'll be a stock-take of our achievements and we're going to be found wanting . . . we're going to come up short. Hence, we're poisoned with a constant urgency to 'catch up' . . . catch up with some distorted notion of who, what and where we think we should be by now . . . the lofty heights of private goodness or public success we should have reached. Oh for sure we'd like to reap the benefits of relaxation, but we can't spare the time for that, not now, not yet, not until some never-never . . . that we won't let come.

Where does it come from?
Maybe parents or teachers or a school ethos . . . some daily atmosphere of unrelenting standards in which, explicit or implied, whatever we did or how we were was never quite good enough by someone else's tape-measure. Or maybe our present perfectionist habits are just the result of an innocent childhood misunderstanding of how lives work.

Working therapeutically with young people as I do from time to time, I see how many individuals in their teens and twenties struggle to cope with the excessive and misleading demands heaped upon them. They are anxious, self-conscious and exhausted, and by age 25 are full of regrets and the fear of hitting thirty. They feel somehow their back was turned when the best years raced by, and they wonder what they're doing wrong because life is rubbing . . . like ill-fitting shoes. On the one hand, many parents and schools expect ever more A-grades from their teenagers, while media messages exert pressure on those same students to excel in physical attractiveness, sporting prowess, and sparkling character. Such over-inflated and often incompatible goals may help to explain why eating disorders, depression, alcoholism, and crime have all risen dramatically since the 1950s, as people of all ages feel anything from shame to anger about not having lived up to expectations – theirs or someone else's.

But the good news is, the *roots of our perfectionism are relatively unimportant to putting it right.*

The antidote:
high-performance comes from being productive not perfectionist

To combat the paralysing effects of perfectionism, one powerful principle to bring to mind is that the more fully-formed attempts we make at any task, the higher the probability of scoring a recognised success. Dean Keith Simonton's analysis of accomplished lives shows this fundamental rule holds fast across all disciplines and applies at any age. Professor Simonton notes, for instance, how Shakespeare wrote his smash hit *Hamlet* one year, and the not nearly so successful *Troilus and Cressida* the next; and though he produced 37 major works, we only really celebrate a quarter of those. This means that this wise old writer simply didn't know, or didn't care, what would fly and what would flop. History shows how every high-achiever relies on this same brand of tenacious productivity to eventually make progress. Their most prized accomplishments are invariably surrounded by a vast number of missed shots. For every golden egg, there's a whole flock of turkeys.

This example tells us that we can counter the scourge of perfectionism by making it our goal to be as *productive* as possible, *not* as perfect as possible, in the sure knowledge of what I'll now call 'The Shakespeare Principle': through high productivity we can still hope to create the occasional gem. Productivity brings a profound pleasure, and that knowing when we've done sufficient is a far FAR more satisfying and productive skill than trying to ace everything.

Overcoming workaholism

If paralysis is one side of the perfectionist coin, then workaholism is the flipside, wherein, far from being paralysed, we feel unable to stop for fear of falling behind or losing out in some way that we can't quite put our finger on. And we can be workaholics in many different ways, of course. Perhaps we work relentlessly at looking our best, or buying the best, or doing our best, or being ever-so tidy, or being cheerful and pleasing others as the life and soul of the party. We know it's perfectionism though, because the activity brings us pain not pleasure. It costs us dearly.

To combat such a workaholic streak, we would do well to ask the following question: *to what extent does the balance of how we spend our time day to day, faithfully reflect who and what we most value in life?* I.e. How healthy is the current ratio between our work compared to our leisure activities for rest and recuperation? Because rather than our guiding thought being *'Do your best!'*, it would prove far more helpful to 'do our best with whatever's left over once we've made ample provision for all of our other needs, passions and responsibilities'. This motto may not fit so neatly on the family crest, not even in Latin, but it makes for much happier living. Six times Tour de France champion, Lance Armstrong, reflects on this trade-off: "For every minute that I improve physically, there are days when I may become 45 seconds less motivated, as I understand more about what achievement can and cannot do for me as a person, and what it costs."

I'm not arguing for mediocrity. Expertise is wonderful stuff, but not at any price. Besides which, perfectionism doesn't mean doing an excellent job. Perfectionism means rarely starting because we fear not reaching our idealised standards. Or it means rarely finishing because we never feel things are good enough yet. Or it means investing far more resources of time, money and energy than the task ever warrants, resulting in a large net loss. This is called a Pyrrhic Victory after the Spartan leader whose troops defeated the invading Romans some 280 years B.C. King Pyrrhus declared the win to have been at so great a cost to his own troops that it could not rightly be called a victory.

Taking action against perfectionism
In the pursuit of a happy and healthy efficiency, we could do the following:

- It will help enormously if we measure ourselves by 'productive output' not mere activity; so we should tend to allot a time-limit within which to complete a task, rather than vaguely saying "I'll do it till it's done".

- We also have to be discriminating, because not all tasks are equally important. Whilst writing this book, I don't put my dishes away in the cupboard, because I don't give a monkey's that they sit there clean and dry on the draining board.

- Let's list the advantages of pushing so hard: *the pay-offs*. Then list the disadvantages: *the costs and losses*. Close relationships, health and passions are the common casualties, yet it is these which bring us our greatest happiness, and our happiness is a guiding light in life.

- If we systematically took our foot off the accelerator by 20%, those we care for will be far happier for it, because they'll get to see more of us and we'll be in a much cheerier mood.

- We need to update the pictures that can crop-up automatically in our mind which are horribly out of date. The pictures of how we once wanted things to be in some apparently perfect world. Those childish mind's eye fantasies in which we're so rich and beautiful and powerful. Far more likely what we wish for now is the satisfying company of good people and time for simple pleasures.

Here is five-time Olympic rowing champion, Steve Redgrave, describing the effects of the training regime he followed for 49 weeks a year during his long career at the top of his sport: "I go round feeling knackered all the time. I have no energy and I'm fighting the margins of being ill and not being ill. I go to dinners and fall asleep. I'm pushing back the boundaries all the time, and training so hard takes a toll on the body. If you feel fit and strong, then there's something wrong. You're not training hard enough . . . In reality, most athletes live on a knife-edge . . . quite healthy, quite ill, tipping one way or the other . . . because they are constantly pushing their body to the limit."

A cautionary tale

Perfectionism got me when I was still in shorts. Six years old and I was worrying what teacher would say about my colouring book. A few years later, once every two weeks, the headmaster would add up all the gold stars awarded for class work and read the results out in morning assembly. For a full five years I came second from last. Eventually I was awarded the 'industry prize', which on reflection can only have been for 'working harder and achieving less ... than any other boy in the school'.

Despite my over-earnest approach, I don't think I ever did hand a piece of homework in on time. Homework is responsible for my uncomfortable feelings on Sunday afternoon on account of all those unfinished essays on things like sugar-beet farming in Tanzania ... or Icelandic caribou. When I was eleven, a teacher wrote that I was "irritatingly juvenile". But he was quite wrong; I was far too serious. Proof in point, I committed my first string of crimes in the name of homework: filching other boys' exercise books from the pile outside the science office, so I could copy their work. But more than once I'd go back to return the books an hour later, and the pile would have been collected for marking, so I was too late! This led to my burying several of these stolen exercise books in a wood near our house. It's just a matter of time before Scotland Yard find them and begin piecing things together.

By the age of 12, I was pulling all-nighters to keep up with the work, and at age 14, I told myself that if I did well in my end of school exams four years later, life would surely be easy for me from then on in. So I held my breath and put happiness on hold. What I didn't realise was that setting distant goals like this is no better than planning to quench your thirst once you reach the mirage. The years passed almost without feature. School lessons that took place when I was eleven, became indistinguishable from the ones seven years on.

I grew up believing so thoroughly in the hocus pocus of trial by examination that I'd shoved my life in the deep freeze to make time for revision. I had taken no interest in the world that didn't contribute to my paper qualifications. My whole existence had been one long exam. Not for one moment did I look up from the grindstone to see the real world. I'd been on a treadmill labouring under the illusion that I'd been sprinting into a glorious future. I'd hoped that raw effort alone would forge my chubby features into heroic profile.

By the time I reached 18, I was suffering from executive burnout. I would not have minded if God's stern voice had come to me in a vision, saying "Could you stop writing and breathing now, this exam is over!" I would put down my leaking fountain pen and, with the smug expectation of St Peter awarding me a B minus, politely die.

In July 2004, the cosmologist Professor Stephen Hawking of Cambridge University concluded a lecture by saying that according to his present calculations *"travel back in time, can't be ruled out"*. When that day cometh, I just hope I'll have the wisdom not to use time-travel simply to go back and finish off my homework from thirty years ago. I hope I've learnt that the best thing to get really good at, is getting on with people.

We can guarantee our self-confidence by building gradually

When it comes to giving a good performance, there are few feelings more useful to us than confidence . . . the confidence that we can deal with setbacks, that we can roll with the blows, that we can rely upon our best friends, and that we can make a positive difference to the world around us. We also need to develop 'our nerve' – to speak in public, to ask for a dance, to suggest a date, to reach for a dream, or to change our life-direction. All this is why self-confidence not only *feels* good, but it actually increases the possibilities we're willing to explore. Says boxing legend and U.N. Messenger of Peace, Muhammad Ali, "It's lack of faith that makes people afraid of meeting challenges, and I believed in myself."

Being confident that we have the internal resources to take on a new challenge and, by dint of our actions, succeed in it, is probably the single most powerful determinant of how much we accomplish. This is because it's so self-motivating. If we think we can change something for the better by drumming up ideas, roping in support, and putting in some effort, this greatly increases the likelihood we'll have a go in the first place. What's more, we'll even be versatile and tenacious in the face of problems and setbacks, all because we believe in ourselves. It just so happens, of course, that such dynamism, ingenuity and perseverance are key ingredients for progress, and it's largely thanks to them that our confidence becomes a self-fulfilling prophecy.

Two times Nobel Scientist, Marie Curie, wrote: "Life is not easy for any of us. But what of that? We must have perseverance and above all confidence in ourselves. We must believe that we are gifted for something and that this thing must be attained."

Not only does a can-do attitude protect us from the paralysing and thus self-defeating pessimism that is all too characteristic of anxiety and depression, but men and women alike declare self-confidence to be one of the most attractive personal qualities in others. And with good reason, because self-assured individuals cheerfully take determined action on all major fronts, and this makes them an inspiration to be around.

How else can we cultivate self-confidence?

By far the most potent method is to set ourselves simple tasks which can be relied upon to give us a taste of success, no matter if it's just a smidgen at this stage. When we witness ourselves succeed, our confidence takes a turn for the better and little by little this enables us to handle ever grander goals. U.S. women's team soccer heroine, Mia Hamm, would agree: "I firmly believe that success breeds success. Once you have achieved something, your confidence begins to build."

Lance Armstrong would add this: "You can't fake confidence, you have to earn it, and if you ask me the only way to do that is work. You have to do the work."

And former South African President and Nobel Peace Laureate, Nelson Mandela, had his own training ground in his thirties, when he spent most evenings at a boxing club. "We each took turns leading the training sessions in order to develop leadership, initiative and self-confidence".

This 'small steps' strategy may not seem like rocket science, but just think what we often do instead. Right from the start we bite off more than we can chew, or draft over-long to-do lists, and the upshot is we never feel we've achieved what we set out to. No matter how much we get done, we never quite finish, and so deny ourselves the satisfaction and self-confidence of knowing that we're in control and can trust ourselves to complete things. Not surprisingly this leaves us irritable and with a sense of hurry and all because we applied the mistaken strategy that says 'If I aim for the stars, at least I'll reach the moon'. It's our old enemy perfectionism again. In fact, we would find far more pleasure and accomplishment if we set much more manageable tasks and harvested the confidence they will reliably bring us.

But let's be sure to stack the odds in our favour by appointing bite-size goals that are focused, tangible and short-range rather than broad, nebulous and distant. In other words, we should commit to a vigorous 20 minute walk three times this coming week, rather than promising to get healthy by Christmas. It's important, too, that we seek frequent feedback on our progress, because measuring improvement is highly motivating and helps guide us to what works best.

With this in mind, it can be really useful to rally around some supporters, who can help us develop our confidence. This helped British runner, Kelly Holmes, to achieve her phenomenal double gold medal win in the 800m and 1500m races at the 2004 Olympics. "I knew I was in the fittest shape of my life but I still needed that self-belief. So I started texting my old coach, Dave Arnold, because he knows me so well ... and he ended up saying that my training times were 'bloody fantastic' and that I had to go for it."

Having a sense of control over the outcome is so very important

The reason that 'building gradually' is so important, is that we thrive when we feel in control, and a sense of control is vital to performing well under pressure. The extraordinary circumstances of individuals and teams in combat can teach us a lot about coping well, no matter how difficult the mission. During the Second World War, the factor of 'feeling in control' explains why solo fighter-pilots displayed less mental trauma than other air crew. Faced with danger, solo flyers always felt they could take direct and effective action by deploying their combat skills. By contrast, the crew in the back of a bomber just had to sit tight through the anti-aircraft flack and the threat of enemy patrols. Such a sense of helplessness can quickly lead to hopelessness, at which point we're prone to give up and suffer serious anxiety and depression. This explains why bomber crews had rates of psychological illness four times higher than the solo pilots who, despite having the same 50/50 odds of survival, could at least take action, and that's what mattered for their state of mind. So much so, that 50 percent of surviving fighter-pilots even *volunteered* for a second tour of combat duty. Nonetheless, the number of bomber crew whose mental illness rendered them unfit for combat was less than one in twenty. Research at the time suggested that the other factors that helped get them through were:

- feeling personally motivated.
- being well trained with lots of practice under highly realistic conditions.
- a calm leader who modeled excellent performance skills.
- a close-knit team spirit.

Bomber crews usually had all of these four factors, and very notably they also claimed that being allowed to sleep for well over a dozen hours or more after a mission was a psychological life-saver.

It could pay us to carefully consider just how we could incorporate all of the above ingredients whenever we're faced with particularly demanding times. Further to this, we should consider how we can inject an element of choice and control into situations where they might not be immediately apparent to us. Here's what golf champion, Tiger Woods, has to say: "It's great to be nervous because that means you care ... The day I'm not nervous is the day I quit, because that's the day I don't care any more about how I perform. I've always been able to handle being nervous by just going through my routine and never deviate from my routine. Everyone has to develop their own routine ... If people get away from their routine, they get out of rhythm and hit bad shot."

Preparing ourselves by finding out what to expect in the testing situation can also give us a sense of control, so we won't be overwhelmed on the day. In addition to which, by focusing our attentions on the activity 100%, we can largely block out the pressures and anxieties, and so calm our nerves. Nobel-winning physicist, Richard Feynman had this to say about public speaking "The moment I start to think about the physics, and have to concentrate on what I'm explaining, nothing else occupies my mind – I'm completely immune to being nervous."

Upgrade our Time-Management

Our lifestyle or ambitions can fast outgrow the time-investment strategies which have served us so well in the past. The trouble with time management, we're never explicitly taught it, we're just expected to pick it up, which means that we may still be using a method that worked for us ten years ago, but is now a handicap. So here's some thoughts:

1: Manage yourself by drawing up a guiding hierarchy of essential goals which best reflect what it is you most value in life, such as loved ones, health, passions, and financial security. Your aim, then, is to invest as much time as possible working at things as high up your priority-list as you can reach. When allotting time to your everyday to-do list, be sure the ratios reflect your guiding hierarchy.

2: Manage those around you and the environment in which you work: by identifying when it is you work best, so as to create and protect your high-performance oases. Let the phones take messages; let the e-mails gather. When requests do finally reach you later in the day, make it your rule never to say yes immediately. Ask yourself first which of your essential goals you'll thus be saying 'no' to? Commitment to your greater cause is the best defence against the distraction and dissipation of your resources.

3: Manage your activities by applying The Pareto Principle which states that 20% of the input produces about 80% of the results. I.e. 80% of your satisfaction or profit from a task will come from just 20% of your investment in it. What you have to discover is which active ingredient is responsible for all that reward. Figure out that one on a regular basis and you can concentrate your energies on what works best. Applying the Pareto Principle can also prevent us from confusing 'urgent' with 'important': *urgent* . . . is the phone screaming at us to answer it . . . or the person who needs an answer by the end of the day. *Important* . . . is to put the phone on automatic-answer so that we can spend some focused time on creating the life we really want to lead.

Unfortunately urgent feels more pressing than important, but let's not be fooled. We have to make sure the stuff that's really important to us is given daily attention. Which is why every morning we should remind ourselves that time management isn't really about time at all, it's about keeping what we truly treasure in life uppermost in our thoughts.

Combining visualisation with relaxation to rehearse our high-performance

We can combine the skills of imagination and relaxation to mentally rehearse any activity so as to strikingly improve our real-life performance, whether in speech-making or deal-brokering, personal relationships or sport.

Proof of the power of this skills-partnership, is that most world-class performers spend nearly as much time imaginatively rehearsing their routines as physically doing them. For example, five times gold medal Olympic rower, Sir Steve Redgrave tells of how the official team psychologist used these techniques to allow the crew to imaginatively rehearse a successful performance.

"He told us about the skills of visualisation and everything fell into place. I had been developing ideas like that myself, naturally, over the years. Either together or separately, we'd sit down and talk through each race and how we saw it developing; we'd then lie down, and Simon would tell us to think about our breathing and relax everything from the toes right up to the head. He would go through each part of the body in turn and get you to relax them. The legs would become leaden. The whole body would feel very heavy. This was purely designed to get you completely relaxed, but in a state where you were still totally aware of what was going on. When we were totally relaxed, Simon would talk to us about what to expect and what we wanted out of the race. It became ingrained deeply into the mind. What Simon said to us was nothing different from what we'd been through as a group before. There was nothing clever or mystical about his words. It concerned the concentration within the warm-up, certain points within the race that he'd pick on, the mental awareness when sitting on the start, after 15 strokes, the stride and the rhythm that you're going to get into. Practical things and tactics. But we were doing this in a totally relaxed state."

The reason this relaxed visualisation works so well, is that our brain doesn't readily discriminate between reality and imagination, which also explains why some memories and premonitions can so unsettle us. In those instances, our brain is reacting as if the imagined event from past or future is actually happening here and now, and so sets off our alarm bells. Tension only serves to thwart the power, speed and accuracy of any physical or mental skill, which is why excessive nervousness makes us stumble over our words, and why we should learn to 'actively relax'.

To harness the benefits of relaxation, we must attend to all three of breath, body and visualisation. First, we inhale slowly and gently through our nose (i.e. mouth closed if possible, so the brain doesn't think we're preparing to gasp in air). Then we exhale even more slowly than we breathed in, (perhaps taking twice as long), as this ratio of slower out than in sends a calming signal to our brain and nervous system. Next, we take each group of body muscles in turn, and first tense them for the count of three . . . and then shake them out before letting them fall as limp as possible. Guard against having hunched shoulders and clenched stomach muscles, and let's not forget our jaw, tongue, and face. Everything needs to fall free and easy.

Now let our imagination waft us away to a favourite oasis of tranquillity, perhaps somewhere out in mother nature. Feel the grass beneath our toes, smell the blossoms, hear the shh of the waves . . . whatever works best for us.

Once we're comfortably relaxed like this, now's the time for skills practice. We vividly imagine ourselves giving a highly successful and enjoyable performance, being sure to view and feel this event from within our own body, rather than seeing it as a detached bystander. Vividly deploy all of our five senses in a systematic, step by step imagining, while aiming to maintain our deep relaxation throughout. We shouldn't rush, and we should be able to feel and see each step of the process being done clearly and correctly. As well as imaginatively rehearsing the specific skills, we could also re-run how it felt in any of our past successes, and also how the general atmosphere will probably be on the day. Our acclimatising ourselves to that background buzz is all part of the preparation.

For significant effects, we should try at least a dozen such low and thorough repetitions, though let's never forget that real-life experience is an unbeatably potent and quite irreplaceable training ground. Nonetheless, imaginative rehearsal represents an extremely useful, low-risk, low-cost experimental laboratory, and is a great back-up when reality is temporarily impractical. (For instance, without our imagination, we simply can't arrange a test audience of 200 people.) I am reminded of singer Celine Dion who says, "Before a concert or a recording, I practiced my songs, a hundred times in my head."

This technique is reliable and powerful and well-worth our investment, and I've seen it work wonders many times (for once terrified souls who needed to give speeches, or oral exams, or sporting performances). It's also been a real boon in my own life. Indeed, I think the positive applications of combining deeply absorbing imaginations with profound relaxation can illustrate one of the fundamental reasons for pursuing the Study of Well-Being: that *feeling good* is not simply a result of good things happening, but can itself be an active cause of them, too, which makes the skills of well-being an invaluable asset in any endeavour.

Make rehearsals highly realistic

Philippe Petit is the French gentleman who, one morning back in 1974, walked between Manhattan's Twin Towers – on a high-wire he had rigged . . . quite without authority . . . *and without a net*. To prepare for such a big walk as that, Petit will rig a longer practice cable than will ever be needed, and will rehearse in all possible conditions: in the dark, and with the sun in his eyes, through wind and rain. When preparing for any event, we all of us have to ready ourselves for distractions and unexpected hiccups, and we need to have practiced working through them. Then the task itself on the day will be little more than a stroll in the park. This is how a professional prepares for their live performances, and this principle of making the practice far more trying than the real thing, is a good one. We should also note that if we don't get it right in training, we won't get it right on the day.

Performance-enhancing drugs

There are none.
Caffeine tablets, several cups of coffee per day, glucose drinks, and all other elicit pick-me-ups, they're all a total sham whose downsides on the day or in the preparation period will far outweigh any promised benefit.

Celine Dion shows admirable clarity on that point. "Drugs and alcohol frighten me because they ruin lives. I just don't see the appeal in putting things up your nose or down your throat that are going to change the way you are. I have never been tempted to go down that route and if that makes me a boring person, I'm not going to apologise because I am very happy with my life."

If we want to give our brain and body some major advantage in a highly competitive situation, we should invest all our efforts in eating well, sleeping well, recuperative exercise, and keeping our spirits up. These activities will send a whole host of beneficial chemicals coursing through our veins and make the best of all our pre-match practice. (My chapter *Nourish and Nurture Beautiful Health* is a guide to the details of what such a healthy regime might include.)

How booze doesn't help: a case study

The thing I most regret about getting drunk on a fairly frequent basis when I was in my late teens and twenties, is that being drunk only ever got in the way of my getting on with someone. When I say 'being drunk', I don't mean lying in the street singing 'Yesh-terday' to passers by. I just mean I'm on my second glass of something and there's a warm glow inside which makes everything seem jollier and more rosy than it really is, and I'm feeling bolder, smarter, funnier and far more attractive with every gulp. It's no accident that British drink-drive laws have a cut-off point of one drink only. Any more than that and our distorted view of everything makes us quite a hazard. Not that anyone has ever advised me to stop or reduce my drinking. I just began to suspect the advantages of getting drunk were far outweighed by the advantages of staying sober. I began to suspect that although booze helped me feel better for a few hours, those feelings came at too high a price. Such possibilities prompted me to do a stock-take of my relationship with alcohol.

Does drink help me be more myself?
No, quite the opposite: the more I drink, the more it flattens out any distinctive and identifying characteristics.

Does drink help me relax and unwind?
Only for the four hours I'm drunk, during which time the alcohol depresses my nervous system so I feel increasingly relaxed and comfortable. But then it stops me sleeping properly because our dream-time brainwaves are completely different once we've had more than one glass of something. This is why drinking always leaves me feeling tired the following day. And that's the trouble: two steps forward, and three steps back.

Does drink help me get on with people?
I think it pays the person we're with a profound compliment when simply by our actions we send the unspoken message that "I don't need to be drunk to enjoy your company... I don't need to be

drunk to relax with you, or to confide in you, or to find what you say interesting, or important, or funny." Being bright and sober in someone's company shows a lot of respect.

Does drink help me with the opposite sex?
Here's how two dates went back in my twenties.

Me drunk:
The girl friend sitting with me in front of the fire seemed to be having trouble getting half an inch down her first glass of wine, whereas I was on my third and telling her about the plot for my feature film idea. In a brief moment of sensitivity, I interrupted my own lecturing to ask her about her relationship with her mum and dad who divorced when she was 7, and her time in hospital . . . but she took too long thinking about it, so for no good reason I began telling her about my school exams and how I was robbed of an A-grade in Economics. Things seemed to be going swimmingly, so I poured myself another glass; but then my date pointed out that she had to go.
   "Don't be stupid, it's not even ten!" I told her.
   She gave me one of those 'continental kisses' on either cheek, and rode off on her bicycle. I shouted out that I'll call her, and she said something in reply, but I didn't quite catch it. I considered finishing off the bottle in front of the fire, but found that I'd drunk it already. So instead, I sat there wondering what was wrong with women today, what with their reluctance to communicate . . . I mean really open up about what's important. I happened to calculate, too, that the evening wasn't cheap, what with the wine and beers and the microwave meals, so no one could say I hadn't tried!

Me sober:
It took several weeks, but finally I persuaded that young lady to give me another chance. We rustled-up dinner together and sipped a glass of wine, but seeing as it was a fine clear night we agreed to go straight out for a long walk. I was just itching to tell her everything I know about the stars and the number of galaxies there are and all of

that, but I sensed there's other stuff she wanted to talk about, so that's exactly what we did. I walked her home slowly, savouring her company, and we arranged to meet again the very next day. On her doorstep, we kissed goodnight . . . this time the kiss was intercontinental . . . and I strode home whistling.

Optimism and joy are far more productive than fear

"To win, you have to dare to lose," says the Norwegian psychology professor, Willi Railo, who has worked alongside Sven-Goran Eriksson coaching the England soccer team. "A winner hates to lose, but is not afraid of losing," and it's this absence of fear about doing the 'wrong thing' which can unleash a performance that has the throttle wide open. It is by these means that high-flyers distinguish themselves, because while reaching for the stars, they do not allow themselves to be daunted by the number of times they fluff it. Failure might infuriate them, but anger *after* the event doesn't handicap the performance. By contrast, if we become afraid of the consequences of failure . . . these might be criticism, embarrassment or blame . . . then this fear will tend to inhibit or even paralyse our skills, and we simply 'choke'. Either that or we play for safety and take too few risks, which only leads to underachievement. Our performances, our career, our whole life could remain lack-lustre because of such self-defeating anxiety. Sven and Railo's answer to such a common phenomenon is to encourage their players to take risks, and they refrain from criticising the mistakes that are an inevitable part of fearless experimentation.

But there are lessons here that reach far beyond the sports field. Time and again, studies show that being optimistic . . . i.e. expecting that things will work out well, and acting positively on account of that expectation . . . is an attitude to life that will halve our risk of dying from both accident and disease. This relationship was born out by the thousand men and women studied in the Netherlands and followed for nine years; just as it was by the work of Harvard psychologist Dr Laura Kubzansky who tracked 1300 men for ten years and found half the rate of heart-disease among those who were curious, hopeful and optimistic about life, compared to the pessimists. This vast difference in health outcomes is as big as the difference between smokers and non-smokers; and is it really a coincidence that Harvard sociologist Professor Robert Putnam observed a very similar health ratio between those people who had been a member of some weekly social activity, and those who hadn't. It seems that not being afraid to mingle in company and make new friends, is literally a life-saver.

The message from the accumulating evidence seems to be 'Far from fearing life, we should stretch ourselves towards it!' But if this is our resolve, then it helps to know how exactly. One sound method is to foster our well-founded hope by identifying several highly motivating goals, and a few realistic but enjoyable routes to achieving each of them. This multiple combination means we're more likely to progress in at least one of our ambitions. (Such as a strategy is, of course, the absolute opposite of putting all our eggs in the same basket, sticking rigidly to a single destination and just one plan.) And it's just possible that if we can muster enough of this health-bringing, progress-making optimism, we can build a bridge that will take us well away from fear of making mistakes all the way through to exuberance...that appetite for life that drives us to explore and pioneer with heart-felt enthusiasm. Exuberance is not to be mistaken for superficial bubbliness, nor the self-possessed out of control state that is mania. Exuberance is pure joie-de-vivre that's being channeled constructively, and acclaimed American psychiatrist, Kay Redfield Jamison, describes its four components as a passion to know more, a playful spirit, empathy with nature, and a sense of joy. We see this quality in writing as various as Charles Dickens and Bill Bryson, or lives as different as Winston Churchill and Claire Rayner.

The fruitfulness of exuberance in contrast to the negative and inhibiting effect of fear, were well illustrated by a famous episode in the life of American physicist, Richard Feynman. His creativity seemed to dry up when at age 27 he became hot property after the Second World War and started receiving fabulous offers from top universities. He so acutely felt the overblown expectations of those around him, that it stopped him in his tracks. Sitting forlorn in the campus cafeteria, his interest happened to be caught by the wobble of a paper plate that a student had thrown high into the air. This inspired some calculations to explain the wobble, just for the sheer fun of it, and it was these diagrams scribbled down over the next few days which later earned him the Nobel Prize, not least because they had major relevance to the stability of rockets and the forthcoming space programme. For me, this life-story proclaims 'Who knows to what heights exuberance might lift us?'

It's important to keep our spirits up

High spirits and good feelings are not only a result of things going well in life, they can also be a potent cause, says University of Michigan's Professor Barbara Fredrickson. Her *Broaden & Build* theory states that pleasing emotions tend to help us think and behave in richer, more creative and constructive ways. For instance, if we feel secure and have a safe haven, we'll be more willing to experiment and explore. Jamie Oliver says about his successful BBC series 'The Naked Chef', "Roping my mates in to help with the show stops me from getting nervous."

By contrast, painful emotions narrow us down to a limited response-repertoire, probably because this focusing of attention has high survival value: we're scared so we freeze or scream or run; we're angry so we threaten or fight.

So, the lesson here is that we should be sure to conjure up highly positive feelings to help us be productive and fluid and creative on the big day. Writer Helen Keller, the first deaf and blind person to attend an American university, would agree: "Optimism is the faith that leads to achievement. Nothing can be done without hope or confidence. No pessimist ever discovered the secret of the stars, or sailed to an uncharted land, or opened a new doorway for the human spirit."

And as history's most successful female tennis champion, Stefanie Graf, put it, "As long as I can focus on enjoying what I'm doing, having fun, I know I'll play well." This principle certainly worked at the 2004 Olympics in Athens, for British runner, Kelly Holmes, who used music to fuel her good spirits and win two gold medals. "When I went to the warm-up track I would listen to Alicia Keys singing *'If I ain't got you'* and I applied the words to the gold medal I wanted. I sang it as I warmed up and it brought tears to my eyes."

The proactive benefits of pleasure and positive feelings have implications for community well-being just as much as for individuals, a point nicely illustrated in the animal kingdom by Professor Barbara Fredrickson recounting how squirrels that have been playmates in their first season of life, are much more likely to risk their own lives by sounding an alarm call to warn their old chums about a predator. The implication is that although the pleasant emotion generated by play may itself be transient, the personality trait that it builds, camaraderie in this case, is long enduring. Naturally, Professor Fredrickson's take-home message is that we should actively foster enjoyable emotions in ourselves and those around us, to better help us thrive and prosper.

On which note, it's rather comforting to know that 'helping others' is one of the most reliable ways to feel good about ourselves. And it just so happens that feeling good makes it all the more likely we'll get a whole bunch of other useful things done as well. Positive feelings are highly-productive, so by helping others we help ourselves. Just another one of Nature's well-rounded relationships.

A checklist of exam preparations

Whether we're taking a professional diploma, or sitting a school examination, 90% of a good performance is achieved well up front through several weeks of planning and rehearsal . . . that's if we want to ensure we make a jolly good job of it, without making our life a misery.

But before I start bullet-pointing three key ingredients for high-performance happiness, there's a wonderful ingredient which would fuel-inject all our efforts, and that is: having someone we really respect agree to monitor our preparations on a regular basis.

Why?

Because it seems to be a law of human nature that for progress to be made, it needs to be measured. What's more, life . . . in this as in all other arenas . . . is best played in partnership, so let's not isolate ourselves.

Now here are my three other suggestions:

- Sometimes we might just do single answers of an hour a piece, but at least once per week we should do the full three-hour monty . . . and we should do this full dress-rehearsal a handful of times in the two weeks before the exam day, so as to acclimatise ourselves to the rigours of writing three questions one after the other. That in itself is a skill: to divide our time equally, and to change our mind-set quickly and easily.

- Be sure we know precisely what skills are going to be rewarded, so we can focus our rehearsals accordingly. For instance, here's my own point of view on university examination papers: The weakest answer to any question is the one that simply describes the problem. The better answer is able to see it from several points of view, perhaps challenging the very premise or scope of the question. But the best answer goes two levels higher. First of all, it outlines what sorts of things need to be done to help unravel the problem and discover new solutions. And, secondly, it draws new connections between unexpected arenas, thus linking up the ideas between two different parts of the course, or even two or more different disciplines. Of course, we'll need to ponder and draft such lofty answers well in advance so we can reel them out on the day.

- When we finally take the stage for real, rather than being tempted to improvise in the panic of the moment, we should aim as far as possible to stick to our routines exactly how we've rehearsed them. Yes, we answer the specific question at hand, rather than the ones we answered in practice, but we should be sure to add all the ingredients with which we've been rehearsing.

As a guiding principle, consider how an Olympic athlete grows *stronger* in training, not weaker, worn-out, or wound-up. In demanding times, we need to rely on a healthy balance of good habits for study and recreation. So we should design for ourselves a training schedule that aims to complete our rehearsals comfortably ahead of any dead-lines, and then resolve to enjoy the journey, because it is the quality and creativity of our preparations which will most determine the big performance.

What's more, if the journey to our achievements and success isn't health-bringing, it won't be sustainable, and our time in the sun will be short lived. And if we don't take the hint from how we're feeling in terms of our happiness and health, we could end up with a chronic fatigue syndrome, debilitating phobias or clinical depression, but in any event, a long spell out of work with an all too genuine sickness that has its roots in a psychological civil war. (*Nick's Special Topic* chapter explores just such psychosomatic problems, and how to deal with them.)

Coping well with success

Success can be hard stuff to handle. Yet, as for so many of life's positives, there's a widely held notion that success can take care of itself and requires no caution. But we would do well to remember that other positives such as unusual beauty or wealth or smarts all come with their own brand of serious pitfalls alongside the opportunities. And like any form of power, these qualities can bring good or ill in equal measure depending how they're channeled. So let's consider some of the tricky situations in which success can land us.

Not an uncommon phenomenon is the individual who enjoys some initial success at something, whether in work, romance, sport or a hobby, but then continues to invest themselves in that same endeavour well past the point at which they are taking satisfaction from it. It's as if their ability to be versatile has been paralysed by other people's demands that they should keep digging where they once struck gold. This is similar to the sort of success that leads us badly off-course because we make the mistake of pursuing something just because we're good at it. Many a medical student became one largely because they were good at science, not realising this requires very different signature strengths from being a junior doctor in an inner city emergency room. A third permutation on this theme is that the skills which earned our initial success may not be the same ones required to keep us there. For instance, we might perform well as the 10 to 1 outsider, but go all to pieces as the odds-on favourite.

A quite different dilemma faces the stars of sport or stage who have found the exhilaration of their time in the spotlight a very difficult high to come down from. Their problem is how to cope with the pains of falling to earth when they so want to stay air-born. It's quite a skill to come off stage and be able to channel so much surplus energy in a benign way.

Still other success stories will suffer 'impostor syndrome', whereby they regard themselves as an ugly fraud who at any moment will be unmasked and found out to be far less impressive than everyone's over-inflated expectations. Such foreboding can bring about some means of self-sabotage in an attempt to end the misery.

And as a last, less dramatic example, there's the youngster who is doing so well at school, that she is left to get on with things by the well-intentioned adults around her. But this can backfire when she ends up equating doing well with feeling invisible and un-valued, at which point she might decide to adopt the strategies of her much-troubled school friend whose misdemeanours get showered with attention.

And as if the above inventory isn't enough, it's not just our own success that requires careful handling. Research by Dr Shelley Gable at UCLA suggests that one of the most positive indications of a strong bond between two people isn't simply their mutual support in troubled times, but also their ability to take joy in each other's successes. It's a surefire sign of a profound friendship when we are as thrilled and delighted as the other person when they win out. Conversely, it bodes very ill if we can't feel excited for them or, worse still, suffer jealousy.

In short, success needs to be ridden with just as much skill and wisdom as failure if we're to thrive in the face of it. In principle, this shouldn't be a problem for us, because building on what we do right, rather than focusing on what we do wrong, is an approach at the very heart of the science of well-being. The idea is that by expanding upon our strengths, we overwhelm our negatives. So how do we build upon an initial success?

While researching among exceptionally high achievers these past ten years, I began to suspect that profound success isn't indicated by the heights we've reached, nor even how far we've come. It's the manner in which we travel that really matters; with what spirit. Are we whistling while we work and appreciative and benevolent? Or are we a miserable soul, or not much better? It also struck me that while making progress should bring us joy, our eventual arrival is, by definition, a pause in the music. We feel the sadness at parting from our travelling companion, and then waking up having got the job or finished it, can be quite alarming. What newly appointed goal is going to set in train an equally worthwhile adventure? This end of journey re-orientation requires our old friend 'versatility', which, as we will see, is not only a key ingredient in resilience to adversity, but also plays a major part in durable success.

Case in point is the research by Harvard psychologist, Daniel Gilbert, which shows that even though it takes several years of teaching for a young American lecturer to finally hear a decision on whether they've been awarded a permanent post or not, in most cases their elation or bitter disappointment takes barely two weeks to wear off. This incredibly short recovery time suggests that our happiness hasn't evolved to be dominated by mere goal-achievement, probably because when it comes to the matter of survive and thrive, 'versatility on route' has far more value to us. Seen from this perspective, there are no real end-points, and success isn't a particular event or a position reached, but rather it's the journey itself. In which case, failure and success look quite alike, since they both present myriad opportunities and pitfalls. Put another way, enjoying our endeavours is the very height of success, and its own best reward. If all we can think about is celebrating once it's all over, then we're probably trying to compensate for insufficient enjoyment on route.

Likewise, happiness is not an end in itself, it's a means by which to guide and motivate our actions so that we make progress towards those things we value most. Success, then, is using our signature strengths in ways that are meaningful to us because of the excitement and satisfaction they bring us. This is why evergreen happiness comes from *creating* rather than *consuming*; and this is why we do well to measure the success of our endeavours by their own rightness for us, not by whether they are acclaimed or rejected. Was van Gogh wrong to paint cypress trees even though the art markets of the time didn't want them? Surely the best judge of our success is ourselves, because only *we* know how well we're responding to our callings, and how much of ourselves we are gladly investing. The reception of our efforts becomes less important the more we put our hearts into something. How true to ourselves are we able to be? Measured in this way, our level of success is less about what we've achieved so far and more about what we're trying to do now: the manner and direction of our journey. So let's consider judging ourselves not by what we have already, but by who and what we hold in such value that we are still striving happily on their behalf.

* * *

Planning for Progress

- In which area of your life is perfectionism holding you back? Which strategies will you use to counter it?

- Where in your life could you increase your sense of control over the outcomes?

- Where could you use 'imaginal rehearsal' to improve your real-life performance?

- In what ways could your own success lead you astray?

* * *

What can Slow our Progress?

How come we can end up so unskilled after years of formal education? Or more particularly, how come I personally grew up so *incompetent* . . . and by incompetent, I mean at age twenty-five I felt completely unemployable.

Now if we were talking chess, posing that question would be the equivalent of the Pawelski Defence known only to a handful of Grand Masters. Because it was with a feeling of pained surprise that at age 25, I finally twigged there was something wrong with the way I was going about things.

This all came as quite a shock, because as a teenage boy watching television, I looked forward to the day when I, too, would be really good at something just like all my tv heroes. I'd be a lycra-wearing Captain from the same academy as James T. Kirk of the Star Ship Enterprise. Or maybe a martini-mixing battlefront surgeon in tribute to Hawkeye & Trapper and my 14 years of *M.A.S.H.* Or even a horse-riding, stetson-wearing homicide detective of the Sam McCloud school of cowboy camp.

I quite simply assumed that my abilities would rise with the tide as I grew older, and I'd inevitably end up expert in something. Hence, when people needed one of the top minds in the country, they'd very quickly call for *Nick Baylis, the expert.*

What in fact happened was, that by the time I reached 25, I could only get work as a waiter . . . and people only called for me when they needed another bread roll.

You see the problem was I simply didn't know enough about anything – *and I mean anything at all.*

This shaming and paining state of affairs got me pondering at 2 o'clock one morning as I worked alone as a catering assistant washing-up a thousand wine glasses after somebody's 21st birthday party. How was it, I wondered, that after all those countless years of schooling and four years of university, I couldn't actually do anything for which anyone would pay more than four bucks an hour, or its equivalent value in yesterday's croissants.

This wasn't what I'd dreamt of at all. Surely by age 25 I was meant to be saving lives, solving murders, storming enemy machine-gun posts, or making scientific breakthroughs. Instead, I spent 12 hours a day as an 'emergency waiter' serving pea & ham soup to scheming lawyers in London restaurants.

Painstakingly that night, like the detective teams I had watched so many times on tv, I pieced together what had happened, and realised I'd made three rookie mistakes. When taken together, these three schoolboy errors well explained what I now call 'My Status Quo of Incompetence'.

MY FIRST MISTAKE: School and The Illusion of Learning
Back in my senior school, between joining at age 11 and leaving at 18, I dutifully did what I was told which generally meant doing a little of everything once or twice per week. This snail's pace of learning was just sufficient so that each week I took one faltering step forward on the path to wisdom, and then in the six days that followed, I totally forgot the smidgen of skill that I'd accidentally acquired, and so took one step back.

Thanks to this illusion of learning, i.e. this simple process of moving forwards and backwards like the tide, I was able to maintain my 'status quo of incompetence'. And when exams came around, I'd cram for them, do fairly well, and then erase all memory of the event with the help of alcohol and the holidays. This whole farce was simply repeated at university, which meant that by the end of it all, I was a completely blank slate. Oh, a couple of things stuck for no good reason and never went away. I knew the Latin word for javelin, and I could recite, *incorrectly*, several lines of Shakespeare. This is a good example of how very often I thought I knew something but didn't – which placed me in a dangerous position of confident stupidity. For instance, that time aged 19 when I spent a whole day in Paris thinking I was charming the socks off a delightful Sorbonne student, who, as she kissed me goodbye, pointed out with an air of despair that her name was pronounced 'Sandrine' and not 'Cendrier' as I'd so seductively been calling her, and that 'cendrier' was the French word for 'ashtray'.

So it was that I left the temple gates of formal education clutching my exam certificates like a gladiator holds his sword, not realising that my 'sword of knowledge' was not only made of floppy plastic, but was also fully retractable.

"I trust good will triumph!" had been the Headmaster's concluding comment on my final school report. Made me sound like *Star Wars*. But the battle was not to be quite so epic. It was just me dressed as a waiter against a galaxy of discarded wine glasses.

MY SECOND MISTAKE: I didn't know it was possible for just about anybody to get really good at something

That 'Illusion of Learning' had so fooled me because I simply didn't know about the importance of frequent and intensive practice, and that my pussyfooting around once or twice a week wasn't going to get me anywhere. And by this accidental omission in my understanding of the world, I grew up believing that to be good at something, even to be passably competent, you either 'had it' or you didn't. Yes, you could work at it, but you'd pretty much be wasting your time, because everyone with 'natural talent' would so easily over-take you on the inside lane and leave you far behind. Sure I knew there was some sort of relationship between practice and improvement, but I didn't appreciate just how trustworthy and useful a relationship that was. I didn't really believe that I could pick any one of my passions and get good at it just as fast as I fancied, simply by putting in the extra hours and effort. I didn't believe that if I worked hard on my game five evenings per week, I'd almost certainly become one of the best players in the school.

MY THIRD MISTAKE: too much television: And this, for me, was the really big mistake, the one I excelled in, because *this* mistake kept the First and Second Mistakes wedged firmly in place.

The trouble with too much television

Watching television is the commonest past-time of the modern world, and the average person will spend more time doing this than in any other activity other than work or sleep. Nothing else has so rapidly and profoundly affected how most of us use our free time. In 1950, barely 10 percent of American homes had television sets, but by 1959, 90 percent did, which is probably the fastest ever spread of any technological innovation. (The uptake of internet availability will rival tv's record, but probably won't beat it.) Nowadays, nearly 99% of British and American households own a television, and the amount each person views has grown by roughly 10% every decade since the 1960s.

Television is tough to control because it taps into our instincts
There is now more than forty years of research in to the effects of television on our lives. Professor Robert Kubey, Director of the Centre for Media Studies at Rutgers University, explains that television taps into our brain's instinctive response to sudden and dramatic changes in our environment, because the cuts, zooms and sudden action all grab our attention whether we like it or not. What's more it immediately relaxes us by distracting us from the present reality with its ready-packaged world. One of the reasons that people view so much more than they intended is because on most occasions the

relaxation immediately evaporates the moment we switch off. (This is quite unlike alternative leisure pursuits which are mentally or physically active, such as walking, gardening, reading or singing. After these, our sense of relaxation can last for many hours.)

Television doesn't help our brain

By measuring electrical brainwave activity, it has been clearly shown that it takes considerably more brain involvement to read a book than to watch television. Reason being that when reading we're creating images in our mind's eye, whereas tv watching is simply the consumption of pre-packaged images. It is poignant indeed that the veteran BBC broadcaster, Terry Wogan, observes how television contracts the imagination and radio expands it. It is for these reasons that many scientists believe that too much tv allows our thinking skills to weaken. And because we're so passive in the face of television – because we're not processing the information by interacting with it, discussing it, or generating responses – we learn very little, no matter how many documentaries we're watching. Documentaries will be interesting, yes, but none of the information will stick for very long, and our interest will only be superficial.

Television doesn't help our body

A Harvard medic specialising in Public Health, Dr Frank Hu, recently published research in *The Journal of the American Medical Association* showing that the amount of time spent watching tv is strongly linked to being over-weight. Dr Hu tracked more than 50,000 women over six years and concluded that *the more you watch, the fatter you get.* This is because people who watch a lot of tv tend to exercise less. They also tend to eat more, not least because of all the commercials for food, yet their metabolic rate is lower compared to someone reading or working on a computer. Thinking brains burn a lot more energy than ones watching tv. Hence, Dr Hu recommends replacing tv with brisk walking for an hour per day.

Television doesn't help our children

No less an institution than The American Academy of Paediatrics recommends that infants under two watch absolutely no television at all. This is because even very young babies just a few weeks old will strain to locate and look at the source of all this light and noise. This explains how a child could grow up expecting television to be a 'natural' part of their environment. Moreover, background tv noise may disrupt children's play and babbling and the inner speech of their thoughts, and all of these subtle activities have key roles in their development. The same, of course, is true for older children who benefit hugely from creating their own imaginative stories and generating their own thoughts rather than consuming off-the-shelf ones. Professors agree that it's the ability of someone to play with their own ideas once they get beyond the bog-standard curriculum, which is the ability that distinguishes the real innovators. That problem-solving creativity needs to be learnt. An hour's silence without the interruption of tv or radio, as we might find on a walk in the country, can provide us with a wonderful oasis in which to think.

We also need to be careful of the values that we're consuming when we watch so much of what comprises mainstream programming. I firmly agree with Body Shop CEO, Anita Roddick, who says that mainstream tv risks "pacifying the mind and perpetuating the myth that material wealth defines self-value and self-worth." That's a speculation, but we know for a fact that in older children, more than two hours per day of television clearly begins to interfere with their school achievement. Time on computer games has many of the same effects and needs to be calculated as part and parcel of this screen time. Learning to self-limit their viewing is a good place for youngsters to start, just like we have to learn to keep a tight rein on how fast we drive or how much alcohol we drink. My personal preference would be for no more than one hour's tv on a week day, and none at all at the weekends, just to show the box who's in charge.

Television doesn't help our social life

Psychologists have observed that when it comes to leisure activities, the more you do of one thing, the more you do of all the others. So if you're big on DIY or going out to the movies, the more likely it is you play sport, host dinner parties, or help out at a voluntary organisation. This equation is very reliable; but when it comes to telly, quite the reverse is true. *We do less of everything.* This explains how, these past 50 years, tv watching has been a major culprit in the severe decline of every other form of positive social involvement, within or outside of the home. Husbands and wives now spend three-fold as much time watching tv as they spend talking together; and six-fold more time watching tv than in community activities. Not surprisingly, there is growing evidence that the channel-hopping short attention span of younger people is also reflected in their having fewer and weaker friendships. It seems they've got used to grazing around the channels for something more exciting, and they tend to do the same with their friends.

Yet how can we be sure that tv watching is to blame?

Lucky for us, back in the 1970s, a team of researchers documented the gradual deterioration of the social-life of an isolated Canadian town when television signals finally made it through to their valley. This naturally occurring phenomenon clearly exposed the detrimental effects of too much tv. The bottom line is that being curled up on the couch with your partner sharing an especially chosen program – that's one thing; but spending all night in front of a flickering light that isn't a log fire, that's quite another. Television should be a nutritious meal we share together, not fast-food we gulp down addictively so as to anaesthetise our hunger for activities and relationships missing in our real life.

The big picture and the small screen

Perhaps the most powerful question to ask ourselves about television, is: *how much does it interfere with what we'd rather be doing.* For instance, the previous chapters in this sections have shown us that it takes about 100 hours to get good enough at a dance style so it feels automatic and we can talk to our partner without treading all over their toes.

Stepping even further back from the tv screen and looking at an even bigger picture, we can see that if we live until we're eighty (which most of us will) and watch tv for two hours per night six days per week (that's one eighth of our waking life, by the way), we would have in the course of a lifetime spent the equivalent of nearly ten solid years of our waking and conscious life watching television. And as we now know, ten years of dedicated practise and we'd have long since been an international authority in our chosen field.

So there's the trade-off: *Do we want ten years of tv, or would we prefer the pride and rewards of expertise?*

We have no choice about whether or not to spend the 25 years we're going to spend in the health-bringing state of sleep, but we do have total choice about that ten years in front of the telly. On our deathbed, are we really going to whisper to our friends: "My only regret is that I didn't catch every episode of *The Simpsons*."
It's a great show, but there are so many other things that deserve to be done . . . and done well.

In the flickering light of my own experience

It's not only the sums and the scientific evidence that shocks me; it's my personal experience of growing up. I wish I was rare in this, but I fear my story is far from unusual, and that I'm part of a generation all but imprisoned by too much telly.

Like so many youngsters between the age of 11 and 18, I spent all evening every evening in front of the television. I would come home from school, have tea, do half an hour's homework, and then watch two or three TV shows. *Moonlighting, Hill Street Blues, Alias Smith & Jones*, there was always something seemingly unmissable. At one time, there was even a stand-off between Star Trek and my hour's piano lesson once per week with Mrs Biggs. I duly weighed up which would be more important to me in later life:

Being able to play Eine Kleine Nachtmusik slowly and badly?

Or being able to deal with alien life forms . . . usually by firing a photon torpedo at them?

Star Trek won hands down and I'm keeping my fingers crossed that

I'll run into some aliens any day now, and three thousand episodes with the crew of *The Enterprise* will finally pay off.

My tv routine meant I was watching three hours on a school night, while at weekends there'd definitely be two or three feature films plus several regular shows (*Happy Days*, *The Waltons*, *Kung Fu*, *The Persuaders*), so that across the course of any seven days my total tv watching would accumulate to at least 20 hours per week. Often more, rarely less.

The reason I was so drawn to these fictional worlds, was that my own real life very often felt frightening and lonely and trivial, which is how real life felt for so many of my friends when growing up as children and teenagers. Tv befriended me and kept me company and made me feel part of something special. And that's the trouble: tv catches us when we're a child and it feels like a good friend, like alcohol can feel like happiness; but the truth is, they're both phonies.

But back then I didn't know this, and much of the time I was far happier in the tv world. This amount of watching meant that American television was in every sense the neighbourhood in which I grew up – the accents and the sirens, the stripmalls and fire-escapes, the college-capers and high-pressure careers. Even today, it doesn't matter whether I arrive in New York or Los Angeles, Philadelphia or San Francisco, those city streets greet me like old friends, and with a happy sigh and a big goofy grin, I say "Boy, it's good to be home!"

And when I'm out among the prairies or mountains or Monument Valley, I have just the same feelings of fond recognition, born of all those hundreds of films and tv shows. One day I'm going to be strolling merrily around the tenements of New York's Hell's Kitchen looking just a tad out of place with my tweeds and a pipe, when I'll bump right into a laundromat robbery and I'll be gunned down. I'll lie there dying on the sidewalk, consoled in the knowledge that my old friends *Starsky & Hutch* are on their way, their red and white car awash with coffee and Dunkin' Doughnuts. My death will not have been in vain; at least it will give the guys a chance to date some super-models wearing 1970s hot-pants who may have seen something. Okay, my big finish won't quite be Butch Cassidy, but it would feel rather apt that it all end there on the streets of my childhood. "Goodnight John-Boy."

That's how fondly in my affections I treasure the very best of television, so it's not easy to say what I'm about to. It feels like I'm 'ratting on the family' and will need to be part of a witness protection program lest Mork & Mindy come after me with meat-cleavers. Nonetheless, there's some tough stuff that has to be said, because tv was such a key factor in my not getting good at anything, and all the science and research we've seen so far doesn't quite capture in full colour exactly how it does that. So here goes:

Television's First Side-Effect: *we think we're learning but we're not.*

Though I knew from watching years of television heroes that I ought to be plucky and creative in the face of life's challenges, I didn't have the first clue about how to muster such qualities. That's because they aren't the sort of details telly bothers to go into. Even if it did, even if I'd only watched documentaries on sharks and jungle survival, it's still that sort of passive learning whereby you just sit silently while you look and listen, and it requires the lowest level of brain activity. (Rather reminds me of my old school). I can say this with some certainty because if tv actually taught you anything, by the age of 18, I'd watched enough episodes of *Hawaii Five-O* to walk straight into the job of Lieutenant on a big city Homicide Unit; and I'd consumed enough M.A.S.H. to be a leading Accident & Emergency surgeon. But no, despite watching over 10,000 hours of television before I hit 18, I wound up without even one usable skill. It was all too clear that tv had been the 'illusion learning'.

Television's Second Side-Effect: *watching tv suffocates all the important stuff.*

While I sat watching television, my real life projects and friendships and boyish ambitions ground to a halt and sat stagnant with me there on the couch. Tv wasn't poisoning me, it didn't have to. Rather it was starving the life out of me by distracting me from doing healthier stuff. Half an hour per night would have left room for other things, but my three hour routine excluded any alternatives. One feature movie at the weekend would have added welcome variety to my view of the world, but I didn't need four. It was wall to wall, vacuum-sealed stupidity. The bottom line is that by watching so much tv, I paralysed myself – brain, body and ambitions.

And that's a real shame, because let's not forget that it takes only 3,000 hours of dedicated practice to turn the everyday novice into an impressive amateur. If I'd just put in the practice, then any skill or knowledge I chose to acquire was mine for the earning. Choose a couple if I wanted! Looking back, I dearly wish I'd swapped a big chunk of that tv time for actually learning to do something. What joy to become a black-belt in both Tango and Kung Fu. What joy to swing a girlfriend head-over-heals without us both ending up in hospital. Still, it's never too late – though if truth be told I'm just at that stage in my dance classes where it looks like I'm trying to tie the girl in knots before the music stops.

Television's Third Side-Effect: *tv ignores the small steps from which all good progress is made.*

It's in the very nature of a screen story to put all the emphasis on dealing with big events and key scenes from glorious adventures rather than the everyday loveliness of the little stuff. Films forget to mention those six years of daily practice that mean the punches can be parried, or the problem solved. And yet it's that everyday little stuff that accumulates to create expertise. Indeed something as seemingly ordinary as water makes up 90% of our body, and just look around you to see how good some people make their water look. It's what we do with the ordinary stuff that matters and makes the difference.

The irony is, of course, that my action heroes would have been the first people to tell me to turn off the telly and go do something with my life. In what seems like several thousand episodes of Star

Trek, I don't remember even one scene in which Captain Kirk spent his Saturday morning slumped in pyjamas watching *The Fonz* while eating five bowls of shreddies.

Nope. My heroes didn't watch life, *they led it* . . . and they were good at it, too. Coming to think of it, they were *expert* – indeed expertise had been staring me in the face all those years I'd been watching the glittering screen. After all, expertise is highly attractive stuff, just as much as physical beauty. We delight in watching a first-class performance, which is why the screen story almost always assumes that somebody is extremely good at something. In fact, the movies make expertise look normal. It's the entry-level requirement for any hero:

In *The Matrix*, someone gets programmed with 20 years of martial arts in the same time it would take to have a hair cut.

Young Buffy can slay vampires while ironing a blouse.

And was there anyone in *Lord of the Rings* who wasn't an absolute ace with an axe, a bow, or a sword the weight of an extra-large anvil.

Even in those films which aspire to root themselves firmly in a more recognisable reality, having 'effortless expertise' is a key requirement for any hero: In *Schindler's List*, the title character is a consummate wheeler-dealer, while in *Saving Private Ryan*, Tom Hanks plays a damn fine Infantry Officer. And in *The Sixth Sense*, Bruce Willis is a child psychiatrist who has just received an award of merit from the city of Philadelphia. It's hard to think of a movie that doesn't rely on someone being unusually good at something, or at least very competent. It's only in comedies that anyone's a big dope. On top of which, screen stories perpetuate the myth that either you have what it takes or you don't, so don't trouble yourself with trying. In the heart-warming tale of *Good Will Hunting*, we join the building-site labourer and part-time janitor played by Matt Damon just minutes before he is discovered as a mathematics genius who'd make Einstein seem like a dullard. This is typical of how the 'talent myth' gets portrayed. Film stories like this let us feel that we haven't got to try because we're just Jane or Johnny next door, and thank God we aren't gifted, otherwise we'd have to get up and do something. Formulas, symphonies, works of art, they could all be such a hassle. But tv quietly reassures us that it's not *our* fault we're so floppy, which all helps justify us watching it by the barrel load.

Discovering the power of passion and practice

As an 18 year old, I went to study Social Sciences at Exeter University. This is when the trouble really took off, because as you'll appreciate from my previous track record of tv and school, I had absolutely no idea how to learn. Any smidgen of achievement had been done by accident or while on autopilot. So once on campus and left to my own devices, it all fell to pieces. At the end of the first year, they asked me to leave on account that I'd failed my exams, not least because someone refused to mark my philosophy paper. Apparently I'd written what was regarded as an obscenity. In fact, it was a misquote of some French philosopher, rather along the lines of my Sandrine-Ashtray mix up, but I don't think the exam committee wanted to hear that. Unfortunately for me, the university changed its mind and I returned to college promising to work flat-out for the next three years. I say this was *unfortunate* because I spent the next three years no more clued-in than when I'd started, and so I finally graduated with the lowest grade of degree they'd awarded in ten years.

Now at this point, the people who believe in 'natural talent and inborn gifts' are grinning smugly, no doubt assuming that it was my being thick-as-two-short-planks that had resulted in my appalling degree performance. Luckily for me, they'd be quite wrong. Better still, I was about to prove it.

Let's wind forward two years ... to that beautiful summer when I was 25 and met a wonderful young German woman called Claudia who had just begun her teacher training. Waiting to go out on our first date, preening myself in front of the mirror, I suddenly felt deeply ashamed of myself to think how she must see me ... full of enthusiasm, semi-employed and not the least bit qualified. I'd had such opportunities, and I'd squandered them. In this frame of mind it was probably no coincidence that just a few days later I stumbled across a book called *The Origins of Exceptional Abilities* by none other than my old tutor from Exeter, Professor Michael Howe. In that moment I wondered what it would take for someone like me to get good at something ... *I mean other than a miracle* ... to get good at something so that someone could be proud of me.

Claudia was my inspiration, I'd realised it was possible, and putting in the time felt easy. A two year correspondence course with the Open University quickly led on to Cambridge for my Masters and PhD. I was ... and still am ... irretrievably stupid according to all and every IQ test; but I didn't let my stupidity stop me. (And let's remember, IQ tests bear no meaningful relationship to our educational or professional success or happiness in life.) I learnt to compensate by teaming up with good people, by enjoying what I did so I wanted to do more, and by believing I could learn to be good at something. That's a pretty powerful recipe. All those people who mistakenly tell us NO, YOU CAN'T, YOU'RE TOO STUPID (and in my life, there've been lots of those), they cannot see in to our hearts and see the passions and the support we can muster among friends or family. They don't appreciate that we're the only person with the power to start or stop ourselves. Our joy in our work will allow us to achieve the goal our own special way.

Why bother to turn the TV off and practice getting good at something?

As I polished a second wine glass, still faced with a thousand, I was finally wise to that one. And ever since that time, I've not had a television in my home, preferring instead to invest in real people and real passions. It was no surprise to me when I learnt that the A-list British actors Joseph and Ralph Fiennes never had a tv on in the house when they were growing up, nor Oscar-winner Julia Roberts, or Virgin entrepreneur Richard Branson. Some people seem to have done very well without it.

Washer-up wins Nobel Prize

Now I don't for one minute suppose The Nobel Prize committee are sitting in a sauna in Sweden reading this chapter out-loud to each other in awed reverence, before dictating a letter that begins: "*Dear*

Dr Baylis, we've seen some clever stuff in our time, but your work on tv's side-effects and The Illusion of Learning is right up there with blue-tack and the bagless Dyson."

But back when I was 25 and working the graveyard shift as an emergency glass-washer, this figuring-out where my boyish ambitions had taken a wrong turn, seemed quite a break-through. Indeed, it would not have felt amiss had I peeled off a pair of bifocals and dabbed my brow with a handkerchief like I was Luciano Pavarotti after a royal performance, nodding modestly in tearful recognition of a standing ovation. The applause would sound perhaps like the beating wings of a thousand doves set free to mark the opening of The Olympic Games.

What I got instead was the bludgeoning voice of my 16 year old supervisor shouting into the chill and empty kitchen: "Get on with those bloody glasses, you dozey git!"

* * *

Planning for Progress

- What would you enjoy doing if you weren't watching tv?

- What more helpful ways could you find to recuperate after a hard day?

- Which reason for kicking tv out of your life rings most true to you? How would you apply that thought when the cravings grab you?

* * *

PART THREE

Helping Mind and Body to Thrive and Flourish

Nourish and Nurture
Beautiful Health

This chapter is all about how we can help our body to cultivate some home-grown, ever-green, deeply-rooted happiness. It's also about all the ways we can be beautiful, inside and out.

It is written in the spirit of *Occam's Razor*, which is the scientific principle which states that when we are faced with two explanations that account equally well for the evidence to hand, we should choose the simpler one. This is because Nature gravitates towards optimum simplicity. Which is why, whenever we're feeling blue, before we go blaming it on our lack of purpose in life, or our difficult past, let's test out some less Byronic explanations such as a deficiency of sleep, nutrition, daylight or exercise.

Some myths about happiness

One could be forgiven for thinking that asking people to rate themselves on a ten-point scale in response to the question *"In general, how happy or unhappy do you usually feel?"* would only lead to wild inaccuracies. But when scientists compare such basic measures to a full-blown psychological assessment, the results are fairly consistent: it would seem we're rather good judges of our happiness. It's also quite clear that happiness isn't just some whimsical concept dreamt up in the 1960s by tripping hippies and advertising agencies. Professor Richard Davidson at the University of Wisconsin-Madison monitored electrical activity in the brain to show how a highly attractive photograph causes a particular portion of our left hemisphere to light up, while an horrific photo stimulates our right side. Indeed, people prone in general to more of this left-brain activity tend to score higher on all counts of good mood, whereas right-siders are notably gloomy. The same is true for new-born babies, so it's not been learned, it's just the way we're wired. The good news is that psychological skills training can alter this left-right activity ratio, but the point for now is that happiness is a very real phenomenon going on in our brain.

Indeed, it seems likely that around 50% of our characteristic level of happiness is an inherited factor. This can be estimated because in 1996, Lykken and Tellegen at Minnesota State University compared an astonishing 663 pairs of identical twins. A further 69 pairs were identical twins who had been *reared apart*, yet these twins still showed at least a 50% similarity in their self-reported happiness, which was a far higher percentage of similarity than for the non-identical twins. Strong evidence indeed that we probably have a genetically predetermined set range. But that said, we should remind ourselves that, as in all aspects of biological inheritance, our genetic potential needs the right environment if it is to unfurl in accordance with our DNA blueprints. So learning to live regularly in the *upper end* of our happiness set-range is where psychological skill and know-how can pay dividends. How well we play the hand we're dealt could dramatically improve how we feel about life.

And there are other reasons to feel we have everything to play for. For instance, surveys show that no stage of life is inherently any happier than another, despite everything our parents told us about our school and college days. If anything, life feels better as we get older. Moreover, intelligence as measured by IQ tests is a very poor predictor of either life success or happiness. And there's little if any difference between male and female average self-ratings, though women seem more prone to intense swings. The bottom line seems to be that life feeling good pays no heed to our age, IQ or gender. *It's open to all-comers.*

Having debunked some of the myths and possible misunderstandings about our individual level of happiness, I'd now like to underline the importance of good quality sleep, nutrition and exercise.

Sleeping well supports *everything*

Good sleep provides a vital foundation for our happiness, so it's worth becoming an expert on this oft forgotten bed-fellow of a much healthier life.

Almost all individuals need eight hours or more each day, but many of us allow ourselves far less. Yet, it is only an unhelpful myth that a high achiever like Winston Churchill or Margaret Thatcher barely slept; they were simply skilled cat-nappers and achieved their full quota that way. Albert Einstein regularly slept for ten hours, and took eleven if he had some really serious thinking to do the following day.

Nowadays, we probably sleep two hours less per night than our grandparent's generation, which leaves western society profoundly sleep-deprived. And what a price we pay . . .

Stanford University psychiatrist, William Dement, has spent nearly 40 years investigating how sleep-deficiency impacts upon our quality of life by negatively affecting our physical health, energy, mood, social relationships, memory, and problem-solving performance. These deficits come about not least because our immunity-boosting, disease-fighting cells drop by over a quarter after just one night's lost sleep, while the stress-inducing hormone cortisol increases by a half. It's also a startling fact that by knocking two hours per night from someone's usual sleep pattern for just one whole week, renders that person as inefficient as someone well over the drink-drive limit. Exactly as if they were drunk, the sleep-deprived person over-estimates their competency and takes ill-considered risks. This is why specialists believe that more accidents both on and off the road are caused by sleep than by alcohol. (One in five adults admit to having fallen asleep at the wheel of a car.) Official disaster inquiries have often blamed 'routine sleep-deprivation' as either the key or major contributor to human-error catastrophes, including those that befell Chernobyl Nuclear Power Plant, the Exxon Valdez oil tanker, and the Challenger Space Shuttle.

Former war reporter and BBC head of news, Kate Adie, is acutely aware of the life-endangering risks associated with sleep-deprivation. "I have always taken the view that it is very dangerous to be very tired. You've got to have your wits about you. I was in and out of Bosnia for four years. Sometimes I just had to get out, or I would have been a liability." No surprise, then, that when Kate wants to relax deeply, she simply goes to sleep.

There are, however, less dramatic but more insidious conse-quences of us cheating on our sleep. It is one of the biggest suspects for triggering migraine and digestive tract problems. Since sleep-deficiency increases our appetite, there has also been speculation that it in part explains the current epidemic of obesity, particularly among children. (One in four adults and children are now 25% or more above their ideal body weight; and it's a problem that's quadrupled in numbers in the past 20 years.) It's equally disturbing to think that good studies have demonstrated important differences in the brains and the intellectual performance of airline crews who have worked tough, long-haul flight schedules for five years or more. It would seem to be for good reasons that our sleeping brain is often more active when we're asleep than when we're awake. It is busy with recuperation, repair work, neutralising negative emotions and processing positive ones. And it really is no coincidence that sleep deprivation is used as a torture and can mimic the effects of severe mental illness. It takes around ten days for an otherwise healthy human to die from lack of sleep, while we can survive several times longer without food, which gives us yet another indication as to sleep's priority importance. It's ironic that we some-times think we're getting more done when we plod on through fatigue. Yet studies at universities from Loughborough through to Stanford show us time and again that because sleepiness makes us less adept at problem-solving, creativity, and modifying our plans, we are in fact far less productive. We are also irritable, sloppy, and reluctant to take on challenges.

The take away message is, we should all sleep eight or more hours in every 24, even if that requires catnapping to make up the difference. Dr Sara Mednick of the Salk Institute in California, is the leading young researcher on power-naps and she advises 30 minutes to a full hour midway through our waking day, usually between two and three o'clock. Dr Mednick says half an hour in our lunch-break would be a fine compromise. This timely nap would not only lead to improved mood, alertness and productivity, but it would also consolidate our learning for physical skills and mental facts. Former U.S. President Bill Clinton said "If I can take a nap, even 15 or 20 minutes in the middle of the day, it is really invigorating to me . . . it really makes all the difference in the world." This strategy certainly worked for a former First Lady and Human Rights activist, Eleanor Roosevelt: "As for relaxation, I have learned to catch a five-minute cat nap in my chair while waiting for someone."

In respect of the above evidence, we could run a little experiment by adding one hour's sleep to our nightly routine, and then monitor the difference it makes.

Bedtime tips
Good shut-eye is all about establishing healthy habits, so I'll set out the cornerstones: We should keep our bed exclusively for sleep (and pre-sleep sex, of course), not as an overflow office or for watching tv. We would also do well to have a pre-sleep ritual, whereby all cares and worries are banned from the bedroom, perhaps with the help of a good book. Then after, a declining body-temperature is a key trigger to dropping off, so a hot drink or bath will help this, as will a slightly cool bedroom . . . because as our body cools we'll become drowsy and drop off. Once the light's out, we should never try to force slumber. If we don't nod off within just 20 minutes, we should get up and go do some dreary chores, such as doing the

dishes, until drowsiness overtakes us, being careful not to accidentally reward our insomnia with any food or pleasurable activity.

Once our sleep routine is in place, we should stick to it. It's
better to go to bed an hour earlier each night rather than to catch up
at the weekend, which only risks disrupting the cycle. That said, we
all sleep differently, and it's a question of adapting our lifestyle and
environment to get the best from our brain and body's own idiosyncratic requirements. It's worth mentioning here that our sleep
pattern is unlikely to be an inherited characteristic, since even
Siamese infant twins who share their genetic make-up and their
major organs and blood supply, can have very different sleep
profiles.

During the course of the day, we should be careful about stim-
ulants like chocolate or caffeinated drinks or even anything sugary.
For some sensitive souls, just one early afternoon coffee can be
enough to spoil sleep several hours later. Likewise, a heavy dinner
within two hours of bedtime is best avoided, and anything more
than one glass of alcohol will interfere with our deep sleep waves
and dreaming. Mobile phones and power lines have been shown to
affect brain activity, so this too is a factor worth considering; and
sometimes the contraceptive pill can throw sleep out of sync.

Still having trouble nodding off?
At any point in time, one in four individuals suffer sleep problems,
which can mean difficulty nodding off, frequent waking, waking too
early, or waking feeling tired. First off, we should try to eliminate
the usual suspects such as nightshift-work, depression, pain, and
excessive stress (and my next three chapters offer clear advice on
this); but if our problems persist, we should see our medical practitioner because anything from vitamin and mineral deficiencies
through to a very specific breathing difficulty called 'sleep apnoea'
could be seriously jeopardising our waking well-being. Apnoea is a
close relation of snoring, and it is thought to affect up to 1 in 20
of the population overall, and 1 in 12 men. It's caused by our breathing channels routinely blocking themselves during sleep, which
makes us wake up hundreds of time a night so as to gasp in air. This

condition brings all the serious effects of sleep deficiency, yet the sufferer may be wholly oblivious to there being a problem . . . hence it goes untreated. Arranging our pillows so that we're forced to sleep on our side is one remedy, but if we suspect we're a sufferer, we should ask our medical practitioner about further measures.

As a last resort, we should also ask our doctor for their thoughts on supplements that can help put our sleep cycle back on a healthy track. Our local health food shop will have non-prescription remedies such as St. John's Wort, Valerian, 5-htp, Hops, and Passion Flower. However, we should bear in mind that popping prescription pills or powerful herbal formulas will present the very same problem as alcohol: they may help *induce* sleep, but they then disrupt some of its health-bringing components, so it's not as refreshing as unassisted slumber, and should be a temporary measure of last resort.

Though our medical practitioner can advise on safe usage, no sleep-aid should ever be taken with alcohol nor kept near children.

Sleep restores our fighting spirit

I've always been one for early to bed and early to rise, so sleep's been a good friend to me over the years. As a young boy, I'd have a new pair of shoes for the first day of school after the summer holidays, so I'd get up at the crack of dawn, put on my uniform and squeak about in them until Mum told me to be quiet. Then I'd get back into bed with all my gear on, and take an occasional peek of pride at my shiny black lace-ups poking out from the other end of the sheets. Even to this day I like sitting up in bed at six in the morning and making plans on pieces of paper. After a good night's sleep, just about anything seems possible. I bet you Lord Nelson only took on the countless ships of the Spanish Armada because he'd got up early and was having a cuppa tea out on deck, pacing around in his carpet slippers so as not to wake the crew. I bet you he gazed out across the waves at the overwhelming odds stacked against him, and thought "Come on then, I'll have the lot of you!" I'd even go so far as to say that some of my best ideas have come about in an early morning bed . . . though there are some girlfriends who would probably disagree with that claim, so I shalln't labour the point.

Broad daylight prevents the blues and feeds the brain

If adequate sleep is extremely good for us, then so are broad daylight and brisk physical activity. They will reliably nurture a happier frame of mind, as they are two of Nature's most potent anti-depressants. You don't need a clinical diagnosis of Seasonal Affective Disorder (a depression whose sole cause is the brain receiving insufficient daylight) to benefit from ensuring your eyes receive *at least an hour's broad daylight* in the gloomier months. If we just add up the minutes we spend per winter weekday out and about in daylight, by stark contrast to being deep indoors or looking out from a train carriage, we might be surprised. Many of us would clock far short of the minimum hour. Hence, up to 10% of the population show a very distinctive mood downturn come the winter, while very many more of us might just feel sluggish, sleepy, hungry for sweet and fatty foods, and can't be bothered to socialise.

By way of a remedy, there are full-spectrum lamps and light bulbs that can produce 10,000 lux (lux is a measure of light intensity), but we could save these for Plan B, because even a rather overcast winter's day produces 10,000 lux, and bright sunshine offers several times that. Why not simply whip-off the Raybans to let in the natural goodness, remembering that mornings are the best time for an hour's light-bath. (Let's remember, though, we should never under any circumstances, look directly at the sun because this will damage our eyes.) Unfortunately, we can't store the benefits of light for the brain, so our light-bath is best done every day. Our mood can lift within 48 hours, thanks to adequate illumination, but it can descend again just as fast if we're starved of this health-bringing brain nutrient.

All this said, we shouldn't take a good thing too far, because going to live in sunnier climes won't automatically bring happiness. Princeton University researchers, David Schkade and Daniel Kahneman (the 2002 Nobel Laureate) have shown that living in the reliably sunny climes of Southern California does not make the residents any happier. People in colder, greyer places think they'd be cheerier in warm ones, but they are mistaken. Once we've had a sufficient dose of daylight, having extra won't make us extra happy.

What happens instead is that we adapt to the good weather completely and very quickly, and it brings no mood benefits then after.

Vigorous exercise lifts our spirits

There's no debate about it: our ability to 'look lively' and get ourselves moving contains powerful medicine; all the best new research indicates it's equally as effective as medications, but with few if any of the side-effects. And it's not just our good moods that'll benefit. Exercise releases serotonin, dopamine and norepinephrine, which are the chemical brain-lubricants for a whole bunch of psychological activities, so exercise can facilitate everything from our social relations and concentration, to self-esteem and dealing with stress. What's more, exercise will combat the feeling of fatigue that can come from stress; and by increasing our blood flow around our brain and body, we are increasing the effects of our good nutrition. Exercise helps us on so many fronts that making it a part of our daily routine is one of life's surest investments. Seventy-something social campaigner and favourite agony aunt, Claire Rayner, is doing just that. "I swim every morning. I do a kilometre."

Throughout his life, former South African President and Nobel Peace Laureate, Nelson Mandela, has been a keen participant of determined physical activity: "I have always believed that exercise is key not only to physical health but to peace of mind ... Exercise dissipates tension, and tension is the enemy of serenity. I found that I worked better and thought more clearly when I was in good physical condition, and so training became one of the inflexible disciplines of my life."

Be forewarned, though, that while introducing extra daylight and physical activity into our daily lives, our greatest challenge will be not allowing ourselves to become disillusioned by the 'growing pains' that beset any new routine. To this end, we need to find an activity that is sufficiently enjoyable in its own right. *And let's keep it simple.* Can we hop off the train a stop early and stride in from there to give ourselves another 20 minutes of the feel-good factors of exercise and light? Will a friend join us? Our life, by natural design, is comprised of habits and patterns, but our conscious plans and efforts can influence which ones take root and for what good purpose

Don't just keep the plants well watered

Our body's water-level is a good metaphor for how little things can impact on our daily life, because minor alterations can have major effects. For instance, being dehydrated can markedly reduce psychological and physical performance. At 1% dehydration, we might feel a tad thirsty if we bothered to think about it; but at 2% we've probably lost one fifth of our physical capacity and co-ordination, and our judgement is impaired. At just 5% below our usual water levels, we'll probably suffer aggressive, irrational behaviour, as well as nausea. This startling fact is why professional athletes are never far from their water bottles. Yet, many of us are prone to run below our optimal mind and body performance simply because we're not keeping a glass of pure water to hand.

But how on earth could we be caught short like this?

It's all too easy. For instance, on holiday in summer, the extra sunshine, altitude, and alcohol can all leach the water; and if we suffer a stomach upset, with vomiting or diarrhoea, we could dehydrate 10 times faster than normal. On the other hand, come winter time, the altitude and cold air of the ski slopes can triple water loss, and that's before you factor-in the extra perspiration. Even on route to the sun or snow, the dry air of aircraft cabins can exacerbate travel fatigue.

Meanwhile, back at home and in daily life, try putting out a saucer of water to see the drying-power of the environment in which you routinely work or sleep, because central heating or air conditioning can have substantial effects. Ironically, when we feel tired in the morning or in the office, we often reach for a cup of tea or coffee, which will only increase our dehydration, as caffeine has a diuretic effect. To counter this, it would be a good idea to double-up and have a cup of water at the same time. Between two and three litres of non-diuretic fluid (such as water) per day would be an average adult requirement under ordinary conditions. We shouldn't simply rely on our sense of thirst because in many adverse conditions, whether illness or exercise, that inner sense might not keep pace with our rapidly changing needs. By the time we're thirsty, we've already misjudged it. Better to gently prehydrate ourselves with half a litre of water an hour before some vigorous exertion, and keep a bottle to hand to sip from regularly. (Be warned, though, that too much water can be life-threatening, because it dilutes our body chemistry, so let's not overdo it.) And finally, when we or a loved-one feel tired or irritable, consider how something as soluble as dehydration may be partly to blame.

Essential thoughts on good eating

Good eating is a habit that can be learned early. No less than a quarter of British children are obese (i.e. they weigh 25% or more above their ideal weight), as are 33% of American children. This compares to only 10% of French youngsters. The specialists suspect that the cause is a highly sedentary lifestyle and over-protective parenting which restricts a child's daily opportunities for exercise like walking or cycling to school, or playing outside of a summer evening. It's a key factor, too, that the French simply eat less calories, not least because they tend to eat slowly which better allows their body to realise when it's been sufficiently fed. On which vital point, nutritionists are at pains to emphasise we should take adequate time to chew our food, because the enzymes in our saliva break it down and make it far more valuable to our body, as well as making each mouthful far more satisfying, which all helps less food go a lot further. Nutritionists also advise us to eat in company when ever possible because it helps balance our approach to food. *The company of caring people is as much an essential sustenance as a good meal, and will stop us trying to fill the emotional gaps with food or drink.*

In considering our nutrition, we should plan for low-sugar, high variety, modestly portioned meals, and be thinking steamed food rather than boiled, with regular snacks consisting of raw fruit and different coloured vegetables and un-salted mixed nuts (allergies allowing). By these means, we're aiming to even-out our blood-sugar level which is so important for not only our energy but our good moods and concentration. In fact, leaving sugar and salt out of our food altogether makes great sense, because so much is hidden in ready-made products by couldn't-care-less manufacturers. All that sugar, salt, and sauce . . . the stuff we add, and the stuff already added . . . serve only to confuse or blunt our body's appetite-control mechanisms. We're best to bin them altogether.

If we eat a vegetarian diet, it's good to know that this needn't compromise building the very finest body we have the genetic blue-prints for, as evidenced by the number of vegetarians who abound in the world of professional sport. Just for example, I might name the former tennis champions Billie Jean King and Martina Navratilova, as well as Dave Scott (Triathlon and six times Iron Man champion) or Edwin Moses (an Olympic gold medalist in the 400 m hurdles who held a ten year undefeated record). And while I'm praising the power of vegetables to support athletic prowess, the evidence for the health-bringing and protective qualities of other plants and foods is extremely promising, and a regular part of one's nutrition could very helpfully include all of the following: garlic and aloe vera, sour milk and yoghurts rich in the live cultures which maintain intestinal health; as well as uncooked olive oil and whole porridge oats. There's a wonderful range of seeds to explore, from pumpkin to sunflower, as well as a full rack of fresh garden herbs that are inex-pensive yet all have well-established nutritional benefits and can add flavour and goodness to our meals.

The good sense of nutritional supplements

Good nutrition can increase our positive moods and mental perfor-mance, whereas even mild deficiencies of the vitamin B range, for instance, can bring varying degrees of irritability, anxiety, insomnia, lethargy, depression, loss of appetite, and poor memory. University of Wales psychologist, Professor David Benton, has been a prolific researcher in this field, and his study of young British adults found that around one third were deficient in one or more of the B vitamins. However, such shortfalls usually come in groups, and iron, zinc, selenium and vitamins A, B and C are commonly low in adults. This isn't so surprising, either, since air pollution, caffeine, alcohol, sugar, headache tablets, the contraceptive pill and many other standard medications can all serve to unbalance our uptake or excretion of vital micro-nutrients. Sadly, too, modern food production methods have dramatically reduced the nutritional content of most foods.

Weight-loss dieting is another way in which adequate nutrition can be compromised; just as vegetarianism can put an individual at risk of anaemia. A survey by Professor Benton found that 50% of women and 10% of men, had border-line iron deficiency levels, a state which can easily mimic the early symptoms of depression.

With all of the above risk factors so prevalent in our everyday lives, it is for good reason that psychiatric hospitals routinely have blood-tests to screen new clients for vitamin and mineral deficiencies. What a tragedy it would be to blame life-events or relationships for our dwindling happiness, if in fact we're simply deficient in some essential nutrients.

So what precautions can we take to prevent deficiencies?

If you're pregnant or on prescription medicine, then consult your medical practitioner because supplements could be seriously hazardous. Otherwise, consider investing in a reputable, high-potency all-in-one vitamin and mineral capsule. Supplements are 'team players', so the total effect of these all-in-one pills will be far more helpful than the sum of their parts. What's more, premium products are far preferable to some economy own-brand from a highstreet chemist that has thrown together a limited range or insufficient dosage or cheaper synthetic ingredients.

In addition to the above, we would be wise to eat a good variety of fresh, oily fish such as sardines, salmon, mackerel and tuna 3 or 4 times per week, or if that's not possible, we should take an omega-3 essential fats supplement readily available in a 1,000mg fish oil capsule. (Please note that fish oil should *not* be confused with *fish-liver oil*, which is high in vitamins A and D which can be toxic in high doses.) The omega-3 oil vegetarian alternatives would be cold-pressed versions of flax oil (also known as linseed), pumpkin seed oil, or hemp oil. These omega-3 fats (no matter in fish or vegetarian form) have been shown to be strongly connected to lifting depression and promoting happier moods, far more effectively it is believed than any existing pharmaceutical alternatives. Moreover, when omega-3 is taken together with oils rich in omega 6 (perhaps in the form of cold-pressed evening primrose oil, or starflower oil, also known as borage oil), the 3 and 6 combination provides an optimum balance. Taking an all-in-one omega oil supplement would be a good way to achieve this.

The newly emerging evidence on the effectiveness of omega oils in preventing and lifting depression might be particularly relevant to a mum with a newborn baby. She should talk to her medical practitioner about the benefits of such oils to make up for the demands that pregnancy will have made on her own body's resources. In essence, the situation is likely to be this: that in feeding and caring for her developing foetus, a pregnant mum will have put her own nutritional resources under a considerable strain, so it's worth considering what part nutrition can play in preventing or alleviating post-natal depression. (Vegetarian sources are probably best so as to prevent any danger of fish oils that might be polluted by heavy metals.)

When it comes to demonstrating nutrition's effects on our everyday moods and behaviour, Bernard Gesch, a pioneering Senior Researcher at Oxford University, has conducted one of the world's most telling studies to date. In 2001, for a nine month period, his team administered seemingly identical daily supplements to 231 inmates at Aylesbury high-security young offenders' prison (all of whom were young men aged 18 to 21). Within two weeks, the prisoners who'd taken a modest but daily dose of 28 *genuine* vitamins and minerals as well as those all-important omega oils 3 and 6, demonstrated a 37% reduction in aggressive behaviour. I.e. the guys on nutritional supplements engaged in 37% less of the sort of serious or violent offences that are very accurately logged by the prison authorities. By comparison, the behaviour of the group of young men on seemingly identical but *fake* pills was quite unchanged. This was an extremely well-designed study, and neither the prison officers nor the young prisoners themselves knew which half of the boys had received 'truly active pills'. In addition, the boys had been randomly allocated to either the genuine or fake group, so the chances of these results being biased in that way, are rather slim. Yet more compelling evidence came about when the experiment was over and the inmates' nutrition went back to normal for all concerned. It was now that the behaviour of the lads who'd received proper supplements quickly deteriorated back to their original levels.

At time of writing, a very similar field experiment is being planned to run among younger teenagers, and the research team fully expect this to show *double* the effect (i.e. nearer a 70% reduction in aggressive behaviour). This would largely be explained by younger teenagers having brains and bodies that are undergoing such rapid growth that it would not be unusual for their needs to outstrip their dietary intake of essential vitamins, minerals, trace elements and essential oils . . . and for these accidental deficiencies to cause behavioural problems.

Such impressive experiments all serve to remind us that for children, teenagers and those in their early twenties, good nutrition is particularly important, because these younger brains and bodies are developing at such a prodigious rate, they need all the help they can get.

Let's be sure to remember, too, that our best efforts towards improved nutrition should go hand-in-hand with increased physical activity, because the more that our nutrient-enriched blood is flowing around our body and brain, the more likely we are to be providing our vital organs with adequate supplies.

Exciting though the above possibilities might be, it's *not* a question of 'the more the better'. We should *always* follow the manufacturer's guidelines when it comes to supplements because it would be far too easy to consume too much vitamin A or D for instance, which would be particularly dangerous for a pregnant woman or a child under 12. It's always worth considering booking an hour's visit with a qualified nutritionist who can help us to proceed safely and effectively in our goal to eat well. For most of us, it might take a year for the full effects, although some mood improvements might become apparent within a month of taking supplements. And let's not think that supplements are an excuse to eat carelessly. On the contrary, they should be seen as a safety-net if our temporary circumstances don't allow for sufficiently healthy meals.

Making progress
With all of the potent foods and supplements I refer to above, we need to explore what suits our body best, so let's proceed with care. For instance, if we're taking supplements we want to give our body every opportunity to get rid of what it doesn't want. So we need to drink a good deal of clean water (not tea, mind, just plain water). But don't drink more than a few sips with meals, because it only dilutes our digestive juices.

While we're about things, why not experiment with giving up caffeine. Steven Spielberg has never had a cup of coffee in his life, but his film career could hardly be described as sluggish. What's more, I don't know anybody who doesn't think their moods, digestion, or headaches don't improve very noticeably when they give up caffeine. After a few days, the benefits seem to over-ride the pangs, and they never look back. To refresh flagging energy, a few minutes exercise and daylight prove excellent pick-me ups, as can a change of task; and a power-nap of 30 minutes would be very restorative, followed perhaps by a peppermint tea. Such changes are well worth considering. Flexibility and variety in our nutrition gives our mind and body the very best chance of good health (in the very same way that flexibility and variety are vital for the health of our thoughts, behaviours, and friendships.) So let's not get stuck in any ruts. Let's spring clean, experiment, push the boundaries . . . and be sure to wean ourselves off any fads and blinkered perspectives. Let's surprise ourselves. Variety is far more than the spice of life, its part and parcel of its very essence.

Physical dynamism beats dieting, any day

If I was better looking, surely I'd be happier . . . almost seems like common sense, doesn't it? But just as extra money makes very little improvement to our happiness once we're above the poverty line, the same goes for good looks. It makes people little or no happier than the rest of us to have wealth or beautiful bodies far above the average. It would seem Nature doesn't want us over-investing ourselves in pursuit of either of them.

Nonetheless, wanting to make progress in all key aspects of our life is one of our deepest-rooted drives, and we need to channel these inborn urges as constructively as possible.

This doesn't mean dieting, which only pits us against our biological defences which are striving to keep our weight between genetically determined upper and lower limits. To this end, our metabolism adjusts itself to keep our body within bounds, and eagerly takes on body-fat to compensate for any perceived famine of the like imitated by a low-calorie diet. This is why more than 90 percent of dieters will inevitably put the weight back on, but meantime the brain suffers nutrient shortages which impair mental performance and leave us irritable, lethargic and depressed. In addition to which, we're designed to become preoccupied with nutrition if supplies are inadequate, and these accumulated stresses might well explain how dieting can bamboozle the brain into bulimia, anorexia, or obesity.

The cruellest twist of this weight-loss wild goose chase, is that we blame ourselves for not being strong-willed enough, and we feel helpless and out of control. Worse still, these negative feelings can easily leak into other arenas of our life such as work or relationships.

It's a good job, then, that nature has given us a far more reliable, enduring, and profoundly satisfying way to improve our bodies. It's called *vigorous physical activity,* but there's an oft-forgotten secret ingredient that allows it to work its wonders: we have to let *pleasure* be the motivation for getting mobile, *not pain,* otherwise our new endeavours will be as short-lived as the diets. This 'pleasure principle' means conjuring up a whole host of appealing ways to put a spring in our step, because we're hard-wired to gravitate towards what pleases us, so the more enjoyable we make our activities, the more likely we'll stick with them.

We could aim to start with a 20-minute daily routine that will perk up our metabolism, build the friendly muscles that burn body-fat, and buoy-up our good moods and thinking capacity for many hours afterwards. Maybe it's dancing around the kitchen, shadow boxing in the bedroom, or striding that last mile into work. Variety is good, and all the better if we can find some pleasant company for it. No matter where we start from fitness-wise, we can guarantee ourselves a sense of progress, satisfaction and well-earned pride, all of which beats the red-herring diets 'hands down'. Once we've worked up an honest appetite, we can thumb our nose at the 'thinning industry' with its artificial sweeteners and counted calories. Nutritious, health-bringing foods are not our enemy, so let's relish eating them . . . slowly and considerately and in good spirits. Be glad of feeling healthier and to blazes with the weighing scales. And should ever we crave the latest diet, let's feed ourselves two thoughts – *enjoyable movement makes the most of our body . . . and happiness is beautiful.*

Listening to our emotional appetites

Let's hear how longtime agony aunt and social campaigner, Claire Rayner, learnt to befriend the body that Mother Nature gave her. "I eat a healthy Mediterranean diet, don't use alcohol and am still the size I am. So bloody what? I have not weighed myself for years (not interested in numbers) and don't give a damn what size is written on a garment's label as long as it fits." This is a great attitude, but Claire has not always possessed such admirable confidence. "Those ever-repeated comments 'My, you're a big girl' used to make some part of my guts seem to shrivel inside me . . . As I got older and watched the way the crowd gathered around the beautiful and the thin, the sense of loneliness and the conviction that I would be lonely all my life filled me with desolation . . . "

For Claire, the turning point was finding the right niche for her particular attributes, when she began training as a nurse. "When I found how much patients appreciated a strong arm to hold them when they were trying to sit up, how many liked having an ample front to lean on when they were feeling sick and I was holding their foreheads, and how many liked to have me alongside to oversee a first postoperative tottering walk to the loo, I began to take pride in the person I was and my size. Interestingly, it was at the same time that the hateful problem (incontinence) that had so stained my young years, finally vanished: a little self-esteem goes a long way!"

Claire's story helps remind us that we can all make a world of difference to how our loved-ones feel about themselves and their bodies. She writes fondly about her husband's role in giving her confidence. "Des made me stop wearing flattie shoes to diminish my height and great bundled dirndl skirts meant to hide my ample hips . . . and the last hint of the power of the beautiful and thin to hurt my feelings, finally trickled away."

Favourite comedian, Dawn French, was fortunate enough to have a Dad whose wonderful words helped forge her healthy attitude to how she looks. Five minutes prior to her first trip to a discotheque when she was just fourteen, her Dad sat her down for a talking to. "He told me I was uncommonly beautiful; that I was the most precious thing in his life, that he prized me above all else, that he was proud to be my father . . . It was my father who taught me to value myself. How wise of my father to say those words to me. It affected my whole life. How could you not come out of it well equipped to deal with life, when you felt so loved and supported."

Once asked how much she weighed, Dawn replied defiantly, "I haven't a clue and I don't give a toss."

Way to go, Dawn! She is still an outspoken role-model for other beautifully big women and has invested in a dedicated clothes shop with attractive designs. She says, "One of the greatest bonuses of finding clothes that fit and flatter, is the self-confidence they can engender in women who have never before enjoyed that experience."

But Dawn has also written about the first and only time when she went on a weight-loss diet. It was in the weeks before her wedding day. "I insisted my wedding dress be made in a size twelve . . . I panicked and went on one of those completely stupid quack diets. . . It was a trap and a lie . . . I had a moment of weakness, thinking perhaps I shouldn't look the way I do. I wasn't unhappy about my weight, but being on a diet certainly made me feel unhappy."

It's not only women who suffer with thinking they're the wrong size or shape. It was only when the Hollywood legend and Second World War bomber pilot, James Stewart, was almost forty that he announced being "at peace with my physique". All of his life before then, he'd run into well-intentioned sports coaches, physical trainers, and military nutritionists who all had their rival theories about how to muscle-up his unusually slender body that weighed just 130 pounds (that 's nine and a bit stone or barely 59 Kgs) on his 6 foot 2 inch frame. From time to time he went along with their body-bulking programs, but at age 40 he said acceptingly "I'll always been conscious of it, I suppose, but I'm not going to let it worry me anymore."

And here's a final word on the matter from America's media tycoon, Oscar-nominated actress and show-host, Oprah Winfrey. She reminds us that over-eating for very many individuals is a lot to do with other emotionally-charged things in our life that we've not been dealing with properly. "The issue is not the food, it's what made you overeat in the first place . . . For me, food was a comfort, pleasure, love, friend, *everything*. I consciously work every day at *not* letting food be a substitute for my emotions."

Oprah has written: "I just wasn't lucky enough to be one of that tiny percentage of dieters who manage to keep the weight off. That's why I've gone on record saying I won't diet anymore. I'm looking for the source of my weight problem, not just the symptoms. I think I will carry the weight until I learn the lesson of why I carry it in the first place . . . When I started gaining the weight back, I felt I had let people down, and that triggered my greatest fear in life: the fear of not being liked, of not being good enough. That one had a bigger hold on me than the weight, although I think they are probably connected."

Physical nourishment cannot work alone

The part played in our happiness and well-being by adequate amounts of sleep, daylight, physical activity and good nutrition would be hard to exaggerate. All of our moods have a physical signature, and any level of anxiety or depression, or love and hope, is accompanied by changes in the chemistry of our body and brain. This is why feeding ourselves with the full range of Mother Nature's recipes will help the restorative process.

But powerful though they are, such nourishing measures are never enough on their own. They can only act as supports and allies to the improvements we initiate in other arenas of life, such as our good relationships and our motivating passions and our sense of progress. The other parts of this book have their own forms of nourishment to offer us, such as loving relationships, a sense of achievement, and plans for the future. Former South African President and Nobel Peace Laureate, Nelson Mandela, has this to say about times when sources of physical nourishment are not available: "The human body has an enormous capacity for adjusting to trying circumstances. I have found that one can bear the unbearable if one can keep one's spirits strong even when one's body is being tested. Strong convictions are the secret of surviving deprivation; your spirit can be full even when your stomach is empty."

Which brings me on to *beauty* . . . in all its forms.

Learning curves

I always thought how pleasing it would feel to be really beautiful . . . head-turningly handsome . . . so the women whose admiration I sought would recoil slightly in open-mouthed awe, which is what I seemed to do when confronted by someone stunning. It took a long time to dawn upon me how my own initial response to someone's physical beauty wore off quite reliably after just a few occasions. Then after I seemed to crave only companionship and a refreshing stream of energy and bright ideas that never ran dry. It was kindness and loving I admired, not sculpted profiles and statuesque poses. It took a long time to dawn upon me that good souls doing passionate things were the most attractive people, all the more so because they didn't give a hoot for who was looking. They weren't on display, they were too busy doing.

There's more than one way to be beautiful

Beauty is a form of energy which radiates from a fine example of absolutely anything, whether a delightful taste, a lovely smell, or a gorgeous sight . . . no matter a face, a mountain, or a dance move. This energy is in effect a form of information; Nature's barcode telling us how healthy that attribute is, because health-bringing things increase the likelihood that we and our genes will survive and thrive.

Harvard Psychologist, Professor Nancy Etcoff, observes that with this vital equation very much in mind, our brain behaves like a highly sensitive radar constantly hunting for the beauty signal. If we're shown the photograph of a face, it takes us less than a fifth of a second to make an accurate judgement of its attractiveness.

Much of the language of this energy is hard-wired and universal which explains why three-month old babies far prefer gazing at conventionally beautiful faces. Likewise, adults from diverse ethnic cultures can all strongly agree on who is exactly how good-looking in other people's populations. Experimental studies have established that the active ingredients of beauty include symmetry and order, proportion and balance.

But here's another transforming thought which puts beauty in a whole new light:
Beauty signals health, that's for sure, but it doesn't *create* health. What's far more likely is that the healthier we become, the more beautiful we appear to whomever is bothering to look. And that principle goes for our personality just as much as our body. *Healthy minds and healthy behaviours are highly attractive.* U.N. campaigner and former fashion model, Waris Dirie, captured this dimension of beauty when she recounted her visit to her native Somalia. "My mother was beautiful to me because of the way she took care of her family and her friends and her animals. Real beauty

is not something you see in a mirror or on the cover of a magazine; it's the way you live your life."

Founding chairwoman for The Declaration of Human Rights, Eleanor Roosevelt, has also testified to this view. "No matter how plain a woman may be, if truth and loyalty are stamped upon her face, all will be attracted to her." This statement is surely heartfelt, as the young Eleanor experienced what she called "the pain of the ugly duckling". She writes, "My mother was troubled by my lack of beauty, and I knew it as a child senses these things."

Since beauty is so powerful and important, we can be thankful that there are so many ways to be beautiful, and so very many sources. For instance, how about beautiful movement – which can be that internal, kinesthetic sense when our own bodies dance or play sport. Our stomach can probably remember the school trampoline or a roller-coaster ride, or the thrill of seeing an art or craft well-performed: Tai Chi, skiing, or pottery.

But though we most readily think of experiencing the energy of beauty through our five physical senses of sight, sound, taste, touch and smell, it would seem that its other dimensions are even more potent. The first deaf and blind person to attend an American university, Helen Keller, poignantly emphasizes this insight. "The best and most beautiful things in the world cannot be seen or even touched. They must be felt with the heart."

Consider, too, how ideas, insights and inventions, can be deemed beautiful. In the international scientific community, Einstein's Theory of Relativity is unanimously praised for its extraordinary beauty. Yale University's David Gelernter, a professor of Computer Science, argues convincingly that 'lust for beauty' has driven the great technological inventions and discoveries, and that technologists, engineers and scientists should be better trained in the conscious appreciation and understanding of beauty. It is no accident, he would claim, that Mitchell's Spitfire with its Merlin engines and distinctive wings, was the finest flying machine of its day, while also seeming wonderful to every eye and ear. Twice winner of the Nobel Prize, scientist Marie Curie said "I am among those who think that science has great beauty."

And just as the plan for a bank robbery, a bridge, or a computer program can all work beautifully, so can a whole personality. Founder of the Body Shop, Anita Roddick would agree whole-heartedly. "Beauty is about ... action, vivaciousness, courage, energy and compassion – all the things that women should be celebrated for. It's not passive ... The best kind of beauty implies self-respect, joy, wonder and inner strength."

The Aboriginal, Cathy Freeman, a retired Olympic champion, has recently done some modelling for an Australian designer. She says, "My main reason for doing the shoot was for these images to hopefully inspire our young indigenous women – that we are beautiful and strong and feminine. We need more confidence, self-belief. We are beautiful and we should feel good about ourselves ... Beauty itself is hard to define. It comes from within – it's kindness, compassion, selflessness and humility. And I think we all possess these qualities to some degree."

It seems, then, we'd be making a great mistake to judge ourselves by the way we look, because that's only a fraction of what true beauty is all about. We know from the studies of many lifetimes that humans find a balance of loving and confidence, and kindness and humour, to be highly attractive and very healthy qualities. It is certainly endearing that the former US Secretary of State, Madeleine Albright, pokes fun at herself by admitting that on her 'bad hair days' she would simply wear her black stetson.

And perhaps the greatest source of beauty, for the sheer intensity and volume of positive emotion it brings our lives, is the beautiful relationship – the one in which we can thrive and flourish and grow beyond ourselves. It seems that Lance Armstrong experienced this at his *fourth* Tour de France win. He writes, "I was inexpressibly proud ... We'd grown stronger as the race went on, more secure in our craft, more patient. I felt a sense of achievement I hadn't felt in any of my previous three Tour victories, *because of the sheer beauty of that team performance.*"

We can all of us foster this multi-dimensional appreciation of the potential for beauty in those we care for. American singer, Madonna, fondly remembers her dance teacher. "I was fourteen, maybe fifteen, and feeling horribly unattractive and unpopular and uninteresting and unfabulous. And Christopher said 'God, you're beautiful'. Well, no one had ever said that to me before. He told me I was special. He taught me to appreciate beauty – not beauty in the conventional sense, but rather beauty of the spirit".

My conclusion from such touching accounts of people's lives is that this fertile energy we call beauty can exist between two living things, or a person and a place, or a person and a skill; and the world becomes only more beautiful the more deeply we understand it. Hence, we will find profound happiness in both nurturing and appreciating diverse beauties in whatever ways we can. Let's be beautiful for what we do and how we do it: our ideas, relationships, skills, and daily spirit.

* * *

Planning for Progress

- How might your life feel different if you went to bed an hour earlier, and took some energetic physical exercise for half an hour each day?

- How could you test out what foods and nutritional supplements work best for you?

- How could you create more beauty in your everyday life?

* * *

Self-Control and Self-Motivation

At my primary school, we weren't allowed to stir our jam into our rice pudding . . . the theory being that if we could resist this urge at age six, it would sow the seeds of self-control for later life. Unfortunately, that rigorous early training proved insufficient for me, and I have had to seek additional strategies to curb my unhelpful cravings. In explaining these, I divide the following chapter into two parts:

Part 1: Self-Control – is about those things we want to do *less* of.
These might include excessive activities such as over-drinking, over-eating, over-spending, over-working, or over-watching television. Or it might include excessive amounts of worry or fantasy or regret.

Part 2: Self-Motivation – is about those things we want to do *more* of.
This list might include anything from exercising more, all the way

through to attending evening classes in whatever takes our fancy.

But let's step back for a moment and look at the bigger picture.

Small changes lead to big gains

Learning how to readily change the way we think and behave is one of our most beneficial skills, because alterations in even our smallest routines can open up unforeseen routes to profound progress.

So I'd like to champion the merit of small steps as the surest way to get ourselves moving. It is by creating an environment and an attitude that allows for change, that small measures can act as a catalyst for much greater improvements. What's more, if we can't be resourceful in the face of a minor temptation or challenge, it's unlikely we will be so in the face of a major one. This is why we have to practice standing up to the small fry if we're to build our skills and resolve for coping with the bigger fish. Once we realise this connection between the little everyday things we do, and the larger characteristics of how we run our life, we realise that doing the right thing by ourselves as regards the small challenges is, in effect, an indispensable rite of passage to being able to deal with life's greater demands.

With this grander mission in mind, our initial aim is to confront our everyday habits and declare our independence from them. In doing so, we're rather like the captain who comes off auto-pilot and takes the controls so as to remind herself who's really in charge of the aircraft. This could translate as a week doing X for the first time, followed by a week without Y, just to experience how things could be done differently, and to show ourselves it's possible to modify the way we're living. Not because anything's broken, but merely on the basis that a change is as good as a rest, and if bodies can suffer from unrelieved repetition, so can minds and lives. There's also a psychological principle that says if we *behave* differently, it helps us to *think* differently, and alternative thinking readily leads to innovative action. Bearing in mind that our knowledge-based society pays quite a premium for original perspectives, this strategy of 'doing things differently' could prove highly profitable on any number of fronts.

There is no aspect of our behaviour to which this approach cannot apply. What and how we eat, the words we use and the way we speak them, our choice of music and our route to work. Some elements of our life will appear to be immutable, but these are probably fewer than we might at first presume. Sometimes even those activities that have been decidedly good for us must be allowed to lie fallow for a while so they can regain their potency . . . just as athletes must occasionally alter their entire training schedule so as to transcend a performance plateau.

So if we usually do aerobics, why not give yoga a whirl. If swimming has been our thing, we could dip into Kung Fu. Rather than a Friday night drink, how about drama classes? The likelihood is we'll gravitate naturally to some of our new approaches, and find a pleasing balance between the comfortably familiar and the rather refreshing. Maybe it's using our left hand rather than our right, or simply holding the phone to our other ear, but these modest changes all help to develop that progress-making quality of versatility.

Now we've established the principle, let's consider our motivations.

Why is feeling in control of ourselves so important?

Self-control and happiness go hand in hand because self-control lets us behave according to our deepest principles and in the best interests of our most treasured goals. Far from being limiting, the skill of self-discipline helps us achieve our heart-felt desires, rather than being a slave to the dictates of temporary appetites.

And the younger we start, the better. A landmark study begun by Dr Walter Mischel at Stanford University playfully challenged some four year olds to sit alone and make themselves wait 15 minutes before eating a marshmallow. Their reward would be a second one.

(As a veteran of the rice-pudding & jam ordeal I mentioned above, my heart goes out to those youngsters.)

Some of the marshmallow children covered their eyes, while others sang songs to distract themselves; but some gave in almost immediately. When researchers revisited these once tiny research participants as teenagers some 14 years later, those who had held out for the second marshmallow were significantly more self-confident, self-motivated, and better able to deal with life's frustrations than the ones who had been more impulsive as preschoolers. Not surprisingly, these characteristics had strongly reflected in their academic achievements: if you didn't know how to resist a marshmallow at age four, it seemed you were unlikely to know how to study for an exam at age eighteen.

And the ability to delay our gratification pays off well beyond the classroom. The Harvard Study of Adult Development tracked the progress of 824 American lifetimes as they unfurled over 60 years, and its longtime director, Professor George Vaillant, concluded the following: one of the five life-coping strategies which characterised the most healthy, happy, and accomplished individuals, *was their ability for self-control.* Put another way, they didn't act impulsively, but rather they dealt with things when and how it suited their best long-term interests. Present pleasures could be resisted for a greater net gain further down the road.

Part 1: Self-Control

I'm going to propose *three* powerful methods for replacing negative habits with positive ones.

FIRST METHOD: A good foundation to help beat the cravings

Slow and gentle breathing, adequate sleep, and self-reward can combine to form a good solid foundation for self-control.

But first off, we should bear in mind that the most important preventative measure is simply to avoid pondering even for a few seconds, the unwanted activity, as this will only fuel painful flames. Distract yourself *immediately* the temptations enter your head, being sure not to dally with an image in your mind or savour the thought of the no-go activity. You'll only be etching its seductions deeper into your system, and that's damage you'll only have to un-do.

However, in the event of a craving grabbing hold, the first thing we can do is focus all of our attention on slowing our breathing by gently inhaling for the count of perhaps 4 beats, and exhaling for the count of 6 beats. This ratio of a longer breath out than in, has the guaranteed effect of calming our nervous system. This slow and gentle breathing is *actively* relaxing us.

Continue with this slowed and gentle breathing while at the same time consciously unclenching all of your muscles. This is another means of sending a signal to your over-aroused nervous system to calm down.

Now's the time to start some encouraging self-talk imagining what your good friends or role-models would be saying to you now if they were standing there beside you. (I'm reminded how US Senator Hillary Rodham Clinton, when faced with testing times, is glad to conjure the spirit and good sense of Eleanor Roosevelt.)

Neutralised by these accumulated steps, our cravings will rarely last beyond 20 minutes. That said, we have to be prepared to wrestle with ourselves to behave the way we want to, and we have to be prepared for several re-matches. As three times British Prime Minister, Lady Margaret Thatcher, observes "You may have to fight a battle more than once to win it."

Rearrange our routines . . . and get lots of sleep

We've seen above how 'self-control' doesn't mean passively 'holding back', it means actively taking counter-measures. With this in mind, to help maintain our progress, we should redesign our daily routines and environment so as to actively avoid the triggers and temptations that might trip us up. We should also note that whether we're saying no to a second piece of cake or fending off alcohol, our amount of self-control tends to operate like a limited source of renewable energy: *the more resisting we do now, the less we'll have for later.* So, at the end of a temptation-filled day, we'll be particularly vulnerable, which is why it's good to know that *sleep* is one excellent way to replenish our self-control. Considering that so many people, young and old, are often an hour or two short of eight hours sleep, we might usefully ponder just how much obesity, heavy drinking and road-rage might be exacerbated by people having exhausted their day's supply of self-control.

Be sure to reward ourselves

When we achieve our first mini target of self-control, perhaps one week being 'habit free', let's be sure we've devised a range of mini rewards that are distinctly positive, rather than simply bingeing on that very thing we've been trying to resist. In any event, far better than using food or alcohol or some such 'passive' prize, we could treat ourselves and a friend to some enjoyable excursion . . . such as swimming, salsa dancing, or a new museum. U.S. Olympic team soccer captain, Mia Hamm, is hot on this point "Once you experience success — and you will if you put in the work — you shouldn't be afraid to celebrate it. Unless you feel good about what you do every day, you won't do it with much conviction or passion. So celebrate what you've accomplished."

SECOND METHOD: Associate the negative habit with negative feelings

This second approach aims to associate the deeply unwanted and unwelcome activity with a wholly negative image and a physical feeling of sickness.

Stage 1: If we're trying to stop ourselves drinking, we would vividly imagine feeling very sick at just the smell (and then the taste) of alcohol. By associating the activity with some extremely negative physical feelings like this, we will quickly weaken our cravings, because the behaviour will be less and less associated with pleasure. The key to this is the vividness of our physical feeling and visual image and our using which ever additional senses drive home the message for us. For instance, work by psychologists in Australia has looked at associating cigarettes with 'white, wriggling maggots'. A horrid image, but an effective one for instantly arousing the would-be smoker's instincts of disgust and revulsion in order to repel their temptations.

It seems timely to observe that one of the ten key thoughts that Oprah Winfrey uses to guide herself is "Rid yourself of your addictions – whether they be food, alcohol, drugs or behaviour habits."

And without a doubt, 'Imaginal Aversion Therapy', as the above method is often termed, has proven a useful weapon against seriously self-damaging behaviours such as smoking and substance abuse, *but I wish to sound a very strong note of caution.* Vividly imagining nausea and disgusting visual images is quite a drastic psychological measure, so we must use the procedure with consideration. It would, for instance, be extremely dangerous and self-damaging to try to associate feeling sick with eating food, in some misguided attempt to lose weight. No. We can only effectively use this method of 'negative associations' for those behaviours for which there is one clearly identifiable 'culprit' for which the likely consequences of not breaking the habit are truly dire. We would also be very wise to seek the guidance and support of a qualified professional in our endeavours to change any such behaviour; and I outline the characteristics of a good working relationship with a therapist in my chapter on *Powerful New Approach to Common Health Problems* and in the chapter called *Nick's Special Topics* towards the end of this book.

Stage 2: Very importantly, we need to be sure we have 'ready-and-waiting' some replacement activities that promise to bring us healthy satisfactions while also serving the purpose of distracting our attention. Perhaps taking a walk, playing sport, or finding some good companionship. The more inventive we are in devising some rewarding alternatives to meet our needs for tension-release, confidence, or companionship, the more successful will be our attempts at behaviour change. This strategy certainly worked for Margaret Thatcher during her student days. "I smoked my first cigarettes. I did not like them much either, thought I knew I would get the taste if I persisted. I decided not to, but to save the money and buy *The Times* every day instead."

THIRD METHOD: Create and channel some self-controlling anger

When it comes to dealing with our painful emotions, happiness is not achieved by avoiding, quelling ,or giving free rein to them; it is achieved by channelling their energy in constructive and helpful directions. One of the best examples of this strategy is the positive use of anger as a powerful tool in putting a stop to our unwanted behaviours and worst habits.

People are often reluctant to talk about the role of anger in their lives, as this emotion is all but taboo because of its association with destructive or violent energy. But this most certainly does not have to be the case; and we will read a little later in this chapter how learn-ing to harness our anger so as to drive forward our good deeds is a crucial skill for the healthy, happy and accomplished life.

But before considering its positive potential, let's first remind ourselves of the typical *misuses* of anger.

If we try to bottle it up, we're prone to develop psychosomatic problems with our eating, digestion, skin, sleep, headaches, or any number of such stress-related symptoms. Diana, Princess of Wales, spoke out boldly so as to highlight the dangers of turning anger in upon ourselves. "When I was bulimic I wasn't angry, because the anger was coming out that way. And it always felt better after I'd been sick . . . and I'd be very passive afterwards. It's a repetitive pattern which is very destructive to yourself."

On the other hand, if we let anger have its own way, this only results in irritability and temper tantrums, aggression and even violence. Both courses – bottling it up or bursting it out – will leave our physical health and interpersonal life suffering badly. Oprah Winfrey cautions us on just that point: "What I've learned about being angry with people is that it generally hurts you more than it hurts them. All the anger that you're trying to vent breeds so much frustration."

A far better approach is trying to de-fuse our anger by actively relaxing mind and body, but sometimes this isn't possible or even appropriate. Sometimes we dearly need to stoke our anger so that we can move decisively to confront and then channel negative forces – forces which might otherwise bully us into unwanted habits such as eating too much, smoking, excessive spending or worrying. What we know for sure if we have a powerful urge to do something, is that there must be quite some energy driving it. In which case, the emotional energy that drives our negative habit is also capable of driving the turbines of whatever positive alternatives we care to undertake. However, to achieve that tidy solution, we have to generate a competing and more powerful force, i.e. some anger that is sufficient to form a dam to re-orient ourselves in a more fruitful direction. Here's an example: I could, for instance, become angry at how getting drunk has too often undermined a promising relationship, or stolen the time and energy I'd intended to spend on better things. I could then fan the flames of my rage by seeing booze as a parasite that leeches my resources away from what I really wish for, fooling me into doing things I don't want to, distracting me from being who I want to be. In that moment of deliberate anger, I'm like an athlete who strategically generates a strong emotion so as to fuel my performance. The purpose of my anger is not self-punishment, but self-assertion, so instead of downing an after-work drink, I use my frustration with alcohol to channel the day's tensions into my doing some enjoyable exercise.

That, then, is the principle. This puts me in mind of a vivid personal anecdote told by Richard Feynman, winner of the 1965 Nobel Prize for Physics. "I was walking along the sidewalk opposite the beach at Copacabana past a bar. I suddenly got this tremendously strong feeling: 'That's *just* what I want; that'll fit just right. I'd just love to have a drink right now! I started to walk into the bar, and I suddenly thought to myself, 'Wait a minute! It's the middle of the afternoon ... Why do you have such a terribly strong feeling that you *have* to have a drink?' – *and I got scared. I never drank again* ... You see, I get such fun out of *thinking*, that I don't want to destroy this most pleasant machine that makes life such a big kick."

It seems to me that to stop himself from drinking, Professor Feynman channelled his fear of undermining in any way his hugely enjoyable mental prowess.

To guard ourselves against being caught out by an unexpected temptation like this, we do well to keep battle-ready by frequently rehearsing how we would cope: imagining first the tricky situation, then conjuring sufficient positive anger to block and then channel our energies into a replacement activity. Once we've experienced ourselves coping in our imaginations, then our ability to succeed in real-life becomes far more likely. Five times Olympic gold medallist, British rower, Sir Steve Redgrave, recounts in his autobiography how he vividly and step by step 'mentally rehearses a successful performance,' and it's the very same technique practiced by all leading performers, whether athletes, musicians, or surgeons.

By these combined means, our anger can, like fear or sadness, form a healthy and useful part of our emotional repertoire, providing psychological energy for useful action. *An important proviso, though, is that we should only direct our anger towards the specific behaviour that's trying to bully us around, and never towards the whole person, no matter if this be ourselves or someone else.* Reason being, that for there to be progress in an un-satisfactory situation, a person needs to feel there is a route by which they can put things right, rather than feeling totally demonised once and forever. Hence, we use anger to attack the problem, *not the person*, on top of which we always make sure there are some clear routes to improvement. On just this point, former U.S. President Bill Clinton said of his violent, alcoholic step-father "I hated what he did, but I never hated him."

This very same principle lies at the heart of Mahatma Gandhi's philosophy of non-violence. "Man and his deed are two distinct things. *'Hate the sin and not the sinner'* is a precept which, though easy enough to understand, is rarely practised, and that is why the poison of hatred spreads in the world . . . It is quite proper to resist and attack a system, but to resist and attack its author is tantamount to resisting and attacking oneself."

Once our anger has been well deployed with laser-like accuracy, our problem behaviour should weaken within just a few days; but we'll still need to keep our resource of anger close to hand to fight any urges to backslide. It's not unusual to have to give up our bad habits several times, as each time we become more proficient at preventing relapses. Try and try again is the motto for all worthwhile endeavours; and as Nobel Peace Laureate Nelson Mandela says, "the greatest glory of living lies not in never falling, but in rising every time you fall".

Defusing our rage

Though our well-channelled anger can serve many purposes, there are times when we will wish to curb our rage. To which end, 'Anger control' uses the very same techniques with which we can soften all of our strong emotions, such as fear, sadness, and sexual arousal.

First, it pays to be aware that irritants such as fatigue, noise, and alcohol will reduce our threshold for anger, so sensible precautions can build strong defences. As a preventative measure, daily physical activity is a great ally. Nelson Mandela recounts how "Many times in the old days I unleashed my anger and frustration on a punch-bag . . . In prison, having an outlet for my frustrations was absolutely essential."

But once our hackles have risen in an unexpected situation, we should strive to delay any response for at least the count of ten so as to allow our nervous system's automatic eruption to gradually subside. Slow and gentle breathing will be our greatest ally in those ten seconds; and breathing more slowly out than in, is the ratio we're looking for. Only then will we begin to think clearly again. If needs be, we should withdraw immediately from the antagonistic situation for several minutes or even hours.

During this 'time out', we shouldn't brood over the infuriating incident, because those mental reruns will only aggravate our nervous system and deepen the irritation. In the first instance, it is better to distract ourselves. Here once again, we would do well to concentrate on actively relaxing: breathing very slowly in, and even slower out, and loosening those muscles in our face, stomach, and shoulders, which so often tense in response to a quarrel.

Veteran BBC broadcaster, Terry Wogan, is certainly on to something when he says, "Losing one's temper is vain self-indulgence, so I don't dwell on things that hurt or damage me."

By the above means we can begin to project a calmer manner that will itself help defuse the situation. But anger control doesn't mean inaction; it means generating ever more beneficial solutions rather than the impulsive and destructive revenges that only throw fuel on an inflamed situation.

Part 2: Self-Motivation

My START formula to get the wheels rolling

Here's a healthy routine for how we could tackle making the improvements we wish for. We are making a mistake if we wait around for the right moment, because our self-motivation most often comes once we're on route, as do the good ideas. It's only by getting started that good things happen.

- S is for Simple, Specific and Straightaway. This is what our goals should be, rather than 'big and vague and all set for sometime never'. We will need to prioritise. What can we do *immediately*? What phonecall, what appointment, what course of action? How soon can we move on this? Naturally enough, our goals will change as we progress, but for now our only aim is to set ourselves in motion.
- T is for Targets. Let's be sure our goals reflect our values. And let's be clear how we will measure our progress. Seeing clear improvement is highly self-motivating, so what benchmarks will we use to monitor our progress? *We* choose the tape-measure by which we appraise ourselves.
- A is for Agree plans with a partner or coach. For instance, let's agree enjoyable routes to satisfying goals. Having someone looking out for us can be very helpful.
- R is for Realistic Plans . . . rather than perfectionist ones. Our pace of progress will increase enormously once we've got the hang of things, so we needn't overdo the first step. R is also for 'Remind ourselves of the times we've succeeded' and forgive ourselves

those that we didn't. We can't make good progress without making mistakes, so let's learn from the cock-ups, then cut ourselves loose from them.

- T is for Time-Limits. The time when we'll weigh up what's been achieved and rethink our strategies in the light of that. What can we do within this the next seven days? When is it reasonable to expect some results?

Harnessing our anger so as to fuel action

If we learn to harness our anger, it can play a profoundly positive role in key aspects of life. We've already seen in the first half of this chapter how it can help stop our unwanted behaviours and redirect the energy that drove them; but what can anger *initiate*?

Daniel Goleman, the psychologist who popularised the term 'Emotional Intelligence' fully acknowledges that anger can be "energizing, even exhilarating" and we see this on the faces of those Olympic competitors whose expressions go from dead calm to an anger-fuelled determination. Case in point is the American, Lance Armstrong, cancer survivor and six times winner of Le Tour de France: as a twelve year old boy angry at his step-father and much else besides, he threw himself into cycling and swimming. This meant riding his bike the five miles each way to the pool for morning swim team practice, 5.30 till 7. Then after school, back he'd peddle for two more hours working out in the water. This intensive routine led to him winning adult triathlons by the age of just 15, and his autobiography explains how "the old wounds and long-ago slights become the stuff of competitive energy."

That same boy could have expressed his rage through self-sabotage . . . hurting himself as a means to hurting others . . . a tactic epitomized by the teenager who drops out to punish his parents. Just as easily, Lance could have become ill-tempered, spiteful or violent; but thankfully his mother helped him transform his anger with her mantra "Make every negative into a positive," and she led by example. As a result of her mentorship and his daily practice, Lance has become a skilful master of his emotions. For example, at the 2000 Tour de France, Lance deliberately conjured up a sense of anger. "'Watch,' I told my friends. 'I'm going to win it again. And you know why? Because none of them think I can. I began *looking* for reasons to be aggravated on the bike; I catalogued each expression of skepticism, every disbelieving remark or expression of uncertainty by an opponent, and used them to challenge myself. I kept a list. It was an old competitive habit that went back to my childhood, when I'd never had as much money as the other kids, or played the right sport. I didn't have the right conventional parents, either. I'd always been underestimated, and I knew how to put it to good use."

Such alchemy as this takes strategy and skill, and the first stage is to construct our goals so that they require positive action rather than putting on the brakes. For example, aim to eat healthily rather than make certain foods taboo; aim to savour the benefits of staying sober rather than banning booze altogether. All the evidence suggests that creating positive targets like this makes their attainment far more likely. What's more, there's a strong link between depression and too many goals that begin *"I must not . . ."*

The second stage for our emotional alchemy is to use our anger to reinforce our sense of resolve, so we can overcome the self-inhibiting inertia, fear and perfectionism that can procrastinate even our most longed-for projects. Well-ridden anger like this can also be used to get us over the painful shyness that makes us afraid to ask questions, dance in public, or declare our passions. We should take heart that former head of BBC News Kate Adie, Oscar-winning actress Julia Roberts, Princess Diana, Special Forces General Sir Peter de la Billiere, Human Rights campaigner Eleanor Roosevelt, and Indian leader Mahatma Gandhi *all* described themselves as being painfully shy, and *all* overcame their inhibitions because their passion for what they believed in and wanted to express was even greater than their self-consciousness or fear of the consequences.

Here, perhaps, is part of what drove Kate Adie. As a university student, Kate spent time studying in Berlin, and there, crossing by train from East to West Germany, she first felt "a sense of rage that ordinary people could be made to suffer humiliation and fear" when she witnessed an East German family being assaulted and intimidated by border guards. "I still feel it very strongly, I can remember that actual moment and I still feel outrage when I see, for example, some bloke who, just because he's got a gun, pushes back a whole crowd who have a legitimate reason to be there, who want to protest, who are doing something to assert their rights. The idea that people can still be bullied in that way, I think is awful, and I feel terribly strongly about it still."

Self-realisation in love and work both require us to channel our anger

There is compelling evidence that learning to acknowledge and positively channel our anger serves a fundamental role in our maturing happiness. Findings from the 824 American lifetimes examined by the Harvard Study of Adult Development strongly suggest that those men and women who either bottled up their frustrations or were prone to explosive outbursts, were at least three times more likely to have unsatisfying careers as well as severely inhibited personal and social lives.

By stark contrast, those adults who learned to harness their anger for creative action that put things right, were characterised by well-established and satisfying careers, emotional and physical intimacy, and happy, healthy lives. The best explanation for this seems to be that telling someone we love them and asking to partner-up, requires bravery and self-assertion. As does demanding suitable recognition for our professional acumen. It seems we need the capacity to feel angry and not just sad when things go wrong, and we need a frustration-burning furnace if we're to drive forward our dreams in life. It certainly took some assertiveness for Dame Cicely Saunders to achieve the foundation of St Christopher's Hospice and the modern hospice movement. "You need a degree of aggression in you to go on doing it and I was certainly conscious that I was treading on people's toes."

Reflecting on the above, it's interesting to note that actress Julia Roberts says of herself, "I have more confidence now to speak up and say, 'You are crossing a line,' as opposed to wanting to please other people at any expense to myself."

And this sentiment echoes the honesty of Oprah Winfrey: "You know what my biggest fault is? *I don't have the courage to be disliked."*

Of course, anger is by no means the only form of creative energy, as evidenced by the supremely motivating power of love and hope and happiness. They are all resources that well deserve our cool-headed consideration. Oprah Winfrey nails it again: "If people want to solve their problems, they must sooner or later reach inward to bring about a positive difference in their lives".

Defusing the fears that hold us back

Fears can often stop us doing things . . . important things . . . such as asking someone for a date, or going for the career that really attracts us. Overcoming our fears is part and parcel of freeing our self-motivation, so let's look at how we can shrink even our biggest nightmares. How, for instance, does the bomb-disposal operator, who is invariably a well-balanced and everyday individual, cope with such a challenge? And what can this teach us about conquering our own fears and phobias?

There are at least two key ingredients in training a bomb-disposal novice. The first is *small team camaraderie*, whereby the squad operates as a tightly knit group of four people who live and work together. The second is *highly realistic training* in which the individual is gradually confronted by increasingly difficult but manageable tasks so that he or she acquires complete confidence in the adequacy of their abilities. So effective is this combined approach, that the vast majority of bomb-squad operators eventually lose all fear.

It's good to know that a civilian version of military methods works equally well for those inflated and debilitating fears of such things as performing in public, enclosed spaces, heights, spiders, the dark, or being alone at home. Not unlike military methods, an effective cure is to very gradually and progressively confront our feared situations. The first of our carefully controlled encounters may be only a picture or a video or simply a well-imagined scenario. From there, we must progress up the ladder step by step to increasingly daring real-life exposures. The key goal at all levels is to remain steadfast in that feared situation until our anxiety completely subsides, which may take just minutes . . . or may take a couple of hours. It can help if a good friend reassures us through the first stages of this process, though ultimately we must be able to accomplish it alone. (The technical term for this whole process is 'gradual desensitisation.) Interestingly, we don't have to use relaxation. If we're finding it impossible to relax, than we should try to use laughter instead . . . reminding ourselves of some hilarious incident or farcical scenario. Laughter and fear are completely incompatible, so if we can get ourselves chuckling, we're definitely winning. This certainly worked for star singer, Celine Dion, at her opening performance at the 1996 Olympic Games: "In Atlanta, a few minutes before I went onstage, I was reminded of the show I did ten years earlier in Quebec when the mayflies flew into my mouth and slid up my skirt. At any other time, we probably wouldn't have thought that this was very funny. But everyone was so tense in the dressing room that just imagining me spitting out mayfly wings sent all of us into wild laughter that lasted right up to the moment when they came to tell us: 'Miss Dion, two minutes.'"

Following the above guidelines, being sure not to rush on to a new stage until we're completely comfortable, we will eventually cope easily with the things we once most feared. Though we may need occasional top-up training sessions, more often than not it is permanently effective. No one can inject us with bravery, but by investing effort in these tried and tested strategies, we can readily achieve it.

This is a rather good time to hear Eleanor Roosevelt's reassuring words: "We do not have to become heroes overnight. Just a step at a time, meeting each thing that comes up, seeing it is not as dreadful as it appeared, discovering we have the strength to stare it down. The encouraging thing is that every time you meet a situation, though you may think at the time it is an impossibility, once you have met it and lived through it you find that forever after you are freer than you ever were before. You gain strength, courage, and confidence by every experience in which you stop to look fear in the face." One of

Eleanor's self-guiding mottos was "You must do the thing you *think* you cannot do."

We need to master 'Time-Travel'

Whether we're building self-control or self-motivation, versatility in our imagination is a mighty valuable skill. It helps us cope with what ever comes our way. It allows us to seize opportunities, survive storms, and adapt to new situations. One of the key skills allowing such versatility is a flexible 'Time-Perspective' which is the term coined by Stanford University's Philip Zimbardo to describe how our focus of attention can be directed towards our past, present or future lives. A recent president of the 160,000 members of the American Psychological Association, Professor Zimbardo claims with good reason that Time-Perspective is a major personality characteristic that just about everyone in psychology has overlooked these past 100 years. He also claims it can make a crucial difference to how well we do in life and how happy we are while we're about it. Indeed, our particular bias to one time-orientation or another can strongly predict everything from our health, income and educational attainments, right through to the personality of our romantic partners. It's powerful stuff.

Of course we need all three of our past, present and future thoughts, but problems occur when we unwittingly allow ourselves to become fixated on one perspective or another. We will often have found ourselves escaping through psychological time or being unwittingly drawn in an unhelpful direction, rather than investing our attentions in the way that's needed.

Too little of the past, and we fail to learn its lessons; too much and we fall foul of depression, or forever bemoan the passing of our hey-day.

Too little present, and we're not savouring the richness of the moment, or giving ourselves fully to a task; too much and we jeopardise our well-being with our 'live for today, hang tomorrow' behaviour.

Too little future, and we can lack the foresight and motivation to plan ahead; too much and we never take enough time to enjoy our achievements or reflect and reminisce. This latter scenario is probably the most typical British malaise.

To restore a healthier balance, Professor Zimbardo advocates that rather than let it be an unconscious habit, we should actively develop a *flexible* Time-Perspective with which we can deftly invest our full attention in learning from and savouring whichever dimension is going to be most helpful and reflect our true values. Our mind is a time machine, but like Dr Who and the Tardis, we must learn to use it wisely.

We need to develop the flexibility of our Time-Perspective so that we can respond more helpfully to the flow of situations which living brings us. Let's take, for example, my indecision over whether to join a new club this season, for weekend rambling, dancing, or landscape painting. By focusing for just five minutes on the past, I can remind myself of how much pleasure I took from being a regular participant in a previous class.

Then, when I begin to get cold feet about turning up to the first session, I immediately focus on the future so as to reassure myself that though the first few meetings will probably feel awkward, in six weeks time I'll be settled in.

And once I'm actually there, I focus solely on the present, throwing myself whole-heartedly into the lesson around me rather than self-consciously holding back to wallow in regret that I didn't do all this when I was a lad of ten.

That, in a nutshell, is how I could strategically deploy my Time-Perspective, rather like using the gears on a bike to get me up and down a hill.

But it needn't be just our own lives we travel forward and back in. We could also imagine how our elderly neighbours might have been when they were our age, or what sort of conversation we would have with a teenager once they're 30. The trick is to make these shifts of Time-Perspective quite deliberate and systematic. It might seem pedantic, but we shouldn't under-estimate how our broad and fluent thinking can become blinkered and blocked because of emotional excitement of one ilk or another. Anxiety, anger, sadness, or romantic attraction will all bring emotional intensity, but in doing so they tend to inhibit our thinking versatility and cause us not to see the fuller range of paths forward in a situation. This explains why, after we confide in a good friend, they can offer several ways of viewing our predicament that somehow evaded us. To free up our thinking, let's first use our old stand-by of drawing-out our breathing to barely one quarter of its usual pace, while also unclenching any bodily tension. Next, we should put ourselves in a distinctly positive mood so as to broaden our horizons and help us be creative. This requires us to recall a particularly pleasing thought to nudge our spirits in the right direction. Relish this gem for just long enough that it puts a smile on our face, then off we go.

When it comes to using Time-Perspective, it's all very well Dr Who-ing around in the Tardis of our imagination, but we don't want to be a time-tourist. Rather than simply observe, we want to immerse ourselves in our imaginative experience so as to better understand the possibilities. It's intensity that's important here, and focused concentration is the key to that. One sure route is to conjure with our senses all the sights, smells, touch and sounds that are redolent of the imagined scenario. Let's try to inhabit it.

The insights afforded by our Time-Perspective explain why many psychologists hold in the highest regard the broader skill of imagining the world from many points of view and manipulating it in our mind's eye. It's real life that benefits from a healthy imagination. In fact, so helpful to us is our imagination in enabling us to swiftly change our thoughts and behaviours, that in *Nick's Special Topic* chapter towards the end of this book, I gladly champion the remarkable role of an often misunderstood means for broadening our psychological, physical and social horizons. It's called Clinical Hypnosis, and is a technique very close to my heart that I believe any of us can benefit from learning.

* * *

Planning for Progress

- How would your life feel different if you changed some of your typical thoughts and behaviours?

- Which of your specific behaviours do you wish to change, and in which order? Set yourself clear and easily achievable goals, so your early success can lead quickly on to more challenging ones.

- What highly motivating thoughts or memories will you draw on to create the energy with which to drive change forward?

* * *

Recuperate and Rekindle

How well we treat ourselves away from the demands of work and our everyday responsibilities, will be the biggest factor affecting our ability to sustain our progress. If we're to thrive and flourish, we would do well to master our time off.

Doing beats having, any day

In a recent study, 60% of the British households surveyed agreed that they cannot afford to buy everything they really need, and this included 40% of households with an income of £50,000 or more. And though in real buying power we earn on average *three times* that of a 1950's generation, there is good evidence that we rate ourselves not one jot happier. Very similar trends are evident throughout Europe, the USA and Japan.

For some time now, we've been spending more and working longer than is good for us, in a misguided attempt to acquire the luxuries that we think will make life better. For instance, credit card debt has trebled in the past seven years, and we probably sleep two hours less per day than our grandparents.

So how can we temper our appetite to consume?

Part of the answer is appreciating that *having* things isn't nearly as satisfying as *doing* things, so pound for pound we're far better investing our money in opportunities to actively participate rather than merely own. Just for example, my present car serves a dozen useful purposes, so I thought about buying a new one. Then it occurred to me that for a fraction of the cost, I could have a pretty wonderful push-bike. My friend, Barbara, peddles seven miles into the office which takes her thirty minutes, and she's grown to love it. She said that there's something so involving about being out in the elements and self-reliant on your own steam-power, that it simply cheers the soul. I got back into cycling after a 15 year sabbatical, and re-learning such skills as hands-free steering and the side-sliding emergency stop have brought me lasting pleasure (and more than a few admiring looks from children on tricycles).

On a related note, it feels great dressing up to the nines when the spirit grabs us, but rather than buying quite so many clothes to look good in, could we buy some more to 'partake in'? I mean the walking boots and wet weather gear that will keep us dry and snug on weekend adventures in the autumn rain... or when cycling into work.

By redirecting some resources like this, we ensure the focus of our lives is *less* passivity and surface appearance, and *more* activity and profound effects. Worth the trouble, because no matter the task, our depth of involvement will largely determine our depth of satisfaction. It seems that we humans have evolved to favour creative activity and thrive on it. Of course, there are times we need to do absolutely nothing but rest up and watch the world go by, but more often than not we benefit from tipping the balance towards taking-part. This is why youngsters who travel overseas as tourists rarely gain nearly as much as those who actually work alongside the locals.

'Creating in preference to consuming' is a principle that can equally invigorate our time investments. We could, perhaps, reduce the shopping hours we'd normally spend looking for luxuries, and use that effort to revitalise what we own already. I mean treasure things rather than trade them in, not least because things well-cared for say more about our true values than any price-tag.

Likewise, we might occasionally forego the reruns of *Casablanca* or *The Great Escape*, and instead pour their inspirational themes into something personal. Maybe a marathon catch-up phonecall with a distant friend, or writing the kind of lengthy, heartfelt letter that was once the pride and joy of parted lovers and prisoners of war.

My call to action, though, comes with one crucial caveat. I'm *not* proposing 'thrills without skills', or anything equivalent to bungey jumping off a bridge. The feelings gained by gulping down such off-the-shelf experiences are too often trivial and fleeting. Far better we build healthy relationships in which our increasing knowledge of a person, a place, a skill, or even ourselves, provides an unceasing source of satisfaction. Reason being, there's quite a sense of progress that comes from 'knowing better' rather than 'buying bigger'. So when next we're tempted to purchase something passive or cosmetic, we could stop and ponder *'Will this really bring as much pleasure as inviting a friend on a weekend course in whatever takes our fancy?'*

Put like that, it might dawn upon us more often than not, that a fourth outfit isn't going to bring us half as much pleasure as embarking upon a course in Italian or art history, and thereby embarking on some whole new depth and dimension to our lives. If it's music we crave, could we join a choir or learn an instrument? Could we decorate our homes with our own attempts at painting, sculpture or poetry? How about drama, gliding, archery . . . or all three at once?

It's the putting effort in that makes things feel good and brings the benefit, just like it's the amount of effort that really tells someone how much we care about them. Time spent on our loved ones is more precious than the most expensive of gifts.

Don't let a calling become an obsession

It's a wonderful thing to feel a calling, whether it's to share our life with someone, raise a family, practice an art, a faith or a profession, or even to live in a particular place. But such a heart-felt desire is only worthy of being dubbed 'a calling' if its pursuit brings us health and happiness. If our going about it damages or unbalances our life in some way so that the costs to us outweigh the benefits, then that activity is tainted with some degree of obsession that is merely masquerading as vocation. Such an obsessive tendency can take many forms, and is just as likely to show itself in some excessive behaviour to do with exercise or household chores, as in some workaholic job routine. Most often such an activity is serving either as an escape from painful emotions, or as an attempt to compensate for them, but no matter which, such an inflexible and airless fixation will be harmful rather than healing.

To guard against such a state of affairs, we need to balance the passion with some other activities which recuperate us, and by doing so allow our pursuit to provide a lifetime of nourishing enjoyment. Let's look at some of the things other people found to balance themselves so they don't burn out:

NASA astronaut and first woman Shuttle Commander, Eileen Collins, enjoys her leisure time. "I have always enjoyed reading, running, astronomy, and golf. Now that I have a child, I spend more time with her activities such as swimming and soccer."

The onetime anti-apartheid activist who went on to become the first democratically elected South African President, Nelson Mandela, writes with great enthusiasm about his boxing training as a younger man in his twenties and thirties. "It was a way of losing myself in something that was not the struggle. After an evening's workout I would wake up the next morning feeling strong and refreshed, ready to take up the fight again."

Likewise, the young Pavarotti played soccer and tennis every spare moment throughout his childhood; and now as a much older man and acclaimed opera singer, he loves being around horses and will go spend some time with them to calm himself before and after performances.

And BBC's veteran reporter and former Head of News, Kate Adie, says this about the good life well beyond work: "I do have a private life. It determinedly takes up a large chunk of my existence. And the job is only there as a job . . . I fit in sailing, singing, average cooking, above-average shopping, theatre, desultory attempts at skiing, antique hunting and a horde of friends who tolerate my odd hours."

Kate's words remind us of the single most powerful key ingredient which can keep the life-work balance right for us: *a good variety of close and nurturing relationships*; the ones that might be found in friends and mentors, partners and companions, parents and children. But, of course, such health-bringing relationships are fed by personal contact, and cannot thrive on a fast-food diet of phone calls, text-messages and e-mails. In the event that our daily activities don't sufficiently embrace who and what we truly value, there are several ways we can foster a healthier balance. First off, we should sit down in person with those who care for us in order to design a schedule that builds-in a range of recuperating social pleasures for our evenings, weekends and holidays. Be warned that without some close allies to monitor our progress, we can all too easily slip back into heart-numbing "busyness" which got us into trouble in the first place. A full life, yes, *but deeply unsatisfying*.

So as to accustom ourselves to investing time in new adventures, we should vividly picture ourselves enjoying the experience. In these mind's eye rehearsals, rather than focus on the final achievements, we should try to relish the thought of taking part. After all, soccer isn't really about the number of goals scored, otherwise we'd go straight to penalty shoot-outs. It's about the ebb and flow of play, and the myriad skills and teamwork involved. The occasional goals are only a means to creating the much more important elements. Likewise, if making love took just 60 seconds from first smile to orgasm-over, it would miss nearly all the pleasure. Nature has designed life so that rather than being dependent on 'end products', most of our happiness is derived from the manner and spirit in which we go about things.

Breaking ourselves of an old cycle of behaviour will probably entail a period of considerable discomfort. For instance, social activities will not feel rewarding until we get to know people, besides which our sub-conscious will be campaigning angrily for a return to its isolating habits. As with fear, this is an alarm bell that should not be allowed to paralyse us. Our personal relationships and shared pleasures will thrive if we invest them with the very same energy and resources we once deployed elsewhere. Rather than wither from this redistribution of our energies, our calling in whatever form will, like a log fire, burn all the more brightly for us letting in some air.

The USA's top woman media pioneer and show host, Oprah Winfrey, has herself told how hard she found it to learn to relax at her rural retreat, rather than be busy. "Those first few weekends it was hard. I felt that I wasn't being productive, that I needed to be doing something. That I needed to hurry up and get back to the city. But I made myself sit still, and I told myself *I am doing something...* And gradually I felt myself going through a transformation. Now I don't want to go back to the city! When I'm pulling into the gate and my dog comes running out to meet me because he knows the sound of the truck, I'm the happiest I've ever been. I walk in the woods. I do Tai Chi Ch'uan by the pond. I get great happiness from having a good book to read and knowing I have the time to curl up in front of the fire with my fuzzy slippers on and finish it. I've realized it's very simple things that make me happy, but that I have to be open to happiness. I have to want to be happy rather than just busy."

Heed our need for balance and variety

Life-balance is when our personal resources are well-matched to the demands upon us. In other words, when our support from friends and mentors, and our skills and experiences, and our ability to recuperate are all well-matched to what life's asking of us. Far from leading to mediocrity, this balance between investing in ourselves compared to expanding our energies, allows us to feel renewed each morning, to learn from our experiences, and to enjoy the journey. BBC veteran broadcaster Terry Wogan is crystal clear on this point:

"If I didn't have the capacity to switch off and relax, I couldn't have survived in this business."

This brings me yet again to a major theme that I hope runs through vividly this whole book: that we should spend more time appreciating the journey and less time anticipating the goal. Otherwise we tend to compromise our present happiness for the sake of some future reward. And getting this right has lots to do with balance. Our goals need to be sufficiently attractive to motivate us, but we shouldn't let them grow too large lest they become like an albatross around our necks. How high we pitch our expectations will affect how much we attempt, how much we achieve and, very importantly, how satisfied we are when we get there. There's a cautionary message in the study by Cornell University researchers who found that Olympic silver medallists were prone to being less happy than bronze medallists because the former felt cheated of a gold, whereas the latter were just glad to be on the podium at all. Focusing in on the positives of a situation rather than the short-comings, doesn't just work for Bronze medallists, it's the principle upon which all good therapy and good teaching can work: *build on the strengths of our situation.* I am reminded of Lance Armstrong's remarkable reaction to not winning the gold medal at the 2000 Olympics in Sydney. "That night, my wife and I and some of our closest friends took a cruise of Sydney Harbour, and we celebrated the fact that there would be other races. I would ride again, into the highest hills, up the pitch of a mountainside, where green leaves quiver in the cold sun."

In achieving such an admirable state of equilibrium as Lance achieved there, we need to seek variety and be versatile. *Variety* because we thrive on a rich mix, whether that be of ideas, activities, friends or foods. *Versatility* because we benefit not from avoiding life's challenges, but from learning to *adapt* in the face of them. For instance, if we spend 60 hours per week desk-bound in commercial conversations and staring at a computer screen, we can be sure that sitting in front of the television is far from the best antidote. What we need to do instead is counter-balance our working-life with an equal and opposite force. Instead of television, it would be far more rewarding if we got outdoors for some highly physical and emotionally expressive pursuits. Perhaps gardening or hill walking, sailing or singing, or the local hare and hounds. But if it's leather-clad dancing and adventures in the city, then so be it, as long as it channels our passions into positive, real-life escapades. And if they're carefully designed to fulfil our deepest needs, these alternative worlds will make our time off-duty all the more refreshing. Not only will they improve our back-on-the-job performance, but it's far more satisfying if we can give ourselves whole-heartedly to the role we're playing at any one time. It seems that the greater the difference between the various parts of our life, the more thoroughly we can play each part and yet still keep mind and body in balance.

Taking time off makes all the difference

Some of the most successful professionals I personally know take at least eight weeks holiday per year, because it keeps them fresh and eager to do quality work, as well as preserving and nurturing their personal relationships. These people also take most of their weekends and their evenings off.

Time out, time off, time away – it all needs consideration if it's to refresh and rekindle us. All the more so since the early 1980s when our office working hours began to rise, a situation now compounded by the ubiquitous reach of business e-mails and mobile phones. It's worth noting that some of the unhappiest people in the Harvard Study of Adult Development rarely if ever took holidays, had hobbies or played sport. Instead, they retreated from work into fantasy worlds which they used to substitute rather than explore real-life possibilities. It's a big mistake. At all ages we benefit from having play-time in the company of others, and we should respect its essential contribution to our well-being by making shared leisure time and holidays a non-negotiable feature of our weekly schedule and yearly calendar.

Here's Oprah Winfrey again: "Every Sunday, I'm having some free time. because I find that if you don't at least give yourself a day to rejuvenate yourself, to revive yourself, just to be silent with yourself, to do nothing, then you end up burning-out really quickly. And there have been times when I didn't do it. *You can tell the times when I don't do it.* And so I try to, on regular basis to give myself a day a week to just do nothing. I have a farm in Indiana. My fiance and I go there and talk about things that are important to us."

When planning our play, the key principle is to create complementary activities that will balance-out our usual routines. Prioritise those things we don't usually do, but would dearly like to. If at all possible we should make those activities social and physical and pitched at a level that well matches whatever resources of energy and skill we can muster at the time. If it's too easy or too demanding, it will feel unsatisfying and deny us the pleasure of being fully absorbed.

And let's not forget to give our head a holiday. Make a pact that for this weekend or longer *"I'll not allow myself to think about so and so, and any mention of 'the other' is strictly out of bounds."* This period of abstinence will remind us just how possible it is to turn the volume down on our habitual worries. What's more, we'll return to the fray with renewed vigour.

A change is as good as a rest

There's a psychological principle that says if we *do* things differently, it helps us to *think* differently, and alternative thinking easily leads to innovative action. Habits are not necessarily bad: they save time and energy, and their daily practice makes us highly proficient. But they play such an important role in our lives, that it pays to be sure they are how we want to behave. Habits should free up time and energy so that our life can grow, they shouldn't restrict it.

So can we challenge our usual patterns? Not because anything's broken, but merely on the basis that a change is as good as a rest. And at best, something highly productive might come of it, not least because our knowledge-based society pays quite a premium for original perspectives. Our aim is to confront our daily habits and declare our independence from them. It's one means of exercising our self-mastery in order to strengthen our creative muscles; but it's about the dos just as much as the don'ts, and it requires finding healthy rewards for ourselves as well as enduring the pains of sacrifice.

In the late 1990s, country and western singer, Emmylou Harris, dissolved the legendary Hot Band after a serious bronchial infection, "It made me realize how hard it was to sing over the top of the electric instruments. And I'd been doing it for 13 or 14 years. It made me come face to face with the fact that I was tired, and I was tired of doing the same thing. Sometimes I think these events happen to us that can initially be looked on as something bad, but they awaken us to something: you have got to make a change . . . because you are a different person and you're in a different place but you're acting as if it was 10 years ago."

There is no aspect of our daily schedule to which this theme cannot apply. What we eat, our route to work, the words we use, and our choice of music. Some elements of our life will be irreplaceable, immutable anchors, but these are fewer than one assumes. Sometimes even those things that have been good for us must be allowed to lie fallow for a while so as to rekindle their potency, just as the athlete must occasionally alter her entire training so as to transcend a plateau. So, if you usually do aerobics, why not give yoga a try. If swimming's your thing, dip into Kung Fu. You're a steady jogger, so try a sprint-walk regime. Bodies can suffer from unrelieved repetition, and so can minds and lives. Rather than a Friday drink, try drama classes. Rather than tv, switch over to dancing. The chances are you'll gravitate naturally to some of your new approaches, and find a pleasing balance between the familiar and the refreshing. For one week or a month perhaps, we could peak without cursing, use our left hand rather than our right, hold the phone to our other ear . . . simply because all of these little changes can help us towards versatility in the bigger arenas of our life.

We can apply the same principle to the changing seasons. For example, how about giving our habits a summertime shake-up. When was the last time you rose with the dawn, not for work mind you, but to go walking? Our good spirits can be very responsive to the season's changes and could greatly benefit from putting our whole body-clock on summertime mode like this. So how could we use the early dawns and late dusks to do something outdoorsy we would never do in the darker months? What a great opportunity to rediscover those others sides of our personality, those passions and plans we've had tucked away all winter. This could mean skinny-dipping on some wilderness river bank, or hiking the hills under a harvest moon? The aim of all this is to revitalise our joie-de-vivre by a shake up in the whole routine. Variety is not just the spice of life, it's fundamentally good for it. We can now appreciate why the key architect of The Declaration of Human Rights, widely regarded as one of the most remarkable American women of her generation, Eleanor Roosevelt, once said "I have only two remedies for weariness; one is relaxation, and the other is change."

Making the most of unexpected time out

In an era characterised by shifting employment needs, 'time out' is occasionally forced upon us, and if we're not careful a few months out of work can seriously undermine our mental and physical well-being. This is largely due to the uncertainty about when we'll be back in business, and not feeling in control of our own future, so to counter these effects we have to do everything possible to bolster our sense of being in command and making progress. We should take heart in knowing that ten percent of the unemployed describe themselves as very happy . . . so it can be done. The best antidote is to pursue clear and achievable goals in arenas that mean a lot to us and bring us pleasure, for example, hobbies, sports, or DIY. Voluntary work can be a great source of satisfaction, particularly if it's social and physical and requires the sorts of skills and judgement which play to our strengths. Whether planting trees, running a club in the local prison, or being a companion to hospice patients, we're hard-wired by evolution to want to be helpful. Better still, the unusual environments can cast a bright new light on our own predicament. Here's an opportunity to step back from the fray and see the bigger picture of our lives so as to consider new directions and strategies. If we get it right, a well-planned and productive period outside of paid work is demonstrably better for our physical and psychological health than a period of insecure and unhappy employment.

We might also bear in mind that some enforced time-out can be just what's needed to open an entirely new life-dimension. The childhood ill health of authors H.G. Wells and Charles Dickens confined them to bed for long periods during which they read and wrote voraciously. Their example is typical of how, in an attempt to stave off loneliness and uncertainty, an enterprising spirit can strike the golden seam of a lifelong passion. Winston Churchill was in his forties when his whole career seemed to run aground. It was then he discovered painting, first with watercolours and then with oils. This captivating pastime was to stay with him for the rest of his life, and we are told that it was the only occupation he pursued in absolute silence.

My final example comes from the life of Muhammad Ali who refused to take part in the Vietnam War: "I asserted my right as a conscientious objector to refuse to be drafted. I was stripped of my heavyweight championship title almost immediately, and boxing commissions around the country refused to give me licenses to fight in their state. My passport was taken from me so I couldn't go overseas to fight. My prime boxing years were denied to me. During those years, I was not allowed to box for money, so I opened a restaurant called Champ Burgers to support my family. I also took a part in a Broadway play. But what I enjoyed more than anything was giving lectures to people as diverse as brothers in Harlem and college students in America's leading universities. When I look back, I see only what I have accomplished. The price I paid was nothing compared to what I gained. I lost the championship title. I lost three and a half of my prime fighting years. I lost financial security and public acclaim, but gained something greater by giving it all up – a title no man or government could ever take away: I was the People's Champion."

Look for the bare necessities . . .
Mother Nature's recipes

The more we learn how to relax our mind and body, the more likely we are to perform well. For instance, top athletes report achieving their peak performances when they feel loose, because the power, speed and accuracy of any physical or mental skill are only thwarted by excessive tension. Think how when we're apprehensive of speaking, we stumble on our words. Besides which, our inability to relax immediately and deeply makes us vulnerable to bad habits and anxiety symptoms in response to stressful situations – resulting in anything from stomach trouble to insomnia, from bingeing to nail-biting, from irritability to exhaustion.

As Eleanor Roosevelt reminds us, "If the capacity for relaxation is there, if you can attain the ability to create your own inner calm, you can get your relaxation as you go along, no matter how active you may be."

In just this spirit of 'relax as you go', golf champion, Tiger Woods, uses the moment before a crucial shot. "Sometimes I'll just take my glove off and feel each little seam inside, just focusing on that. It helps take my mind away from the situation. When you're standing over a shot it can be pretty tense. One thing I've realized is that it's impossible to stay focused for four or five hours. You can give yourself a headache or burn out or lose your concentration toward the end of the round. Talking to other players is my way of not overextending my mind by focusing on one thing too long. My dad has always been a big believer in smelling the roses. I didn't understand that till I got older. It was his way of saying, "Don't focus on the task too long or you'll burn yourself out." It was a great lesson, and it was also his way of saying the only real focus you should have is when you're getting ready to play the shot. Talk to your caddie; talk to the crowd; look at other things. The game of golf is very beautiful; enjoy it."

So, to foster relaxation, we combine two complementary approaches. The first is mental imagery: letting our imagination put us in a calming place of our own invention. Focus our attention completely, because this should be Shangri-la for all our five senses: feel the grass beneath our toes, smell the blossoms, hear the waves. Will we swim in warm waters, stroll among bluebells, or soar like a bird between clouds? This is our treasure island where stress can't reach us.

The second skill is physical relaxation. We should concentrate on our breathing: slow inhale, even slower out, relishing the rhythm. Then take each group of body muscles in turn, and either tense them tight or shake them out for a few seconds. Then let them relax and grow ever more limp for half a minute. We should progress from our toes all the way up to our face, jaw, tongue and lips. All told, this is a 15 minute round-trip, but daily practice will bring improvements to repay us ten fold through restful sleep, more energy, better moods, and being able to cope without resorting to quick-fixes. We should aim to reach a level of skill whereby we can actively relax any part of our body and reach our mental oasis in a matter of moments.

Oprah Winfrey has made a similar type of relaxation part of her daily routine. "It is constant work staying on target and coming from a centered place. I meditate in the morning, in one form or another. Sometimes it's a formal ten minutes sitting quiet in a room."

And while we're talking about relaxation, when was the last time you sang out loud at the top of your lungs? After all, singing is part of our evolutionary history as social animals for whom voice is the key means of communication. The singing voice reverberates through our chests and skull. It's massaging us from the inside. We sing around campfires and when travelling in our cars and taking showers. I think we'd feel even better if we sang more often.

"I'm singing in the rain, just singing in the rain, what a wonderful feeling – I'm happy again!"

What's good to hear is that scientists at the Goethe University of Frankfurt would say that Gene Kelly's elevated spirits while singing that song, were only to be expected. Reason being is these researchers took saliva samples of singers in an amateur choir before and after an hour's rehearsal of Mozart's Requiem. They found that the singing had dramatically stimulated the immune system that fights disease, as well as notably improving the performers' mood. By comparison, when the choir listened to a recording of themselves, there were no significant effects. This has led the study's director, Professor Gunter Kreutz to propose that singing is at least as beneficial to one's body and mood as forms of meditation and light exercise. Likewise, London University scientists, Drs

Elizabeth Valentine and Claire Evans, compared the effects of half an hour's solo singing, choral singing and swimming, and found that all three activities reduced tension and improved energy, mood and heart-rate. Swimming had the largest effects, but there was little difference between choral and solo singing, which suggests that singing's benefits go far beyond its social factors.

Professor Gene Cohen of George Washington University has followed a group calling themselves the Senior Singers Chorale, whose ages range from 65 to 96. Compared with their elderly neighbours, the senior singers suffer less depression, require fewer visits with the doctor, take fewer medications and partake in more activities. Such findings will come as no surprise to Graham Welch, Chair of Music Education at the University of London, who says that singing, particularly as part of a group, can express a full range of emotions as well as exercising major muscle groups and increasing oxygenated blood-flow. Better still, it's not just the singer who benefits. Studies suggest that hearing singing voices can contribute to premature babies being able to leave Intensive Care a few days earlier than they would otherwise. At the very least, it appears to improve the infants' heart rate and breathing. The remedial effect of musical sounds is also evident in a study by The International Society for Music in Medicine, that looked at ninety-thousand patients in post-operative phases of surgery. Nearly all the patients said listening to their own choice of music during their recovery helped them relax, a claim substantiated by their using 50% less of the recommended dose of sedatives.

So the message is clear. Our singing voice should not be confined to bathrooms and car journeys when an old favourite comes on the radio. Let's join a local choir in time for Christmas, or a Gilbert and Sullivan light opera. Let's team up for some a'cappella or search out some Blues or Soul. But whatever we do, at work or at play, let's practice using song to reflect and to rally our spirits. And if someone demands of us, "What is there to sing about?" we might well borrow the words of the mandolin playing Captain Correlli when he is held at gunpoint by the passionate young Greek woman who asks him how he can sing when there are people dying in the world war that has come to her islands. The Italian Captain replies in all earnestness: "There is singing when babies are baptized; when you celebrate a marriage; men sing as they work; soldiers sing as they march into battle; and there is singing when people die. I have always found something in life worth singing about, and for that I cannot apologize."

Using laughter as a powerful pick-me-up

'Firm-up your farce and tone-up your titters' is another one of the clearer messages from modern medical research. And with clipboards in hand and no hint of a grin, leading psychologists would place 'a good sense of humour' firmly among the key characteristics common to nearly all happy, healthy, and accomplished individuals.

But it has to be the right sort of humour. We should mature out of malicious joking and strive instead to under-cut our own foibles and pains with some wit at our own expense. This skill is worth developing not least because studies have shown that when a self-effacing funny comment accompanies a person's photograph, the individual is reliably rated as more attractive.

But increased attractiveness is only one of the plus-points of good humour. In 1979, an acclaimed American journalist and one-time winner of the U.N. Peace Medal, Norman Cousins, published *Anatomy of An Illness.* He recounts how he'd been diagnosed with a paralysing degenerative disease, but shunned mainstream medicine as to put himself on an intensive daily diet of amusing books and movies. He claimed laughter saved his life, and he went on to live another 25 years.

Since then, highly credible scientists such as Stanford University's William Fry, a psychiatrist and pioneering researcher in the therapeutic use of humour, have strongly championed laughter's health-bringing properties. Numerous experiments have demonstrated its effects on the body's level of chemicals known to be connected to immunity-boosting and pain reduction. Humour also comes very close to producing the exact physical opposites of stress; for instance the blood-levels of the stress-hormones, cortisol and adrenaline, drop significantly. This is nicely illustrated by how patients post-surgery ask for significantly less pain-killers if they view comic films.

Further confirmation comes from Harvard's Tom Perls and Margery Silver studying individuals who live 100 years and more, which is just one in 10,000 of us. A lively sense of humour is a notable skill among these human Volvos who, far from falling apart with their old age, often have the keen wits and physical faculties of a much younger age group. Perls and Silver conclude that humour, as well as conferring bodily benefits, is simply a good indicator of how creative and flexible the person is in their approach to problem-solving when faced with fortune's slings and arrows; humour lets us roll with the blows.

Former U.S. President, Ronald Reagan, a staunch Republican, famously took this approach to life. On 30 March 1981 while in Washington, Ronald was shot in the chest by a delusional attacker. Shortly before surgery to remove the bullet from his chest (which had barely missed his heart) he remarked to his surgeons, "I hope you're all Republicans!" Likewise, Senator Hillary Rodham Clinton says of her time as First Lady: "Laughing at myself was an essential survival tool."

At first glance, there would seem to be some tragic exceptions to the strong connection between humour, health and happiness. However, it is the brain disorder called manic-depression and its resulting emotional roller-coaster that invariably explains the dire problems that were faced by such comedians as Tony Hancock. (Modern drug treatments can now very effectively control this brain-function abnormality.)

The accumulated evidence is clearly telling us that laughter isn't a luxury, it's a fundamental building-block of all round health and happiness. So when was the last time you did the comedy equivalent of a three mile run, or circuit-training for your funny-bone? Whether we're giving a talk, unwinding after work, or ready for sleep, getting ourselves to chuckle will relax us very nicely, so we would do well to have a few favourite scenes we can readily bring to mind. For me, Bill Bryson's American travel diary, *The Lost Continent,* could make me laugh out loud at my own funeral – which is good to know, because there's a scene involving a poodle in the movie, *Something About Mary*, that damn near kills me every time I think of it.

My conclusion: though 'being unexpected' is certainly a key requirement for a real rib-tickler, we should put ourselves at risk of laughing far more often. Note, too, that we're a thirty times more likely to laugh when we're in company than on our own – which to me is just another example of how Mother Nature is urging us to team-up so at to enjoy life more.

The restorative powers of the natural environment

We all appreciate that getting closer to nature is good for us, but let's just remind ourselves of its full potential. The evidence to date comes from small-scale studies that have struggled to monitor the myriad factors that could affect a person's well-being. Even so, the findings are intriguing. In 1984, Texas-based Environmental Psychologist, Roger Ulrich, studied the post-surgery notes of 23 gall-bladder patients each of whom had a room with a view of a small copse of trees. He then made a comparison with 23 very similar patients recovering in near identical rooms in the same hospital, whose windows looked onto a brick wall. Ulrich discovered that those who had a room with a view were discharged one day earlier on average (after 8 days not 9) and used considerably less of the powerful pain-killer medication. These may only be modest improvements, but then again the view of the trees was equally limited.

This link between having a window looking on to nature and having improved physical and psychological health, is a phenomenon true for families living in inner city housing estates just as much as for prisoners in high-security cells. Professor Ulrich has also observed that open-heart surgery patients recovering in rooms decorated by art depicting some form of natural water feature, have lower post-operative anxiety than patients exposed to pictures of other natural scenes or no art at all. Particularly telling is how the highest levels of patient anxiety were associated with abstract paintings.

Though these studies do not demonstrate conclusively that views of nature improve well-being, they strongly suggest it, and lend support to the Pulitzer Prize winning Harvard Sociobiologist, Edward Wilson, who coined the term 'biophilia' for what he believes to be the in-born affinity that we humans feel for the living world around us.

So how might the natural environment be achieving its calming and recuperative effects?
First of all, our attention is drawn outwards to the fauna and flora, rather than ruminating introvertedly on our worries. We feel engrossed but in an un-demanding way that apparently helps rest and restore our thinking capacities. It also seems likely that we are subtly reminded how life is seasonal and regenerative and that good things aren't always dead and gone, but might only be lying dormant and awaiting some nurturing sunshine. We can understand why Nelson Mandela always relished gardening and fought for permission to create his own allotment on the prison colony of Robben Island. "To plant a seed, watch it grow, to tend it and then harvest it, offered a simple but enduring satisfaction. The sense of being the custodian of this small patch of earth offered a small taste of freedom."

In respect of all the above, I think it behoves us to cultivate our very own series of experiments. Do we feel any better for a brisk walk around the park at lunchtime? Do we sleep any sounder for a half-hour stroll before bed? Does it noticeably enhance the month ahead if we go 'walkabout' one weekend? And if we were to plan a wilderness adventure, what would be our chosen tonic: a seascape or the open savannah, the river bank or the mountain trail?

Urban cowboy
The good that can come of unfamiliar settings, puts me in mind of the time as a young man that I went West ... West in search of young women with whom to frolick on beaches and discuss philosophy. I was 19 years of age, had just left boys' school, and I'd answered an advert for a pool-boy required by a ranch in Wyoming.

I really wanted Californian beaches, of course, but all the jobs had been taken by those ahead of me... which was just about everyone . . . so manning a swimming pool out west would have to do.

In eager anticipation of all the social occasions to which I'd be cordially invited, I packed my suitcase full of bow ties, silk underwear, fancy waistcoats, suits and dinner jackets, indeed all the apparel that a member of the Royal family might require if they were doing a tour of the Commonwealth. Somewhere in my deluded teenage mind, I saw myself not so much as a pool-boy, as an Ambassador for Britain.

It's hard to know for sure what the pair of twenty-year old Wyoming cowboys must have made of me as I arrived by Greyhound coach in their little village that lay 16 miles from their cattle ranch, the biggest in the state. They'd been snowed-up all winter, and were still blinking at the freshness of the mellowing April world. I must have come as quite a shock as they saw me step down from the bus, wearing a crumpled suit and my school tie after 24 hours of travel. I wheeled my two suitcases towards them. Their raised eyebrows were, I recall, the only give-away that I was totally 'unexpected'.

To their enormous credit, I never once felt scared or intimidated in their company. Oh for sure, I felt out of my depth and terribly adrift and meaningless . . . but never bullied. They were kind and gentle souls despite their side-arms and pump-action shotguns and talk of beer and brawls.

It wasn't them that scared me. It was the mountains.

As a boy from the flat farmlands of Hertfordshire, I'd never been in close proximity to so much geography before, yet every morning I pulled back the door to my tiny log cabin and was met not by an English postman, but by the Little Big Horn Mountains towering above me. I had to crook my head back to see their snow-capped peaks. I could even make out families of coyotes and small herds of elk up there in the pockets of mist that drifted like gunsmoke around the higher slopes. For a boy brought up on the fast-food world of *Starsky and Hutch* or the lugubrious safety of Latin lessons in over-heated classrooms, that landscape was . . . and I choose my words carefully . . . awe-inspiring and overpowering. The sheer force of Nature seemed to x-ray me as I stood there cold and skinny in my M & S boxer shorts, and I felt *insufficient*. Was it any wonder? I had dreamt of LA girls on roller-skates, and hot dates at drive-in movies. Instead, I got *The Last of the Mohicans* meets *Apocalypse Now* . . . only with cows standing in for the helicopters.

But that was then, and now I've learnt that the mountains and the wilderness are there to nurture us. Like big old trees, they were once a home to us some six million years ago, and just a like loving mum, they're still taking care of us after all this time.

* * *

Planning for Progress

- How could you increase your all-round performance by improving the quality of your rest and recuperation?

- What new activities could you take up to better counterbalance the everyday demands upon you?

- What tired old habits could you rest for a while, so as to benefit from doing things differently?

* * *

Powerful New Approaches to Common Health Problems

This chapter is about the very latest approaches to some tricky health problems, ones that might take both physical and psychological forms. I also suggest how to find a suitable therapist. Most of all, though, it's about our attitude to making progress in the face of our problems, and this is where I'll begin.

Some key principles when tackling problems

The skills we learn in facing up to and tackling problems will stand us in extremely good stead in every other arena of our daily lives. For instance, in personal relationships and our working world we will be more methodical, more exploratory, eager to be well-informed, ready to challenge so called expert or final opinions, and more able to keep ourselves going in the face of life's inevitable setbacks. We will also be more sympathetic to others facing up to problems for the first time, and more able to mentor them. Rather than weaken us, the journey will make us strong. As six times winner of

Le Tour de France and testicular cancer survivor, Lance Armstrong, reminds us, "It's an absolutely important human experience to be ill . . . It can change your life . . . and it can change other lives, too."

Olympic rowing champion Steve Redgrave was diagnosed with diabetes three years prior to his record-breaking fifth consecutive win at the Sydney Olympics in 2004. "At first I went into a denial phase - you do not want to accept that it is happening to you." But true to character, Steve turned the struggle to his advantage. "I'm a better athlete than I was at any other Olympics, because I'm mentally stronger. And that's because of the hard times."

Inspired by those personal accounts, when faced with health problems we could endeavour to do the following:

Team-up with a healthy range of good friends and expert professionals for the encouragement, and for the fresh ideas and different perspectives. The temptation is to soldier on alone, or see the topic as taboo, or feel as if we're whinging. Everyone but everyone has experience of some really troubling problems, so we're not the odd one out. Here's Lance Armstrong again. "We don't do anything alone, none of us. I certainly didn't fight cancer alone, or regain my health through some extraordinary solo effort. I survived with the help of six different doctors, four chemo-cycles, three surgeons, a devoted mother, dozens of tirelessly caring friends, and several much-cussed-at nurses."

Research what's known about the problem: It helps if we make ourselves an expert on the problem, by checking it out on the internet, and finding out about the very latest book. If we're to make headway, we need to be prepared to experiment and to broaden our horizons. No one is going to be nearly as interested in solving our problem as we are, so it's *we* who must set the pace of progress. We can all take inspiration from the sheer determination and resourcefulness of the social campaigner, Claire Rayner, when she was a nurse of just twenty-seven years of age, and yet to become Britain's favourite agony aunt. She and her husband had been waiting months for Claire to become pregnant, only to be faced with two tragic miscarriages. At that time, back in the late 1950s, much less was known about fertility, and Claire had already seen *five* different doctors who'd been unable to help. At that point, she decided, "This was getting ridiculous. I needed to do some studying on my own account." Having done a great deal of reading in her spare time, Claire then booked a private appointment with the best specialist in London, and firmly requested that she be given a very particular medical test. Claire's reward for her tenacity was that her own diagnosis was duly confirmed and this finally allowed for effective treatment. She'd solved her very own mystery, and her daughter, Amanda, became the first of her three children.

It can also be reassuring to know that we're not the first to be tackling the problem. Media pioneer, Oscar-nominated actress and talk show host, Oprah Winfrey, recounts this common worry. "In my loneliest and most frustrating moments, I felt I was the only person who had it this bad with weight. I felt like everyone else had been able to control theirs, but not me." To quell those feelings, self-help groups are good for a sense of companionship, and they often can list well-known or historical figures who faced the same challenges as we have. This all helps put the thing in perspective. It might be first time around for us, but it's good to know that we're fighting a fairly classical enemy and are following in the footsteps of some good people who have proven the problem can be overcome.

Seek out increasingly expert professional opinions: We need the input of experienced professionals, and we should tenaciously seek the advice from specialists in different fields until we find someone who can help us beat the thing. Let's also bear in mind that the approach taken by British or American practitioners might be lagging five years behind what has been discovered in other parts of the world. (Time and again in my own work I come across effective techniques that are not yet common practise in the UK for a range of barely explicable reasons that have nothing to do with safety or efficacy. So let's be a truly 'world-class' explorer when we're seeking improvements . . . and the internet, if we're discerning about the quality of websites, can be so helpful in this.)

Take multiple approaches at the same time: There are no magic silver bullets, and most solutions to most problems require *a combination of powerful measures* that when taken together are sufficient to improve things dramatically. Also, we should not forget that science tends to be interested in averages and trends which represent what works for the average and for the majority. As individuals, we might well fall outside the statistical average, and so we need to explore and experiment to find out what works for us personally. (However, it might be that a medical practitioner advises us it's dangerous to mix our remedies . . . as might be the case if we mixed two forms of medication.)

Set small manageable goals so as to build our confidence: We can always increase our pace and our ambitions once we've built some sense of being in control of progress. At the same time we can set clear dates by which time we want something to have improved, so that we can measure our progress or change our approach if something isn't working fast enough for us. Let's not forget to celebrate achieving our sub-goals such as a new insight, finding a new ally, or finally having some small impact upon the problem.

Keep cheerful: We should take holidays off from fighting the problem, and motivate ourselves by imagining how good progress is going to feel once our new approaches begin to bite. Keeping ourselves in good spirits will enable us to recover in the face of set-backs, and to be resourceful in getting around brick walls and locked doors.

I say again: We should not be aiming to isolate ourselves with our 'self-help', we should be aiming to 'team up' . . . with good professionals, good friends, good books, and with good organisations.

Making progress with a Coach, Counsellor or Psychotherapist

A safe 'rule of thumb' is that if some of what we think or feel or do is getting in the way of our everyday life, or limiting the best of our heart-felt ambitions, then it's time to seek professional support. After all, we see specialists to maintain our teeth, eyes and the rest of our body, even to repair our cars, so it makes good sense to see someone who has made a full time profession out of overcoming problems and enjoying life.

We'd be in very good company

"The best thing I did was I get into therapy. That was really valuable." That's what veteran singer Bruce Springsteen had to say on the subject of tackling his life problems.

Golf champion Tiger Woods has told his own story. "My mom, who is Thai, tried to teach me her native language when I was young, but we found out I had a learning disability that caused me to stutter. . . . I couldn't even read out loud to myself . . . It was hard, friends would make fun of me, but I had to get over it. I went to a special school and learned how to speak again and was able to conquer my fears."

American comedian and actress, Ellen Degeneres, says this about her decision to come out publicly as a gay woman: "I was in therapy at the time, I got in touch with my feelings of my pain, which I hadn't been in my entire life. I started realising what a huge source of pain that was for me to constantly worry about. I finally decided to come out and it made sense for the tv character I was playing to come out as well . . . To be 37 years old and be feeling this sense of shame, that nobody would like me if they found out I was gay, it's a pretty emotional thing to expose yourself to. But I grew up, and I got rid of that shame and found a new sense of pride. I didn't have anything to hide."

Princess Diana sought help for the emotional problems that were resulting in her bulimia and suicidal feelings. She said her therapist asked 'How many times have you tried to do yourself in?'

"I thought, 'I don't believe this question,' so I heard myself say 'Four or five times'. He asked all these questions and I was able to be completely honest with him and I spent a couple of hours with him and he said 'I'm going to come and see you once a week for an hour and we're just going to talk it through.' He helped me get back my self-esteem and he gave me books to read. He said 'In six months time you won't recognize yourself. If you can keep your food down, you will change completely.' I must say, it's like being born again . . ."

And for a final example of someone who benefited from professional guidance in her emotional life, former BBC Head of News, Kate Adie, used the help of a counsellor for several months when she decided to trace her birth mother. Kate had always known she was adopted, but in 1991, aged 46 and signing-on to cover the Gulf War, she was asked to fill in a form that included 'Next of Kin'. "I realised that . . . I didn't actually have any relatives. That was it. And then I said to myself, 'Nonsense, I do know there are people'. So when I came back, a friend who was very kind put me in touch with a counsellor. This is the proper way to do it."

What to expect

An effective course of therapeutic training can often require less than a dozen one-hour or 90-minute training sessions, plus some daily homework assignments. With the help of a professional, we'll soon learn skills that put us back in charge, in much the same way that specific physical exercises help us regain the full use of a muscle after we've suffered an injury, or in the way that sports or music coaching will help us stride ahead. It's well worth the effort so as to lead our life the way we want to. A good coach or therapist will help us get the most from our mind and emotions and the opportunities and relationships in our everyday life.

We could even consider taking a friend. They can either be an ally to us, or we could team up on a goal we both have in common: for instance, to give up smoking or alcohol.

Identifying a psychotherapist

There's no point in me naming types of therapy, because a good therapist will use a range of different approaches (perhaps Cognitive-Behavioural or Multimodal Therapy) and a range of specific techniques (such as hypnosis, or roleplay, Socratic questioning or systematic desensitisation). What the good therapist will aim to do is tailor-make a training program to suit our personality and our particular needs at the time.

A recommendation from one of our own friends is a good starting point for choosing a therapist, but our needs might be very different from theirs. A good fit between the client's needs and the coach's skills and approach is the most important thing.

Alas, membership of a particular organisation or qualifying society is no guarantee that a coach or therapist is going to be good, or as good as they were when they qualified, or any good for our particular case. So we would do well to look for recent, present-day evidence that they're a good practitioner. A good therapist takes themselves on training courses to keep-up with skilfully applying useful new approaches and techniques. We should politely inquire when was the last formal training course or workshop our therapist went on. A one week refresher course within the past year is encouraging. A weekend conference ten years ago is not. A good therapist will be pleased and proud to recount their most recent training experience, because a good therapist is enthusiastic about learning more about their craft in the company of their peers, rather than seeing that as a chore. Our attention to their suitability will be a reassuring sign to a good therapist that when it comes to getting better, we really mean business.

What therapy might involve

In *Nick's Special Topic* chapter later in the book, I go into quite some detail as to some of the approaches we might reasonably encounter in working with a good psychotherapist . . . a checklist for when you think you've found someone to visit. Here are three examples to give you a sense of these:

- Look for rapport: we need to feel comfortable with the person we'll be working with, and feel that they have our best interests at heart. We need to feel that they rather like us, and that they certainly respect us for making an effort to improve our situation. They should also radiate lots of positive energy, and be optimistic but realistic in their plans about helping us make major strides.

- We and our therapist are allies ... just like a hill-walker and a native guide who can help us through some unfamiliar and difficult terrain. We don't want a 'You doctor Me patient' sort of relationship. It's a highly collaborative process and requires our highly active participation. We should bring a note pad and a pen because good therapy requires us to be very active in our listening, thinking and explaining. To draw a comparison with making physical improvements, psychotherapy is like having a work-out with an instructor at our side guiding and encouraging our activities. By stark contrast, it is not at all like having a massage or visiting our dentist whereby we just turn up and let it happen with little effort required from us. On the contrary, good therapy will motivate us to tackle the problem with skill and confidence. For instance, we might practise role-plays so as to rehearse different ways of dealing with tricky situations. We should always feel well supported by our therapist, but we should also feel that we're leading the charge.

- The more honest and clear we can be in our explanations of our present problem and hopes for the future, the better chance of progress. The therapist will dwell relatively little on the past, because it's what we do now and in the near future which will determine how fast and how effectively we get better. *(However, there are excellent techniques to neutralise traumas from our past, which do not require us to recount the initial incident; so we shouldn't worry that effective therapy need entail any upsetting blow-by-blow disclosures of painful past experiences.)*

(Remember there are a dozen more points on this subject in the chapter called *Nick's Special Topic*.)

Confronting common problems with new approaches

The following section looks at some new approaches to some rather common but very troubling health problems (psychological and physical) each of which affects very many individuals at one time or another. This means even if *we* don't have the problem, someone among our closest friends or family probably does.

- Depression
- Anxiety (which can take many forms)
- Shyness
- Emotional Trauma
- Migraines
- Digestive problems
- Pre-menstrual syndrome or tension

The ideas below are not by any means meant as the last word on the subject. Far from it. They are simply a starting place for us to find out more about what's troubling us, and are intended merely as an intriguing insight that might bring us renewed hope that things could get better if we broaden our horizons and begin to team up with specialist therapists.

Taking action to prevent and lift depression

For the one in four of us who will become seriously depressed at some point in our lives, the average age of a first major depression is 14 years old. Back in the 1960s, an individual would be nearer 30. It seems that life is rather more demanding and less protective than once it was.

Depression is a much over-used word, but a genuine depression is when everything in life feels lack-lustre and miserable. Not just one arena, *but everything*. And it won't lift even after a few days. As well as being characterised by low moods, it can show itself as irritability, sleep problems, and lack of appetite for food and all of life's other pleasures.

It's worth bearing in mind that feeling miserable is most often a healthy response to the rut we're in, simply Nature's way of telling us to make important improvements or take new directions or perspectives. So rather than reach for a quick-fix to numb the pain in one form or another (alcohol, tv, too many cakes, or trying to buy our way out of the blues with spending sprees), we would do far better to apply Nature's own-brand remedies. For instance, just as depression can have physical and psychological symptoms, its remedies can likewise be both physical and psychological, as we're about to see. Here's my own checklist of powerful allies in both preventing and fighting-off the blues.

Increase our physical activity: When it comes to our understanding of physical activity, Loughborough University's School of Sport and Exercise Sciences is arguably one of the best centres in the world, and its long-time head, Professor Stuart Biddle, has been a pioneer among the 1,000 or so studies to date which have all agreed the following: to beat the blues, vigorous physical activity can be part of the prevention and part of the cure. More than one excellent study has found physical activity just as good as all the new fangled pharmaceuticals that are intended to lift depression, besides which the drugs tend to have side-effects and also leave us vulnerable to recurrent episodes.

All of our moods, whether joyous or painful, operate largely through the chemical and electrical mechanisms which run our mind and body. Exercise helps change this chemistry and so changes how we feel.

It's good to know then that just a 10 minute brisk walk will mean more energy and less tension even two hours later. 60 minutes exercise will have substantial mood benefits that last all day and probably through to the next. And the more we invest, the more we'll gain. Vigorously exercising for 45 minutes three times per week for 16 weeks has been shown equally effective as the leading anti-depressant medication for depression, and yet the exercise achieves this with few if any side-effects. In fact, exercise both reduces anxiety and increases happiness, so imagine what a daily routine could achieve. This is why half an hour, five days out of seven, is the recommended maintenance dose.

Ellen Degeneres had this to say about exercise in the aftermath of her girlfriend leaving her back in 2000: "It feels like your insides are cracking open. I hadn't experienced it before. I had never had my heart broken. And it feels like you cannot go on. And I would sit and literally not know where the day went. The sun would come up and the sun would go down, and I didn't notice because I was just staring at the wall. I didn't leave my house. I would go through days of crying. It felt like I would never live again. I decided the best revenge is living well. So I decided, I'm going to get up and I'm going to start working-out every single day because I know that makes me feel good. No, I didn't feel like getting up and going to the gym and working out, but I just had to do something to take care of myself, and I couldn't make myself feel better in any other way, other than physically. So I worked out with a trainer every single day. And it started making me feel better... Somehow it does something to you inside. It reminds you in the smallest way that your whole life isn't about this pain. It sounds silly, but it really does."

Worry won't solve anything but it will ruin our sleep: When depressed, our sleep is likely to be disturbed, probably characterised by waking very early and not being able to get back to sleep again; and also waking feeling exhausted. This is very likely caused by us 'ruminating' during the daytime, i.e. churning over worries unhappily in our mind. If we can prevent ourselves from ruminating in this way during our waking hours, then our brain will not have to work nearly so hard at night to neutralise all those 'red-alert worry-lights' that have been turned on in our brain during the day. We can prevent such rumination by distracting ourselves with enjoyable and immediately satisfying tasks, or by finding company to talk with about cheerier things. UN Ambassador and former US First Lady, Eleanor Roosevelt, took just that approach. "If I feel depressed, I go to work." Likewise, Claire Rayner, experienced clinical depression in her teenage years, and explains, "I learned the uses of distraction. The worse I felt, the more important it was to have lots of books to read, and read I did at great speed, but not missing a single word. By the end of two or three marathon sessions, I would feel much better able to cope."

Another powerful approach is to set aside an hour every day to problem-solve our worries, but make them out-of-bounds at all other times of the day. Our aim is to prevent them sprawling and by doing so dragging down other arenas of our life.

Improve our social life: All by itself, building a better social life of rewarding personal relationships is probably the strongest and most reliable source of improving our physical and psychological health. We are highly social animals and thrive in the company of others, whereas loneliness can lead to ruminating and looking inwards, so let's make every effort to team up. Joining a local club, voluntary society or neighbourhood group can introduce us to a healthy variety of new personalities and points of view.

Identify some pleasurable activities for ourselves: engage our brain in happily pursuing them. Our brains and bodies are never happier than when on route, preferably in someone's good company. Helping another person always feel good, so does walking in the country or cooking food together. We need to ask ourselves what have we enjoyed in the past, and how could we reintroduce such things into our daily lives.

Learn to be more optimistic: If we learn to be optimistic, (i.e. routinely expecting things to go well if we make some smart efforts) we will benefit greatly in every arena of our lives: study and work, personal relationships, and our physical and psychological health. We will live longer, healthier and happier. *That's not optimistic thinking, that's a fact.* And the good news is that optimism is a skill we can all acquire. Essentially, we need to generate at least three different *positive* ways of looking at a problem. We might also remind ourselves that depression is not simply a result of something that happens to us, because it's not uncommon for someone to lose their job, or to lose a loved one, and yet they do not become depressed. This is because depression is our reaction to something, and so it lies within our power to change this reaction by generating positive thoughts and activities. By way of example, British middle distance runner, Kelly Holmes, has admitted the dream of future Olympic glory in Athens stopped her quitting the sport a couple of years before when she was recovering from chronic fatigue syndrome. "I could have given up. I had depression, *everything*. But I felt in my heart one day it might happen."

Reconsider our goals: A fabulous psychiatrist called Randolph Nesse at Michigan University is arguing that depression can sometimes serve the strongly beneficial purpose of telling us to stop our activities and reconsider. Professor Nesse proposes that depression could be a healthy response to our unhelpful tendency to set ourselves goals that are too large and too distant. All the evidence suggests we derive far more satisfaction from pursuing highly manageable, shorter-term goals, indeed multiple goals so long as they are all pulling in compatible directions. Professor Nesse notes how Homo Sapiens demonstrate a profound capacity for deep emotional and often lifelong commitments to other individuals, and to our vocation, and to the place we call home . . . and that our brains are well designed for intimate relationships *not* over-blown ambitions.

Diana, Princess of Wales, suffered post-natal depression and said this of the experience: "You'd wake up in the morning feeling you didn't want to get out of bed, you felt misunderstood, and just very, very low in yourself. I had never had a depression in my life. But then when I analysed it I could see that the changes I'd made in the last year had all caught up with me, and my body had said 'We want a rest.' "

Good nutrition: Omega-3 fats (no matter in fish oil or vegetarian form) have been shown to be strongly connected to lifting depression and promoting happier moods, far more effectively, it is believed, than any existing pharmaceutical alternatives. Moreover, when omega-3 is taken together with oils rich in omega-6, the combination provides an optimum balance. Taking a good quality an all-in-one 3 and 6 omega oil supplement would be one good way to achieve this. These omega oils may be particularly important for pregnant mums as a guard against post-natal depression, *but a medical practitioner's advice on what supplements may be warranted is always necessary for a pregnant or breast-feeding mother.*

In addition to the importance of omega oils, surveys have found that 50% of women and 10% of men had border-line iron deficiency levels, a state which can easily mimic the early symptoms of depression. It is not for nothing that out-patient hospitals dealing with depression will routinely conduct blood-tests to screen new clients for vitamin and mineral deficiencies.

Adequate daylight: Our brain needs at least an hour per day of broad daylight, and in winter times, if this is hard to come by, we should consider investing in a good quality Seasonal Affective Disorder lamp, one that can deliver an adequate dose of 10,000 lux of light. (Lux is a measurement of light intensity.)

See a professional therapist: All of the above are intended as complementary approaches to the guidance we could receive from a therapist. I've addressed this above and in the *Nick's Special Topic* chapter in the back of the book; and let's take courage from knowing that celebrated author Joanne K. Rowling, Olympic champion Kelly Holmes, and Princess Diana, are just three of many people who have benefited greatly from seeing a psychotherapist for their depression. More of this in the paragraphs below.

Considering prescription medication: I'm not against using prescription anti-depressant medication when the combination of the circumstances and the individual require it, but I think their effects for each and everyone of us needs to be frequently monitored by the medical practitioner who prescribes them. I fear they have too often been over-used and their usefulness to the individual patient has been inadequately monitored by some over-burdened medical professionals. What seems very likely is that depression reoccurs far more often after medication than after psychotherapy. Medication might be appropriate for short-term symptom relief over a few months, but we should be very cautious of its longer-term use. In any event, such medication should only be one of the whole complement of dynamic approaches I have outlined above.

Herbal remedies: St. John's Wort is a herb that has been shown to be equally effective (without the side-effects) of the best known anti-depressants. We must be proceed wisely though, because herbs have active ingredients just like a prescription drug, and should be treated with caution and respect. But it seems that St. John's Wort is, for many people, far more brain-friendly and body-friendly than prescription anti-depressants. There are other herbs with a good reputation for anti-depressant qualities, well worth finding out about.

Our willingness to bring variety and a spirit of exploration to our particular problem, will be powerful allies to us. By combining the various methods above, we increase the chance that our rich combination of approaches will make rapid improvements.

From Personal Experience
When faced with depression, let's remember, we're not alone:

Sir Winston Churchill and Marie Curie, twice winner of the Nobel Prize, suffered black days of depression, but were nonetheless able to lead extraordinary lives.

Indigenous Australian runner, Cathy Freeman, tells how she suffered depression after her gold medal win at the 2000 Olympics in Sydney, in some part due to the expectations she felt were thrust upon her. "Training became just a waste of time, a waste of energy. I wanted to sleep instead of getting back on the track. It was actually quite scary. For the first time in my life I was relinquishing something that I thought I could never do without: *running fast.*" Cathy's manager spotted the tell-tale symptoms of depression and convinced her to see a psychologist who helped her move on in her life. Now that she's retired, Cathy has recalibrated her goals. "Connecting with people is my new passion now," and is involved with an Australian foundation called I*nspire* which reaches out to young people in rural regions who are having a tough time coping with life.

Ellen Degeneres had her TV show cancelled after she came out as a gay woman. "I went through a very tough period after the show got cancelled . . . I worked for 20 years to get to where I was and suddenly just by revealing this one thing that I was scared to reveal, everything was wiped out. It's your biggest fear. I went through a pretty deep depression for a while, and didn't know if I was going to be able to make it back out." Ellen has now been able to rekindle her career and reach extraordinary new heights, not least because of her enchanting performance as the voice of the fish, Dory, in the block-busting movie, *Finding Nemo,* and her award-winning new talk show, *Ellen.*

Children's writer, Joanne K. Rowling was a young mum struggling to make ends meet for herself and her infant daughter, when she suffered a bout of clinical depression. "I never expected to mess up so badly that I would find myself in an unheated, mouse-infested flat, looking after my daughter . . . I didn't suffer depression for very long, but I vividly recollect what it felt like. It is that absence of being able to envisage that you will ever be cheerful again. The absence of hope." Joanne's experience made a lasting impact on her and inspired the Dementors, who suck all the joy and life out of the prisoners in her Harry Potter novels. It was for her daughter's sake that she sought counselling. "She was my touchstone. If it hadn't been for her, I probably would never have had the courage to go to the doctor and say I needed to talk about things." It also helped that Joanne was working on her novel. "Writing was very helpful to my sanity. It gave me something to focus on." By the end of that period, she had put her name down for a course to qualify as a senior school teacher that next year, a course in which she eventually shone. Joanne now uses her fame and fortune to support charities that help young mums in need, which is a fine example of how even our roughest times can be put on the furnace so as to fuel positive actions.

When it comes to anxiety, there's more than one sort

The Harvard researchers, Drs Tom Perls and Margery Silver, specialise in studying those individuals who have reached 100 years of age in exceptionally good psychological and physical health. The researchers describe worry as an 'ageing accelerator' because anxious states produce the sort of battle-ready chemicals which, if prolonged, can be harmful to digestion, skin, heart, and brain. This is why coping well with stress is a crucial skill. We might not avoid life's slings and arrows, but we can sure learn how to deal with them.

Everyday anxiety, such as run of the mill worries and apprehensions, respond very well to gentle, slow breathing for at least ten minutes, twice per day. This is because our rate of breathing affects what state our brain is in, i.e. relaxed or tense. To complement our relaxed breathing, we can take each of our muscle groups in turn, tensing them for three long seconds, and then releasing the muscles to a very relaxed state. Take twice as long for releasing as for tensing. We should do this for each muscle group of our body: arms, legs, stomach, and so on . . . including our face.

Anxiety Disorders

Everyday worries are one thing, but 'Anxiety Disorders' are a very uncomfortable state of unease which prevents us enjoying and progressing in our everyday lives. Such disorders can come in several different forms, and although 21st century psychology now knows how to make very major improvements in most cases, this entirely relies upon us correctly identifying the type of anxiety. This is why it's important to team up with a professional clinician who can distinguish one ilk from another and which approach is most appropriate for it.

The following section explores six different types of anxiety, so at least we know what we're up against. That said, no matter which brand of anxiety we're suffering from, in the great majority of cases, psychological measures are better than drug-therapy by a considerable distance, very largely because people treated with drug therapies are prone to relapse soon after they cease taking the medication.

Phobia is an unreasonable and excessive fear of quite particular things such as the dark, spiders, cats, crowds, heights, flying, or being home alone. This will usually be due to some incident in which we have learnt, perhaps unwittingly, to fear something. To tackle phobias, the treatment of choice is systematic desensitisation, though methods such as 'flooding' or 'reality testing' are equally good in most cases.

Social Phobia is an excessive fear of feeling humiliation or embarrassment in public. (For children this might mean a phobia about how their peers will judge them.) This is strongly related to shyness.

Agoraphobia (from the Greek meaning 'fear of the marketplace') can often develop out of Panic Disorder (see below), but can also be unrelated. We become irrationally afraid of falling ill or needing help or being caught short while out and about in some public space where we would be helpless, yet no one would help us. Physical symptoms might include dizziness, nausea or fainting.

Panic Disorder is an overwhelming fear that some catastrophe will befall us. There's a range of physical symptoms such as shortness of breath, dizziness, racing heart, chest pains, nausea, or a cold sweat. We fear that we literally might die, or go mad, or lose control. We might also fear we are suffering from some severe medical problem, or are having a heart attack or a stroke. The attack begins abruptly, peaks within about ten minutes, and then subsides gradually.

General Anxiety Disorder is a situation in which most of our day, *everyday*, for week after week, is filled with a sense of worry and anxiousness. We're jittery, on edge, tense and nervous, and this state is likely to leave us tired, irritable and sleeping poorly.

Obsessive-Compulsive Disorder is characterised by repetitive thoughts or images or impulses that we find very hard to resist. These might include repetitive washing or cleaning, or checking that taps are turned off, or saying a lucky mantra, or thinking a particular thought. We know the frequency of such thoughts or behaviours are excessive and unreasonable, but we are unable to stop them intruding much of the time. The purpose being served by these compulsive rituals of mind or body, is to reduce our sense of anxiety, though this underlying goal might not always be obvious to us.

From the small list above, we can perhaps appreciate how important it is to find a clinician who knows how to help us deal best with whichever type of anxiety is troubling us. The worse thing we can do is allow the problem to force us to avoid situations or distort our life in a vain attempt to postpone confronting the problem. If we act to see a professional immediately, we could make major improvements in just a handful of sessions, even with some very long-standing and debilitating problems. The reward for our enterprise will be our ability to work unhampered towards our heart-felt ambitions and, of course, freedom from the anxiety itself. A psychological approach called Cognitive-Behavioural Therapy, particularly when supported by the techniques of Clinical Hypnosis (see in later section) has proven very effective for anxiety in all of its forms.

Let's take inspiration from boxing legend, Muhammad Ali, who confides, "The one thing that I have always feared is airplanes. For a while I was serious about not going to Italy for the 1960 Olympics, and then I thought about what my father said, 'Always confront the things you fear.' I realized that we are only brave when we have something to lose and we still try. We can't be brave without fear. I realized that this was one of those important moments when I would have to make a choice . . . and I knew it would have a great impact on my life. If I didn't get on that plane, I couldn't win the gold medal. If I had not faced that fear and gone on to win the gold medal at the Olympics, I might not have become the heavyweight champion of the world. If I let fear stand in my way, I would never have accomplished anything important in my life. Having made the decision, I was soon on my way to Italy."

Overcoming shyness

Shyness is a tough jailor that can considerably hinder our enjoyment and progress in life. If we're shy, though we might crave companionship, we cannot easily or freely declare our true hopes and hungers, nor ask questions or invite mentorship. We might also be timid about expressing our heart-felt affection, or be overly wary of accepting affection from others because we fear that we'll only prove to be a disappointment to them. Shyness can indirectly bring us even more pain if we try to bolster ourselves with alcohol, or occasionally blow our tops with ill-judged outbursts of self-expression. We might even end up resenting those who don't seem to suffer shyness. If any of these symptoms rings a bell of recognition, it might come as some reassurance that the BBC's Kate Adie, General Sir Peter de la Billiere formerly of the Special Air Service, and Indian spiritual and political leader, Mahatma Ghandi, are just three individuals among many who have led lives as inspiring pioneers, yet they have all written about having to overcome their considerable shyness. In fact most people in one type of situation or at one time of life, have been painfully held back by shyness, and a large minority are shy in just about every situation which involves presenting themselves to unfamiliar people in some context.

Shyness is a phobia, that's to say it's an over-blown and unhelpful fear derived from our conscious and subconscious sources. In the case of shyness, we fear being evaluated by our audience very likely because we fear being disapproved of or even humiliated on account of our appearance, our ideas, or our mode of expression. Paradoxically, our excessive anxiety to do well and create a good impression, will not only inhibit our performance, it will also put our audience on edge. And as with any other phobia, we can accidentally allow it to dictate how we lead our lives, perhaps by narrowing our educational or career horizons, or negatively affecting how we behave in our social and personal lives. However, we shouldn't think that the opposite of shyness is showing off, since the need to be the centre of attention is simply another form of being overly anxious about the impression we're creating, and to all intents and purposes the exhibitionist is woefully subservient to other people's assessment.

The true opposite of shyness is being able to forget ourselves so completely that we can enter the psychological 'flow' state characterised by focusing our attention entirely on the task and so increasing the likelihood that we will perform at the height of our abilities. All the better if we can put our audience so at ease that they forget themselves, too, so that the content is at the forefront of everyone's mind.

So how do we achieve such a useful level of skill?
First, it helps to recognise that a phobia, like any other bully, often operates as part of a little gang of life-restricting behaviours. For instance, shyness is a close relative of perfectionism, so we might harbour an exaggerated need to do things just right. Shyness might also signal a lack of self-worth, fearing that we've nothing much to offer. And this tendency to focus on negative possibilities rather than positives ones, probably indicates a pessimistic perspective on life that will also undermine our everyday endeavours.

When faced with bullies, the more we try to dodge and avoid them, the more restricting they become. By far our best bet is to arm ourselves with some relevant know-how and then face up to those things that bring us dread. The good news is that when it comes to tackling shyness, what's known as cognitive-behavioural therapy can be an ally to us in challenging all of our self-defeating assumptions which more often than not are rooted in the out-of-date thinking habits from our earlier life experiences. As soon as we resolutely challenge their accuracy, then after our out-of-proportion fears, perfectionism, pessimism and self-consciousness will begin to melt away. By using imaginative role-play or a state of hypnosis, we can experience some success in ever more demanding situations, and so gradually desensitise ourselves to being observed or evaluated. We then move on to some manageable real life try-outs which by then will have lost much of their sting. Throughout all of this, we'll be aiming to associate the once feared situations with new feelings of physical relaxation and emotional pleasure. Such work is the bread and butter of any good coach or therapist, and the more daily practice we put in to performing in a calm and enjoyable and un-selfconscious way, the more pleasure we'll bring ourselves and our audience.

Neutralising the negative emotions of trauma

Perhaps we've suffered some single event (e.g. a car crash or physical assault), or perhaps the suffering was recurrent and long-term (e.g. childhood bullying). Either way, these experiences can sometimes cause psychological trauma (also referred to as Post-Traumatic Stress Disorder or PTSD) which might lead to any number of physical or psychological symptoms, ranging from persistent anxiety to emotional numbness, and from sleeplessness to loss of appetite. What has happened, is at the time of its occurrence, that initiating incident was perceived by our brain as being intensely negative, and this negative feeling has lodged like a piece of emotional shrapnel in our memories. From then on it can handicap our progress in life. Here, former US President Bill Clinton recounts how difficult he found it to write his autobiography because of a traumatic incident in his own childhood. "I did have periods when I had to just get up and drop it — it was just too hot. I have that pretty gripping scene in the early part of the book where my stepfather was drunk and he had the gun in his hand and he shot it off, and my mother and I were standing in the hall and the bullet goes in the wall between us. I felt it all over again. It was frightening."

PTSD very often goes undiagnosed or untreated. This is no longer necessary, because there are *two* therapies for PTSD that are not yet widely adopted, but which are very promising for certain individuals under certain conditions. These are the Rewind Technique, and EMDR.

Rewind Technique
The therapy is known variously as the Rewind Technique or V-K Dissociation or even The Fast Phobia Cure (but this last name is a bit confusing, because it's effective with so much more than phobias.) This technique can be used for fully-blown PTSD or to detraumatise (i.e. neutralise the negative emotions) the worst instances of a phobia or a panic attack. It can aid in all of the other anxiety disorders, simply by means of re-associating a vividly imagined version of the once feared stimulus with a highly relaxed state, rather than an anxious one.

I do not recount the technique in any detail here, because it is far more safe and effective if carried out with a therapist whose been thoroughly trained in its proper use. That said, the technique itself is simple, straightforward and reliable, and is founded on good psychological principles. In a nutshell, it involves us being helped to achieve a deep state of relaxation before rerunning the traumatic scene backwards and forwards in our mind's eye . . . several times one after the other and at varying speeds . . . as if we're watching it on a video screen. Throughout these self-generated screenings backwards and forwards of the traumatising scenes, we aim to remain very calm and deeply relaxed in mind and body. Eventually the negative emotions will fade away, and our response to the scene becomes neutral. All of this procedure is achieved with the guidance of the therapist reassuring us and calming us if we become over-anxious. At its best, this technique will help us to find complete relief from flashbacks, and enable us to speak about the trauma or traumas without alarm or anxiety. We should also acquire a more positive mood and confidence for life generally.

Very importantly, in using this rewind technique, the therapist does not need to know any of the details of the trauma. Being able to keep completely private the intimate and distressing details of our traumatising incident, can be a very reassuring aspect of this technique.

EMDR (Eye Movement Desensitisation and Reprocessing)

This is another technique well worth considering. It has elements related to the Rewind Technique (just mentioned above) but is also substantially different. In broad terms, it works like this: while we recall the trauma, both visually in our imagination and also its emotional and physical elements, the therapist moves a finger back and forth rapidly just a foot or so in front of our face, so that it can be followed by our eyes while our head remains still. The therapist's finger or pen might make any number of these rapid left-right passes in front of our eyes. With rests in between, this process is repeated several times while the therapist encourages us to focus on the thoughts, emotions and physical feelings attached to the memory. Research so far suggests that the eye movement stimulates our brain in a way which helps us to better access and digest deeply upsetting emotions. It also seems the case that eye movement isn't necessary, and that any form of body movement, tapping our fingers for instance, that stimulates first the left and then the right side of the brain in quick succession, is equally effective. Results have been encouraging for otherwise difficult cases, but the procedure must be carried out by a clinician properly trained in its use, (commonly referred to as Level 2 EMDR training, not simply Level 1 or Intermediate training), and one who also possesses a good background of clinical training in general diagnosis and a range of therapeutic alternatives.

Making counter-attacks on migraines

Migraines affect about 12% of the population in the Western world. If you or one of your loved ones are suffering from migraines, you'll know only too well that they can be excruciatingly painful and can severely interfere with your day-to-day life. Unfortunately, however, according to the British Migraine Action Association, around 60% of migraine sufferers have never consulted their healthcare provider, either because they don't like to trouble anyone, or they believe that nothing can be done to help them. Often their experience of a previously prescribed treatment is that it did not help and so they have not felt it worthwhile to go back. Rather than suffer in silence like this, better to seek out a specialist migraine clinic, the like of which are now available in many countries. In the U.K. alone, there are more than 20 such clinics providing specialist advice and treatment to sufferers about the new and increasingly effective drug treatments that are coming out every few months.

Seeking help is all the more important, because migraines may not be a series of attacks, but unbeknown to the sufferer they might be the symptoms of a progressive brain disease which doubles the likelihood of stroke in sufferers. The risk analysis comes from a review conducted by a group of Canadian, Spanish, and American scientists of fourteen studies on the link between migraines and stroke. In particular, people whose migraines are accompanied by auras, lights or other visual disturbances, are at somewhat higher risk of a future stroke than are those whose migraines do not produce auras. In addition, female migraine sufferers who take oral contraceptives have eight times greater odds of a stroke. Smoking is still a bigger risk factor for stroke, but if you are a migraine sufferer, it might be sensible to discuss with your doctor whether you might be at risk, and if so, how this risk can be managed, both by cutting down other risk factors for stroke, such as high blood pressure, and by finding ways to reduce the number and severity of the attacks.

On a far more cheerful note, it is exciting to learn that acupuncture has proved to be a powerful ally in the fight against migraine. In a study of more than 300 sufferers in England and Wales in 2004, half the patients received up to 12 acupuncture treatments over three months, as opposed to conventional medication from their doctor. Those who received the acupuncture had on average 22 fewer days of headache a year, took 15 per cent fewer days off work, and used 15 per cent fewer drugs. It is reassuring to know that these results are consistent with numerous similar studies carried out in Italy, Germany and Denmark over the past ten years. It would seem there's no better time than now to discuss the possibilities of acupuncture or other alternative migraine remedies.

Controlling unhelpful yeasts in our digestive system

Candidiasis is the term for unhelpful types or quantities of yeast in our digestive system, which can spread to many other parts of our body. This is why symptoms are various, and might comprise one or more of the following: a difficult digestion, asthma or fatigue, cravings for sweet foods (or bread or alcohol), recurrent infections, allergies or sensitivities, and skin problems such as acne, mouth-ulcers, rashes, thrush or cystitis. It can also be the root cause of aches and pains (particularly of the back and neck), or migraines, pre-menstrual syndrome or depression. In children, infections of the eyes, nose and throat may be recurrent, or there may even be behavioural problems such as hyperactivity, irritability or severe tiredness.

As you can imagine, it's the sheer variety of symptoms that can allow this increasingly common problem to go misdiagnosed.

What causes it? In physical terms, candidiasis is an overgrowth of an otherwise friendly yeast which inhabits our digestive system. This could be for a number of reasons, and opinion is divided. It could be due to taking the contraceptive pill or Hormone Replacement Therapy, since these both can alter the body's natural balance, as can any strong prescription medicines. Or it might be the sorts of foods we commonly eat, if they're high in sugar or yeasts. On the other hand, the yeast overgrowth could be due to a bout of illness or psychological stress or insufficient sleep. It's worth giving some thoughts to possible causes because we'll want to remove these as part of putting things right.

What to do? We should make an appointment with a properly qualified nutritionist who is experienced and interested in evaluating and treating our candida. Candida is a resilient problem and will come back with a vengeance if we don't approach it wisely. Our nutritionist will be able to make a correct diagnosis of whether we have candidiasis and in what form. They can then help us determine the likely cause, and the best way forward. This is definitely *not* something we should try to treat ourselves, at least not until we are being guided by an experienced practitioner, because candidiasis tends to be too complicated. We need a tailor-made approach. Things could show encouraging improvement within a week or two, but it might be a year before we're really back in charge of it. Seeing a qualified nutritionist every 6 weeks or couple of months will help us keep on track.

Once we're working with a nutritionist, we need to read up about it and be prepared to be tenacious on several different fronts at the same time, just as we should with any problem. That means improving our lifestyle, the foods we eat, (and those we should probably avoid such as sugary, yeasty or fermented foods like breads, mushrooms, some sauces, vinegars and alcohol.) We might also need to take a range of nutritional supplements and probiotics (friendly bacteria) that will help re-populate our body with friendly bacteria.

On a final note, I cannot over-emphasise the likely underlying role played by psychological stress or distress as a root cause of candidiasis, i.e. our deep-seated emotional troubles and/or over-demanding schedule can themselves create a physical climate within our body in which candida can run out of control. The direct physical measures as outlined above may alleviate the symptoms, but it is only by addressing the root cause of how we feel and how we lead our everyday emotional life, that we will be able to sustain improvements and restore a healthy digestive balance.

Rediscovering an ancient remedy for Pre-Menstrual Syndrome

Claire Rayner writes about her teenage years in the 1940s: "If I was ever going to have a row with someone, or get into trouble, it was always in that few days before a period. But who knew about PMS then?" Fortunately, medical research has caught up considerably since Claire's day, and now PMS is a recognised condition estimated to affect up to 75% of women during their childbearing years, and is characterised by a range of physical and psychological symptoms that occur throughout the menstrual cycle. The symptoms usually begin somewhere between five and eleven days before the start of menstruation, and usually stop when menstruation begins, or shortly thereafter. Of the 75% of women who suffer PMS, more than one third report symptoms that are severe enough to affect their daily activities. No one knows the exact cause, but several factors may contribute to the condition, such as cyclic changes in hormones, chemical changes in the brain, and low levels of vitamins and minerals in one's daily diet. This presents a great challenge to medical practitioners who often need to resort to a range of conventional and alternative remedies to help women alleviate specific symptoms such as irritability or bloating.

Germany seems to be leading the way with research on a traditional herbal remedy called Chasteberry, or 'Agnus castus' to use its botanical name. Chasteberries grow on the chaste tree, a large shrub indigenous to southern Europe, the Mediterranean region, and Asia. In those regions, chasteberry has been used since ancient Greek times as a treatment for menstrual problems and was a mainstay of monastic medicine, hence its name. The dried ripe berries contain a mixture of powerful ingredients that appear to alter our release of reproductive hormones and so relieve PMS.

In a recent study in Germany of 170 women diagnosed with PMS, half received chasteberry extract and the other half received placebos (which are fake pills to test whether it's just wishful thinking that will lead to improvements). Over the course of three menstrual cycles, more than half the women using chasteberry had a 50% reduction in their levels of irritability, anger, headaches, and breast fullness, when compared with women taking the dummy tablets.

In two earlier German surveys involving 1,500 women, one-third of the women had complete relief from PMS symptoms, while another 57% reported significant improvements. This led doctors to rate 'chasteberry extract' as being good or very good 90% of the time. Recent clinical studies in Switzerland and Turkey have confirmed the benefits of chasteberry and the near absence of side-effects. It is also reassuring that conventional medical practice in Germany approves chasteberry for menstrual irregularities, breast pain, and premenstrual complaints.

(As always, it is important that you consult your clinician before deciding on which route to take, and pregnant women or women taking hormone therapies of any kind should *not* use chasteberry.)

Considering alternative therapies

We would always do well to consult our mainstream medical practitioner as a first port of call, before considering who else we could go to for a professional opinion. However, we need to bear in mind that a practitioner trained in one therapeutic approach may not have sufficient information or incentive to recommend that we go try a practitioner trained in another approach. This means that our doctor, or acupuncturist, or psychotherapist simply may not volunteer what else and who else might work very well for us. This shouldn't really present a problem, because we always need to be proactive in asking around for advice from a range of health centres and self-help groups, as well as exploring the possibilities by reading up-to-date books on alternative approaches, and searching on the internet to see what might be happening abroad. We should remember that countries like the UK, the USA, Germany and Japan are quite different from each other in the directions they've taken with a whole range of orthodox and complementary approaches. For instance, in Japan, powerful therapeutic magnets are commonly used to alleviate long-lasting aches and pains that don't respond to other treatments. In Germany, many herbs can be prescribed by general practitioners, such as St. John's Wort for depression.

Once we've identified some promising avenues, we need to make sure that our intended practitioner has good qualifications appropriate to their specialism, whether that's hypnosis, homeopathy or kinesiology. It's very important that we know whether the individual possesses a practitioner's diploma issued by a well-established institution, or whether they merely have an introductory weekend workshop 'attendance certificate'. To do this check properly, we need to contact their diploma-awarding body and confirm the length and level of training that such a qualification has required. We also need to confirm with the institution that they have that person on their books as registered to practice, and whether or not that individual is recognised as having an area of expertise appropriate to our problem. (They may well not, but it would be nice to know if such specific experts actually exist and, if so, how they might be found. For instance, some psychologists using hypnosis will specialise solely in the treatment of Irritable Bowel Syndrome or depression.)

By way of example of what we might expect, homeopathy in the UK would normally mean at least a two year full-time course to become a well-qualified practitioner, and has a very promising reputation among the healing professions, having shown itself helpful for a significant number of people and with a range of resistant problems . . . from sleep or skin problems, through to depression and pain. By contrast to the entire discipline that is homeopathy, the very particular therapeutic skill of hypnosis is more likely to require perhaps three working weeks of intensively supervised training and examinations as well as extensive homework to enable individuals who are already experienced nurses, dentists, doctors or psychotherapists to reach a reasonable practitioner standard. (More on hypnosis below.)

The final judgement is ours to make, but if we are thorough in our investigations, at least we will be making a more enlightened decision. What we're trying to avoid by all these efforts is having a bad experience with an inadequately trained and poorly experienced practitioner whose incompetence puts us off the whole idea of finding a solution. We want to give the new approach a really fair chance at helping us, to which end just a couple of sessions with someone really good at what they do is likely to be far more helpful than any amount of sessions with someone still learning the ropes. We owe it to ourselves and our spirit of exploration to be really thorough.

The cure does not necessarily indicate the cause

Just because a cure is physical, does not mean the problem was. For instance, frequent and vigorous physical activity may lift depression, but that is not to say lack of physical activity has necessarily caused that depression. Similarly, the fact that hypnosis may alleviate a problem, simply indicates to us how the mind can strongly influence the body. After all, when we're embarrassed, we might blush; if we're anxious, we might stammer on our words; if we have a phobia we might recoil in fear from something harmless. Putting this idea in a line: the cause and the cure do not have to be from the same camp, they simply have to cross paths.

Hypnosis is a highly effective technique for a range of problems

Hypnosis has been used safely and effectively for well over 50 years in western medicine, and its powerful therapeutic role is now fully recognised by the American Psychological Association. This side of the Atlantic, one of the UK's leading psychology departments, University College London, has taught a professional post-graduate diploma course since the early 1990s, for use largely by psychologists, medical doctors, nurses and dentists. Moreover, coaches to Olympic athletes will routinely use hypnosis to reinforce the effect of their psychological and physical training strategies.

What is it?

Hypnosis is not a therapy in itself, it's a particular technique, a way of doing therapy that can be used to enhance various different approaches. Because it's a tool rather than a broader diagnostic approach, hypnosis can only be useful once an experienced psycho-therapist has diagnosed the particular problem or set of problems, and suggested how to tackle them. Hypnosis can then help to deliver those helpful strategies, but it can't replace them. This is why it takes an experienced psychotherapist to know what role hypnosis can play in this whole process.

Hypnosis is the Greek word meaning sleep, but in fact, when we're in a hypnotic trance state, we're far from asleep. Our attention is simply very focused, and whatever we're imagining feels very real. We will not do or say anything we don't want to, and we'll not get trapped in that state. Far from being passive automatons, we're very able to explore new possibilities and conjure scenes.

As part of our daily lives, we go in and out of such focused trances of concentration all of the time, for example when we're very intently focused on some internal thought or activity, disconnected from background realities, having tuned out all the distractions. Reading a book or daydreaming to music, anything in which the surroundings fade away and we're focused ... or 'entranced'. That focus of our attention can be on positive events that might conjure optimism, relaxation or some productive activity ... or that focus can be on negative events that might muster feelings of anger, regret or shame. Hence, the depressed or anxious person is already in their own hypnotic trance: focused on one unhelpful thought or activity. In which case, the therapist needs to help them release their unhelpfully narrowed attention and take a more positive perspective. For instance, I might give up my recurrent regrets about the past, and with the help of the therapist start feeling enthusiastic about what I can do in the present to improve my future possibilities.

When it comes down to it, *all* hypnosis is self-hypnosis … it's something we do to ourselves, and the therapist is merely guiding us in helpfully using the technique. In terms of exactly how it works, scientists aren't quite sure yet, but it seems likely that when we're in trance, our *conscious* mind is taking a backseat, and the *subconscious* mind is far more open to new ideas and new ways of doing things. That's why hypnosis can help break unwanted habits and build new ones, even such seemingly automatic activities as our speech or digestion.

Some myths

We don't have to be relaxed to be in a hypnotic state; nor do we need a good imagination or a particular type of personality. It can't help us remember the past any more accurately, nor do we genuinely regress to our past lives. When in a hypnotic state, we are vividly imagining things rather than remembering them.

Some facts

Clinical Hypnosis, when used to deliver appropriate therapeutic goals and strategies has proved to be extremely effective. Here's a small sample of its treatment areas:

Depression: Hypnosis has been shown to be very useful if combined with Cognitive Behavioural Therapy for the treatment of depression, as well as for anxiety and phobias and Post Traumatic Stress Disorder.

Irritable Bowel Syndrome: characterised by difficult and distressing digestive problems of one form or another, such as painful stomach cramps, abdominal bloating, diarrhoea, or constipation. It's estimated that one in four adult women probably suffer from some problematic level of symptoms. Studies show that over 75% of people with IBS can find circa 90% relief of all their symptoms; and five year follow-ups of people who've worked on their problem with self-hypnosis suggest the great majority of people maintain these gains, and some improve upon them.

Pain Reduction: Hypnosis has been shown to be highly effective in substantially reducing pain, for instance, in surgical operations, dentistry, or births conducted without the use of anaesthetics. It can provide relief for a large majority of participants, and can be used for both short term and long term pain conditions.

Stopping Smoking: In the great majority of studies, 50% or more of patients give up and remain non-smokers after between just one and three hours of one-to-one anti-smoking therapy that is rooted strongly in hypnosis.

Hypnosis is a state of mind in which to explore and experience positive possibilities

Hypnosis provides vivid imaginal experiences (visual, emotional and physical) in which we can try out new ways of behaving, or responding. This imaginal work is a state in which we can rehearse new skills safely, easily, and confidently. We can use this state to reframe the problem, by which I mean see it from another perspective. We can use it to improve our horizons of what's possible and expectations of what will happen. And we can also use our imaginations to travel forward into the future to vividly experience living without our inhibiting symptoms. In hypnosis, the extinction of symptoms can be experienced so convincingly, that it makes putting that reality into action far more possible. To increase the effectiveness of the technique, the therapist will draw upon our particular strengths and likes along with our personal experiences so as to weave these into our mental rehearsals. Coaching for executives and athletes particularly uses this method of building on our strengths. It allows us to surpass invisible and unrecognised subconscious barriers that may be holding us back. Five times gold medal Olympic rower, Sir Steve Redgrave tells of how his coach used an hypnotic technique to allow his team to imaginally rehearse a successful performance. It can be equally effective in building our self-confidence for public speaking or social occasions.

In conclusion

Hypnosis isn't a cure, it's the tool with which a therapist and client can work together to help solve the problem. It's never the sole treatment, but it does bring powerful experiences to help change our thoughts and behaviour. Hence, we need a good diagnosis of the problem, leading to a good treatment strategy, and only then can the tool of hypnosis be used effectively. Hypnosis has been shown to be a powerful supplement to cognitive-behavioural approaches, so a therapist skilled in both Cognitive Behavioural Therapy and Clinical Hypnosis will be at an advantage in helping us.

(You can read a lot more on the subject of the sub-conscious mind and hypnosis in the chapter called *Nick's Special Topic*. To locate a therapist well-qualified in hypnosis, see the Notes in the Further Information section.)

Delaying action against a problem only makes things worse

It can seem at the time that ignoring a problem reduces its effect upon our life. We feel that if we box it up, stash it away, and avoid situations that bring it to the fore, that we are somehow getting the better of it. But this can be a dangerous illusion. In addition, it's all too easy for a serious problem to have an unexpected and invisible effect upon the directions we take in life . . . rather like a powerful magnet can dramatically influence the reading that a compass gives. By avoiding tackling a problem, it's all too easy for us to start planning our daily lives to minimise our contact with it. Then we start bearing it in mind when we make new relationships, and end up bending our ambitions and career directions so as not to provoke it. What's happening here is that the problem is subtly bullying us and penning us in. Under its unhelpful influence, our whole life grows in a distorted way reflecting the problem that like a parasite is sapping our energy and confidence.

Very often these subtly invasive distortions of our everyday life are considerably more damaging and inhibiting than the original problem. Whether it's a medical problem like an injured muscle, or a psychological problem like a powerful fear, by compensating for it, we can accidentally and unwittingly do ourselves more harm.

Not only that, but we learn a really unhelpful lesson: we learn that some problems are too big too handle and that all we can do is bury our head in the sand. So the next time something uncomfortable turns up . . . and we rarely have to wait too long . . . we may be tempted to give it our usual treatment, *and run the other way.* That's why our best strategy every time is to team-up with good people to tenaciously get the long and the short of a problem. We might not solve a problem but we can benefit enormously in mind and spirit by being resourceful and ingenious in our making progress. By doing so, we are part athlete, part explorer, part scientist, part fighter, part astronaut, and part 'escaped prisoner'. If we learn to help ourselves, we can learn to help others and become ever more a power of good to those around us.

* * *

Planning for Progress

- Which persistent health problems could you tackle with some new approaches?

- Who do you know who might be grateful to learn about these promising new solutions?

- Where could you find the very latest information about your problem and possible solutions?

* * *

PART FOUR

Choosing and Changing our Journeys and Life Directions

Making a Good Living

What we decide to do with our life, where and with whom, will all require some of the biggest decisions we'll ever have to make. This chapter considers some guiding principles and key factors we might like to keep in mind.

Coping well with all the choices

How often do you feel overwhelmed by the number of options that confront you in every arena of life, from college and career, to home and partner? Professor Barry Schwartz of Swarthmore College in Pennsylvania has deftly unmasked a growing epidemic – *too much choice.*

The problem largely arises because many of us have grown up attempting to make fully informed decisions when faced with a choice. Such a personality is termed a 'maximiser', and to some extent we're all prone to behave this way. But increasingly we tend to encounter such an excessive range of alternatives and such an ocean of information, that the perfectionist goal of finding 'the best' becomes quite paralysing and depressing. The problem being that when confronted with 50 brands of new television to choose from, all offering different combinations of pros and cons, it could take literally weeks to convince ourselves we have found the best possible deal. It seems that the worldwide web and manufacturing advances have meant that choices have increased several hundred fold for most items and experiences, but our rule-of-thumb strategies for making decisions haven't kept pace. Moreover, the cumulative effect of these ever-multiplying choices in every aspect of our life, is causing people substantial problems and dissatisfaction. We just don't know how to deal with it.

A telling example of this phenomenon is the tidy experiment that posed as a promotion offering exotic jams. When six jams were on offer, 30% of customers actually bought a jar, whereas among the comparison group confronted by 24 jams, only 3% of could-be customers made a purchase. Choice-overload quite simply put people off.

In the same way, many graduates hang painfully back from entering one of a hundred professions, because they just can't choose and are scared to commit. Even more alarming is the insidious impact of the 'maximiser strategy' upon our closest relationships, which ordinarily prove to be our richest single source of happiness and well-being. In any partnership, our own wishes must be tempered with consideration for the other person, but when so much of our world is selling us the lie that 'greater choice is synonymous with greater freedom', the boundaries and commitments of a close relationship can begin to niggle. What can happen is that, overwhelmed by the number of choices, we end up committing to no one and nothing because we can't bear the thought of not netting the best deal. This 'fear of choosing' can have profound consequences: we daren't buy the house we like in case there's a better one just around the corner; we don't marry the person we love for fear there's a more perfect match waiting somewhere down the road. Either that, or once we've made the choice, we suffer a lurking sense of dissatisfaction. What's more, society so highly prizes breadth of choice, that it's easy for us to make unhelpful assumptions, such as

"There is no excuse for second-best in a world where so much is possible. And there is certainly no excuse for unhappiness."

I'm reminded of a time when I, for one, was totally bewildered by too many options. As an undergraduate lad working at the Wimbledon Tennis Championships many years ago, by some wonderful stroke of luck I was allotted the whole two weeks as the only male waiter working alongside 24 female students. Like a boy in a sweet shop, I was so overwhelmed by the delightful choices that seemed to present themselves, I just couldn't make up my mind who to ask for a date. I'd only whittled the field down to about half a dozen, before the Wimbledon fortnight was over, and by which time the women had all decided that I didn't deserve any of them. Frustrating stuff, I can tell you. *"New balls, please!"*

Making smart decisions quick and easy

By way of an antidote to this condition, what Professor Barry Schwartz does brilliantly is attack the conventional wisdom that . . .

- the more choices we have, the better off we are.
- the best way to get good results is to have very high standards.
- it's always good to have a way to back out of a decision.

To help immunize ourselves against toxic levels of choice, Professor Schwartz suggests that first of all need to be clear about our values and priorities and key motivations in life, so we can reserve our decision-time and high standards for those handful of life's more important matters. Rather than being succoured into making choices about trivia, we're better served by self-made rules that deal swiftly with all situations of a similar ilk, such as "Visiting just two stores is quite enough for a choice of frying pan . . . refrigerator . . . and all the rest of that stuff. We could spend a week identifying the world's finest toaster, but life's too short."

When decisions are genuinely necessary, we might bear in mind that Nobel Laureate Professor Herbert Simon, observed that once we weigh-up the costs in time, money and anguish of becoming well-informed about the numerous options, it turns out that the clever strategy is to gladly accept the first one that satisfies our minimum criteria. And this principle is the bedrock of making good choices. With the great majority of choices in life 'good enough will do just fine' and will net us far greater happiness than some exhausting search for 'the best.' Our time and energy is better invested in our life's true priorities.

In all of this, let's be sure to keep our expectations deliberately modest, rather than teasing ourselves with extravagant fantasy scenarios which will only undermine the eventual reality. And let's remind ourselves that if lottery winners adapt to their windfall millions within a year, *which they reliably do*, then we can definitely adjust to the wrong colour kettle. So why agonize? Nobel Laureate psychology professor, Daniel Kahneman, won his prize for alerting economists to his observation that people are awfully bad at making accurate predictions about what will bring them most happiness and satisfaction. Life, ours included, defies accurate prediction.

Professor Schwarz offers this rule of thumb: we should not shy away from making non-reversible decisions, because not having the niggling option of backing-out will itself increase the likelihood of our finding lasting satisfaction. This focused commitment will be further helped if we mentally remove ourselves from the marketplace and pay absolutely no attention to 'new & improved' models. Computer pioneer, Bill Gates, is making just such a point when he recommends, "Don't make the same decision twice. Spend time and thought to make a solid decision the first time so that you don't revisit the issue unnecessarily. If you're too willing to reopen issues, it interferes not only with your execution but also with your motivation to make a decision in the first place. After all, why bother deciding an issue if it isn't really decided."

To deepen the roots of our decisions, we should resist comparing ourselves enviously to other people, not least because we'll most likely have a very different configuration of values and goals which will make any comparison quite meaningless, though no less disturbing to us. The only comparison necessary is with ourselves: are we making progress in our life's key relationships . . . our companions, our skills, the place we call home.

What will also help our sense of satisfaction is frequently and actively savouring the benefits of our chosen route rather than regretting the roads not taken. Actively appreciating what we have already, in terms of possessions or memories, skills or relationships, will provide far more net happiness than rushing to get our hands on some seemingly better choice. A good example of this is British athlete, Kelly Holmes, who won the hearts of the public by winning the 800m and the 1500m at the 2004 Olympics. Kelly says, "Looking back now it would be easy to say that if it hadn't been for being in the Armed Forces I might have gone to the Olympics in 1992. But at the time, my heart told me that I wanted to be in the Army, and that is what I did. I thoroughly enjoyed my time there, so I have no regrets – it was just the path I chose."

What can happen if we don't choose?

When I was at senior school, the so-called 'Careers Room' was unlocked just one lunchtime per week, but most of the material had already been stolen by previous generations. The only information boxes containing anything of note were for all those jobs you wouldn't possibly want to do, like 'Food Catering for the Oil-Rig Industry'.

This didn't bother me much because by the time I reached university, I felt that I didn't need Careers Counselling because I already knew exactly what I wanted to be: a 'Playboy' . . . as personified most endearingly by Tony Curtis and Roger Moore in the 1970's television series, *The Persuaders*. Just like those tv heroes, I wanted a Lamborghini, tight leather driving gloves, and young bikinied lovers. I also wanted to be a spy on Her Majesty's Secret Service, like James Bond. I happily imagined how my Russian counter-part Natasha and I would sip hot chocolate in mountain cafes, and then I'd snowplough cautiously after her as she skimmed down the mountain in a haze of white powder.

No one had told me about the working world, or maybe they did, and I didn't believe them. As graduation approached, would-be employers said if I played my cards right, I could have a future with them. My fear was, that if I went into their offices for ten years, I wouldn't even have a past . . . because my working days would be so alike they'd be quite indistinguishable.

Dear God, what had happened? When I was younger I used to dream that I had special powers and that such things couldn't happen to me. I wanted my life to be special, not off-the-shelf and over-the-counter and EEC-approved . . . replaceable, exchangeable, earthed.

I didn't want a job, I wanted a destiny!

But instead of carving one, I graduated that summer and hung around my home town wondering what to do next. After a year of this, I'd had enough of launderettes and my fridge always empty, and checking for the price on a tin of soup. I'd bump into someone's mum in the supermarket and find myself telling her that I'd just started my own electronics company. My basket full of baked beans and reduced-to-sell sausages would tell her quite another story. Heading home, I'd look up from the pavement and watch the planes overhead and wish to God I could be in one of those Jumbos and off to Australia or somewhere special. The closest I'd come to Australia was a bag of sultanas.

That is what can happen if we don't choose a future for ourselves: it comes for us anyway and drags us out from our hiding place and bullies us around.

So how might we earn a truly happy living?

How to earn a happy living is one of the founding questions of The Study of Well-Being. Let's remind ourselves of some guiding principles, one being that no time of life is intended to be sacrificed in the service of any other. For instance, schooldays shouldn't be treated as a training ground for adult careers, as if they're an executive training course. Schooldays have intrinsic value and if we encourage a youngster to enjoy them for their own sake, then schooldays will naturally lead in pleasing directions and procure helpful skills.

The same goes for every stage of life. If we compromise our focus, we will never fully engage with today nor explore our passions because we'll be too busy looking over the shoulder of the here and now in the hope of catching sight of a seemingly more important tomorrow. By studying lives that go well, we see that in every new chapter of life it makes good sense to set out do something we thoroughly enjoy, and to let enjoyment be our priority before any consideration of likely salary or social status.

Likewise, Nobel Laureate, Francis Crick, who co-discovered the structure of DNA from which all human life is formed, is very typical of successful individuals when he rated his 'enjoyment of work' as the characteristic most responsible for his remarkable achievements . . . and he placed this ahead of 32 other possible factors such as so-called talent.

In a quite different arena of life, General Sir Peter de la Billiere recounts how, as a young soldier, he was raring to transfer into the Special Air Service because of the exciting work it promised him, even though back in those days that maverick regiment was considered a career cul-de-sac. That's not dissimilar to Joanne K. Rowling being warned by her publisher when she started the Harry Potter saga, that there was absolutely no money in children's books. And I'm reminded, too, of the deeply intelligent passion personified by a young American woman (just one of many women studied by Harvard University) whose qualifications and abilities would have taken her far in any field, so she chose to be a homemaker. "A home where my husband and children will be free and happy, and one they will consider the centre and not the boundary of their affections." She achieved her ambition with flying colours.

Here then is the nub of the matter: the heartfelt motivation that comes from doing what truly enthralls and enthuses us is the key ingredient of every successful endeavour. One of the world's most successful media personalities, Oprah Winfrey, underlines that point: "If you are willing to align with whatever your dream or vision is for yourself, then you can do great things in life".

In all of our honest self-evaluation, we would do well to take account of our idiosyncracies and unusualness, both the positives and negatives, and wonder how we can channel these differences to our advantage. The head of Virgin, Richard Branson, suffered a knee injury that foreclosed on his sporting prowess, while his dyslexia scuppered his school work. But the boy Richard had learnt the joys of business from his irrepressibly canny mum, and he was cooking up money-making ventures from his earliest teens. Oprah Winfrey was equally rewarded for playing to her true strengths. She says "I remember being taken off the air in Baltimore and being told that I was no longer fit for television and that I could not anchor the news because I would cry for the people in the stories, which really wasn't very effective as a news reporter. And it wasn't until I was demoted as an on-air anchor woman and thrown into the talk-show arena to get rid of me, that I allowed my own truth to come through . . . And so I took what had been a mistake, what had been perceived as a failure, and turned it into a talk-show career that's done OK for me!"

To thrive, we need to feel in control

Let your heart choose the direction, and let your head handle the journey. This is a fine way to go on, but we must also 'craft the graft' to bring out the best in ourselves. And when crafting a job, the single most important factor for our head to bear in mind is this: *the more we feel in control of our work, the more we will thrive.* By that I mean, we need to feel capable of affecting the outcome, feel sufficiently skilled to do a decent job, and feel able to go about it in a way that suits us.

Time and again the 'feeling in control' factor has proven invaluable for anyone facing a challenge. In the 1960s, Volvo factory workers formed into teams which became responsible for building entire cars, rather than having separate individuals contribute just one tiny aspect to a production line. The rise in camaraderie, a more interesting variety of skills, and a greater sense of pride and recognition, were the psychological consequences that paid tangible dividends to all involved.

The same magic works in white-collar professions. In the 1990s, psychology professors Charles Harrington and Susan Boardman at New York's Columbia University examined the lives of 60 highly accomplished adults (age 40 to 55) who had overcome the odds of their impoverished backgrounds to become top lawyers, medics, scientists and business tycoons. The researchers then compared this group with 40 highly accomplished adults from backgrounds that were clearly privileged. One key factor distinguished the hotshots who had blossomed despite major disadvantages. Yep, it was that old fashioned feeling of 'being in control', in respect of which we would do well to build this factor into any job description, and let ourselves be the sculptors of our own success.

A sense of being in command of our own fate is important for other reasons, too. A landmark study of 10,000 British civil servants concluded that our sense of control over our working life could halve the rates of serious illness such as heart disease and depression. Not surprisingly, it was the lower status grades who suffered the most from too little sense of being in control of their own lives: those who got told how they worked, when, and with whom. This finding underscores the accumulating evidence that feeling powerless will depress our immune system, whereas feeling in charge of our life boosts it.

The positive role of self-assertion is also reflected in findings from The Harvard Study of Adult Development in which 824 American lifetimes were studied as they unfurled over 60 years. The study identified four ingredients that comprise a career that feels successful: *we need to enjoy it, be competent in it, feel committed and feel adequately rewarded.* Because a career with these characteristics requires the self-confidence and self-assertion that allows us to make our mark in the world, it's not surprising that individuals who deal with their anger either by burying it, or through uncontrolled outbursts, are likely to have poor career development. On the other hand, anger that we cleverly channel to drive our progress, is one of the defining personality hallmarks of healthy and satisfying careers.

What sort of work would suit us?

Where to begin?

I've championed it above, and I'll do so again here in recognition of its fundamental importance: *motivation that comes from inside is the first key ingredient to every successful endeavour.* Recognise your passions – recognise what you like to think about, what you like to read about out, and what you do with your own free time. That's powerful stuff whatever it is, so don't dismiss it, it may hold the key to your future. Nobel scientist, Professor Gertrude Elion, advised just this in a lecture to her students: "It is important to go into work you would like to do. Then it doesn't seem like work. You sometimes feel it's almost too good to be true that someone will pay you for enjoying yourself."

Find out what thrills you, what intrigues you, what brings you pride. What questions about any aspect of life or the universe absolutely enthrall you? What do you willingly do with your own free time? What books do you hungrily read and what fills your daydreams? *There's your direction!*

Here's a beautiful personal history told in interview by the NASA Space Shuttle Commander and mother of two, Eileen Collins: "I have *always* loved flying, ever since I was a small child and growing up in Elmira in New York State. Elmira, with its Harris Hill, is the glider-soaring capital of America, and I was very fortunate to have grown up in that area. I went to summer camp near the Soaring Museum and the glider field. My family never had the money to get me flying lessons or even a ride in an airplane, but my desire to fly just continued to build. And when I got a job at age 16, I started saving money. Eventually I had saved up $1,000 and I took that to my local airport, at age 19, and I asked them to teach me how to fly. Very timid, very shy, you know there are no other women up there. This was a guy thing, but I wanted to do it anyway. My flight instructor was a former F-4 pilot from Vietnam, and he really inspired me. I went on to military flying. It turned out that the year I started military pilot training for the Air Force, 1978, was the same year that NASA took their first women into the Shuttle program. The six women that were in the first Shuttle class became role models to me. They were Mission Specialists, but I knew that I wanted to be a pilot. I knew that this program existed, and that's when I decided that someday I was going to go on and fly as an astronaut. Flying is a challenge, and I found it was something that I could do well. I was never very good at sports in school; as much as I tried, that just wasn't my thing. But I found that I could fly and I could do this well, so that's why I chose flying as my career. Taking flying and interspersing it with my desire to learn about subjects that I was interested in — astronomy, the history of the space program – meant being an astronaut was the perfect job for me."

Honesty, role-models and exploration

I hope that a key theme is emerging here: through all of our explorations and false starts, we've got to fight against the urge to try to say and do what other people want of us, because down that path only misery lies for all concerned. We have to do things for the passion in our own heart. We only make the most of our life if we feel it really is *our* life 100% and we get to choose which direction it goes in and what roads it takes. This is why we must never lose sight of those things that are fundamentally important to us, and use them as landmarks to help keep our bearings on route. When we're choosing a job, rather than only asking what we want to do, we would do well to ask what sort of person we want to become. And let's not forget to seek out role models. Olympic champion, Cathy Freeman, has found it daunting to retire from competitive running. "And the future? Well, it is a bit scary. It's like I'm stepping away from a safe environment into the wilderness." As Cathy is forging a new professional identity, she has become strongly involved with a range of charitable and indigenous causes, such as the Inspire Foundation, which reaches out to young people in rural regions who are having a tough time coping with life. "The reason I got involved with Inspire was because of Jack Heath, he's the founder of 'Inspire'. I felt immediately comfortable with Jack. You surround yourself with people you want to be like in order to find your dreams and goals."

To look at it in another way, we do best to prioritise the journey rather than allowing ultimate goals to dictate the route we take. Oscar-winning actress, Julia Roberts, takes just such a view. "I don't have specific goals. I suppose my desire is just evolution and growth". In this spirit, we should allow the sorts of loving relationships and fulfilling experiences we would wish for on route to influence us far more than our final objectives, which might be a qualification or greater income. Because if we do it the other way around, and let our long-distance destinations determine how we lead our day to day lives, we not only risk having an unenjoyable journey, but we also risk ending up somewhere we won't be happy. There will always be tough days or even awful weeks, but three miserable months on the trot is almost certainly telling us to make major changes.

So, rather than looking to the future at job titles and income, we'd do better to ask how we want to live our life, at least for the time being, as far as we can see. I am reminded that when the young Mia Hamm took up soccer in the 1970s, the sport wasn't yet popular in the USA; she was playing simply for the love and companionship of the game. Then the sport became Olympic, she went on to captain a winning team, and then after it was the public recognition and financial reward which sought *her* out, rather than the other way around.

In all of this, we need to be asking ourselves what are our present values and priorities. And which of our principles are we prepared to act upon? What sort of companions and experiences are we looking for? At this point, it helps to imagine the everyday nature of what we might do, the more detail the better: the country, the colleagues, the clothes, the vocabulary, the hours, the indoors and outdoors, the movements and emotions of a typical day. This is the personality of the job. The good news is that most professions are sufficiently flexible these days that we can create ourselves a tailor-made environment.

Let's be careful though. Impressions of what a particular industry or a company is like, are very often false. Parents, friends and teachers can be out-of-date in their views of what a particular world is really like. Or their judgement might be clouded by their own personal experiences; or they may simply be scared of losing us to something unfamiliar. There are usually places to suit a wide variety of personalities within any one organisation, and it's a question of exploring them. We can best put ourselves in the picture by talking to people who actually do the job everyday, and by experiencing the environment first hand through work-shadowing or internships. Film-making might seem great until we've hung around a cold set all day for a thirty-second shot that ends up on the cutting-room floor, and we have to do the same thing four weeks running. Worse still, it's a very hard world in which to make any headway. Just one in fifty of the really good and capable producers and directors will end up making dozens of documentaries or movies, while the other forty-nine not-so-fortunate individuals spend most of their careers making corporate training videos or, if they finally get lucky, tv commercials for toilet paper. It's timely to note here that Britain's first woman Speaker of The House of Commons, Dame Betty Boothroyd, was a dancer in the London West End before turning to politics. She quickly felt out of her depth and later wrote "I foolishly thought that 'show business' was going to be terribly exciting and glamorous. But it was just like politics – damned hard work."

Choosing paths forward is a good time to be honest with oneself, and honest with those people from whom we invite mentorship. And we shouldn't worry too much about not having sufficient experience. Here's what Oprah had to say on setting up a magazine: "What has been an advantage . . . is the fact that I had no magazine experience. Zip. Zilch. None. Zero. And so I came in with an open mind about what could and could not be done. And I still maintain an open mind."

We can only progress if we're moving

There are probably at least a dozen trades and professions that would each be just as right for us as another. So it makes no sense to imprison ourselves with the notion that there's one thing we're made for, and if we can't do that it's not worth bothering. With a little creativity, if one door slams in our face we can invariably drum up an even more attractive alternative. The trick is to be open to discoveries and surprises. Let's not have too fixed a notion of the path: if we like performing to an attentive audience, that could make us a good teacher, a barrister, an actor or a sales executive, yet each of these professions offers quite different styles of life and a sense of who and what we are. A case in point is Dawn French. Here's what she says she would do if she wasn't a comedian. "I would definitely be a teacher which is what I'm properly trained to do. I enjoyed teaching very much. I taught from 11 up to 18... Drama and English."

Once we've got a direction, rather than hold out for a dream job, it's much better to make progress. A career, rather like a car, is far easier to steer once it's actually moving. We can't expect to get the right job first time around, so we need to be prepared to change, whether that's after a few weeks or months or years. On route we acquire certain transferable skills, perhaps with computers, people or presentations, that we can always take with us into another line of work. With each new experience we encounter, our propensities develop and so do our needs and aspirations.

What it wouldn't be wise to do is wait around for our one big break, because the study of accomplished lifetimes shows that such quantum leaps are an illusion, and that progress far more often relies on the accumulation of small and uncertain steps. Former U.S. Secretary of State, Madeleine Albright, launched her career only in her forties, after her painful divorce. "It took me a long time to figure out what I was doing. Since I had begun my volunteer work in those first years after returning to Washington, I had been proceeding a stepping-stone at a time. It didn't matter that they had been placed at random and were sometimes slippery. I concentrated on doing every job well. And when the crossing became hardest, there were friends there to help me retain my balance."

And there really is no such thing as the best college or the top career. What we should be looking for is the one that matches our particular strengths and needs for the time being. It's about 'the happiest fit'.

Be prepared to change direction on route

We haven't got to settle on passions that will suit us for a lifetime. Their purpose is to spur highly determined and positive action and this alone makes them very useful feelings. If the reality of doing them is a disappointment, that's okay because as soon as the disappointment has made itself plain, the healthy personality will immediately take action... either to add the missing ingredients, or admit to the misunderstanding and change tack. As Britain's best loved gardener, Alan Titchmarch reflects, "It's only now, when I come to write it down, that the course of my life seems to have been carefully mapped out. But not by me. Not consciously, at any rate."

And as Gertrude Elion says: "I think that people need a goal, but I don't think they have to feel that goal is immovable. They might find a better goal along the way."

The life of former nurse and Britain's favourite advice columnist, Claire Rayner, illustrates just such a natural evolution of her career as she speaks about her vocation for helping others. Note, too, how nothing of her experience and joy went to waste. "I loved the hospitals! I felt comfortable there and I fitted in a treat. Even when I came out to have my own baby, I still missed it, which is why I started writing, really. Much of what I was writing was what I knew – it was nursing stuff, childcare and teaching – I'd been teaching people as part of my job for donkeys years."

So let's be sure to keep versatile, because it is estimated that in 16 years time the microchip will be 1,000 times more powerful than it is today. This startling prediction is a reminder that our world is changing so rapidly that we simply can't follow a blueprint of how to conduct our life, we have to be prepared to adapt and to know *how* to adapt. Former First Lady Eleanor Roosevelt puts it rather neatly: "If life were predictable, it would cease to be life."

A life tends to change direction much more quickly now than they ever have in the past. What we want to do now might not be what we want to do in five or even just two years time. So we mustn't be afraid of making a new choice. It is vital to know what we don't like, just as much as what you do, so we shouldn't regret even the 'miserable' experiences. The important thing is that we own up to being unhappy and act positively to improve things. Michigan University psychiatrist, Professor Randolph Nesse, has documented how so much unhappiness and even mental illness comes from setting ourselves just one rigid and over-ambitious target which we then pursue self-destructively despite the journey proving unsatisfying and the destination unreachable. He says that the pain of the subsequent depression is simply telling us to stop peddling in order to rethink. This is why I suggest that rather than allowing our eventual destinations to dictate our journeys, we could instead prioritise the types of experiences we would wish for. We could decide that savouring our closest companions and giving more time to laughter, exercise, sleep and self-mastery, are highly rewarding goals in themselves and should not be sacrificed in our outcome-focused pursuit of pay-rises, promotion, and material luxuries. Life is full of opportunities, and we do ourselves no favours at all by appointing one narrow target, and one way towards it, because this only leads us to ignore all the adventures that we might subtly be invited on either side. Better to think which directions and which journeys best reflect our present values and priorities, passions and intuitions ... rather than adhering to some pre-determined and perhaps out-dated plans. The ability to intelligently surrender one goal in favour of another more realisable one that offers us a more enjoyable journey, is a key ingredient for psychological good health and happiness.

Of course, if we haven't thought our values and priorities through, we'll be pulled all over the place by our short term appetites for one thing or another; but if we've settled some fundamentals in our mind, we'll always be heading in a generally healthy direction.

And let's rest assured that there is absolutely no stigma in changing targets, fields or careers. It has been the hallmark of very many accomplished people. As an undergraduate at MIT, the future Nobel Prize winner, Richard Feynman, changed from Mathematics to Electrical Engineering and only then to Physics. In much the same way that Britain's first woman Prime Minister, Margaret Thatcher, studied chemistry at Oxford and then went into law and then politics. And Bill Gates had the wisdom to leave Harvard after the first year so as to set up his Mircrosoft business with a lifelong friend. Change should bring progress, that's all that's important. We just keep doing it while it's enjoyable, that could be our rule. Let our passion decide how long we'll continue.

Six-times Tour de France winner, Lance Armstrong, has this to say: "What will keep me in the saddle, is happiness. The way I ride has always been based on a simple fact: *I love riding my bike*. It's just too hard to do it otherwise. How long will I continue to love it at the world-class level? That needs to be checked regularly. I can't answer that or guarantee it."

Let university come later, when you feel good'n'ready

On the face of it, my formal education had taken various well-intentioned precautions to prepare me for the demands of both the man-made working world and the natural one. But the sad fact is, almost none of it would prove itself relevant to anything I'd encounter. Symbolic of this mismatch between my school education and real life were the survival lessons in the school swimming pool when I was 10 years old. While furiously treading-water, we had to inflate our pyjama bottoms and wrap them around our necks to serve as life jackets . . . presumably in case someone left the bathroom tap on overnight and we woke up afloat like ship-wreck survivors. Well, that particular disaster scenario never happened, though others certainly did for which I was not nearly so well prepared.

These shortfalls in the formal education system is in part why I think there are real drawbacks with going straight off to university after high school, rather than experiencing some form of apprenticeship in the working world for a couple of years or more. In fact, my own experience of university serves a good example of the sorts of things that can go wrong if we go off to college at the wrong time to suit us. When I arrived there, age 18, everyone was pretty much the same as me, with broadly similar life backgrounds, so there was a real shortage of advice or mentorship from anyone even five years older. Lecturers, tutors and researchers were then, and are now, far too busy to give young people the attention they need and deserve, so there was simply no one to learn from. By contrast, in the working world, there's a far more natural mix of ages and experiences, and far more on-the-job mentorship, so our learning curve is going to be all the better for it.

My second point would be that we learn best when we're hungry for something, and not embarrassed to ask questions or make mistakes. At age 18, I was tired of learning from books, and yet I was too afraid to ask anything for the sheer terror of looking stupid. All of this meant the opportunities of university sailed over my head. So if I had my time again, I wouldn't go to college until I had a much better idea of what parts of the working world intrigued me. I think I could get that information by embarking on a series of 'compact careers' in promising arenas. Just as a for instance, in Britain it takes only a few months to train as a police constable ready to take one's place on the beat under the mentorship of a more experienced colleague. That sort of work would certainly have been an eye opener for a naïve lad like me.

And even when I got to university, I'd definitely want to have a part-time job while I was studying. Having another life beyond the campus, some form of working identity, is worth its weight in gold. I recall former US President Ronald Reagan telling how he spent his college summers as a lifeguard, and that he never lost the sense of pride which that responsible role had given him.

I appreciate that the clubs and societies of college life are often lauded as its great strength, but these are features that we should foster throughout our whole life not just in those three or four years. It was in a misguided attempt to get sensible and grow up after graduating, that I put away my football and my dreams of flying planes and making films. But years later, I've got those passions right back out again because I realise they are an essential part of me and cannot be discarded.

In summary then, I'm not saying we shouldn't go to university, I'm simply saying we shouldn't go until we're truly fired-up about wanting to learn something that universities are particularly good at teaching; and not until we have acquired the personal confidence to put our best intentions into practice.

Finding the right size pond in which to feel valued

It's a wonderful thing to feel appreciated (it's equally nice to make someone else feel the very same way), but in much of the western world today, feeling special is in short supply. When a neighbourhood is stable and close-knit, in the way that was portrayed in *The*

Waltons or *It's a Wonderful Life*, people know us well enough to value us for our positive contribution to their everyday world. By stark contrast, in a more disjoint and anonymous social environment, where we don't feel people know us well enough, we try to broadcast our uniqueness and true worth through more immediate if superficial means, such as brands, qualifications and job-titles. We are social animals and it is natural that such emblems of identity have always been important to us, but the balance is shifting too heavily in their favour and it's making us ill. We're directing too large a percentage of our personal resources into acquiring these secondary characteristics rather than investing in the first-hand caring relationships for which we're truly hungry. In our struggle to earn more money and status to bolster our public image, we neglect the intimacies of our personal human bonds, and wind up feeling lonely, unappreciated, and insecure.

It's this phenomenon that explains much of the epidemic increase in a self-defeating workaholism, and the reliance on alcohol and other drugs for the cosmetic pleasures they temporarily bring. And it is for these reasons that being a much-valued fish in a very small pond will feel a whole lot better than suspecting you're just another shark somewhere bigger.

The mass media is often blamed for stoking our appetite for material things by showing us the air-brushed lives of super-celebrities; but this isn't a sufficient explanation for the malaise that has taken hold. After all, we've always known there are the 'haves' and the 'have nots', but most of the reason that disparities in wealth and opportunity are able to hurt us more now, is because our all-important sense of identity, of being cared for and valued, has been deeply eroded by the changing nature of families and communities and working life. Our communities are full of people passing through within a year or two, so we don't get to know each other as our human spirit needs to. Which is why there's a lot to be said for putting down roots and making the best of our local world. The more we feel valued, understood, and cherished by those around us, then the less time, money and energy we have to spend on all the substitutes . . . the brands, the beauty products and the showing off.

There would be less need for all that flimflam, because we wouldn't be fooling anybody. If people didn't know us personally, they'd know someone who did. Our good deeds would go before us.

The message seems to be that it can pay dividends to work on the principle that 'intimate is beautiful', because it doesn't matter if it's school or university or the working world, it's not much fun feeling invisible, and it will not bring the best out in us. So there's a real case for the benefits of small clubs, small teams, small work units. We need to feel we can make an important difference, which means that the pond we move in has to be big enough so that we can learn from a range of people, but not so big as to make us feel insignificant. Finding the right size arena all depends on our present level of experience and our present confidence. By illustration of this point, it's worth noting that the economist, Professor Robert Frank, has observed very convincingly how in terms of our own sense of happiness, it feels far better to be the third highest-paid lawyer in a small firm and earn 30,000 a year, than to be just somewhere in the middle of the pack in a large firm even though we might be making 40,000 a year. Likewise, emigrating somewhere which offers a higher standard of living as part of the standard package, Sweden perhaps, won't in itself help us feel any better about what we've achieved in life. Just as with the lawyer's salary example, it seems that we get much of our buzz from seeing our situation improve relative to those immediately around us. But if friends and neighbours are doing equally well, we won't feel any happier in the lap of luxury. This interesting phenomenon just underlines the theme that our sense of achievement and status, which all contribute very considerably to our happiness, rely on us choosing a size of pond that we can feel important in.

And it's not that we need to be saving lives or working in education, medicine or the church for our life to feel useful and valuable to the people around us. It's just that it feels very good to have a reason-for-being that is greater than ourselves, and that reason might simply come through actively loving our partner, child, friend, vocation, or spiritual faith. The active ingredient is realising that what we do has impact and importance beyond ourselves – that we make an original difference to the well-being of our everyday world.

Paying too high a price for an increased income

Should we take on more work for the sake of greater income? In answer to this classic quandary, the psychological evidence would strongly predict that if we're safely above the poverty line, and not harangued by major debt, even shed-loads of money will not make any permanent difference to how happy we rate ourselves. The most impressive voice on this subject, Professor Ed Diener of the University of Illinois at Urbana-Champaign, surveyed 49 of *Forbes* magazine's top 100 wealthiest Americans, and found them only very slightly happier than the average Joe. Moreover, multi-million lottery winners return to their original level of happiness within the year. Sounds astonishing doesn't it, but this unexpected outcome has been researched time and again and is highly convincing. It would seem Mother Nature has supplied us with an in-built mechanism to swiftly habituate us to many extreme circumstances, whether good or bad, and this 'return to normal' motivates us to pick ourselves up and progress our lives. For instance, several studies have observed that well within one year of an individual being rendered paraplegic or quadriplegic by an accident or illness, those same individuals rated themselves almost as happy with life as they were before.

However, the net outcome of this human ability for rapid adaptation to our circumstances, is complicated by another factor. Professor Daniel Gilbert of Harvard has established that we are really quite poor judges of how long the pleasures and pains of major life-changes will last. The result of our characteristic 'cost-benefit' miscalculations is that we tend to over-invest ourselves in trying to acquire certain things at the expense of others, and we end up worse off because of it. Put another way, our inaccurate predictions can lead us to distort our jounreys in the pursuit of goals that falsely promise greater gains. For instance, Professor John Helliwell of the University of British Columbia has shown that even a 30% drop in our income causes us far less emotional pain than the all-too-common casualties of chasing extra money. Such casualties might include job insecurity and unemployment, a substantial decline in our health, or even separation from our partner and divorce. The message is clear: it just isn't worth jeopardising the well-being of our other life-dimensions, such as friendship, home, health and hobbies, for the sake of extra money.

For my own part, having studied extremely high-achievers in myriad professional worlds these past ten years, I'm now far less impressed by how high someone has risen in their field, than by the quality of their journey getting there. What has it cost them and their loved ones? What life-skills has it taught them? There is nothing impressive about becoming a well-respected professional if we compromise our health and personal relationships. That's not what life's about, because there's a net loss. The downsides and misery outweigh several times the gains and glories. What struck me, too, about my very high-achievers in interview, is that I very often heard them say: "the success came *because* I was enjoying myself; and my family has been by far and away the most rewarding and important thing to me."

Even Albert Einstein warned us against mistaking the means for the ends, but we *do* benefit from reminders, so here's mine: We earn money to live, not live to earn money, and once we cross the threshold of having sufficient finance for our basic needs, we should immediately direct our surplus energies to more fruitful pursuits. Happiness depends not on our purchasing power, but on how well we invest our time. The accumulated positive feelings from several meaningful relationships and activities will very likely prove far more rewarding than putting our hopes in that one squeaky basket labelled 'big bucks!' And if, like me, you're itching to pull an *Italian Job*, an *Ocean's Eleven*, or a *Butch Cassidy*, then let's just remember *it's not about the money*.

The Study of Well-Being can pay its way at work

The word health means whole, so when we're hoping to make improvements to our work performance and working life, we would do well to take an wholistic approach. By this, I mean we need to take into consideration at least the following four dimensions:

- How our mind and body can dramatically affect each other in both positive and negative ways.
- How our conscious and sub-conscious goals and strategies need to work in harmony. (This is covered in detail in *Nick's Special Topic* chapter towards the end of the book.)
- How the individual can be made more comfortable in a team. (For instance, we might want to be cautious of promotions that might elevate us out of our arena of expertise and signature strengths. It might sometimes be better if we look for rewards and recognition that leave us in a social environment similar to the one in which we've flourished.)
- Consider how to improve not just work-time but break-time, commute-time and personal-time. This big picture approach will mean that our on-the-job performance will rise with the tide of a generally happier life.

The combined effect of applying all four of these principles at once will be greater than the sum of the parts.

Applying the principles

Positive emotions help sustain high performance, which is why The Study of Well-Being can pay its way in every environment from the workplace to the schoolroom. The key reason is that happiness is not only a result of things going well, it is also a cause of them, which makes it a very useful feeling to cultivate. High spirits will help us function better physically, be more productive, open-minded, creative in our problem-solving, resilient in adversity, and benevolent to others. All skills that will tangibly benefit the bottom line of any work environment. By contrast, when our mood is negative, perhaps because we're anxious, depressed, or angry, then our thought and action repertoire is typically narrow, rigid, and inward looking.

It also seems that the sort of resilient personality who can bounce back quickly after a major setback, does so largely because they quickly generate positive emotions which serve as a physical and psychological antidote to bad news. What's more, the most resilient people don't just cultivate positive emotions in themselves, they also inspire such emotions in the people around them, and so create a sort of social cocoon of buoyant and supportive individuals. Such clever observations have been the pioneering work of Michigan University's Professor Barbara Fredickson.

In a similar vein, her colleagues, Marcial Losada and Emily Heaphy, studied 60 management teams drafting annual strategic plans. They found that the teams whose fortunes later flourished were the ones who had a ratio of at least three positive comments to every negative one. Likewise, Washington University's John Gottman found a five to one ratio of positive to negative comments in the discussions between marriage partners who achieved lasting and satisfying marriages, compared to those who ran aground. What this accumulated evidence suggests is that whingeing doesn't pay, whereas positive messages promote positive outcomes.

And here's some more food for thought: research by Nobel Prize winning psychologist, Professor Kahneman, has shown that high-points and endings are what we remember when evaluating an event. So perhaps taking 10 minutes to end each working day by recalling what has gone really well, is one way in which we could foster a sense of greater satisfaction.

Far better, too, if incentive schemes reward us with extra time to develop a good range of close personal relationships, and time to explore our social hobbies and passions. This might mean golf or hill-walking, amateur dramatics or gardening, but the research confirms what we always suspected: that such extra-curricular pursuits, far from detracting from our work performance, are a positive complement to it because they serve to refresh us. So the new scheme, swim-club and five-aside team are a shrewd investment for all concerned. What's more, a relaxed body sends relaxing signals to our brain, and a relaxed brain is fast, versatile and creative. Suddenly we feel fine about taking on difficult business, and our good cheer is conveyed in a tone of voice and physical bearing that is its own self-fulfilling prophecy.

On a strongly related subject, tempting though it is to regard money or promotion as highly motivating forms of reward, studies suggest that what would actually brings us the deepest and most enduring satisfaction is the respect and appreciation of our work-mates. So when the time comes to recognise innovative ideas and prowess, rather than risk accidentally isolating the star individual by antagonising their colleagues who didn't do as well, it's far better to award something which benefits *everyone*. This might mean a cele-bratory picnic, new badminton equipment, or lush landscape posters to cover bare walls. This way, the individual is very publicly thanked and lauded, but doesn't become a target for jealousy. Nonetheless, anyone freeloading will get the clear message that by not contribut-ing, they're missing out on a lot of positive attention. Such an inclu-sive reward policy draws on the principle that some of the richest sources of well-being are social activities which help us feel more connected to others and foster our sense of being a valued member of a community whether through our work, family or neighbourhood. This is why it's so unhelpful that the school and university exam sys-tem is almost exclusively focused on individual performance rather than on what partnerships of two or more people can achieve. After all, teaming up to take on life is what humans are designed for, which helps explain the fact that when people tell researchers they have a best friend at work, this happy state of affairs invariably coincides with better productivity and health.

Other strategies can be guided by what we know about human well-being. For instance, if one of those workforce rewards was to be some bags of soil, seeds and tools to form a garden allotment, then break-times could be spent in the company of friends while also getting some fresh air, exercise, and daylight, along with the profound pleasure of growing the flowers and vegetables that could then grace desks and canteen tables.

On a quite different tack, when it comes to structuring the working day, our physical and psychological health quickly degen-erate if we don't have a sense of control over our own destiny but feel instead that we're just following bullying orders. What we need is to feel that what we do makes a difference to our situation. Better still, if we're left free to pace ourselves to suit our energies, attention and enthusiasm at different times of the day, we're likely to achieve more without burning out. This being in control of our situation is

closely linked to our self-respect, i.e. we can feel important and valuable because we feel we can make a difference to the world around
us. But for this, we need the freedom to use our initiative in a task
and to feel personally responsible for the outcome.

The positives of 'feeling in control' work equally well for the
daily commute, because traffic jams and train delays can be a source
of enormous frustration. So, to encourage some physically beneficial
alternatives, a really considerate employer would make provisions
for bicycles, clothes lockers and power-showers.

However, if our work environment doesn't support our social,
physical and psychological well-being on conscious and subliminal
levels like this, then our subconscious will soon flag its discontent
through psychosomatic illnesses. In response to these, we tend to self-
medicate, often with too much alcohol, or taking sick days in front of
the tv, none of which helps us recuperate. On the other hand, our
workplace could develop a life-enhancing culture, perhaps assisted by
a small lending library of books and videos and some workshops on
relaxation and the other building blocks of life feeling better. Once
we're accruing new ideas like this, the advantages will multiply expo-
nentially, because we will as a matter of course share these skills and
insights with our partner, child and best mates, who will also begin to
benefit. By these means, the personality we bring to work each day
will be deriving ever more pleasure and support from our personal life.

By appreciating the connectedness of things in the ways suggested above, our place of work can become a catalyst for progress
in every aspect of our life, and this progress is balanced by a sense of
stability because we're far less tempted to change jobs. So it is that
by fostering educational and working cultures that respect the
whole person and our wider life, we can all harness our need and
capacity for a sense of progress, and the organisation's fortunes will
flourish alongside the individual's.

Choosing *where* we live, to fit *how* we live

When next we find ourselves people-watching in some foreign quarter, it's worth pondering how countries compare in the happiness

league tables. How come the average individual in Denmark, Iceland, Sweden, the Netherlands, Switzerland and Australia invariably rate themselves as rather happy with life, while Britain barely makes it into the top ten and is always behind the US? How come Italy, France and Germany always languish a full 10% below the happiness self-ratings of the front runners? The key factor certainly isn't average income, nor is it the weather.

What's more, these national averages tend to hold for all sections of the population, irrespective of gender and age. I.e. schoolboys and grandmas alike, if Danish, are likely to declare themselves a darn sight happier than their French counterparts. Indeed, 60% of Danes rate themselves as very satisfied with life, compared to 45% of Netherlanders, 30% of Brits, and just 15% of French people. Someone even calculated that a Dane would have to be divorced, unemployed, broke and sick before he would rate himself as dissatisfied as a Frenchman.

These strong patterns of the past thirty years are not simply a quirk of vocabulary or a nuance of translation. We know this, because regardless of whether the Swiss research participant are speakers of German, French or Italian, on average the Swiss self-rating for satisfaction with life is a good 10% higher than their neighbours in Germany, France or Italy. So it's not a simple language issue. That said, it could very well be cultural traditions that are skewing the survey figures. For instance, in community-oriented cultures such as Japan and China, the well-being of the group is held as far more important than any individual's happiness, which is quite different from the culture personified by much of Britain. What's also muddying the waters, is cultural taboos on emotional expression. For instance, in Japan, it's impolite to show negative facial expressions in public, sadness for example; whereas in China it's not done to look too pleased with life, since unpleasant emotions are stoically regarded as the norm. It's plausible, then, that similar cultural differences are subtly operating among western countries and are affecting the self-ratings of various nations. In Latin American countries and the US, there is a particularly strong emphasis on the appearance of cheerfulness, less so in northern Europe. So it's more than likely that in answering survey questions, people are slanting their answers towards the beliefs and practices of their wider culture, rather than offering an entirely personal evaluation.

In an attempt to gain a truer picture of a population's overall satisfaction, psychologists have compared national rates of depression, alcoholism and suicide. If you think the percentage differences in the self-reported happiness of western nations seem surprisingly large, then it's even more of a quandary that Denmark's suicide rate is at least three times higher than Britain's, and alcoholism in Italy is a shocking six times higher than here. But then again, in the past forty years, there's been a ten fold increase in depression among the seemingly cheerful Americans. Intriguingly, that figure is a whopping ten times higher than among the 8,000 or so people of the Old Order Amish community in the countryside near Philadelphia, who live a close-knit, un-modernised existence, where depression is extremely rare.

While we're waiting for the scientists to pin down the whys and wherefores of these anomalies, perhaps our best bet is to find the right niche in which our values and goals well match those of the local community. For instance, Norway, Australia and the Netherlands don't allow the working day to be all-consuming in the way that much of North America does; on the other hand, if a lasting marriage is our hope, let's beware the near 50% divorce rate of the ambient culture in Sweden. Then again, if we're entering a risky profession, we might bear in mind that the Netherlands offers the security of a high level of benefits for the unemployed. On which point, it's worth noting that if things are going well for us, we'll feel even better in an individualistic society where we can bask in our success, but in bad times, we'll feel glad of a community spirit. So we can see how different stages of our life or career might be better suited to different surroundings.

When making the calculations about going abroad, let's just remind ourselves that there will be real and emotional costs connected to leaving our homeland, and we have to feel these will be greatly outweighed by the benefits of our new destination. Let's ponder, too, how we could readily find very different cultures and atmospheres and environments all existing cheek by jowl in the very same city . . . maybe even our own. So maybe moving across town is all that's really necessary.

That said, American travel writer Bill Bryson settled in England as a young man, and he illustrates how a new country can perhaps bring to life one of our dormant signature strengths. This is what he says about his exposure to British humour. "It was as if I was sort of wired for this but the connection had never been made. Back in Iowa you didn't get that kind of humor. So it was as if a switch had been flipped and I suddenly had neural circuits lighting up. I thought: God, this is great. I love it . . . I've always felt very lucky that I had this chance to be part of two cultures'."

Once we've found the right type of soil in which to plant our roots, we can set about growing our own happiness – by involving ourselves deeply in a trusting, neighbourly community; by finding and shaping an enjoyable job offering stable employment; by investing in loving, lasting partnerships; and by creating a strong sense of meaning and purpose in our daily lives. Such endeavours have long since proven themselves an international passport to a happier life.

* * *

Planning for Progress

- What choices do you need to make that would help you move on in life?

- How could your working life better reflect your heart-felt values and most profound pleasures?

- What sorts of experiences and whose points of view would you really appreciate?

* * *

Growing Strong
in the Face of Adversity

It's not the troubles we run into, it's what we do about them which determines their net effect upon our lives. Rather as a plane can most easily take off when facing into the wind, it seems that by facing and surmounting problems we can grow not only stronger but happier than if our journey had been uneventful. An appreciation of this open-ended relationship between the initial circumstances and the eventual outcome, forms the very bedrock of lives that flourish.

Intrigued by those individuals who have learned to turn pain into opportunity, psychologists are beginning to identify at least two dimensions of our personality which can benefit from deeply troubled times.

The first is in terms of the sheer strength and determination of our character. Double Olympic gold medallist, Kelly Holmes, suffered several major injuries as well as chronic fatigue syndrome in the years before her twin victories in Athens 2004. "All the ups and downs I've had, I think they've made me the athlete I am . . . made me stronger." Kelly's assessment echoes her fellow runner, the indigenous Australian gold medal sprinter, Cathy Freeman, who lit the Olympic flame at Sydney in 2000. "Somewhere deep inside, I'd absorbed all the pain and suffering my people had endured and turned it into a source of strength." Cathy achieved this alchemy by channeling the energy of pain into her passion for athletics. "You can draw energy from what has happened in your life, the tragedies and successes. When you combine it all at the right moment, it propels you forward."

The second possibility from hardship is our development of a more helpful and satisfying life-perspective. Hillary Clinton said this in the wake of her father's death: "When our hearts are raw with grief, we are more vulnerable to hurt, but also more open to new perceptions." Her insight is born out by the work of Peter Herschbach at The Technical University of Munich: one half of 385 women cancer patients said that in the aftermath of their illness they lived more intensively, with more compassion, and with a better relationship with their partner. Those findings tally closely with studies showing that half the men who survive a first heart-attack will report strong beneficial effects on their values and life-philosophies, and a decade later those same 50% will be less likely to have suffered a second attack. There is, then, accumulating evidence from this pioneering research into 'post-traumatic personal development', to suggest that self-rated quality of life after recovery from physical or psychological problems, can for some individuals actually be higher than for those who have never fallen so ill. Could it be that first-hand knowledge of misery can be our incentive to master happiness?

By considering the capacity for good that pain holds within it, I do not wish to suggest that any less can come of joy. Hardship has no monopoly on the production of greatness. For instance, Charles Darwin had a remarkably happy up-bringing, doted on by his older sisters, his widowed father, and his colourful relatives. Likewise, Albert Einstein was raised amid a richly supportive extended family. And the actor James Stewart grew up in heart-warming small town circumstances which preceded his becoming not only one of the finest movie stars of a golden era, but also an 8th Army airforce officer who led wartime bomber crews on numerous dangerous missions.

There is ample evidence that the pleasures of a wonderful youth can produce some exceptionally positive skills and personalities. I simply conclude that intense experiences, whether misery or joy, can provide the raw materials for some very fine things. With this thought in mind, we might be less apprehensive of what emotions life may bring us, and take heart from the Human Rights pioneer, Eleanor Roosevelt's shrewd observation which could apply equally well to all of us: "A woman is a like a teabag. You never know how strong she is until she's in hot water."

Let's ask for help

This hopes to be a 'helpful book' rather than a 'self-help book'. By that I mean that if we have a problem or a goal, we will not keep it secretly to ourselves and starve it of the oxygen of other people's encouragement and good ideas. I hope we will not only share our problems and our ambitions with friends, but also with a range of specialists in our areas of interest. And once we've got the hang of things, I hope that we will use our experience of tackling problems and enjoying journeys so as to help others who might be facing similar challenges.

The more it scares us to ask for help, the more we have to gain by doing so. The fear or shame or despair we feel in confiding our troubles in another, are not signals warning us not to, they are simply saying 'This is important, so pay attention'. As it happens, squaring up to our troubles, when we've rallied the support of the right allies, is one of the healthiest ways of getting on in life.

By stark contrast, an ignored or inadequately resolved problem may not only hold us back, it will more than likely drag every other aspect of our life out of kilter. This phenomenon simply reflects the profoundly holistic, interwoven nature of our well-being. We can't just vacuum-seal some part of our psychology and stick it in the deep freeze. Better we face up to things.

Even so, us chaps in particular, no matter we're 6 or 76, can be reluctant to ask for the benefit of someone's experience when we're faced with something tricky. But I'm reminded of how General Sir Peter de la Billiere, who spent nearly all of his career in the Special Air Service and whose autobiography is poignantly called *Looking For Trouble*, says that the worst thing we can do is soldier on alone if there's a problem in our lives. Far wiser to call in the support of some good people, team-up, and work it through. That's intelligent bravery. By contrast, a stiff upper-lip only results in stagnant thinking, because when we're either worried or sad our problem-solving skills typically become narrowed and inflexible. In such a state of mind, we tend to overlook promising new approaches and can't see the bigger picture; whereas with the help of two or more heads, it's very likely that we'll drum up far better solutions.

There is no problem that is not improved by our asking for help. It could be health scares or sexual anxieties, money worries or a relationship impasse, but having had the privilege of interviewing hundreds of individuals in all walks of life and of all ages these past ten years, I am left in no doubt that the more personal the problem feels, the more universal it is likely to be. All of us, but all of us, have had a host of show-downs with our health, deeply unhelpful habits, and our closest companions.

Whatever it is, we're rather prone to leave asking for help as a last resort – as if an act of desperation. But such a strategy is self-defeating, and the truth is, it's never too early to invite support. As soon as trouble comes over the horizon, that's the best time to call in the cavalry. If we say "I'll see if I can solve it on my own", we miss the opportunity to team-up with some potential allies and get off to a flying start. After all, the best time to discuss routes forward is before the journey, not half way through. But equally, it's never too late to tackle a problem, and just because something has been hanging around our necks for twenty years or even forty, doesn't mean we can't start to put it right first thing Monday morning. (Where I personally like to begin is: "Could you help me think through a rather stubborn problem, because I'd very much value your thoughts on it".)

We should aim to be discriminating in whom we confide. After all, we are likely to need experienced know-how as well as moral support. The bolder and more inventive our search for the right source of help, the better quality will be the eventual choice of solutions. In our quest for wise counsel, we need to own up to how even our best friends and family can, quite unwittingly, be jamming our problem in place . . . perhaps by their well-meaning acceptance of it, by their turning a blind-eye, or by treating something as taboo and not to be talked about so as to spare anyone's pain or embarrassment. That's why we might require a confidante well outside of our usual circle, someone who can see the whole picture through fresh eyes, and help us to do the same. On top of which, we will probably have to broach things with several people before we hit upon something that works for us. *Persistence* should be our watchword.

But if asking for help is such a darn good idea, what holds us back?

Maybe some negative thinking gets the better of us, such as we don't want to be a nuisance, don't want to admit that something's got us down, don't want the embarrassment of being thought needy or incompetent. But our reservations are mistaken on at least three counts:

- Asking for help is not the same as acting helpless. Quite the contrary, it can demonstrate our fighting spirit. In the snakes and ladders of life, we grow strong not in spite of fighting problems but *because* of fighting problems. The struggle strengthens us. But there's no rule that says we must do it alone. And let's be honest: what passes for a spirit of independence may in fact be masking our childish need to appear perfect. Or maybe we're just putting up with the problem as a form of self-punishment. In any event, the best self-help is partnering up because our problem-solving will improve by leaps and bounds as we talk things through with a healthy range of thoughtful souls.
- We should keep in mind that it's not the problem that does the damage, *it's what we do about it*. If we wall it away, it can go rotten on us; but if we open it up to fresh air and bright light, it can heal and we can learn from it. What's more, by asking for help, we

can be a role-model of inspiration for those around us, sending a message that progress in life is not about concealing our demons.

- We owe it to those we love and are loved by to help ourselves move on in life, and partnering-up shoulder to shoulder in a spirit of exploration is at the very heart of well-being.

Besides which, the sooner we deal with our own adversities, the sooner we have the pleasure of helping others who might be suffering the same or a similar predicament.

Let's take inspiration from other lives

We could, for instance, read the autobiographies of those people we most admire. This way, we can read in helpful detail how their progress in life was not overnight or unearned, as it can so often appear from afar, but was in fact a natural development of their determined practice, passion, and enduring positive relationships. Gertrude Elion, winner of the 1988 Nobel Prize in medicine, was inspired by reading about other scientists. "I read about Marie Curie, of course. That said to me that a woman can do it, too. There was also a book called *Microbe Hunters* ... which dealt with a lot of very exciting discoveries by people in chemistry, physics, and biology. These were biographical sketches, not just about their discoveries, but about their lives ... Paul Ehrlich, Louis Pasteur ... and what wonderful things they were able to accomplish from very poor surroundings. Each one had an entirely exciting life, a lot of struggle but a lot of satisfaction, a lot of achievement. That book gave me the feeling that it was alright to struggle, it was alright for it to be hard. It didn't have to come easily."

American Comedian and talk-show host, Ellen Degeneres, drew courage for her coming out as a gay woman, from the example of Mrs Rosa Parks, who back in the 1950s famously challenged America's racial segregation laws of the time by refusing to give up her seat for a white passenger and move to the back of the bus. Ellen said of her coming-out experience: "Everything that I ever feared happened to me: I lost my show. I've been attacked like hell. I went from making a lot of money on a sitcom to making no money . . . I don't feel resentful about what happened . . . I am grateful that I had the opportunity to touch others . . . to change people's minds."

Oscar-nominated actress for her role in *The Color Purple*, US media pioneer, and acclaimed talk-show host, Oprah Winfrey has this to say about being inspired by others. "I had authors who were my role models. Maya Angelou was a role model for me. Growing up, reading her book, *I Know Why the Cage Birds Sing* really opened up my life in a way that made me think for the first time that being colored and being poor had some validation." Oprah says she felt the very same way when she read the revelation of sexual abuse in another book. "I read the first page of *The Color Purple*, put the book down, and wept. I could not believe it, that someone had put this in writing. It was unbelievable . . . to know that you are not the only one. Because all this time, you have carried this burden. You think nobody else in the world has been through this. Nobody else is as bad as you. And then you discover that you are not so bad after all. It's an amazing thing."

A sense of mission and standing strong

Many times in these pages I have said that we are at our very best when we're willing to experiment with new approaches to old problems, to take another perspective, and to consider how to do things differently. The ability to take a new position on things when circumstances warrant it is the hallmark of a resourceful personality, and is one of the most useful tools in the backpack of any one of us hiking in the hills of happiness and hoping to do right by our fellow travellers.

But for this versatility to be bona fide, for it to have a heart and soul, we have to be prepared to take a stance when circumstances demand it, a stance that might go against the grain of everyone around us. In the classic 1950s movie, *Bad Day at Black Rock*, the ex-serviceman played by Spencer Tracy climbs down from a train to stand thick-set in a black suit and hat, the very embodiment of a passionate energy, like volcanic lava solidified. He has arrived in a small town to go find and thank the Japanese-American who had saved his life in a Pacific Island battle. But all is not well, and everyone from the drunken sheriff to the local bully are hiding something. Now Tracy has a choice: call a cab, and leave town, determined to write a long letter of heart-felt thanks to his missing saviour and let the mail service take care of the problem. Or . . . he can personally do something about it. 'Do' is the key word here. Psychologists pay only cautious attention to what people say, because self-motivated action gives a far better indication of the level of genuine feeling and intent. Our deeds, if we're in sync with ourselves, reveal our priorities . . . our rank-ordering of values. In this movie, our man Spencer Tracy is one hundred percent in sync with himself, and decides he'll stick around. He sets himself the task of finding out what's become of his old comrade, and his inner spirit of doing the right thing is quite unstoppable despite all the efforts of a cast of heavies lined up against him. Tracy's role portrays the notion that 'If we think our cause is worth it, no sacrifice is too great'; and I suspect that acknowledging this is a key to us finding the inner strength to make headway in life. We have to believe that our cause is deserving of our best efforts. Clearly identifying the people, skills and places that inspire in us this tenacious level of commitment will in the long run make everything far easier and more satisfying. Likewise, our life will feel all the more right for us once we clearly identify those parts of ourselves which we truly wish to foster.

Coming forward now to a modern independent movie, *My Life Without Me,* we meet an impoverished young American women in her twenties shortly before she is diagnosed with a highly aggressive liver cancer, and given only weeks to live. She is a mother of two little children, and is a also a wife, so without divulging her fatal condition, she sets about making provision for her family's future. She deftly arranges that her young husband innocently develops a mutually supportive friendship with the young single woman in the trailer-home next door. Then she secretly makes a series of audiotapes for the two children, tapes that they can listen to on their birthdays up until they're eighteen. What comes across so endearingly is that this woman has set herself a mission, and this sense of good purpose helps protect her from self-pity and the innate tragedy of the situation. In fact, her sense of good purpose leaves her very much alive.

Can we reconsider our sadness?

For the science of happiness, sadness is not the opposite and is not the enemy. To appreciate happiness, we all need sadness to reawaken our capacity and appetite for joy. Together they form an ebb and flow of pleasing and painful emotions, wholly complementary to each other. They both promote our well-being. Of course, sadness is not to be mistaken for depression, that state in which our emotions are stuck in despair; and happiness is not to be confused with mania, in which our exuberance is trapped in over-drive and self-destructive levels of out-of-control optimism. By contrast to these two unhelpful and inflexible attitudes, feeling happy or sad is our free and dynamic response to living life hour by hour, and so can serve to both guide and motivate us. A heavy heart might be painful, but it serves a healthy purpose.

By way of analogy, the very same principles apply to our essential need to say 'no' as often as necessary. Being positive in life is not about saying 'yes I'd love to' every time someone offers us something. No is not the opposite of yes, and is no less dynamic. In fact, no makes yes possible by keeping our powder dry. Our ability to make a discriminating decision between two or more choices is the very root of wisdom and opens up all sorts of possibilities as to how else to invest ourselves. And when it's someone saying no to us, then despite the initial sting, their rejection nonetheless leaves us open to pursue a whole range of alternatives. Like sadness, the word 'no' can be highly fertile and sow the seeds for a whole lot that's positive.

For sure, feeling sadness and hearing 'no' may bring us pain, but our ability to tolerate pain and press on in spite of it, is one of the key strengths that allows us to learn and progress. For instance, the embarrassment at performing a new skill badly; the pain of disagreement or feeling rejected and lonely. But this pain can be a sensitive indicator of what's important to us, and be a source of energy to do something about it. Yes, I could all too easily anaesthetise my sadness at my absent friend by watching a movie or drinking some wine. On the other hand, I could use that sadness to write that friend a letter. Like any hunger of the body or soul, sadness is not a feeling to be carelessly extinguished, but is something to be fed just the right nourishment. To use another analogy, we might put out a fire because we're afraid of the flames, or we could choose to see by it, cook by it, and sit and be warmed by it. So rather than running from sadness, we might wonder what that distinctive hunger is telling us. At the very least, sadness is an indication that we care; a seal of authenticity. But it's one thing to care, it's another thing to know what to do about it. If we can hang in there long enough to consider and explore that painful feeling, we might be able to tease out what positive action is called for. With such benefits in mind, our pain in whatever form may not be telling us to stop in our tracks, or to reach for some pills; it might simply be saying 'this matter deserves our care and attention.'

Let's focus on what's helpful

The likelihood is that someone we know well is quite depressed, even though they might be hiding it. I wrote above that depression not sadness is the enemy of happiness, and it's in everyone's interests to develop the skills that can cure and prevent depression, since these are the very same skills that can enhance our quality of life no matter our starting point.

As a rule of thumb, we're depressed if for several consecutive weeks our once enjoyable activities fail to bring us pleasure, and we've been resoundingly down in the dumps, with life feeling like one long grind. Only one quarter of individuals who suffer this very debilitating state actually seek help for it, not least because depression is characterised by a lack of motivation and a pessimistic outlook. For these same reasons, a sufferer will tend to drop out of psychotherapy within a couple of sessions because they persuade themselves that their situation is hopeless. Yet, the reality is, no matter the cause of our depression, and there can be many, if we practice a good range of well-proven approaches, we've every chance of initiating a full recovery.

Several times this book has championed the depression-busting ability of 45 minutes sweat-breaking physical exercise three times a week, plus lots of sunlight and adequate omega oils to correctly nourish the brain. We know, too, there is nothing better for our well-being than frequently attending social clubs and friendly societies of every sort for the healthy mix of relationships they readily foster. And when it comes to our thinking-skills, learning to be vigorously optimistic about investing our efforts in life will bring us resounding benefits on all fronts: our health, relationships, and accomplishments. In fact, so vital is our style of thinking to our sense of happiness, that I'd like to add some additional thinking-strategies to our checklist.

My first proposition is simply that we need to get good at ignoring unhelpful criticism and negative thoughts and feelings. This goes as much for our home-made voices of doom and gloom as for the stuff thrown our way by the world around us. We all of us have self-critical thoughts that skitter through our mind, thoughts worth no more attention than if they were shouted by a drunk in the street. We all of us have half-formed feelings of foreboding in our stomach, and occasionally feel spiteful, violent, envious, and suspicious. But these are just the sparks, noise and exhaust-fumes of a human brain thinking. Likewise, if we're looking for them, everyday life is liberally peppered with negative attitudes towards us whether it be the disapproving stare, the irritable tone, the dismissive gesture, the jealous put-down, or the officious rejection. The good news is that in the face of all that negativity, our own and other people's, we do have a choice whether to focus on it or not, and our accumulated choices powerfully determine our quality of life. Reason being that what we focus on, whether in ourselves or in the world around us, will provide the raw ingredients for how we think, feel and behave. So it pays us to be extremely discriminating and to cherry-pick the helpful and self-motivating thoughts, and quite simply bat the others away without a second glance. To do this, we might need to laugh at the negatives, rebuff them with counter-examples, or simply distract ourselves; but whatever we do, let's not linger on what isn't helpful to us.

We can learn to choose

It's not our past which most determines the possibilities open to us, it's what we choose here and now to make happen in our present and future. Put another way, our potential is far greater than the sum of our previous experiences, or our job title, bank balance, or physical appearance. It is the actions and attitudes we generate today that have the greatest power to represent us to the world, to bring us pleasure, and to improve our horizons in life. After all, we can initiate conversations, make plans and get moving. Viewed this way, our present and future behaviour appear to be our most intriguing and attractive personal qualities, and well worth investing in.

It is the ability to focus our attention on such self-motivating thoughts as these, rather than being mesmerised by negatives, which rests at the very heart of a healthy approach to life. And it's never too early to acquire such thinking skills because studies show that anxiety-prone children . . . anxious about their performance, about adult approval, or about life generally . . . are at high risk of depression some ten years later. In all of us, the well-honed ability to take helpful perspectives is a characteristic which clearly distinguishes the thinking of those who thrive from those who flounder in terms of health, accomplishment and high spirits. This is because when we face the uncertainties in daily life . . . and almost every moment of life has numerous unpredictable elements . . . the healthily optimistic person looks towards the brighter possibilities and acts accordingly. But if we're depressed, we tend to look backwards ruminating about past negative experiences, which leads us to conjure only pessimistic visions of the future. Not surprisingly, our focus on past negatives makes it extremely hard to stride forwards confidently. We're far better off to look to the present and future and to develop our skills at ducking and weaving around the flack, so as to get our spirits to where we want them to be. For instance, we can choose to ponder and relish our friend or partner's finest qualities rather than their shortfalls; and we can foster our realistic hopes rather than our farfetched forebodings.

Once we've got the hang of usefully re-deploying our focus of attention, we can start balancing other aspects of our thinking. If we're unhelpfully inward looking, we can start taking greater interest in things around us. If we're overly concerned about other people's opinions of us, we can turn the volume down on that. If we are too much at the beck and call of our emotions, we can engage our rational side rather more often.

Sleep is another arena that our re-focusing skills can improve upon. If we're depressed, we'll more than likely be waking several times a night or far too early in the morning; and, if anxiety is part of the problem, then we'll have real trouble getting off to sleep in the first place. Studies show that if our sleep returns to a healthy rhythm we tend to stay depression-free, so it's very important that our bed-time is not worry-time. To this end, we need to distract ourselves, perhaps with a good book, and make it a firm rule to banish thoughts of anything but gentle pleasures from our pre-sleep routine. Which brings us back to the essential idea that, for the most part in life, we have far greater ability to choose, and for far greater effect, than we might sometimes realise.

Finding life in death

Just as happiness needs sadness to help us appreciate it, so life needs death. Something to push against; the opposition. Far from being malevolent, death is simply a necessary counterpoint if life is to have meaning. After all, if our time for living was not finite and uncertain, we'd feel no imperative to 'carpe diem'.

Mulling such thoughts, I went to spend a day at St Christopher's Hospice in East London. It felt like my first day at Feltham Young Offenders Prison ten years before, because on both occasions I was apprehensive of what I might find, and on both occasions I was much inspired by the good spirits of the individuals who chose to work within such seemingly forebidding circumstances. I left St Christopher's, as I always left Feltham, feeling wiser and happier than when I arrived.

Dame Cicely Saunders is founder of the modern hospice movement, although she attributes its inspiration to David Tasma, a refugee from the Warsaw ghetto. In the London of 1947, this terminally ill 40 year old bequeathed to his young carer the sum of 500 pounds, saying "I'll be a window in your home". Cicely tells how "It took me 19 years to build a home around that window, but the core principles of our approach were borne out of my conversations with him as he was dying. David Tasma, who thought he'd made no impact on the world by his life, started a movement."

This beautiful story bears testimony to the words of 18th century Irish philosopher, Edmund Burke: *"No one could make a greater mistake than he who did nothing because he could only do a little."* There are now some 250 hospices around the UK, providing the model for many similar retreats in over 100 countries. They take a resoundingly holistic approach to the dying individual, not only applying their expert pain management but also being considerate of their patient's fears and regrets, and the practical and emotional needs of the family. Their service earns a modest income from the NHS, but they rely heavily on voluntary workers and donations, which is why Dame Cicely urges us to phone our local hospice and simply ask "Is there anything that somebody with my particular background can offer you?"

And who better than Cicely to understand that it can be hard to initiate things. In the years that followed David Tasma's death, it was only with the encouragement of a mentor that she took the brave step at age 33 of training as a doctor so she could better implement her audacious plans for an entirely new approach to terminally ill individuals. It was her same bold and enterprising spirit that took her to America in 1963 to learn about break-throughs in pain control.

Many years on, and from her richness of experience beside the death bed, Cicely says reassuringly "There can be something very creative about bereavement"; and from my own study of lives, I'd say her thought is embodied in the achievements of Aboriginal Australian Olympic runner, Cathy Freeman, who at the age of 16 lost a loved one. "A defining moment was when I saw my sister's casket lowered into the ground. I was in so much pain but I gained so much strength and I think that made me determined to make the most of who I was and what I had. I took that energy and all of the passion and it fed my soul."

For sure, bereavement is one of life's most painful emotions, but psychology has shown us that grieving does not necessarily lead to depression. For a healthy recovery, it helps us to have the example of those who have experienced bereavement and are living happily now. It also helps to have at least one close and confiding relationship in which we can talk openly about the pain of loss. Most of all, it seems we will cope well if those we live among need us to. By letting go of one much loved individual, our heart and hopes are set free to embrace another, and life renews itself.

Squaring ourselves with our past, present and future

'Health' comes from the Old English word meaning 'wholeness'; and the verb 'to heal' literally means 'to make whole'. This idea that health is something 'fully-rounded' helps remind us why fostering greater happiness in ourselves requires us to improve our relationship with our life in each of its three time dimensions – past, present and future.

Finding happiness in the present by fully engaging

Body Shop entrepreneur, Anita Roddick, says simply, "When you make a mistake you have to face up to the fact and take immediate steps to change course." And sure enough psychology would agree with her: *If we're feeling low and put upon by the world, let's get busy.*

Despite its popularity, a glass of wine in front of the telly isn't the best way to feel better in the here and now. We're much better off being fully absorbed in some mental or physical activity that requires far greater involvement. This is because our human brain has evolved to be a rapacious problem-solver, but rapidly finding itself in a comparatively danger-free environment, it often has a lot of spare capacity. This means that if we don't present ourselves with a positive but demanding task, our brain goes looking for trouble, and that's how regrets about the past and worries about future can run away with us. So the Nobel Scientist, Marie Curie, instinctively did the right thing after the tragic death of her young husband in a car accident. "I am working in the laboratory all day long, it is all I can do; I am better off there than anywhere else." This has something of the same strategy adopted by former British Prime Minister Margaret Thatcher: "Throughout my deliberately busy life I had been able to find solace for personal disappointments by forgetting the past and taking up some new venture. Work was my secret elixir."

Fortunately, the concepts of 'flow' and 'signature strengths' offer two closely related strategies that can promote our total absorption in the moment.

American psychology professor, Mihaly Csikszentmihalyi (pronounced cheeks-sent-me-high), first coined the term 'flow' for that intensely positive state achieved when our skill and energy levels well match the task we're engaged in, so that we skate close to the edge of our ability and have to concentrate absolutely. The goals must be clear and immediate, and so must the feedback on our performance. This is why playing a musical instrument or a sport are such common sources of flow, but if we're cream-crackered at the end of the day, so is reading a good book. If the elements are right, we will experience a complete lack of self-consciousness, and time will pass unmeasured in a warm and lasting glow of satisfaction.

I'm reminded of how H.G. Wells (author of *War of The Worlds*, and *The Time Machine*) and Charles Dickens (author of *Great Expectations* and *Oliver Twist*) suffered childhood ill-health which confined them both to bed for long periods. They used this time to immerse themselves in good literature and read well beyond their boyish years, building up skills that were to fabulously transform their later years. This observation seems to bear out something six times Tour de France champion, Lance Armstrong has written about his suffering cancer. "It taught me that sometimes the experience of losing things, whether health or a home or an old sense of self, has its own value in the scheme of a life."

What's most likely to promote this productive 'flow' state of pleasing engagement with the here and now, is reducing our passive pursuits such as tv, and replacing them with the activities that deploy one or more of our 'signature strengths' – which are any skills (physical or mental) so pleasurable to exercise that we feel invigorated rather than drained by doing them. Be it gardening, cooking, pitching for business or playing the fool . . . it's that small handful of activities at which we excel and relish above all others. The flow-inducing power of signature strengths explains why my Monday evening soccer with some like-minded comedians, leaves me feeling chipper well into the week, whereas Friday night's drinks have worn-off even before dawn.

Let's savour our blessings
Taking five minutes to note and savour what's going well in our life, is a daily routine that can make a tangible difference to our all round well-being, particularly in times of trouble. American psychology professors, Robert Emmons and Michael McCullough, are pioneering the experimental work in this field with some promising results. For instance, they asked one group of research participants to keep a journal of things for which they were thankful, while other groups wrote about neutral subjects or their life's daily hassles. Ten weeks later, the 'blessing-counters' tended to exercise more, report fewer physical ills, be more optimistic about the upcoming week, and feel better about their lives in general. In addition to which they were more likely to offer emotional support or practical help to someone with a problem, while also mustering greater enthusiasm, determination and energy for their own important goals.

None of these benefits should really surprise us because savouring one's blessings is the polar opposite of rumination – which means turning over and over in one's mind some negative thought or incident – and rumination is one of the surest ways to depression. But what the new research serves to remind us is that to encourage our well-being requires us not merely to reduce our negatives practices, but to actively pursue our life-enhancing ones. It reminds us that our psychological health is not so much a reflection of what we do wrong, as what we do right.

So in every day terms, how might I personally cultivate the practice of thankfulness for what's felt good or is going well? To cheer my spirits before sitting down to lunch, I could take a full five minutes to look back over the morning and cherry-pick some pleasures: I could relish the conversation I had with a friend, and watching that squirrel rummaging in the grass, and my tickling the cat Moses over the road who seemed genuinely pleased to see me. I use these little memories to beat away any urge to rue the feeling that I'm behind in my work or haven't had closure on a couple of problems. By focusing my attention on the recent positives, and by replaying those experiences and pondering their goodness, I help put myself in a better mood; and a better mood is one powerful means by which I can become more productive, more open to change, and more willing to take on challenges. I can use the same five minute procedure to prevent myself becoming irritated or glum on the journey home, and again at bedtime to ready myself for sleep. I simply savour the sunset I saw from the train window, and the kind e-mail I received earlier. This way, I give no quarter to the sort of negatives that might disturb my slumber.

Oprah Winfrey has just such a routine in place and she recently recommended it to the graduating women of Wellesley College: "Keep a grateful journal. Every night, list five things that happened this day, that you are grateful for. What it will begin to do is to change your perspective of your day and your life. I believe that if you can learn to focus on what you have, you will always see that the universe is abundant and you will have more. If you concentrate and focus in your life on what you don't have, you will never have enough. *Be grateful.*"

It's worth noting here that American Professors Fred Bryant and Joseph Veroff suggest we learn to savour more expertly, i.e. to better appreciate who we are and what we have, akin to when we close our eyes to relish the taste of something, rather than concentrating on teeing up the next mouthful. This way, a little can be made to count for a lot more. The researchers advise that we reduce our future-mesmerised multi-tasking, and instead systematically savour any chosen moment by examining it with each of our five senses in turn. They note, too, that discussing a past or present pleasure with someone is usually the leading means of heightening its intensity, reminding us of the time-honoured principle that 'a joy shared is a joy doubled'. Best of all if we can savour the everyday positive experiences such as a loving gesture, a social activity, or our natural environment – those freely available experiences which can so readily bring an affirming sense of intimacy in our relationship with life.

Deaf and blind since infancy, Helen Keller had wise words on this subject. "Keep your face to the sunshine and you cannot see the shadow." She also had the following to say about her own restrictions. "Everything has its wonders, even darkness and silence, and I learn, whatever state I may be in, therein to be content . . . . I seldom think of my limitations, and they never make me sad. Perhaps there is just a touch of yearning at times; but it is vague, like a breeze among flowers."

We each of us has the power to help our loved ones see the wonder in their lives, just by asking the right questions. One evening shortly after her painful divorce, former US Secretary of State Madeleine Albright was having dinner with some of her female friends, where they were talking about their personal lives. "As I listened, I was fascinated by these women's problems and a bit jealous – especially of those who were married. Then one of my friends turned to me and said, 'Madeleine, you're the one who has it all. You've been married, you have three fabulous daughters, a great job. How did you do it?' I was stunned, I realised that I had fallen into self-pity, focusing not on what I had but on what I had lost. I have never forgotten that evening. Before that episode I felt I had no advice to offer younger women because I had failed. This discussion had banished those thoughts."

Feeling happy about the future

We're about to be reminded once again of the central theme of this chapter: how it's not what experiences we have in life that determine whether we're happy or sad or thrive or flounder, *it's what attitude we take to those experiences.*

Irrepressible optimism is widely regarded by psychologists as one of the most beneficial personality traits . . . and thankfully it's one we can readily learn.

Optimism is simply taking the attitude that things can and will improve if we put some effort in. Hundreds of studies demonstrate that compared to pessimists, optimists are higher achievers both at work and on the playing field, as well as enjoying better physical health, faster recovery from illness, and suffering much less anxiety and depression. U.N. ambassador and former fashion model, Waris Dirie, recognized the wisdom in her mother's perspective on life when she returned to her native Somalia: "My mother didn't look old to me, the wrinkles around her forehead give her a great dignity. *It tells you that hardship is not the same as worries.*"

The health benefits of optimism accrue for a host of reasons. First, optimists have more friends and social supports, not least because they're such cheerful souls to be around. They also do more self-care activities such as exercise because they believe it all helps; and meantime their generally buoyant mood boosts their immune system. On top of which, optimists involve themselves more actively with everyday life because they believe their endeavours will eventually reap rewards. Indeed, their worldly success is largely because they persevere in the face of life's routine setbacks and major blows, and this Robert-the-Bruce 'dynamic resilience' often becomes a self-fulfilling prophecy. Mo Mowlam, the Former Northern Ireland Secretary of State who fought her cancer while simultaneously brokering the beginnings of peace, would certainly agree: "I always look on the bright side – one of my characteristics that helped produce good results."

It's no coincidence that the ten percent of would-be army officers who each year drop out of the United States Military Academy at West Point are very largely pessimists. So, too, are many lawyers, because the job requires they anticipate every possible negative scenario, and this aptitude is very likely why they have such a high incidence of anxiety and depression. It seems that lawyers can find their cloud-filled perspective hard to turn off when they leave the office. By contrast, the best sales people are unrelenting optimists, because they tell themselves the next big deal is just around the corner.

But the stakes can be even higher than career success. A team led by the longtime Director of Clinical Psychology at the University of Michigan, Professor Chris Peterson, studied 1,000 individuals across 50 years. The pessimists had an increased likelihood of early death, but rather than the cancer and heart-attacks usually associated with the trait, *'accidental death'* was the most frequent culprit. Peterson's team concluded that the character trait of pessimism led to a fatalistic, careless lifestyle which led the individuals to put themselves in harm's way. Optimists, on the other hand, habitually put themselves in situations with a high risk of good things happening. It's a fascinating thought that our attitude to life alters the settings in which we put ourselves, not just how we behave once we get there. Lance Armstrong nails this: "The way you live your life, the perspective you select, is a choice you make every single day when you wake up. It's yours to decide."

Nice to know, then, that we can all learn to be more optimistic. The University of Pennsylvania's *Penn Resiliency Project* directed by psychologists Karen Reivich, Jane Gillham and Martin Seligman, provides 12 two-hour training sessions that teach optimism to teenagers. This course *halves* the incidence and severity of depression, and long-term follow-ups over several years show that the gains to the individual youngsters *increase* rather than fade. I.e. Once they get the hang of optimism, they start applying it more often.

The key ingredient in learning optimism is this: how we explain to ourselves the causes and implications of things going wrong. When things go badly, we should be sure to generate realistic explanations for just how temporary and specific the causes were, which means that if we rework the problem with some inventive new approaches, we'll probably pull through. On the other hand, when things go *well*, we should look for evidence that they did so for reasons that are permanent and characteristic of every aspect of our life. In short, we've got to play the wily courtroom lawyer who always has a counter-argument to win-over the jury in our favour.

All this said, let's keep flexible in our relationship with 'possible futures'. For sure, viewing the world through rose-tinted bifocals will help keep our spirits up so we can soldier on. But it's important to note that pessimism usually sees the harsh realities of a situation far more accurately, so we need to practice flexible optimism in circumstances when the cost of mis-forecasting the likely outcomes could be disastrously high. For instance, if we were considering drink-driving, unsafe sex, or a major investment of our time or money, then it's vital to envisage some worse-case scenarios so as to prompt some smart precautions. But if we're simply churning out ideas, taking a shot at goal, or asking for a date, that's when strategically deploying a can-do gung-ho attitude will actively help achieve our goals, because we'll press on in good spirits.

Giving ourselves every reason to become more hopeful
Professor Rick Snyder, who has spent much of his career as Director of Clinical Psychology at the University of Kansas, believes three ingredients reliably increase our sense of hope in all and any endeavour.

1: Multiple goals
Number one is to appoint sufficiently attractive and self-motivating goals for each of our key life arenas. It's essential to generate several goals in each category, albeit rank-ordered by preference, rather than fixating on just one lone objective. Snyder suggests that a healthily, hopeful individual might have on average *six* goals on their horizon, spread across different arenas of their life. Boxing champion and UN Messenger of Peace, Muhammad Ali, is clear on this very same point: "What keeps me going is goals!"

We should also break the end goal in to shorter term sub-goals as stepping stones: goals for this hour, this afternoon, this week. These sub-goals serve not only to make us consider how, realistically, we are going to step-by-step achieve our aims, but they also serve to indicate what progress we're making on route.

2: Multiple routes forward
Our second task is to generate several possible pathways towards each goal, so that if needs be we can - swap to an alternative trail to

the same eventual objective. This variety guards against our progress being blocked. We'll always be able to make headway via one route or another, so we need never feel stagnant or trapped. In this, as in all things, tenacity and persistence are characterised by genuine progress, not simply a stubborn repetition of failing techniques. Note how it is the *multiple* nature of our goals and pathways which is the key to building a resilient sense of hope. This underscores the theme of variety and versatility. *Variety* – because we thrive on a rich mix, whether that be of ideas, activities, friends or foods. *Versatility* – because life benefits not from attempting to avoid challenging situations, but from learning to thrive in the face of them. This requires us to be flexible in how we think and behave.

3: Self-confidence

Our third task is to foster a strong sense of self-confidence in our ability to succeed, by recalling previous successes, by arranging to learn any requisite new skills, and by actively inviting help and mentorship.

Applying systematically these three components: multiple goals, multiple routes, and fostering self-confidence – can significantly increase our likelihood of success, and meantime we'll be a good deal happier and healthier for being more hopeful. Helen Keller puts this very poetically: "To keep our faces toward change, and behave like free spirits in the presence of fate, is strength undefeatable."

Squaring ourselves with a painful past

When things have gone wrong, we can sometimes feel that we're going to be permanently scarred or damaged or hurt . . . haunted, as it were, by the bad patch. This is far from how it needs to be, and we can take some active steps to prevent that.

One of the biggest enemies of happiness is rumination about the past – obsessively churning over time and time again our negative memories and partly digested thoughts, rather than putting things to rest. Such morbid analysis is a breeding ground for bitterness, regret, sadness and shame. Rumination is a deeply unhelpful habit not unconnected to the common misunderstanding that if we express a negative feeling, no matter rage or misery, it will free that emotion and return us to neutral. *There is not a jot of evidence to support this myth.* Quite the contrary: dwelling on or airing our negative feelings serves only to increase the pains they cause us. Yet, if left unstirred, they fade away. (The one exception to this rule is when someone is traumatised; but I address the extraordinary phenomena of traumatising experiences and detraumatising techniques, in my chapter called *Powerful New Approaches to Common Health Problems.*)

So how to combat the self-torturing rumination and emotional dramatics that can so poison happiness? Well, Professor Martin Seligman at the University of Pennsylvania is arguably one of the world's leading researchers on coping with depression, and he says that insufficient appreciation and savouring of the good events in our past, and overemphasis of the bad ones, are the two culprits that undermine serenity, contentment and satisfaction. So here's what to do about it:

Firstly, we shouldn't replay images of our negative past. This is not denial, this is simply removing the oxygen of attention that will reheat the emotional embers. On this point, Helen Keller, who triumphed over her deafness and blindness, reminds us, "When one door of happiness closes, another opens; but often we look so long at the closed door that we do not see the one which has been opened for us."

The only condition under which we should revisit a grim episode is to learn some lessons that we can directly translate into 'solution-focused action' – because such action is the very antithesis of rumination.

Secondly, we should allocate a particular time of the week for this lesson-learning, action-oriented backward glance, rather than allowing negative memories to intrude whenever it suits them. Sounds like a small point, but in the Harvard Study of Adult Development, one of the coping-strategies that characterised the most healthy, happy and successful individuals, was their ability to put-off thinking about something until a better time to do so.

Thirdly and finally, when painful memories do ambush us, we

must repel them immediately by conjuring positive thoughts incompatible with the negative ones. For this, we need a handful of ready-made, heart-warming memories on emergency stand-by to evoke a profound sense of pride or pleasure.

Let's just remind ourselves: *the past doesn't own us*

It's good to know that Professor George Vaillant's Harvard study of 824 American lifetimes unfurling over the course of more than 60 years (this is the very same study I've just mentioned above), confidently concludes that our skills for coping, enjoying, and doing good, each have the capacity to improve greatly throughout a lifetime. A personality need not bear the bitter fruits of a grim childhood nor be shackled by the mistakes of young adulthood. Painful memories can lessen and heal if we persevere with self-healing choices in how we lead our everyday life. The past may seem to stack the odds, but it can never dictate the next steps we take.

A quite different study of 700 eminent individuals from all walks of life in the 20th century, recounts how three-quarters of them had suffered a childhood troubled by something – whether by poverty, by a broken home, by rejecting or over-possessive or dominating parents, by financial hardships, by physical handicaps, or by parental dissatisfaction over the child's school failures or vocational choices. Yet those same beleaguered childhoods nonetheless grew up into adult lives that rose to great heights.

It seems that if we can learn to channel it, adversity can become the wind beneath our wings. Oscar-winning actress Julia Roberts says wisely "It's not just great teachers that sometimes shape your life. Sometimes it's the *absence* of great teachers that shapes your life . . . and being ignored can be just as good for a person as being lauded."

A case in point of how we can reject a painful past and forge much of our own future, is Claire Rayner who became first a nurse and then Britain's best loved advice columnist, and now a social campaigner. "The first fifteen to twenty years of my life were pretty grotty . . . but once I'd escaped from the awfulness of my childhood, I had nowhere to go but up, and up I went like a cork . . . It is sur-

prising what can be salvaged from a life, however inauspiciously it
begins. . . . You can't spend your adult life grieving for the child you
once were: it is wasteful and pointless, and obliterates the present,
which is meant to be your time to live happily. That child who was
you is long gone, dead in fact, and the best you can do for him or her
is to make the best of the life that you have now."

Put regret to good work

In the 1946 Frank Capra classic, *It's a Wonderful Life*, the smalltown
good guy played by James Stewart, runs into some seemingly insur-
mountable problems and, blinded by his rage and despair, wishes
he'd never been born. At this point, an apprentice angel called
Clarence persuades St Peter to let this tortured soul see how his little town would have turned out much the worse if James Stewart
hadn't been around to make a wonderful difference.

And so begins a 'what if' scenario so beloved of stories the
world over. It's probably no accident that this theme proves so
popular, because our human brain is highly adept at pondering the
'what ifs' of life. After all, this is the raw material of our imaginations. And 'what if' thinking is rarely more powerful than when in
the form of hope and regret, the latter of which is most often viewed
as a self-punishing mug's game and best avoided.

It's good news, then, that psychology professor Neal Roese at
Illinois University takes a refreshingly positive perspective on that
pain of loss in the pit of our stomach. He builds his case on the key
observation that although in the shorter term we regret the things
we've done, as time passes we increasingly regret the things we didn't
do but could have. This characteristic is evident in studies as far a
field as the US, Russia, China and Japan, and it probably reflects the
following phenomena. As time passes, we're very good at seeing the
silver lining in our gaffs, but we also start to see the bigger picture of
our life-course, and realise that trying something bold but risky
wouldn't have been so bad after all, even if it hadn't worked out. In
essence, psychology would agree with America's former President,
Theodore Roosevelt, in declaring "Far better it is to dare mighty
things, even though chequered by failure, than to dwell in that per-

petual twilight that knows not victory nor defeat." In respect of this, Professor Roese suggests we view regret as a natural warning bell to say we're missing out on a longed-for course of action.

From this point onwards, Roese's argument seems to rest upon our familiar friend, one of the first principles of the human condition: *it's not making mistakes that's a problem, it's our response to them which allows the mistakes to lead to a net loss or a net gain.* For although it can look as if a lifetime can be dramatically shaped by single events or turning points, on closer inspection we can see that our lives are far more sculpted by our characteristic and habitual skills and strategies for coping with setbacks and generating opportunities. Most often it is *these* that will determine our outcomes, rather than the events that befall us. Accordingly, for regret to be productive rather than toxic, we should harness our pain to spur the versatile, creative actions that will put right what feels wrong. We must create a future that compensates for the past in some positive way.

The professor's proposal reflects a theme than comes up time and again in the strategies of a psychologically healthy person: *harnessing painful emotions* . . . such as anger, fear, or loneliness . . . so as to produce positive, creative action. We should ask what the emotion is telling us, and then, rather than repress, ignore or ruminate on such powerful and potentially destructive feelings, we should saddle them and ride them in the directions we long to go. Media pioneer and philanthropist, Oprah Winfrey, has this to say "Although there may be tragedy in your life, there's always a possibility to triumph. It doesn't matter who you are, where you come from. The ability to triumph begins with you. Always."

As with just about everything else in life, moderation is the most productive approach. Too much looking back and pondering what might have been will risk depression. Not enough, and we neither learn from our mistakes, nor feel urged to act to remedy them. Hence, Roese counsels that for regret to be productive, it needs to be sharply felt but short-lived, rather than being allowed to linger. Used in the correct dosage and in the right way, regret can prove itself a welcome nourishment.

In the last minutes of *Casablanca*, Humphrey Bogart tells

Ingrid Bergman to get on a plane or ". . . you'll regret it. Maybe not today. Maybe not tomorrow. But soon . . . and for the rest of your life." Well, in the light of our capacity for harnessing regret, I'd say Bogart was under-estimating the emotional alchemy that can turn regrets for the past into hopes for the future. So, when some promising course of action calls to our heart (in contrast to our temporary appetites), we should take it. Be it the kiss ventured, the friendship offered, a career explored, or an adventure undertaken, we should remind ourselves that if all we risk is embarrassment or a painful sense of setback, these aches will quickly fade, and by the very act of trying, our spirit is making progress.

I am moved by the sentiments of former US Secretary of State, Madeleine Albright: "I was taught to strive not because there were any guarantees of success, but because the act of striving is in itself the only way to keep faith with life."

* * *

Planning for Progress

- Who could you ask for help and on what topics? And to whom could you offer help?

- How are you going to improve your relationship with your past, your present, and your future?

- What regrets about things not done could you channel into positive future action?

- Whose life, and how exactly they coped with it, would you like to read more about?

* * *

Reinventing Ourselves and Reinvesting in Life

Is it time to change?

Imagine you met yourself out walking in the wilds one afternoon, and fell into friendly and frank conversation over many miles. Imagine you told yourself your own life story, would you like what you heard?

Sometimes we realise that we've paddled ourselves into a dead end, and we've got to do something about it. Sometimes tinkering won't do and we need to completely redesign our approach to life, our goals and our journeys. Sometimes we need to reinvent ourselves.

Let's be clear though, that new outfits, new hair-dos, new looks . . . are not what reinventing oneself is all about. If all we change is the outside, it's just a disguise. But if we change ourselves on the inside, then all the other stuff will follow suit. All the other stuff becomes the tools of our trade and a natural extension of our best ambitions. Let's not forget that we're aiming to *make* a difference, not just look different.

We want to redesign how we cope with life and the world around us.

We want to change the environments into which we put ourselves. And we want to rethink the company we keep.

In truth, self-reinvention is not invention at all, it's about owning up to and giving air to another part of ourselves that's been resting dormant or that we've only just developed. It's about reworking our list of priorities in life, and it's about acting upon them.

There have certainly been times in my own life when I've felt the need for considerable change. When I first left university, I worked for a time as a waiter in a top private hospital, up on the cancer ward. Philosophically this was a testing time for me. Monday I'd be sharing a laugh with Mrs Jones in room 14, and the next day she'd be at death's door. Her priest would request some water so as to administer The Last Rights, and I'd find myself asking "still or sparkling?" Worse than that, my fellow waiters and I were all on the minimum wage, so when people died, we'd 'forget' to tell the kitchens for a couple of days so Chef would keep sending up the cordon bleu meals which we happily polished off. But I was well aware that eating a dead person's dinner was in breach of all sorts of moral codes. Brushing aside these uncomfortable thoughts, I'd sneak off for a smoke in the gent's loo, but then I'd catch myself in the mirror . . . me in my white nylon shirt and clip-on bow tie and my hair sticking up stupidly where I'd slept on it. *How had it come to this*, I wondered? *And what was all this death meant to tell me?*

Evolution not Revolution

One key proviso is this: improvement doesn't mean throwing the good out with the bad, or blaming those around us. Improvement means building on the positives so that the whole situation is made better for everyone involved. Very often it's not a question of giving things up, so much as adding things on, i.e. a new dimension to one's life through new skills, experiences and relationships. To this end, we need to be discriminating in our approaches, rather than all-or-nothing. We dump the negatives but take the positives with us: our hopes, our allies, our skills, passions and cherished memories.

It's encouraging to note that the healthiest people in the Harvard Study of Adult Development were highly adept at channeling their passions so as not to let them overturn the apple cart, while nonetheless allowing them to drive some sort of productive and positive action which cleverly pays heed to our callings. For instance, rather than give up our day job to become a struggling actor, we would join an amateur dramatics class three evenings per week.

So let's not tear in recklessly. *Evolution rather than revolution.* Evolution is organic and more gradual and comes from inside us, building on what feels good and does good. It gives us time to balance one change with another. So if we give up boozing, we could take up dancing. Our evolution will probably require us to develop some additional skills, perhaps more self-confidence or a new language or a particular qualification. Rather tellingly, revolution does not require any such progress, and so not surprisingly, revolution is destructive and hurtful of oneself and those around us.

So let's set out to thoughtfully explore the different directions we could take, and be prepared to investigate and experiment. We could also consider who might guide us or be allies through our period of metamorphosis. If there are no mentors to hand, perhaps there are autobiographies of individuals we admire for how they have lived their lives. It can prove very encouraging to see in detail how life has looked through other people's eyes.

Replacing our negative patterns

The Science of Well-Being isn't about fine tuning, it's about engineering profound and lasting improvements. But Homo Sapiens, as well as being social animals, are essentially creatures of habit. And if a sense of progress is one of life's most satisfying feelings, then being trapped in a long-term pattern of unhelpful behaviour is one of the most frustrating. The trouble is, in the course of growing-up we become accustomed to certain roles, even downright unpleasant ones, that we usually learn within our family or at school.

Thereafter, when facing new challenges, we can unwittingly repeat those same survival strategies which we devised in sheer panic as a child or teenager under stress. These patterns are like magnets whose invisible force pulls us off course. As a consequence, we automatically recreate a cycle of relationships, jobs, or lifestyles that at best are self-inhibiting, and at worst are self-destructive.

Such ingrained habits can manifest in myriad ways: perhaps in the course of disagreements we are too quick to appease . . . or overly aggressive. In personal relationships, we might tend to be emotionally cold . . . or too clingy. Or maybe we are untidy to a fault . . . or neurotically pristine. It could also be just a nagging sense of being an outsider . . . or a failure . . . or something of a fraud.

If we look more closely at our relationship repertoire, we may also observe that we tend towards one or more of three self-defeating strategies:

- We acquiesce to all our old familiar roles because we mistakenly think they reflect our own true self and so can't be changed.
- We try to escape the emotional pains of our flawed relationships, either by keeping everyone at an emotional arm's length, or by anaesthetising ourselves through compulsive bingeing on anything from food and fantasy, to exercise and work.
- We try to compensate for the negative feelings from our past, but in doing so we over-compensate, and ironically it's this that alienates the new people in our lives. So, if we were shy or ashamed or fearful when younger, we might now act showy, arrogant or even bullying.

If we can recognise ourselves in any of the above, there are some simple steps to help develop more rewarding ways of relating to the world.

First, we could weigh-up the pros and cons of our habitual behaviour, and why it's worth changing. What purpose did it once serve, and what's still jamming it in place? Rather than trying to attribute blame, we could simply take full responsibility for improvement.

We can call the bluff of out-dated fears by systematically experimenting with alternative ways of doing things. Now's the time to use the well-honed skills from some other arena of our life to serve as duckboards taking us into new territory. For instance, enjoying people's company or the great outdoors can be the means by which we get ourselves into regular exercise.

It will also help us to visualise in rich detail how we'd prefer to behave, imitating the best examples from those we've seen around us. We should be sure to support our imaginative rehearsals with deeply relaxed muscles and the slowest, most gentle breathing. Combining these ingredients helps us acquire skills at the level of our sub-conscious auto-pilot which is exactly where our old behaviours are deeply rooted. And if we have images from the past that flash demoralisingly into our mind, we should reshape those images just like a film director reshooting the scene so as to give it a happier ending.

As with anything we wish to become proficient in, a little practice every day will work very well, whereas occasional tweaks won't change anything. Our subconscious, in a misguided attempt to maintain the status quo of the old habits, will probably try some sabotage. It's as if something inside us is working on the principle of 'Better the devil we know than the wild blue yonder'. We must spot these negative feelings and seemingly accidental distractions for what they are, and keep progressing. As in all learning situations, our rate of improvement will be directly proportional to our willingness to experiment with how we think and behave, and our willingness to tough it out when feeling uncomfortable with acting in unfamiliar ways.

Let's free up our rigid thinking

Being able to see a problem from several perspectives, and then being able to generate several solutions, is one of the strongest hallmarks of a healthy and powerful mind. But psychologists can list at least twelve unhelpful attitudes which too often scupper our accurate and flexible assessment of a situation. Which of the following ring bells of recognition for you?

- All or nothing thinking: "If I can't do it perfectly, I shan't bother at all."
- Catastrophizing: "I forgot to add parsley, so the dinner's a complete disaster."
- Overgeneralizing: "I *always* mess up like this."
- Name calling: "I didn't simply make a mistake, I'm a complete bloody idiot."
- Exaggerating: "I'll never meet anyone as wonderful again."
- Emotional Reasoning: "I want this so much that it's simply bound to work out."
- Dismissing the positives: "Oh yes, I got the job, but I expect they were desperate."
- Wishful Thinking: "If I only spoke German and a bit of Japanese, it would have all worked out fine."
- Fortune Telling: "This presentation will be a disaster, I just know it."
- Mind Reading: "I can just tell by his smile he doesn't like me."
- Taking things personally: "She walked right past me in the street as if she didn't see me. I'm trying to think what I've done wrong."
- Taking the blame: "When I phoned, she sounded very rushed, so I feel awful at having bothered her."

Then, of course, there's the 'Thought Police' words which try so hard to outlaw any alternative ways of thinking . . . words such as *never, nobody, always, must* which we routinely over use. It's rare that life benefits from us approaching things so rigidly.

We might only occasionally fall into the above thinking pitfalls, but like a pilot doing preflight checks, it can pay to systematically go through such a list when considering an important matter. And if this all sounds like little more than common sense, then you're in full agreement with Albert Einstein who concluded that "the whole of science is nothing more than a refinement of everyday thinking."

Changing our tune

We feel emotions in response to our thoughts, so by improving what we think, we can improve how we feel. The trouble is, as outlined in the section above, many of our inner thoughts about ourselves and our world are long-ingrained, automatic habits that are out-dated, inaccurate and inhibiting. What we need instead is for our inner voice to become our strongest ally, particularly since there's so much media that is deliberately undermining our confidence just in order to sell us something. One powerful remedy works as follows: when we feel our mood swing to the negative – perhaps sad, angry, anxious, or embarrassed – we should immediately ask ourselves what demoralising thought, memory, or mental image provoked our knee-jerk reaction. Then our job is to cross-examine it, demanding to see the up-to-date evidence that supports our pessimism. Too often we're acting on false presumptions, or are criticising ourselves in unfair ways we'd never inflict upon others. Equally important in this self-monitoring, is to note the uplifting thoughts that give wings to our good spirits, so we can encourage ourselves when times require.

Reassessing our stock responses can up-grade all aspects of our life: attitudes to exercise, to the way we look, to how we behave and with whom. Our task is to shed the skin of the personality we might once have inhabited but is no longer working for us. Our reward will be the fresh and conscious choices which truly reflect our full, up-to-date range of life experiences. People take cues about how to treat us, from how we treat ourselves, so it pays to keep the self-talk warm and helpful. Work at it every day and, like any bully, our self-bullying voices will soon fade away. We'll reap the benefits because our feelings will affect our performance, which is why Olympic coaches consider the well-honed ability to improve one's mood, to be the hallmark of the gold medallist.

The seeds of change

So how else can we develop far more mature, effective, and satisfying strategies of relating to the world? First off, we could recognise what brings us satisfaction and joy, and then commit ourselves to expanding those positives.

We've probably been this way as long as we can remember, so we're going to have to attempt manageable challenges first of all, and leave the tougher stuff until we've built up some muscles. The bad days will be when we're tired or under pressure or feeling under the weather, but setbacks won't mean we're back to square one. Once we're familiar with our goals and inhibitions, next time will be easier. Such a self-help approach can be very effective, but if progress is unsatisfactory, we should take ourselves to a specialist, just like we would do to make major improvements to our health, our teeth, or our car. Let's remind ourselves that it isn't selfish or self-obsession to invest in our personality like this. After all, our everyday behaviour has profound effects on those we love, so for their sake, we want to make progress.

My story, much like any other

At the age of 10, from one moment to the next, I lost control of my speech. Before this sudden change in my situation, I was a child who spoke fluently and eagerly, much to the annoyance of my schoolteachers. Then one fine morning, I was startled by a perfectly pleasant teacher shouting at me to be quiet and, for the first and only time in my life, I suffered some sort of difficulty breathing that literally knocked me to the floor. When I got up off the ground two minutes later, I could barely get a word out. It's as if an incompetent electrician had rewired my brain, and the unconscious co-ordination that speech requires had all gone to pieces. I was stammering on every word.

My faltering speech caused hilarity among my classmates, and a deeply worried look in the eyes of adults, so within twenty-four hours I had decided it was better to conceal this unwelcome addition to my schoolboy vocabulary. I learned either to swap the words I *wanted* to say for the ones I felt able to, or I avoided speech situations altogether. These simple strategies worked a treat. No one seemed to notice that one moment I was an unstoppably blabby ten year old who might well have been a student at The Barbara Streisand School of Melodrama . . . and 24 hours later I became a silent, thoughtful boy who seemed to be modeling himself on Clint Eastwood.

Maybe they thought I'd matured.

What I actually did was muddle through, which at age ten is easier than you think. People expect you to be shy, and your speech to be uncertain. But as I grew towards the end of my teenage years the true extent of this long-concealed impediment threatened to cripple all my ambitions for becoming a man. The world expected a chap to give talks and make phonecalls and speak up for himself. But on a bad day, I couldn't guarantee I'd be able say my own name, let alone my girlfriend's. Worse still, I knew of no men, or at least *no heroes*, who stammered . . . *or so I thought.* What I didn't realise was that my difficulties speaking placed me in the excellent company of Sir Winston Churchill, Charles Darwin, and many other individuals by whose lives I might have been much inspired. But unaware of these role models, I was saddened and deeply frightened by my firmly shackled speech. I wondered how there could there be any place for me in the adult world. Surely my dreams of being a jet pilot or a medical doctor or a business man or just about anything at all would simply run aground just as soon as I opened my mouth. School had been a place where everyone knew me and I knew the ropes and most days I could duck and weave around my hidden problem. But university at age 18 threatened to be a far more demanding world, and I was unwittingly faced with a big dilemma.

Deal with reality or run from it?

Without making any conscious decision on the matter, *I ran.* And in my attempt to run from my fear and sadness at what felt like a difficult present and a bleak future, I increasingly resorted to homemade fantasy-world scenarios which offered the glories I couldn't hope to fulfill in my real life. Pretty soon I was immersing myself in the pleasures of my imagination four or more hours per day. There at least I could be an accomplished speaker with a fabulous voice, and just for good measure I imagined I was 'desperately handsome and a highly skilled professional'. What made it all the easier was that escaping into make-believe like this was already quite familiar to me. After all, I'd been watching three hours of television every night since I was 11, thereby skating on the thin ice of a life that rather favoured unreal worlds. But, by the time I arrived at university, I didn't need a television, because I simply used my imagination to escape reality altogether, and there was nowhere I couldn't do it: walking to and from home, sitting at the back of the lecture class, first thing in the morning, and last thing at night. I squeezed reality in around my fictional life, not the other way around.

If I'd been drinking from a vodka bottle, smoking dope, or playing computer games several hours a day, then somebody might have noticed. *I might have noticed.* But fantasising felt quite natural, or at least comfortable, and was easy to conceal. And although fantasising was my true forte, I had other well developed 'quick-fixes' with which to distort the world around me so things seemed better, albeit only for the short term. For instance, if I didn't feel an account of my real life was going to be good enough for my listener, then I'd exaggerate or lie about it. I also made grandiose plans which I'd only follow up with half-baked efforts towards them. Reality was a lot of trouble, and I didn't feel up to the job.

It's not the original problem that does the damage

My strategy of escaping into fantasy and quick-fixes when reality proved difficult, was to cause me unimagined problems. Sure, having trouble speaking made life a little tricky: not being able to ask a question in class, and barely being able to make a phonecall or introduce myself in a job interview. But what was ten times more damaging . . . what held me back and drew my life wildly off course . . . was the effect this problem had on my relationship with reality. Reality is an environment that puts up a lot of resistance to our making progress, and consequently it helps build the mental muscles for problem-solving. But by stark contrast, fantasy is a zero-gravity environment in which anything is possible, so our problem-solving skills begin to wither away if we spend too long there. My addiction to fantasy in those teenage and university years meant that I lacked the real-life coping skills and step-by-step planning to make any headway. Yet, as a university student, I had little or no insight in to my fantasy life's role in my real-life problems. I didn't realise that by escaping from reality or resorting to quick-fixes, I was depriving myself of the opportunity not just to cope with adversity but to grow strong in the face of it. In fact, by my evasions and quick-fixes I was making my real life an ever harder place in which to feel comfortable and hopeful.

This simple theme could run though every chapter of this book: our well-being is not determined by what happens in our life . . . the progress or the set backs . . . it's what we do with them that matters.

For any child or teenager, a fear and dissatisfaction with real life can come from being bullied, or from a serious illness, or a traumatic experience, or a depressed parent, or any number of emotional pains that every life is heir to. What determines whether these pains lead eventually to positives or negatives, is wholly dependent on whether our responses serve to strengthen us, or weaken us. So it was, that as a direct result of my resorting to fantasy and quick-fixes whenever a cloud appeared, I made little progress in my university studies, my personal relationships stagnated, and I shunned employment after graduation. Though I felt desperate to achieve in the real world, my vague goals were always wildly ambitious because I so wanted them to compensate for the humiliations and desperations of my word-stealing stammer. It was not by accident that I left university with the lowest class of degree that the psychology department had given in the previous ten years. I was, however, a specialist in at least one thing: *make-believe worlds.* Combine this with not being able to talk very well, and it is not entirely surprising that I began to write fiction . . . novels and film scripts that would never find a publisher. It's not that I wanted to write particularly . . . I wanted to *live* . . . but real life seemed all but impenetrable, so writing it was.
It's not the original problem that does the damage. It's what we do about it.

Cut forward several years . . .

. . . and I'm walking into a high security Young Offender Prison in West London. I'd asked Channel 4 Television, Levi's Jeans, and the producers of *Four Weddings and a Funeral* to sponsor me to work for several months as a creative writing tutor in Europe's largest prison for serious offenders age 18 to 21. But I got more than I bargained for, because while talking to these young inmates about their imaginations and the creative storylines that ran inside their heads, I quickly realised that the very same reality-escaping fantasies that had so imprisoned my own life, had imprisoned theirs. They were using, and had always used, exactly the same escapist thoughts and quick-fix behaviours to run from anything that made them uncomfortable or threatened emotional pain.

I'd assumed that my escapist strategies had been one of a kind. My own original property. But here was my enemy cloned a hundred times in these imprisoned lives.

I'd recently been studying a correspondence course on 'the psychology of crime' through the Open University, so I went to a specialist library to read up on what those young inmates and I were suffering from. To my astonishment, there was nothing in any of the mainstream books on psychology or psychiatry, crime or education. The words fantasy and daydreaming weren't even mentioned in any indexes, they were deemed so totally irrelevant to people's lives.

This knocked me back a little. Maybe I was mistaken. Maybe I was making it all up, and this 'escaping from reality' thing was some sort of psychological mirage.

So I phoned a dear friend . . . a guy I'd grown up with in my teenage years . . . someone who had found real life a rather daunting place just like I had . . . and I asked him straight up front just how much he once used daydreams and fantasies so as to escape his reality.

There was a long, startled pause . . . not least because this is something we'd never spoken of in the twenty-five years of our close companionship. And then he told me everything . . . word for word he described the very same reality-escapes and quick-fixes that I had used. The fantasy and tv, the lying and exaggerating, the grand plans and putting things off and ignoring serious problems. In the next hour we nailed our enemy, move for move.

I immediately phoned another friend whose awkward life-history looked as if it might also fit the bill, and he bravely revealed a whole private collection of secret evasions and quick-fixes when reality got tough. And just like the rest of us, this misguided defense-mechanism had cost him a heavy price in terms of the well-being of his personal and professional life.

Wow. The impact of these realisations made me both excited and angry.

I was excited because I'd recognised the profile of reality-evasions and quick-fixes there in the prison cells as those young inmates recounted their lifestories, and I had seen that it wasn't just them and me but perhaps a whole bunch of other people who had fallen foul of such unhelpful coping strategies.

Yet I was angry, too, because something had so clearly stopped us from engaging well with real life, and yet there was no mention of it in the very places where it might prove useful.

This simply wouldn't do.

Like the Count of Monte Cristo imprisoned for twenty years, I wanted my revenge. It was then I realised how this revenge could come from my hunting down and publicly unmasking this long-hidden problem.

Imprisoned Young Offenders and The Grenadier Guards

It was with quite a sense of mission that I applied to Cambridge University to do a masters degree. For 12 weeks that autumn I worked as a 'volunteer research assistant' in the hope that the Cambridge lecturers would consider awarding me a place. Thankfully they did, and as part of my masters course I had to do a piece of research. Here was my chance. I wanted more evidence that whether you chose to escape reality or invest in it was a strategy that could seriously affect where you ended up in real life. So I conducted face to face interviews two hours long with each of nine convicted young prisoners serving long sentences for serious crimes of theft, robbery and violence. For comparison with these prisoners, I conducted identical interviews with ten enlisted men (i.e. the lowest rank of soldier) from The Grenadier Guards. This is an elite British army regiment world-famous for their combat excellence, red uniforms, bearskin hats, and guarding the royal residences in times of peace.

The Grenadier Guardsmen and prisoners alike were all male, aged 18 to 21, all strongly oriented towards physical activities, and all had grown-up in grimly impoverished circumstances. However, the interviews illuminated a startling contrast between the early teenage years of these two groups. Those young men who became Grenadier Guardsmen claimed they hadn't resorted to high levels of quick-fixing and reality-evading whether via fantasy or drug-abuse. By contrast, the prisoners' self-reported that their resort to quick-fixing and evading had been a dominant trait in their lives for many years before their convictions, though they were adamant that the loneliness and stress of incarceration had certainly inflamed these escapist pursuits. Their autobiographical accounts also suggested that their quick-fixing and reality-evading as children and young teenagers was initially in response to emotional pain and a sense of inadequacy, though eventually these unhelpful strategies appeared to create problems all of their own making.

By contrast to the prisoners, it seemed that for the Grenadier Guardsmen, the real-life prospect of belonging to a world-renowned army regiment was sufficiently attractive to them that they strategically deployed their fiction and daydreaming in a reality-investing way to help self-motivate themselves to adhere to the healthier lifestyles which would realise their ambitions. When they did use fantasy, it was only to relieve boredom rather than to escape emotional pain; and it was notable, too, that their alcohol use, though heavy, had a purely social purpose, in stark contrast to the way prisoners had always used alcohol or drugs to evade their reality rather than improve it.

As for an explanation of the differences between how the two groups had coped with growing up in a particularly tough environment, I noted that in all ten cases, the Guardsmen spoke of an adult mentor (i.e. someone other than their mum or dad) who took a benevolent interest in their ambitions. This informal mentor who took the youngster under their wing, appeared to be a key factor in those boys identifying their goal of becoming Guardsmen, and in helping them on their journey over the several years until they joined the regiment.

A paper trail from the past

In the Cambridge libraries, I soon discovered that I wasn't the only person to have seen the potential problems of too much fantasy. Others had spotted something awry. . .

I was intrigued to read an account by the 30 year director of the Harvard Study of Adult Development, Professor George E. Vaillant, who wrote gravely of the Harvard graduates that he personally interviewed and evaluated when they were eventually in their late forties: "Nine of the ninety-five men that I studied used fantasy often. None of them engaged in games with others, none had close friends, and only four stayed in touch with their parents or siblings." Vaillant was in no doubt that these nine men had led unfulfilled and lonely lives. And since they had all been part of a remarkable research project that had studied them since their late teens . . . with medical assessments, questionnaires and psychological interviews . . . Professor Vaillant's assessment was pretty convincing.

Even more intriguingly, the professor went on to illustrate the dangers of excessive fantasising by using the historical case-study of the mid-Victorian nursing heroine, Florence Nightingale, who is even today a household name for her work in the Crimean War. Back in 1855, Nightingale's innovative sanitary measures reduced the mortality rate caused by dysentery among hospitalised British soldiers, from 40% to 2%. But this same real-life heroine had in her twenties felt quite overwhelmed by what she called the "petty grinding tyranny" of a well-to-do woman's Victorian life. In her anger and frustration, the young Florence had escaped into fantasy. Vaillant writes "As early as age 23, she recognised the extent to which the habit that she termed 'dreaming' had enslaved her". Vaillant then quotes her biographer, Cecil Woodham-Smith: "Sometimes she could not control herself and she gave way with the shameful ecstasy of the drug-taker". According to Woodham-Smith, by the time Florence was 28, "dreaming became uncontrollable. She fell into trances in which hours were blotted out. She lost sense of time and place against her will." Indeed, so disillusioned was she by the frustrations of real life, that by age 31 she wrote in her diary, "I see nothing desirable but death". Yet, just four years later, Florence was heading a team of 38 nurses in a battlefield hospital. Vaillant suggests that this transformation was only made possible by a process of channeling her potentially self-destructive emotions into positive but satisfying means of real-life expression.

But there the paper-trail pretty much ended. No other researchers, therapists or educators had ever written about the dangers of escapist and avoidant lives, at least not as anything other than an extremely rare phenomenon; but this didn't fit at all with my own understanding of it. My work with the Feltham prisoners and the Grenadier Guards had given me a glimpse of exactly how it was that our lives could either thrive or run aground in the face of problems. But what I found hidden away in the library books or research papers wasn't nearly enough to confirm my suspicions. The published observations were like a few unconnected segment in a thousand-piece puzzle. I felt that something connected these clues together . . . the fantasies . . . the drinking . . . the tv watching . . . and all the other unhelpful reality-evasions and quick-fixes that distance us from real life. But if I wanted to put an explanation out there in the mainstream books for parents, educators and psychologists so that something like this wouldn't bushwhack other lives, I would have to embark upon a much larger investigation.

My full scale exploration

By now I'd developed a theory that we each and every one of us has a *'Relationship with Reality'* which affects how we cope with everyday life. There seemed to be three distinctive ways of coping which I called Reality-Investing, Quick-Fixing, and Reality-Evading. I felt that viewing people through the lens of this Relationship with Reality idea could help explain the sorts of things we think and do everyday (such as fantasising, watching tv, and drinking alcohol). These activities may seem insignificant and unrelated at first glance but, on closer consideration, are united by their common goal in terms of reality . . . whether to evade it, quick-fix it, or invest in it. In fact, these everyday activities accumulate to form our characteristic style of dealing with real life, and thereby have substantial effects on our well-being . . . physical, psychological and social.

What's more, I felt sure that individuals who were particularly prone to quick-fixes and reality-evading would have faired considerably worse in life when compared to individuals who were characterised by a greater amount of reality investment.

To test my theory, I embarked upon a PhD at Cambridge so as to investigate my ideas among young men and women in their late teens and early 20s. I chose four groups of people who had achieved very different things with their lives so far:

One group comprised 82 'High Academic Achievers' who were all Oxford or Cambridge undergraduates, an even mix of men and women. Winning a place at an Oxbridge university commonly requires at least three A-grades at school-leaving age, which is close to the maximum achievable mark. The vast majority of these individuals had also publicly excelled in some other performance arena such as sport or music.

A second group was made up of 14 'High Physical Achievers' from Britain's Royal Marine Commandos. A commando is a small force of soldiers operating covertly, and 'The Corps', as it is known, is widely regarded as an elite, special forces regiment. These were enlisted men, i.e. non-officer ranks, who were very much sports-oriented and had only the most basic academic qualifications. I deliberately chose these young men because they were very likely to come from the same unprivileged backgrounds not dissimilar on the face of it to the young men who wound up in prison.

My third group consisted of 75 'Moderate-Achievers' all of whom were men and women undergraduates drawn from a university with modest admissions requirements (two C-grades); and these individuals did not regard themselves as having yet obtained a high-level of achievement in any other performance arena such as sport or music.

My last group was formed by 68 'Under-Achievers' (i.e. Imprisoned Young Offenders). All were serving sentences ranging from one to four years for crimes that ranged from drug-dealing to armed bank robbery.

All of the above individuals completed an identical questionnaire that took on average 20 minutes. Below, I give a glimpse of the sort of results that came from it. In this extract, you'll see that the questions focused on escapist fantasy and wishful daydreaming, and this is because I regarded these as useful indicators of an individual's Relationship with Reality.

The amount of time they spent in fantasy worlds
I asked every member of each group the following question:

> How much 'escapist fantasy' do you do in a day, from waking-up first thing, to falling asleep last thing at night. (I mean escapist fantasies about things that you know will never happen, but you imagine it purely for pleasure. An example might be fantasising about dating a favourite film star.)

The following results were a first rough indicator to me that my different groups were using vastly different levels of escapist thinking.

- The Oxbridge Undergradutes said 30 minutes of fantasy.
- The Royal Marine Commandos said 30 minutes of fantasy.
- The Moderate Achievers said 60 minutes.
- The Under-Achievers (the young men in prison) said 180 minutes (i.e. Prisoners were using escapist fantasising for *three* hours per day.)

It was quite striking how the High-Achievers (no matter they be Oxbridge undergraduates or Royal Marine Commandos) reported doing half as much fantasy as the Moderate Achievers, and just *one sixth* as much as the imprisoned Under-Achievers.

Also notable was that men and women used fantasy and daydreaming in much the same quantities as each other.

What did they use fantasy and daydreaming for?
It seemed that for the great majority of these young men and women
across all four groups, their use of fantasy and daydreaming served
some important functions and played a powerful role in their thinking lives. Firstly, they described them as being a vital 'safety-valve'
for their unfulfilled needs and desires. In fact many individuals felt
they had almost irresistible urges to fantasise or daydream about
certain favourite things. They often worried they did too much of it
for their own good, and that sometimes their fantasies were too
extreme. This worried them because they felt that too much daydreaming and fantasy made it hard for reality to compete, and many
admitted that they had often dreamt so high, imagined so much, that
real life (real lovers, real jobs) seemed quite a let down.

I then asked whether there were any features that made the
experience of real life more enjoyable than fantasy and fiction. In
reply, it was widely felt that what makes real life special and irreplaceable is a good relationship with someone with whom we can
share our experiences. Better still, in real life we can directly affect
other people by our activities. Real life is also intriguingly unpredictable, and produces a superior intensity and durability of feelings.
What's more, real-life activities permit very pleasurable 'reminisc-
ing', whereas we tend not to reminisce about fantasy scenarios.

It was becoming clearer to me that although fantasy worlds
could play a major role in many young people's lives, sometimes for
better but often for worse, they nonetheless felt that reality still had
some unique and highly-prized attributes.

In their own voices
I interviewed many of these young men and women one-to-one and
for two hours each. The following two quotes are highly illustrative of
how the 'Academic High-Achievers' used fantasy and daydreaming.

At 18, J. declined the opportunity to become a concert-level
musician and went on to take an Oxbridge first class degree, before
joining one of the world's top investment banks. At age 22 he said,
"Fantasising? No I don't do that."

R. went on to an Oxbridge Ph.D. in science and then pursued a career in an extremely competitive corporate world. At age 21 he said: "I might do half an hour's escapist fantasy in a week. It's been that way since I was 13 or so."

I suspect that they were under-estimating quite how much they did, because the anonymous questionnaires showed a slightly higher amount of weekly fantasy-use for people in their sort of highly accomplished positions, but their statements weren't far off.

Compare their estimates, though, with the following quotes which are strongly illustrative of the imprisoned young men when thinking back over their growing-up years as teenage schoolboys long before prison:

One young prisoner revealed "It got to the point where I'd come home from school and just fantasise for hours. I was fantasising too much and I wasn't actually doing anything. I couldn't keep it out. Real life couldn't compete."

Another inmate recalled "I had quite a few different fantasy worlds. No one realised what was going on."

During our chats, I noted that the *Terminator 2* film character played by Arnold Schwarzenegger in 1991, was far and away the most popular fiction character for these imprisoned young men. I suspect this was because the character called Terminator 2 was not only a *physically and emotionally invincible robot* with the exact same qualities these pained and frightened boys would wish for themselves, but the Terminator 2 robot has been sent back through time to protect and befriend a 14 year old boy who has no father. I believe this role of surrogate Dad made that character all the more psychologically resonant and satisfying for these young inmates, above and beyond any other tough-guy film character. This is a reminder to us of how our taste for fiction can often reflect our inner needs.

Prison only makes things worse

16 of the 18 imprisoned Young-Offenders I interviewed also self-reported that their fantasy use increased in prison in both frequency and intensity and its themes became more extreme and ever-more divorced from likelihood of enactment in reality. In addition to

which, fiction materials such as TV and glossy magazines assumed an inflated value to the user. When I asked the question: *How does your imagination change in prison?* a young prisoner told me, "My imagination has got more intense and bizarre. I do it pretty much most of the day. Because I'm doing a lot of it, it has to get a little bit stronger each time to keep the buzz up."

It may not be surprising that imprisoned youngsters testify to using extreme amounts of fantasy and daydreams. After all, on a bad day, a prisoner can spend all but one hour confined in his cell. However, it is certainly surprising how this psychological phenomenon has never received more than a paragraph or so of comment in the mainstream literature that examines the causes of crime. It is, too, a tragic irony that what these youngsters need is to become more involved in positive social relationships, yet what prison produces in them instead is the emotional pain of fear, anger, shame and sensory deprivation that fuels the social detachment of their escapist fantasies.

So how is *your* Relationship with Reality?

In the light of my PhD research, I was able to develop a fuller picture of our Relationship with Reality. The following pages offer an illustrative but by no means exhaustive list of the sort of thoughts and behaviours that commonly characterise the three main styles of coping with real life: reality-investing, quick-fixes, and reality-evading. This is not to say that any particular type of thought or action is in itself negative or positive, because it is only the specific context in which they are used which can determine this.

But first I have a particularly searching question for you to keep in mind as you read the descriptions:

Can you see yourself . . . or someone you know well . . . in the following descriptions ?

Reality-Investing

This is characterised by thoughts and actions that serve to bring about lasting improvement in our experience of real life. These may or may not bring about immediate improvement, but the investor expects a net gain over the longer term.

Typical reality-investing thoughts might commonly include:

- Step-by-step planning, the goals of which are likely to be achieved (e.g. making a realistic to-do list at the beginning of the day).
- Day-to-day problem solving: negotiating the physical, psychological and social demands of carrying out the to-do list, in a way that does not compromise or jeopardise our longer-term well-being.
- Mental rehearsal with the intention of improving the real-life performance of a future task.
- Wishful daydreaming for self-motivation; i.e. generating pleasurable thoughts about possible future scenarios so that those daydreams are pursued with more determination in real life.
- Escapist fantasies of impossible scenarios being used simply to rest or refresh our mental energies, so we can better engage with real-life action.
- Creative fantasies of seemingly impossible scenarios that eventually form the catalyst or inspiration for some real-life goals or solutions that had not previously been considered.

Typical reality-investing behaviours

- Investing in long-term, healthy, nurturing relationships.
- Asking for some help or advice when faced with major problems.
- Day-to-day practical activities that aim for longer-term benefits (such as getting important jobs done.)
- Self-improving health regimes (perhaps concerning nutrition, exercise, and adequate sleep).
- Self-improving educational regimes to acquire useful skills, knowledge and qualifications.
- Consuming fiction and other forms of art so as to guide or inspire our reality investment (For instance, reading fiction to inspire our real-life action; or using music to self-motivate, as in aerobics).

In summary of reality-investing: this is characteristic of those personalities who considerably advantage themselves through engaging with real life in ways that eventually pay a net profit of rewarding real life outcomes.

Six times winner of Le Tour de France bike race, Lance Armstrong, could be a poster-boy for reality engagement. "A far more difficult test of endurance than a bike race is how you handle the smaller, common circumstances of your days; the more mundane difficulty of trying to make your life work." He writes, "I want to feel this life as it occurs. Not as it might have occurred. Or as it could have been, *if only*. I want to feel it, as it is: naked or clothed; barefoot or wearing shoes; cold, hot, complicated, simple, fearful, happy, discontented, exhilarated, fruitful, selfish, giving and feeling."

And here follow the voices of two remarkable women who resolutely transformed their daydreams into self-motivation for their real-life exploits:

Britain's first woman Prime Minister, Margaret Thatcher, was the daughter of a humble greengrocer, but having grown up in small-town Grantham she writes this of her frequent visits to the cinema: "I roamed to the most fabulous realms of the imagination. It gave me the determination to roam in reality one day."

Likewise for the young Claire Rayner who would go on to become a nurse, the country's favourite agony aunt, and a campaigner for numerous charities. "Back in the early days of the war, daydreaming was my comfort and salvation, and I suspect the source of my decision to take some control over what was happening to me. In my daydreams I could do all sorts of clever and exciting things. *Why shouldn't I try to do them for real?* So I set about the practical details."

Quick-Fixes

These are characterised by the sorts of impulsive thoughts and behaviours that temporarily blur, skew or distort our perception of reality, though they stop short of disengaging us from it. Instant improvement is the primary aim, and though this may bring temporary relief from our emotional pains or frustrations, the downside is that they may jeopardise or damage our medium and longer term real-life well-being.

Typical quick-fix thoughts might commonly include:

- Wishful daydreaming that doesn't lead to action. We deliberately generate pleasurable thoughts about possible future scenarios or outcomes, but with little or no attempt to make the daydream a reality.
- Grandiose or unrealistic plans: plans which are either never attempted in real life, or that fail, because they are wildly unrealistic.
- Lying or exaggerating, thereby creating the temporary illusion of real life being better than it is.
- Postponing a challenging situation so as to avoid dealing with the emotional discomfort.

Typical quick-fix behaviours:

- Excessive consumption of high-calorie but low-nutrition 'junk foods'; or eating well beyond our nutritional requirements to an extent that risks obesity.
- A bulimic or anorexic relationship with food.
- Abuse of high-risk body-building steroids to rapidly gain muscle bulk and strength, despite the physical and psychological health risks. Compulsive exercise can also be part of this behaviour.
- Abuse of high-risk, mood-improving substances such as alcohol, speed, ecstasy, or cocaine, so as to enhance our immediate experience of real life.
- Ill-considered sexual relations.

- Impulsive forms of gambling, crime, and aggression.

In summary of quick-fix characteristics: these are un-constructive engagements with real life which reflect a short-termism that, in the longer run, generates only increased pain and set-backs.

Reality-Evading

This is characterised by thoughts and behaviours that are inadvertently or deliberately used to block-out or escape our first-hand experience of real life.

Typical reality-evading thoughts might commonly include:

- Escapist fantasies that never lead back to real life. These fantasies are tailor-made to temporarily satisfy our emotional needs.
- Constant denial, to ourselves or others, of our real-life circumstances. This denial is being used to evade the emotional pain generated by owning-up to how things are. We are literally living a lie.

Typical reality-evading behaviours:

- Consuming fiction with the purpose of escaping real life. This might include television, videos, cinema, novels, glossy magazines, and fantasy computer games.
- Listening to music with the purpose of blocking-out reality, or to support our self-generated internal fantasy world (i.e. music becomes a soundtrack for the fantasy movie playing in our mind's eye.)
- Habitually ignoring the problems in our lives so as not to have to deal with them.
- Keeping real people at arm's length by not developing any close or intimate relationships, because close relationships might bind us to reality.
- Abusing substances with a strong potential for reality-disengaging effects, such as heroin and LSD, or drinking oneself to oblivion.

In summary of reality-evading traits: their core purpose is to disengage the individual as completely as possible from an emotionally painful, threatening, or simply unsatisfying real life.

We can clearly see elements of such 'disengagement' in the childhood of the legendary horse-trainer and foster parent, Monty Roberts, who grew up around a brutal and dangerous father. "During my childhood I lived in two distinctly separate worlds, one with horses, the other one with people. My world with horses was one of comfort and understanding, but with people I felt isolated and alone."

Reality-evasion was also used under very similar circumstances by former US President, Bill Clinton. He has written of how, from a very young age and growing up in a home blighted by his alcoholic and dangerously abusive step-father, he learned to lead what he calls 'parallel lives'. "When I was a child, my *outside* life was filled with friends and fun, learning and doing. My *internal* life was full of uncertainty, anger and a dread of ever-looming violence. No one can live parallel lives with complete success; the two have to intersect." Bill has since explained that "whenever I was angry or exhausted or under great stress, I was more likely to make a mistake, to run back into the dark alley of my 'parallel lives'."

Partial problems and disguised evasions

It seems more than likely that most of us will use a reality-investing style in some arenas of our life, e.g. academic and working life, but use a quick-fix or evading-style in other arenas, for instance in our sexual and romantic life. There are also less apparent ways to evade reality than I have listed above. For instance, the sort of obsessive working that compromises our health or our closest relationships; or the sort of perfectionism which means important projects either don't get started, don't get finished, or in getting done almost destroy our well-being. We might also be far too secretive about a serious problem or illness. These three traits: workaholism masquerading as passion, perfectionism masquerading as determination, and self-isolating secrecy masquerading as independence, these are all in essence reality-evasions and our real life will suffer very severely if we persist in them.

Here are two quite different voices telling a strikingly similar tale:

Film director Steven Spielberg said of himself many years ago: "Life has finally caught up with me. I've spent so many years hiding from pain and fear behind a camera. I avoided all the growing-up pains by being too busy making movies. So right now, in my early thirties, I'm experiencing delayed adolescence . . . I didn't escape suffering, I only delayed it."

We can now appreciate why Bruce Springsteen said "I see that two of the best days of my life were the day I picked up the guitar, *and the day that I learned how to put it down* . . . I realized my real life is waiting to be lived. All the love and the hope and the sorrow and sadness – that's all over there, waiting to be lived. And I could ignore it and push it aside, or I could say yes to it. But to say yes to part of it, is to say yes to all of it. That's why people say *no* to all of it. That's why people say no, I'll skip the happiness as long as I don't have to feel the pain . . . And that was *my* specialty . . . keeping my distance so that if I lost something, it wouldn't hurt that much. And you can do that, but you're never going to have anything." Then Bruce very happily became a father. "You're afraid to love something so much . . . but then you realise you've got to be able to accept and live with that world of fear, that world of doubt of the future. And you've got to give it all today and not hold back."

Where does a negative Relationship with Reality come from?

Emotionally hurtful experiences or deeply unsatisfying lives are probably the major reason for withdrawing into ourselves by one means or another, and very often it seems reality-evasion is just an inadvertent habit or unhelpful strategy left over from a daunting childhood. Research suggests that almost everyone has the urge to flee life's slings and arrows with some evasive quick-fix, but the lucky ones are those who appreciate how things are only made worse that way. That said, as is the case with much alcohol dependency, the abuse of a drug can accidentally take a hold without there being any prior emotional problem. Likewise, an innocently acquired escapist or quick-fix style may be quite capable of initiating its own downward spiral of real-life problems.

When considering the root causes of a negative Relationship with Reality, it's interesting to note that a husband and wife team of psychiatrists, Mildred and Victor Goertzel, studied the biographies of several hundred extremely eminent people, in which they noticed the following about the fiction authors and the actors among their sample. "All those who now traffic in fantasy remember their homes as having tragic elements." But that said, we shouldn't jump to the conclusion that consuming fiction books or films necessarily indicates unhappiness, or leads to an unhelpful Relationship with Reality. Good fiction can give a highly accurate picture of how the world really is. It's *how* we use these things which matters. The defining characteristic of a positive relationship is *a lasting improvement in our well-being*. With this in mind, we might use reality-evading (e.g. escapist fantasy) for short periods so as to protect our mental well-being from an overly demanding real life, and this strategy may well allow us to return mentally refreshed to far more effective engagements with reality. Similarly, we might use a modest consumption of alcohol as part of our social life. But note how in doing so, the ultimate intention and likely effect is to enhance our performance in the real world, as opposed to not caring about the consequences. It is this caring about lasting progress in real life that is the hallmark of a person that has a truly positive Relationship with Reality.

By contrast, a negative Relationship with Reality would be characterised by someone simply trying to improve their immediate feelings with no care for the longer term impact upon their real-life well-being. Sometimes the trade-off is conscious (e.g. by abusing alcohol), but sometimes it is unwitting (e.g. by abusing fantasy).

Our imagination offers wonderful possibilities

I should also add that I do not mean to demonise our imaginations (which might also be called our 'creativity'). Imagination is the all-purpose thinking tool we use to conjure possibilities and problem-solve with the help of 'What if' scenarios. It might be used to generate fantasies or daydreams, but equally it might be used to solve real-life problems. Imagination's distinctly positive potential is well-observed by the quantum physicist and Nobel Laureate, Max Planck, who wrote in his autobiography that "the scientist must have a vivid intuitive imagination, for new ideas are not generated by deduction, but by an artistically creative imagination." Or, as boxing champion and UN Messenger of Peace, Muhammad Ali, puts it: "The man who has no imagination, has no wings." Akin to these inspirational and experimental roles of imagination, is imaginal rehearsal, i.e. the detailed practicing of tasks in our imagination as opposed to actual movement, which has been shown to improve skilled performance almost as much as real-life practice. Moreover, imagination in the form of 'therapist-guided positive imagery' also serves an invaluable role in the clinical use of hypnosis which has proven itself such a powerful tool in therapy and training. So let me be clear: imagination is a fabulous resource in all of us, but we need to use it wisely . . . because it can work for us, or against us.

The young Eleanor Roosevelt, who went on to be the key personality behind the drafting of the Universal Declaration of Human Rights in 1948, had as a child developed a rich fantasy life to escape her unhappiness. As an adult, she wrote "Unless it is checked, imagination can remain only a means of escape; but if it is nourished and directed, it can become a flame that lights the way to new things, new ideas, new experiences."

How can we improve our Relationship with Reality?
My own escape from the prison I had made of my imagination, came in my mid-twenties, a few years on from my university days. In final desperation at my decaying reality, I stopped running from the demands of real life. This decision to 're-engage' was helped immeasurably by my falling in love with an extraordinary young German woman, since it quickly became clear to me that reality was the only place where she and I could share the world together. What's more, by contrast to her own well-developed skills and confidence in foreign languages and sport, I was ashamed of how little I'd made of myself. I realised that evasion wasn't the answer. Inspired by *her*

good nature, I left my desert island and set sail for the real world.

My own life-story is typical of the 'late bloomers' who I interviewed during my research work. These were individuals whose teenage years and twenties were blighted by a strongly negative Relationship with Reality which rapidly became distinctly positive once the individual encountered sufficiently nurturing circumstances. Stories of healing were most often characterised by at least three ingredients: They needed a deeply rewarding personal relationship with someone whose own life was a model of reality-investment. They also needed a good range of goals that were meaningful to them and readily achievable. And they needed some taste of their ability to improve their circumstances by taking on challenges.

I'm grateful for the key lesson of my own journey: that it is only our response to problems that determines their eventual effect upon us, not the problems themselves. It was not my stammer that slowed down my life-development for 20 years, it was how I dealt with it. What was, in retrospect, far more damaging to my happiness and life-directions, was my deeply negative Relationship with Reality. My fear and shame caused me to escape into fantasy and quick-fixes and, by so doing, I starved and distorted my real-life relationships.

That whole experience has been crucial to my understanding of how lives run into trouble: the initial problem might be a bullying parent, or a physical handicap or an emotional upset . . . just as the unhelpful coping-strategy can be lying, or violence, or alcohol, or trying to be perfect, or trying to please . . . but whatever form that coping strategy takes, it distorts the whole natural balance of our lives. This is why it is vital that when faced with a problem, we address it as soon and directly as we can, and seek support in doing so from friends, mentors or professionals so that it doesn't have a domino effect upon us. We also need to keep our eyes open for those around us who could do with our back-up, because if they learn to apply helpful coping strategies which develop their skills and confidence, then their problems and challenges can lead them to thrive and flourish even in the face of adversity.

What sort of life do we want to lead?

It's going to be sometime before studies can confirm or disprove my observations, but I strongly suspect that *balance* is the goal: a healthy ratio between our Investing, Quick-Fixes and Evading. Such a balance requires us to be flexible, deftly adjusting our style to suit the circumstances. We might use fantasy and fiction to refresh our spirits, or to inspire us or to protect us from overload; but we're better off returning quickly to the sheer potency, unpredictability, and camaraderie provided by a positive Relationship with Reality.

Consideration of our Relationship with Reality seems particularly relevant to a way of life characterised by ever increasing ways to digitally distort the world, or to communicate via phones and computers, or to alter our mood and perception through taking some drug or another. It seems vital that each of us consider the distinctive strengths and benefits of using, *and not using,* such developments.

How highly do we prize reality, and sobriety, and having someone physically with us by comparison with the technological alternatives?

In short, what sort of life do we wish to lead?

For as digital and drug technologies become ever more powerful and pervasive, our best hope of them genuinely enhancing our quality of life is for us to be ever more ingenious in how we use the innovations. Given that we're such highly social animals, how can we use technology to enhance our real-life relationships, rather than allowing technology to accidentally diminish or dilute their strength, breadth and intimacy? How can we harness inventions to physically bring us together, rather than keep us apart?

We need to be equally ingenious in how we use our fantasies and fictions. The challenge we all face is how to allow our imagination to inspire new ways of interacting with the world, rather than have imagination simply replace or undermine our activities. We are undoubtedly driven by evolution to weave fabulous fireside stories and to invent new technologies, but in doing so, let's not lose sight of their higher purpose: the progress and intimacy of our full-blooded, in-the-flesh relationships with the real world around us.

* * *

Planning for Progress

- Under what circumstances, and in what parts of your life, are you most likely to invest, quick-fix or evade?

- How could you improve your Relationship with Reality?

- How could you help a loved one better engage with their real life?

* * *

Nick's Special Topic

By harmonising the workings of our mind and body, our conscious and sub-conscious, we can greatly increase our potential for progress. I feel that a good rapport between these four dimensions is so important to enjoying life, that it seems only fair to call it a 'special topic'. The following sections explain the hows and whys of fostering these remarkable relationships within ourselves, and their capacity to enhance our health, happiness and accomplishments.

1) Psychosomatic illness and our sub-conscious mind
2) How learning self-hypnosis can dramatically improve our health, happiness and high-performance
3) Working well with a coach or therapist
4) Treating the root causes of our troubles rather than individual symptoms

Psychosomatic illness
and our sub-conscious mind

Psychosomatic illnesses are very real physical symptoms that are unconsciously caused by our psychological unhappiness or stress. The word psycho-somatic simply means mind-body. If our mind is not happy it will express this through our body, in the same way our body lets our mind know if it's in pain. So psychosomatic symptoms occur when our psychological distress takes bodily form.

Our sub-conscious holds the keys

Our subconscious mind holds the keys to achieving satisfying and sustainable improvements in our life. This is because our sub-conscious is a storehouse of all the habits and assumptions acquired from our previous experiences, kept in a place that is ordinarily out of reach of our self-awareness. But don't picture the subconscious gathering dust like some attic treasure trove. It's far more like the engine, propeller and rudder of a boat responsible for driving and steering our craft even though these mechanisms are well out of sight beneath the waves. We're up on deck, sure enough, but not always at the helm. This is why, when we consciously try to change ourselves, we sometimes find our behaviours returning to their original course as if they were dutifully following a route map to which we're not yet privy. On such occasions, though we might in all honesty be telling ourselves and other people that we want one thing, our subconscious may crave quite another. Sometimes, to know how we truly feel about something or someone, we simply have to wait and see how we behave. That's why psychotherapy is always asking *'When don't the symptoms occur? When do things improve? When have you been happy and well?'* Because it's at those times that our sub-conscious mind is probably getting enough of what it really wants, so those occasions hold all the clues as to what melody our subconscious is dancing.

The result of these miscommunications and power struggles

between different parts of our mind, can have dramatic impact on our progress and well-being. For instance, it's been observed that athletes will sometimes practice too little before a big competition, and thereby significantly reduce their chances of success. One explanation for this paradox seems to be that some part of their mind doesn't want to think that their score on the big day will represent as good as they've got to give, and that their peak performance isn't good enough. The clarity of that realisation would present too great a blow for them, so their subconscious seeks to provide a safety-buffer for their self-image by subtly instigating a sub-optimal training routine which will be their excuse if things go pear-shaped.

It's the tug of war between our conscious wishes and our subconscious fears that sometimes accounts for why it can be so difficult to bring about change in ourselves. Though its always aiming to act in our best interests, the goals and strategies of our subconscious mind can sometimes be the out-of-date or misguided product of our immature or emergency responses to some significant past experiences.

Fortunately, psychology has learnt a few means of resolving at least some of the occasional conflicts between the different parts of our mind. Case in point is the therapeutic technique often called 'paradoxical intention' whereby we do the very thing we've been trying not to. So let's say we often feel an anxious compulsion to repeatedly check that the front door is locked, our therapist would encourage us to very deliberately check it time after time, no matter it be a hundred and fifty times one after the other, until we're quite sick of doing so and grind to an angry halt. Or, as another for instance, if we're prone to lie in bed at night worrying, what we do instead is very deliberately try to stay awake and do lots of disagreeable chores. It seems that our brain soon gets the message that the negative habit which has been bullying us, is most unwelcome.

However, it's not always so easy to put things right. Sometimes our subconscious seems to accept the shortcomings of its strategy and welcomes the new way of doing things. Other times, we might overcome one problem symptom, only to find it replaced by another because our subconscious has some pressing agenda that we're not yet recognising. For instance, a seemingly independent little boy may, deep down, want more parental attention and reassurance, and so while asleep at night wets his bed as a means to getting it. If cured of that by some electronic buzzer that wakes him when he wets, he may soon develop a skin complaint as a substitute signal for his unhappiness. It's only when the little boy receives sufficient attention and support for all the positive things he's doing in life, that his subconscious will be comfortable turning itself to other matters.

But there may be times when our subconscious harbours priorities or presumptions that are profoundly out of sync with our conscious goals and strategies. In which case, our subconscious may go to very considerable lengths to get its way ... and this might include self-sabotage. We're all quite capable of some 'own worst enemy' antics, whereby we do something daft that puts us at a considerable disadvantage despite our protestations that we want to do our best. Perhaps we go out partying into the early hours just a day or two before a big performance, or we leave our preparations to the very last minute. Perhaps we endlessly postpone some longed-for activity, or aim our ambitions low, or always manage to come second in the face of competition. Whatever surprise problem we trip ourselves up with, it holds progress back in some dimension of our life: career, social, educational, or physical. And it's our covert agenda that explains the paradoxical sense of relief when our undercover wishes becomes a self-fulfilling prophecy and things don't work out for us. We might even find ourselves almost gloating because we felt in our guts that 'things were too good to be true, could never last for long, bound to go wrong, ... it always does for me'. In truth, it was our feeling of 'I told you so' that has itself played a major role in engineering the failure. Some part of our subconscious mind harbours some out of date and misguided notion and is surreptitiously making us act upon it. In some individuals, this subliminal strategy of self-handicapping can escalate into seriously reckless or self-destructive behaviour that is subconsciously designed to end in disaster. Alternatively, our subconscious might simply bring on such a degree of depression or psychosomatic illness that it stops us in our tracks and forces us to reconsider the direction and pace of our journey in life.

I don't mean to suggest that the subconscious is always being unhelpful. This is the same part of our mind that allows us to drive safely on automatic pilot, that solves problems overnight, or cleverly senses something not right in a situation. So an equally likely scenario is that our all too conscious mind has made some poorly conceived plans that are not sufficiently playing to our heart-felt needs and desires, in which case our subconscious is doing us a very good turn in causing us to re-evaluate. My only contention is that it's important to have the two levels of our mind working in sync if we're to make lasting progress that's deeply satisfying.

So how can we restore a healthy working harmony?

Psychology has several well-recognised approaches, and here's three examples: 1) pure and traditional psychoanalysis studies our dreams and a free association of our thoughts to help reveal and then release the problematic contents of our subconscious. 2) a more cognitive approach would look for our tell-tale automatic thoughts, feelings, and images that simultaneously occur in response to certain trigger situations, because these knee-jerk responses will indicate our 'core beliefs' about ourselves and how we perceive the workings of the world. Once we've diagnosed what rules of thumb we're using to deal with life, we can then arrange to test out their accuracy and helpfulness and so bring them up to date if needs be. 3) clinical hypnosis offers a swift and effective way of accessing our subconscious so as to understand our subliminal beliefs and motivations, and then improve upon these by experiencing through a state of heightened imagination how real life could go better.

No matter the approach we take, alone or with the help of a therapist, it is by recognising and working sympathetically with the goals and strategies of our subconscious mind, that we can perhaps foster a deeper happiness.

The extent of the problem

It's quite likely that at least half of a GP's patients are suffering from at least one psychosomatic disorder, i.e. a very real physical problem that our subconscious mind has created in response to some form of psychological distress. The sort of classic 'conversion disorders' resulting from extreme psychological trauma would be paralysis, blindness, or loss of speech. But far more common among many of us is having a small cluster of less severe symptoms, albeit demoralising, debilitating and long-term. These might include digestive troubles and sleep disturbances, skin complaints and hair loss, asthma and nausea, frequent colds and constant fatigue, or problems with our sexual and reproductive abilities. Unexplained pain, particularly if it moves around the body, can be another characteristic symptom, perhaps involving migraines, lower back pain, and aching limbs. Our subconscious can either wholly create such physical woes, or exacerbate existing ones.

Far fetched?

Think how we'll blush or perspire in response to social anxieties, just as fear might cause us to suffer shortness of breath or stomach ache. If we receive shocking news, our nose might bleed or we'll simply faint. Psychosomatic complaints are merely a longer-term, less obvious manifestation of our mind and emotions effecting the workings of our body.

So what might be the psychological purpose of producing these tangible ills? *"The heart has its reasons of which reason does not know,"* wrote the 17th century scientist-philosopher, Blaise Pascal, helping to remind us that despite our conscious and unconscious trying to be rational, our rationality does not rule the roost. It has to power-share and negotiate not only with our physical sensations but also our emotions...and for emotions I could equally say heart and soul. Hence, one explanation for psychosomatic symptoms is that unbeknown to that tiny fraction of our brain activity that is conscious, our vast subconscious mind is trying to deter us from what it regards, mistakenly or otherwise, as one or more of three evils:

1) that we're going the wrong direction in life,
2) travelling at a self-damaging pace,
3) keeping poor company.

Another strong possibility is that our subconscious is creating these physical ills as a means of channeling a deeply felt emotion such as anger, fear, shame or despair, that we don't feel at liberty to consciously own up to, let alone express openly and directly. If this involuntary blocking of some taboo emotion sounds an unrealistic explanation, let's remember that if times required it 80 percent of us have the potential to block much of our sensation of physical pain simply by using self-hypnosis to control how much information reaches our conscious awareness. So it is that our sub-conscious may express its alarm or unhappiness in physical symptoms or unhelpful behaviour, because direct expression is too daunting. When we think that Albert Einstein taught us that energy can change form but it cannot be lost, is it so outlandish that the energy of emotional hurt becomes the energy of physical hurt?

Of course, in principle, it's very important to establish that there is no medical condition underlying a physical problem. But this is a tall order, not least because we, the patients, are rarely conscious of our own deeply buried psychological disquiet. Even if our GP *does* suspect the mind's initiating role in our physical symptoms, at least one third of us refuse to see a mental health professional because we think it's a slur on our sanity. But nothing could be further from the truth. Our body expressing our mind's concerns like this is in no sense malingering nor mental illness. On the contrary, it's our healthy brain using all the means at its disposal to signal to us, and to those who love us, that there are some un-aired feelings that need addressing. Mother Nature meant our body to care for our brain, and vice versa, and it's only an historical accident that has seen the healing professions of medicine and psychology artificially separated, and be less effective for it. The mind and body, science and arts, may stand apart in academic and professional training, but in our real life they walk hand in hand at all times. An appreciation of this relationship can help make our psychosomatic distress signals a rather less common occurrence.

Emotional pain . . . in the flesh
Here are two very personal accounts from remarkable individuals

whose physical and psychological health experiences well illustrate
the central themes of this special topic:

Whilst on tour in Quebec, singer Celine Dion suffered severe
inflammation of her vocal chords. She confesses that from that
career-threatening trauma, she eventually learned a great deal that
would change her whole approach to life and to herself. "The problem was fatigue, overwork, pressure, and constant stress. I was
beginning to feel that I'd gone too far, too fast. I had to realize that
somewhere inside of me, there was a tired and puzzled little girl I
hadn't been paying attention to or listening to for quite a while.
Now she was making signs to me, reminding me of her needs. This
little girl had no need for applause and ovations, no desire to give the
biggest concert in the world. She just wanted a little peace and a little rest. So, I'd never let myself get overtired again. From then on,
I'd make it my duty to sleep well and for a long time, to relax, to
unwind a much as possible from all stress. I'd also eat well, not too
much and only good things. I was also going to laugh a lot and be
happy, because it's well known that laughter and happiness are good
for the health and are enemies of stress. You have to be in shape to
find peace, beauty, strength, and rest in yourself."

American comedian and talk-show host, Ellen Degeneres,
testifies to very considerable emotional and physical benefits from
coming to terms with a deep-seated fear in her life: how people
would react when she told them she was gay. "I feel stronger. I feel
more daring, more confident. I think that by facing all these fears
and all these obstacles that were thrown at me by coming out, it
forced me to grow in ways that I never would have grown. It's taken
me on a journey that I never would have gone on. I think anytime
you face some type of fear, you're going to grow in some way.
You're going to learn more about who you are in a tough spot. For
me, this has been the most freeing experience because people can't
hurt me anymore. I don't have to worry about somebody saying
something about me. Literally as soon as I made this decision, I lost
weight, and my skin has cleared up. I don't have anything to be
scared of."

The strengths and weaknesses of our intuitions

Decisions made in an intuitive instant can be every bit as helpful as decisions made after a far more conscious, careful and comprehensive gathering of the evidence; it's simply a matter of knowing which to use and when. This is the intriguing message of Malcolm Gladwell, an acclaimed commentator on business and science, who has championed a better understanding of our intuitive responses. (Visit www.Gladwell.com) Just as lateral-thinking psychologist Edward de Bono suggests we make more progress if we systematically adopt half a dozen different thinking hats to solve a problem, for instance being first daring then cautious, then logical followed by emotional, so Gladwell suggests we can learn to make better use of our snap-judgements. He notes that at speeds far faster than our conscious mind is able to monitor, our sub-conscious will process a wealth of data so as to warn of danger, create solutions, or instigate action. It's this that creates our intuitive feeling about anything from a new relationship or a business deal through to a high-pressure life or death situation.

Subliminal it might be, but this rapid-response processing can be highly effective. Nonetheless it can also be fallible, and what Gladwell takes pains to point out is that when our immediate unconscious reactions go awry and risk misleading us, they do so for quite particular and characteristic reasons. This means that by being aware of the likely causes of error, we should be able to guard against them.

Exemplifying such errors, laboratory experiments have shown that our responses to a situation can be manipulated by a technique called priming whereby our sub-conscious is fed with ingredients that predispose us to behave in a certain way. For instance, typically forward young New Yorkers were covertly subdued into waiting patiently because they'd just completed a word puzzle that had deliberately embedded within it cues like polite, courteous and considerate. For much the same reasons, elderly people did far worse on a memory test when demoralising words very negatively associated with aging, such as doddering and senile, were flashed on screen so fast that they were only available to the individual's sub-conscious. And if any of us are made to feel frustration before taking a problem-solving test, we'll invariably do worse than if we're coaxed into feeling cheerful. Such effects are all to do with 'priming the sub-conscious', and there are boundless implications of acknowledging the phenomenon. One tidy example: 30 years ago, American orchestras started using screens when choosing new musicians because judges were demonstrably biased by an individual's physical appearance. When screens hid the contestant so only audible musicianship could win someone the job, many more women were hired.

From the world of psychotherapy, too, there is substantial evidence to support the proposition that our sub-conscious harbours a host of presumptions and bias responses of which we may not be consciously aware even though they may considerably affect our dealings with the world. An individual can be invited to talk about topics or relationships they consciously rate as innocuous, only to discover that the sensitive machines monitoring their skin temperature, heart rate and blood pressure, tell a very different story, clearly indicating covert distress when a particular subject is raised. It would seem that only their sub-conscious is aware of their disquiet. In respect of such a variety of compelling evidence, Gladwell invites us to become more appreciative of the unconscious processes we call intuition, and how to deploy these to make better decisions.

Reading the signs

When it comes to the funny look on our face, research suggests that we have a voluntary system of facial muscles under our conscious control, as well as an involuntary one reflecting our sub-conscious feelings. As a means of personal survival, individuals who've grown up with some form of threat from violence or emotional bullying, have often become highly adept at reading facial expressions. But the skill is learnable at any age, and the so called Facial Action Coding System has, for instance, been used to train Californian police officers to recognise the involuntary clues to someone's emotional state. It requires just a few hours to improve the accuracy of our readings once the facial giveaways are better understood. Likewise, it was simple enough for researchers at Berkeley to learn to distinguish the genuine joy expressed by the so called 'Duchenne smile' as distinct from a forced grin. The real thing is characterised by the involuntary crinkling or crows feet around the eyes that's very hard to fake. The researchers then sorted through a collection of 140 women's college graduation photographs from thirty years before. They discovered that the genuine smilers at age 21, when interviewed in depth at age 52 declared themselves to be more happily married and satisfied with life by comparison to the women who'd just been putting a brave face on that graduation snap. The lesson I take from this haunting study, is that we need to find things to genuinely smile about, because there's no faking the all-round good effects to which genuine joy is heir to, and our forced grin isn't fooling anyone's sub-conscious radar, least of all our own.

Reading facial expressions is just one example of how we might benefit from better appreciating our brain's automatic operations. Here's another: during moments of extreme personal threat, police officers and fire-fighters, soldiers and fighter-pilots all report at least the following three phenomena: 1) they have tunnel vision that focuses very clearly on the source of danger; 2) they see activities as if in slow-motion; 3) the sound of events is reduced almost to silence. What's happening is that the sub-conscious autopilot of the brain is limiting any sensory information that it deems superfluous to our survival. And it's this distillation process filtering out all but the most vital incoming data, which allows our subconscious to make split-second decisions. This psychological ability can be a life-saver, but if activated in the wrong situation it can also cause us serious problems. Similar sorts of phenomena are true for all of us when we're extremely aroused, no matter by joy, anger, fear, excitement, or sexual arousal. Our thinking will be blinkered rather than seeing the bigger picture, and we simply won't be receptive to advice or alternative courses of action. It's to prevent this cutting-in of the brain's emergency system in unwarranted situations, that many police forces in the USA are not allowed to engage in high-speed chases. We, too, by recognising that these characteristic sub-conscious responses are brought about by moments of excessive stimulation, can either remove ourselves from the situation altogether, or use deep, slow breathing and muscle relaxation to help regain a higher level of conscious control. This isn't to say that conscious thinking is any better than automatic, but each has its place.

Well-Being skills training

Mind and body can interact to promote health or cause illness. The skills of well-being are ones we can all learn, and should preferably be taught quite systematically in primary school so children grow up knowing how to calm themselves and cope in tricky situations by channeling their energies rather than bottling stuff in unhelpful ways that might cause them troubles later. *But it's never too late. . .*

Preventing psycho-somatic illness in the work place
Teach First is the pioneering charity that each year places hundreds of top graduates in some of London's most challenging inner-city secondary schools. During this time, they qualify as teachers, are trained in leadership skills, and are mentored not only by an experienced teacher, but by an experienced manager from any one of Britain's leading companies. After their two year teaching stint, the individual can either progress with their fast-track school career, or enter the world of high-powered business. Teach First have asked me to give an annual training seminar in the skills of well-being for those extraordinary young women and men who face such a demanding mission.

The thinking is this: if we don't possess sufficient know-how to take care of our all-round well-being, both in and out of the workplace, it's more than likely our own sub-conscious will begin signalng us, or in effect, *sabotaging us*. This can take the form of any number of very real physical symptoms all intended to have us rethink our way of living. So here's a flavour of the sorts of approaches that can reduce the likelihood of a psychological civil war.

Let's look first at insufficient sleep. If we're tired, we behave very much like a drunk person: though our problem-solving and decision-making skills are woefully impoverished, we nonetheless feel excessively confident in our flawed abilities. This toxic mix explains why the official reports on most major disasters, from Chernobyl and Exxon's oil tanker through to the Challenger Shuttle, cite sleep deprivation as their leading cause. Former U.S. President Bill Clinton observes in his autobiography that the vast majority of his biggest mistakes, personal and professional, occurred when he was excessively tired. The fact is, just about all of us need circa 8 hours sleep per night, and it's good to know that a 30 minute afternoon nap will do much to rekindle our mood and energy and our physical and mental agility. The great ally of sleep is vigorous physical exercise; and 45 minutes of sweat-producing activity three times per week is still the best known prevention and cure for depression. Whether it's striding to work, or playing frequent sport, putting our body through its daily paces is an absolute necessity for our psychological well-being.

As part and parcel of this reciprocal relationship, our mind's skill can readily nurture our body's health. Professor Richard Davidson of the University of Wisconsin-Madison trained 25 individuals in mindfulness meditation intended to produce extremely positive and relaxing emotions. After a seven hour initiation and a total of eight weekly classes, they continued to practice for one hour a day. Lo and behold, the greater their ability to produce positive emotions that were clearly measurable on a range of brain-scans, the greater was their production of health-protecting antibodies when they were injected with a flu virus. This form of mind-training is closely related to the highly targeted self-hypnosis skills that not only help our conscious and sub-conscious goals and strategies work more harmoniously, but which also influence our automatic bodily functions such as digestion, heart-rate, immune and nervous systems. Sustainable high performance is made all the more likely by this form of holistic and considerate personal development. In fact, by using self-hypnosis we can move forward in every aspect of our life, and work-performance will rise with the tide. The net result can mean an improvement in working-world skills and a reduction in stress-related illness.

One of the underlying messages emerging from the well-being research is not to let ourselves be swept along in a rush and hurry, cash and carry, 'greed for speed' existence. Whether we're kissing or conversing, eating or driving, teaching or learning, let's try doing it gently and with greater depth. Slower motion for more profound progress is a strategy as old as the hare and tortoise folktale, but it still applies. Let's not push life, let's lead it.

How learning Self-Hypnosis can dramatically improve our health, happiness and high performance

I had tears in my eyes as I watched a young woman psychologist working with the seriously ill children who chattered away while they ever so calmly injected themselves with big needles and power-ful chemicals. These youngsters had been taught self-hypnosis and could largely anaesthetise themselves against the gauntlet of painful medical procedures and the fear and nausea that accompanied their physical therapies. In their calm faces, I felt that I was watching psy-chology at its best, as it reached out a helping hand, right out to the very edge of our understanding.

Adults can equally benefit from self-hypnosis as a well-proven means of managing acute pain, perhaps from childbirth or dental treatment, or the long-term pain of cancer. It can also provide a low-cost, no side-effects but nonetheless enduring therapy for many people's asthma, skin complaints, difficult digestion, sleep disorders, depression and anxiety. It's clear that a whole range of conditions can respond well to the daily application of self-hypnosis, though a good diagnosis is a crucial starting place. After all, it could be disastrous to reduce a stomach pain or a sense of fear, if in fact these symptoms are the life-saving alarm signals for something far more life-threatening.

Yet, when used appropriately, hypnosis isn't only a remedy for health problems and bad habits, it can also greatly enhance our quality of life. These remedial and enhancement roles are both possible because it provides a state in which our minds are unusually versatile, one in which we can improve our relationship with our past, present and future.

So what exactly is it?

Let's start from the premise that we're in a psychological trance whenever we are thoroughly engrossed in some activity such as reading a good book or vividly remembering something as if reliving it. And sometimes these trance states can be negative, perhaps when our own inner voice and imaginal experiences persuade us to feel guilty, furious, depressed or fearful. What hypnosis does is harness our natural ability to enter a versatile and imaginative mental state, and then guides us with helpful suggestions strategically designed to facilitate positive change. *And change will lead to insight, far more often than insight will lead to change*, said the American psychiatrist, Dr Milton H. Erikson, considered one of the 20th Century's most inspiring exponents of hypnosis. This is why the self-generated, deeply absorbing, virtual-reality experience can be so helpful. By imaginatively experiencing how things could be if they got better, we allow our psychological horizons and expectations to improve to such an extent that we think, behave, and perceive things differently, and even our automatic bodily functions may respond accordingly.

Though science is still some way from a thorough understanding, it seems that suggestions received while hypnotised allow us to alter sensory information at a very late stage of mental processing. So, even though the information intended to signal pain has been physically retrieved by our sense of touch, it is being manipulated in our brain further up the chain of command just before it becomes a conscious experience. This would explain why my heart-rate will still automatically rise in response to some physical injury, even though I won't be conscious of any searing sting.

And here's another piece of the puzzle: when we scan the brain activity of someone hearing a particular sound, the scan is closely akin to a person in hypnosis asked to conjure the same sound. Intriguingly, those scans are quite different from the person whose simply asked to imagine that sound as vividly as possible. Now is this because of the sheer depth of involvement of the hypnotised person? Or have they entered a palpably different state, in the same way that someone asleep has completely different brainwaves from someone relaxing with their eyes closed? The jury is still out on that one.

However, there is no evidence that hypnosis can bring about any super-human feats, either physical or mental, such as extra-ordinary strength or memory. That said, self-hypnosis can very successfully use our mind to provide a vivid and versatile practice environment in which to rehearse ways of dealing with situations. This is why it can so dramatically increase our confidence, our calmness, and our willingness to try things out in real life. By these means, our social, psychological and physical skills can all benefit. In fact, hypnosis reminds me that by using our brains and bodies harmoniously, we can transcend the horizons of what we personally thought we were capable of.

So why is this powerful technique still regarded with such suspicion by Britain's mainstream healthcare services, and where in our daily lives could we usefully apply it?

After all, in our workplace and on the sports field, in educational settings just as much as in health care services, self-hypnosis could make a big difference. It can provide a low cost, low risk, virtual training environment in which to practice key skills: preventing and relieving stress and anxiety; building the confidence for public speaking and performances; developing our optimism and over-coming our inertia. Better still, improving these skills can help in our social and personal lives not only our working ones. For young children, it can develop their focusing of attention, and be a means of dealing with bad dreams, bed-wetting, and fear of school. It can also help women prepare for all aspects of pregnancy and childbirth. Yet, most dramatically in my experience, hypnosis can help neutralise the emotional traumas from some accident, incident, or period in our past that may have left us slow to engage with or develop certain aspects of our present life. Hypnosis can help us move on.

Which is why it's so regrettable that despite being well-established in the USA since 1958, here in the UK almost 50 years on, hypnosis is rarely a sanctioned procedure for an NHS psycho-therapy unit or for medical procedures. This reluctance reflects a long history of professional rivalries far more than any scientific reservations, but it certainly doesn't help that the practice of hypnosis is still unregulated. After all, it's a profoundly powerful tool and so only as safe and effective as the practitioner using it. As the law stands, *anyone* can call themselves a hypnotherapist, but this doesn't necessarily mean they have adequate training in the technique, nor training in the vital medical or psychological diagnoses and treatment plans for which hypnosis can only be an aid, not a replacement.

The UK's centre of excellence in research, training, and clinical practice is the University College London Hypnosis Unit, founded in 1993 by Professor David Oakley, and co-directed with Val Walters. As well as seeing NHS and private patients, the unit trains psychologists, nurses, doctors, surgeons and dentists. In addition, the British Society of Experimental and Clinical Hypnosis, or our local GP's surgery, can point us towards trusted practitioners.

Who ever we work with as clients in a coaching or therapeutic capacity, it is likely we will be learning self-hypnosis from session one. This will enable us to devise the increasingly tailored experiences that are essential if we're to maintain our improvements and progress. Refining this naturally occurring personal resource so as to enhance our daily life, seems to me an opportunity well worth finding out about.

Working well with a coach or therapist

The hypnosis technique I describe in the previous section is only one of several powerful and well-proven approaches that we might reasonably encounter in working with a good psychotherapist. Here is a checklist of some key characteristics we should be looking for.

- A good rapport: we need to feel comfortable with the person we'll be working with, and feel that they have our best interests at heart. We need to feel that they rather like us, and that they certainly respect us for making an effort to improve our situation. They should also radiate lots of positive energy, and be optimistic about helping us make major strides.
- We and our therapist are allies ... just like a hill-walker and a native guide, and they can help us through some unfamiliar and difficult terrain. We don't want a 'You doctor Me patient' sort of relationship. It's a highly collaborative process and requires our highly active participation. We should bring a note pad and a pen because good therapy requires us to be very active in our listening, thinking and explaining. To draw a comparison with making physical improvements, psychotherapy is like having a work-out with an instructor at our side guiding and encouraging our activities; it is not at all like having a massage or visiting our dentist whereby we just turn up and let it happen with little effort required from us. On the contrary, good therapy will motivate us to tackle the problem with skill and confidence. For instance, we might practise role-plays so as to rehearse different ways of dealing with tricky situations. We should always feel well supported by our therapist, but we should also feel that we're leading the charge.
- The more honest and clear we can be in our explanations of our present problem and hopes for the future, the better chance of progress. The therapist will dwell little on the past, because it's what we do now and in the near future which will determine how fast and how effectively we get better. (*However, there are excellent techniques to neutralise traumas from our past, which do not*

require us to recount the initial incident; so we shouldn't worry that effective therapy need entail upsetting blow by blow disclosures of painful past experiences.)

- If we turn up for therapy tired, late, or un-prepared, then this is telling us we're trying to squeeze it in around everything else. We should be sure to own up to our lack of motivation or organisation with our therapist, because these symptoms are probably part of the problem.

- We might be asked to fill in a questionnaire or two that will help give our therapist a better overview of some part of our personality or behaviour. This is akin to a surgeon taking an x-ray to get the bigger picture of what might be going on. Or perhaps the therapist will simply ask us a whole range of exploratory questions as part of the initial interview. Our therapist is looking for patterns and processes hiding in among the sea of details in our everyday life.

- We will probably learn how to actively relax our muscles, because relaxed muscles are a signal to the brain to calm itself . . . and a calm brain is the most efficient brain for learning and creative problem-solving. Just think how our mind can go quite blank if we're put on the spot and under pressure, yet by contrast, if we take a couple of days off from fretting over a problem, some helpful solution can happily emerge. This is because relaxation is a highly productive mental and physical state.

- We learn by doing, not simply pondering or discussing. In respect of this fact, effective therapy is always 'positive action oriented'. By contrast to simply discussing the problem or rehashing the past, the effective therapist requires us to take active steps to change the way we're thinking, feeling and behaving. We'll be asked to agree to some clear and achievable goals each week, things we'll need to practice or achieve before next week's session, such as doing new stuff, or doing old stuff differently. It's important that we see our power to change our experience of life for the better. Even choosing small tasks at first and building up, these target activities might be uncomfortable or even quite daunting, but facing up to these fears will be the beginning of our journey to full health. The therapist might even accompany us on particular tasks, to support and guide us in these early stages. The aim of these assignments is to build up our confidence and know-how as we go. 90% of improvements will come from work we do outside the therapy room, and the more we practice, the faster we'll improve. Our time with our coach is largely for guidance, information and encouragement.

- Our therapist won't provide answers, so much as ask us searching questions and teach us the skills of discovering helpful answers. These will give us the confidence and direction so that we know how to find out things for ourselves, and to plan our routes forward. They'll help us learn to be good explorers and good problem-solvers.

- Along the route to major improvements, we are going to make mistakes, have bad days and temporary setbacks. These are an inevitable part of progress. In fact, if we're not tripping up, it's probably because we're not pushing our boundaries . . . and we want to push our boundaries because we want to start thinking and behaving in more helpful and enjoyable ways. So mistakes, bruises, and setbacks come with the territory in any enterprise in which we're determined to make progress. Picking ourselves up and pressing on in good cheer will be a helpful attitude to muster. The bigger our spirit of healthy exploration, the better things will be.

- Our therapist may wish to tape some or all of the session so that we can take the tape away with us and play it during the week. By these means, the issues that were discussed have a chance to sink in, and no important insights get lost or overlooked. Audio-taping can be particularly important when using hypnosis as a tool, and daily use of the audiotape for several weeks might be a key means to making dramatic and lasting improvements. It would be quite reasonable for the therapist to ask us to bring our own blank audiotape, because by this little effort on our part they can see we're taking full-responsibility for getting better.

- Except on rare or exceptional occasions, we should always leave the therapist's room feeling hopeful and happier than when we arrived. If we feel in an emotional mess or deeply confused, then that therapeutic relationship isn't working. Immediately own up to this with the therapist, and see if you can work swiftly to put that right.

- It might well take a total of 12 or more sessions with our therapist to really get to grips with a problem, but after six sessions it should have become clear to us and our therapist that we can see encouraging signs that progress is on the way, even if that progress isn't always smooth and unfaltering. If we've not made appreciable gains within the first half-dozen of our one hour sessions, then it's time to review the situation very clearly and candidly with our therapist.

- Rest assured that there are at least half-a-dozen well-established psychotherapeutic approaches to problems, all of which can be highly effective, but not one of which can offer skills which cover even half of the possible psychological problems. So, a failure to progress could mean a wrong fit between us and our therapist . . . or it could mean a wrong fit between the therapeutic approach and our problem.

- We should bear in mind that 'improvement is a process' that may take a few months and several combined approaches. Whereas one therapist may help us identify the core of a problem and help us make some headway, it might be necessary to go to a second and third specialist for us to make further gains. This second therapist might be more specialist in a particular approach or technical skill. For instance, someone qualified and experienced in using Clinical Hypnosis may be needed to help with our difficult digestive problems, but only once a cognitive-behavioural specialist has identified and helped resolve some of the underlying causes as regards our relationships with some key people and the way we cope with everyday life. Six months down the line, we might need to go back to a therapist for a few top-up sessions. This would be quite normal.

- With the help of our therapist, we should quickly develop a sense of a profoundly promising future for ourselves (and for our loved ones who will benefit from our revitalised outlook on life). For instance, we might start pondering happily about all the lovely individuals we don't even know yet, who we have yet to meet, but who will become good friends or mentors in the months and years to come. We should feel, too, that the past has no power over us, no power to determine how we go on from here, not if we're prepared to improve the way we do things. Our actions of today and tomorrow are not only more powerful than mere words, they're more powerful than the past.

Treating the root causes rather than the individual symptoms

Modern life is getting on top of us

'How to achieve your goals in life, and 'How to enjoy the journey' were the two questions at the heart of my YoungLives research when, on the brink of the new millennium, I set out to garner the experience and insights of some of the most accomplished individuals of their generation, ranging in age between 16 and 78. My team and I visited leading schools, blue chip companies, and elite organisations, from the Royal Marines to the Royal College of Art. I asked each establishment to invite a handful of their most out-standing members to take part, in addition to which I went on to interview several dozen well known individuals whose work offered helpful perspectives on how lives go well. These voices ranged from the authors Nick Hornby (*High Fidelity*), Helen Fielding (*Bridget Jones's Diary*) and Bill Bryson (*The Lost Continent*), through to Gary Lineker (England soccer captain in the 1990s), Kate Adie (former BBC head of news) and General de La Billiere (formerly of The Special Air Service).

That research was attempting to systematically and sensitively harvest some lifeskills know-how and hard-won wisdom, but the responses also highlighted a chain reaction taking place across British society, that seems to go something like this: the processing power of the microchip doubles about every 18 months, and the ensuing developments in our personal and working environments place ever greater demands upon individuals of all ages. The challenges presented by this phenomenon are exacerbated because the technology-driven life pressure significantly lessens the time offered for mentorship and emotional support by parents, extended family, teachers and trainers.

These prevailing conditions lead to particular psychological hungers, and we can see these strongly reflected in the block-buster feature films of the present era. For example, hunger for mentorship is dramatised in everything from *The Sixth Sense* to *Star Wars*, and from The Lion King to Finding Nemo. Meanwhile, fear of an apocalyptic future with out-of-control technology is epitomised in *The Matrix Trilogy* that took over from the *Terminator* epic. When faced with overwhelming troubles, we tend to seek refuge and comfort in a nostalgia for times past, and this is catered for by a host of stories from the *Titanic* saga through to *Austin Powers*. What's more, we long for some magical solutions, and these are dished up in spadefuls by *Lord of the Rings* and *Harry Potter*.

Film themes aside, our modern-day culture of 'high demands yet low support' seems to be spurring a gentle revolution whereby an ever growing minority of individuals are increasingly redressing their life-balance towards personal development, relationships and passions, in preference to income, status and ownership. One indication of this is that major companies are finding it harder to retain their young executives who want to down-size their working hours, while senior employees are eagerly taking early retirement. But while society waits for this sea change to take a hold, maybe there's things we can do to help keep a good work-life balance.

What we can do to improve the balance in our 21st Century life?

How about Western governments stop using economic growth as the exclusive index of national prosperity, and include their citizens' self-reported levels of well-being and quality of life? In fact, that's the advice of policy-influencing social scientists such as Daniel Kahneman and Ed Diener in the US, and David Halpern and Richard Layard in the UK; and it's for good reason.

My personal take on 21st Century living is this: fuelled by ever accelerating technological developments, the demands of our modern-day life are far over-stretching the psychological resources of most individuals, and we're hurting because of it. In response to this epidemic of lifestyle imbalance, governments have treated symptoms rather than causes, succeeding only in replacing one psychosomatic disorder with another. For instance, in the early 1950s, eight in ten British men smoked and almost as many women. Yet, 50 years of health campaigns have only succeeded in replacing smoking with obesity as the greatest threat to all round health, so that nowadays one in four men, women and children would be described by their GP as being at least 25 percent overweight. That means a quadrupling of obesity in the past twenty years. This is bad news because obesity increases our vulnerability to serious medical conditions like diabetes, heart disease, cancer and arthritis. It would have take many generations for this new national epidemic to have been brought about by changes in our genetic blueprint, so the problem is almost certainly a result of something we're doing wrong in our everyday life – very probably our national tendency to over-eat and yet be decreasingly active.

There's other evidence to support my proposal that we're simply substituting one unhelpful habit for another, while the underlying problem remains our under-appreciation of our essential human needs. Note how the prison of poverty has simply been bought-off by the worry of credit card debt. And though less of us cause havoc through drunk driving, now it's our tiredness behind the wheel that is the main cause of accidents. Yes, safety-belts prevent us going through the windscreen, but they've not stopped us jumping out of our cars to club each other. And even if we make it home, we too often use our technology-created free time to sit for hours in front of some screen or another, which simply doesn't recuperate us.

I don't mean to suggest that technology is the trouble, rather it's our unwise application of it which deserves the blame. Our around-town transport system is just such an example of how we and our governments have let the selfish application of technology ride rough-shod over our community's best interests. In terms of its cycling population, my home town Cambridge is the Amsterdam of England, yet even here there aren't nearly enough genuine cycle paths, i.e. the ones that dual as extra-wide pedestrian pavements, and are safely off the road. Push-bikes and motor vehicles self-evidently don't mix, and understandably parents feel the urge to ferry their children to and fro.

But rather than wait around helplessly for town planners to make a difference, how about school students take the initiative and gently jog the few miles to school, then shower and change on site. After all, a posse of teenagers properly kitted out for all weathers could easily keep each other company and cover three or four miles in forty-five minutes. From everything we know about the benefits of frequent exercise, we know that their moods, learning abilities and bodies would all benefit enormously. What's more, the sense of being in control and under their own steam like this, is demonstrably good for the psyche. With depression, substance abuse, bulimia and obesity threatening all of our young people, we'd be doing them a timely good turn by making such a school run 'de rigueur'. And by rejecting the sedentary alternatives, they'd be striking at one of the root causes of the lifestyle overload. There'd be grumbling from some quarters, of course, but people grumbled at safety-belt laws and called them 'nannying interference', until they fully realised the full extent of their life-preserving benefits. So, could a merry band of innovative students, parents, and teachers take up the gauntlet and show us the way?

If we step back for a moment and look at the traffic situation, and the obesity crisis, and a whole lot bunch of other stress-related problems besides, they rather beg the question: *how did such an unhelpful state of affairs come about in the first place?* The problem seems to be that though, in principle, technology is there to serve us, too often we let it run ahead of us and out of control. Take, for instance, America's experience of handguns kept around the home for self-protection. Statistics show they are more likely to kill or injure a member of the household in an accident, assault or suicide, than ever being used on an intruder.

So how can we tackle the root cause of our own population metaphorically shooting itself in the foot when faced with the accelerating rate of digital, mechanical and pharmaceutical invention?

One solution from the science of well-being would be for educational institutions to be freed from competing so overwhelmingly on conventional subject grades. Instead, they could equally be judged by the progress their students make in their ability to generate their own lasting happiness, health and positive social involvement. A well-being focused education like this, promises far greater benefits for Britain's social and economic prosperity, and far fewer casualties in terms of psychological stress and physical sickness. Technology has brought some fabulous developments, but in school, college and the workplace we might all cope better with modern life by learning much more about the nourishment our human nature requires for the healthy development of our mind, body, and spirit. This appreciation might prevent our drive for invention from trampling over our more important human needs.

Living off-the-record

Here follows an example of how new technologies can perhaps have accidental impacts upon that invisible but potent rapport that needs to exist between our conscious and sub-conscious mind.

What might be the well-being effects of effortlessly recording every sight and sound of our daily life? Because by 2006, there'll be a device the size of a lapel-badge commercially available to the general public, that will automatically take several thousand digital snaps per day, to be down-loaded for whatever purpose comes to mind. It goes without saying that there are a whole legion of horribly intrusive uses that such technology can be put to, because this is undoubtedly a wolf in sheep's clothing . . . the forerunner of the cut-price spy camera . . . whereby everyone can covertly keep tabs on any one else they care to, in home or work or school or absolutely anywhere we want to intrude upon. Quite how our personalities will react to every one spying on everyone else's most intimate business, doesn't bear thinking upon, though I can't help but imagine there will be quite an uncomfortable transition period which will make people shouting too loudly into their mobile phones . . . seem as a mole-hill is to a mountain.

That said, there must also be countless truly helpful applications of this stunning technology, but what might be the psychological downsides of us making or viewing such indiscriminate marathon recordings of our everyday lives. For sure, a photo of a loved one can conjure wonderful memories, as can the home movies of some golden days that we roll out after dinner once a year. But the new nanotechnology recorder is at the very least intended to automatically capture a large percentage of our daily life on a near perpetual basis. Even with this seemingly benign prospect, I have some very strong reservations.

My first thought is that too much time spent looking backwards at life, is time we might better spend moving forward. No matter it be pleasurable or painful, if the past is left to exist as a simple memory, it gradually fades and we feel the hunger to invest anew in our present and our future, and that's how we progress. Such a healthy process requires us to be active participants far more often than mere observers, because progress comes from actually doing not simply knowing. In which case, could all this new data be a paralysing distraction?

My second reservation wonders why our human brain has had several million years to develop a flawless memory, yet clearly hasn't. There's no such thing as a photographic memory for what actually happened, we have only our perceptions of it at the time, infused with emotion and loaded with bias. And when it comes to recollection, our memory for things is something we make there and then like baking a cake, rather than something we pull out of the cupboard ready-made. And this highly creative process of recording and recollecting experiences might actually serve a very healthy purpose, because this malleability allows us by one means or another to reconcile ourselves with the past and move on. My question is, will such all-seeing digital recorders do something akin to sealing our past in plastic and, by doing so, diminish our ability to digest it?

My third reservation is that for things to be beautiful, they need to be seen in a suitable way. For instance, a beautiful face if seen from afar cannot easily be discerned as attractive. Put that same face under the magnifying glass, and all we can see are open pores and tiny hairs. Only when viewed within a suitable range does the beauty become apparent. And isn't our whole life a lot like this? If we over-examine our relationships, our hobbies, our job, we can all too easily squeeze the joy out of them. To get the best from something, we have to respect its limitations and enjoy it the way nature intended us to, even if that means 'once only' and without a rewind button.

Bearing on all of the above thoughts is this final one: that our enduring love of story-telling, whether in the form of novels or films or fireside tales, is rooted in the way that stories leave room for our own interpretation and for filling in the gaps in any way that suits us. It would seem our experience of life is meant to be worn loosely, and flows better that way.

* * *

Planning for Progress

- Do you suffer from psychological or physical symptoms which might possibly have their cause and their cure in your sub-conscious mind?

- Could you contact your doctor's surgery or www.bsech.com so as to be put in touch with a therapist qualified and experienced in Clinical Hypnosis as part of their wider training?

- What changes could you make to your daily lifestyle that would better harmonise your mind and body, your conscious and sub-conscious? How could your friends and family benefit from these possibilities?

* * *

Some Final Thoughts and a Starting Place

Looking Forward to the Future

Bring me my bow of burning gold,
Bring me my arrows of desire,
Bring me my spear, oh clouds unfold,
Bring me my chariot of fire.

(William Blake)
1757–1827

Progress in life is about our attitude not our age

Youthfulness and maturity are not about being or looking younger
or older, they are about how we choose to behave and in what
spirit. Hence me arguing that it's not our age that's important, *it's
our attitude.*

Such considerations are not just word-play or armchair philosophy, because at Canada's McGill University, Dr Sonia Lupien has
shown that a positive attitude to ageing can affect how long and how
healthily we live. And a positive attitude is well-warranted, because
studies have now revealed that though a small minority of people
start life with poor health and decline severely across the years, the

great majority of us will enjoy very reasonable health with only minor problems until the day we die. UN Ambassador Eleanor Roosevelt well exemplifies this: she had barely ever been ill, suffering just a few minor ailments, until just a few weeks before her death at age 78.

Even better, an analysis of eminent lives by University of California professor of psychology, Dean Keith Simonton, confirms that old age need not bring any decline in one's progress and accomplishments. Our brain is extremely malleable and at any age we benefit from stimulating ourselves with new learning, whether physical or intellectual. For instance, if musicians in their 70s keep practicing, they remain almost as dextrous in body and brain as much younger souls, and their depth of experience more than makes up for any shortfall. As long as we pay heed to the principle of 'use it or lose it', for every hill we go over (metaphorically), it seems that the sheer exercise it provides means we'll probably have the where-with-all to enjoy climbing another. Sadly, Pablo Picasso admitted he allowed himself to stagnate in later years and even joked bitterly that he was painting fakes of himself. By contrast, Verdi's writing of time-honoured operas spanned 50 years largely because he remained so determined to develop and keep versatile by exposing himself to new and diverse ideas.

Yes, it seems pure mathematicians do some of their finest work in their 20s, while athletes very often peak in their early thirties. We might also note that the Fifth Symphony, the Sistine Chapel, and Hamlet were all works of art achieved by individuals in their late 30s. However, Winston Churchill was 65 when he set out to lead Britain against the Nazis in The Second World War, and Titian was almost 90 when he painted his masterpiece, *Christ Crowned with Thorns*. In short, life tends to get better the more skills we acquire for living it, and age has little bearing on this reliable equation.

Here's one tiny example of how computer pioneer, Bill Gates, translates the spirit of progress into his everyday life. "I make a point to read at least one news weekly from cover to cover, because it broadens my interests. If I only read what intrigues me, then I'd finish the magazine the very same person I was before I started. So I read it all."

By contrast, if we don't learn how to progress our relationship with life, it doesn't get any easier or any more enjoyable. This begins to explain why countless studies have shown that no time of life is intrinsically happier than any other, no matter childhood, college days, or retirement. Nature does not intend that being young be simply a rehearsal for adulthood, nor that aging be the price we pay for living. Aging is not a disease nor does it bring inevitable decline. Aging is an opportunity – it's more time with which to make a difference to how good life feels for ourselves and for those around us.

Eleanor Roosevelt wrote: "I could not, at any age, be content to take my place by the fireside and simply look on. Life was meant to be lived. Curiosity must be kept alive. One must never, for whatever reason, turn one's back on life."

To which end, aging is in need of youthfulness, because youthfulness is an approach to living, not a facial product. It is the passion to progress rather than be stagnant. It is curious and inquiring rather than blinkered and closed. It is flexible and adaptable rather than rigid and backward looking. Rather than pomposity, youthfulness has humour. Rather than regret and fear, it has cheerful optimism. And it's a skill we learn, just as we have to learn maturity. For all of these reasons and more besides, youthfulness is beautiful; but neither youth nor beauty pay heed to age, just as wisdom is not the preserve of the old. We only progress if we make good of our experiences in life, learning to turn the lemons into lemonade, and to make hay when the sun shines.

I'm sure we've all met someone impressively old who has awed us with their youthful spirit even in the face of life's adversities. One such soul for me is my friend Sarah's grandma who, after 88 years and a stroke, was still an inspiration for all the youthfulness she brought to life. It seems that if we keep working at it, some wisdom will come with age, and surely Winston Churchill was on to something when he wrote, "We are all happier in many ways when we are old than when we are young."

With all of the above in mind, I for one, have decided I don't need to be young again. What I aspire to be instead, is more youthful and more mature, because youthfulness and maturity dance hand in hand. In fact, as each season passes, I find myself happily agreeing with American poet, Henry Longfellow who wrote:

For age is opportunity no less than youth itself, though in another dress; and as the evening twilight slips away, the sky is filled with stars, invisible by day.

So what's on your to-do list?

Now's as good a time as any to draw up a To-Do List of the relationships, activities, and hopes that we hold most dear.

- Which personal relationships do you wish to develop – from among your existing ones, and the ones you've not even begun yet?
- What skills of mind and body would you most like to learn – social, physical, personal and professional?
- Where do you wish to visit or even live – which cities, landscapes and special places?
- What new or rare experiences would you like to savour – the social events, the emotional feelings, and physical sensations?

It will pay to put your emphasis very much on 'enduring relationships' . . . with people, places and skills . . . rather than on one-off experiences which can leave us feeling rather hollow. If we're having any trouble drumming-up some stomach-tingling ideas, the following might help:

- In your favourite daydreams, what delightful things do you most eagerly imagine?
- What are the professions, hobbies, relationships and surroundings of your favourite characters from films, novels and biographies?
- If you suddenly found yourself on your death-bed, but with sufficient time to ponder and compose your thoughts, what things would you most regret not having done in life?
- So, if you had just two years left to live, with whom and how would you spend that time?

The former U.S. Secretary of State and United Nations Ambassador, Madeleine Albright, wrote that "Enthusiasm created from the heart, guides the whole person", and for sure it will be our searingly honest responses to such questions as these above, that will point towards our heart-felt passions buried beneath the paraphernalia of everyday living. Watching more tv or traipsing around the stores will not appear on our wish-list, not if it's a genuine summary of our innermost desires. Much more likely our answers will reflect those sides of our personality and inner callings that we've never fully explored. Let's take heart from the words of another former U.N. Ambassador, Eleanor Roosevelt: "The future belongs to those who believe in the beauty of their dreams".

How good can life get, and how good can we get at living it?

Let's refresh our memories for some of the key characteristics common to lives that seem to be both 'feeling good' and 'doing good', i.e. the common denominators of lives well lived:

Partner-up with like-hearted souls because good companions are our greatest source of happiness in life, and greatest comfort in hard times. Our learning to develop intimacy and appreciation will bring a profound sense of progress. Find people to be passionate about; love generously, and let ourselves be loved. I like the words of U.S. Senator Hillary Rodham Clinton: "Bill and I started a conversation in the spring of 1971, and more than 30 years later, we're still talking."

Let's grab a good hold of real life rather than disengaging our mind and body through television, alcohol, fantasy or anything else that puts distance between us and the real world. The greater the intimacy with a good person, skill or place, the greater the pleasure. Reality is the only place we can share life with the people for whom we care and care for us.

Let our goals in life be to enjoy the various journeys we embark upon – the relationships, the adventures, the learning. Let's not sacrifice the pleasure and goodness of our journeys for the sake of distant goals and glittering medals. Living well is about quality not quantity, so let's not rush. Develop our passions for those things that thrill us. Listen to our heart and our intuitions, and then let our head handle the organisation required to put things into practise. Seek to create happiness in everything we do, because joy is a fuel for good for things, not simply a result of them. Learning to turn a chore into something cheerful is a life-transforming skill. Golf champion Tiger Woods always found a way to turn several hours of golf practise into playful fun; and in a survey of Nobel Prize winners, they placed 'sheer joy and playfulness' at the very top of the list of 30 factors that had helped them excel.

Seek to grow strong in the face of adversity. We progress not by avoiding life's challenges but by learning to create something good from a piece of bad luck. Recall how Monty Roberts transformed the experience of being bullied in his childhood, into a profoundly caring way of training horses; and how Nobel Laureate, Gertrude Elion, was inspired to become an innovative scientist by seeing people she loved die from disease.

Explore and experiment with who we are and how we behave. Test things out, do things differently, act immediately to channel our passions and tackle our problems. Duck and weave to keep making progress. Political and spiritual leader, Mahatma Gandhi, regarded his whole life as a series of experiments. Joanne Rowling tried writing two novels for adults before she finally had the idea for Harry Potter.

Harmonise the workings of our mind and body, and our conscious and sub-conscious mind. This coordinated approach to life will allow us to feel so much more at home inside of ourselves, and our lasting progress will be so much swifter. The starting place for this is an appreciation of how our body can heal our thoughts and emotions, just as our mind can heal and train our body. Developing the skills of self-hypnosis is just one means by which to achieve such a happy alliance.

Make connections with the world around us. Let's consider what people are going to need most of these next few years? How can we create a valuable role for ourselves? For Anita Roddick it was world-friendly ways of producing bodycare products; and Princess Diana discovered greater happiness and self-respect in her caring for those in need.

It seems that if we're doing *what* we love with *whom* we love, we're never on the wrong road.

* * *

EPILOGUE
The Journey of a Lifetime

A deeply satisfying sense of progress in life is possible for all of us, and the journey itself . . . the exploration and companionship along the way . . . is where all the joy lies.

These past ten years, I have had the privilege of hearing individuals trying to make sense of their lives, and I am still delighted and inspired by what I have heard. I could not wish for a more enjoyable endeavour than exploring and recounting such universal voyages.

It was sunny July when I began writing this book, and sitting in front of a log fire on New Year's Eve, I'm mulling over two particular thoughts.

Number one, is that my sole resolution for the year ahead is simply this: I'm going to explore how good life can get, and how good we can get at living it. Everything else, all other goals, are well served by that guiding light. To this end, rather than commit to any pre-determined plans of action, I will endeavour to experiment and be flexible, and to see the bigger picture of how every one thing can help every other.

Thought number two comes from the observation that much of life is unpredictable. In fact, I can rely on it being so. For instance, I know for sure the year ahead will bring mistakes, disappointments and setbacks, and some tears I didn't see coming. There will be painful losses, sad partings, and problems near insoluble. So it's a surefire certainty that I'll have to pick myself off the floor on countless occasions. But I've no hard feelings, because that's just life going about its business, like a river running. And that same river will just as surely bring forth unforeseen friendships, ad-lib laughter, and some very welcome kisses that weren't on my calendar. I ponder, too, at the partnerships and projects, the special new places, and the songs I'll be singing as I cycle to work that haven't even been written yet. The future... and the people with whom I'll share it... are quite unimaginable. Such an unexpected life is downright refreshing, and not having it all mapped out in our diaries means we can be full of hope and wonder as we set out to investigate.

Bon voyage!

Nick Baylis, New Year's Eve
Cambridge, England.

* * *

Heart-Felt Thanks

While writing *Wonderful Lives*, I have been guided at all times by the goodwill of loving friends. I'm deeply proud of knowing these individuals, and I'd like to thank each one of them for making this book possible. I may have seemed like a lone traveler, but my companions have been legion.

First and foremost, Dr Anja Minnich, who worked with me side by side every day for nine months. There's not a paragraph within these pages that Anja didn't improve upon. Anja, my dear friend, you made the journey wonderful.

Maria Loades, the Cambridge graduate who is training as a Clinical Psychologist and has a particular interest in how combining psychology with horse riding can be used to help troubled youngsters. It was Maria who interviewed Mr Monty Roberts, the real-life horse-whisperer. Maria was a vital part of the book project for 10 full weeks, and a fabulous researcher. Her bold new ideas were always welcome.

Cerstin Henning, my Cologne-based educational and creative consultant whose unparalleled teaching experience, vibrant originality, treasured friendship, and home cooking, were always an inspiration and enormous help.

Dr Sarah Fitzharding, the Cambridge-kid turned Manhattan-hotshot who rode with me side by side through my masters and doctorate. Despite the Atlantic Ocean between us, Sarah has been the most loving companion on all my projects ever since we first teamed up.

Mrs Samantha Morley, my very own baby sister. Thanks for talking such sense to me, Sam, and keeping my spirits up, and bailing me out in troubled times. A brother appreciates these things more than words can say.

The following ladies also made transforming contributions to my numerous drafts and first ideas. Their wise intuitions made all the difference: **Caroline Kelham; Dr Pascale Bouger; Dr Constanze Güthenke; Lucy Stewart; Ursel Braun; Edye Hoffmann; Dr Manuela Varzescu;** and my youngest editor, **Katherine Jackson.**

To each one of the wonderful women I've named above, I'd like to say this:
On the yellow brick road of writing this book, you have been like Dorothy to me, just as surely as I have been the Tin Man, the Lion, and the Scarecrow, in search of tenderness and courage and wisdom.
You have also been the Holly Go-Lightly of my journey, softly singing *Moon River* to help me write. You deserve to breakfast at Tiffany's for all your care and kindness.

To be fair, a few fellas have also provided their thoughts and encouragement right from day one:

Dr James C. Oleson, a dear friend of many years, who happens to be an outstanding lawyer and is presently a Fellow of the U.S. Supreme Court in Washington D.C.

Paul Carpenter, the software design consultant whose gentle insights into the themes of the book, and timely expertise with computers, were always appreciated.

Erling Kagge, the Norwegian polar explorer, publisher, and patron of the arts who, with the kindness of friendship, took me walking in the mountains after I handed in this book.

Tobias Wolff of Stanford University, for writing the deeply moving books that kept me good company: *School Ties, In Pharaoh's Army,* and *This Boy's Life.*

My grateful acknowledgement of professional contributions

James Collard of *The Times Magazine,* for being such a considerate and supportive editor on my *Science of Happiness* columns these past two years.

Brandy Donough of the Burlington Press, Cambridge, for her irrepressible enthusiasm that carried the project through from choosing the right paper to delivering the finished books.

Lawrence Coulson, the contemporary English artist, for his fabulous landscape painting, *Blaze of Glory,* which I'm delighted to have for the book's front cover.

And most of all, Professor Felicia A. Huppert for being my companion in The Science of Well-Being and Positive Psychology here at Cambridge University. It was Felicia who led Professor Barry Keverne and I at The Royal Society Discussion Meeting in 2003. Her dynamism and generosity of spirit are an inspiration to me.

* * *

Further Information

Nick's Potted Biog

* * *

My Previous Projects

Trail-Blazers in Feltham Young Offenders Prison
The YoungLives Research Project
Philosophical Transactions of The Royal Society
The Science of Well-Being, Oxford University Press

* * *

Chapter Notes

Where to find more about the leading researchers
whose ideas are the bricks and mortar of this book.

* * *

Index of Key Words and Themes

* * *

50 Wonderful Lives

Introducing the much admired individuals
whose personal stories bring the research findings to life.

* * *

Four of my Favourite Benevolent Organisations

Teach First; St Christopher's Hospice;
The Prince's Trust; The Open University

* * *

Making Connections

What positive moves could we now make . . . and with whom?

* * *

Nick's Potted Biog

Present Day

Since autumn 2001, I have had the privilege of being Britain's first lecturer in Positive Psychology, teaching within the Department of Social and Developmental Psychology which is part of The Faculty of Social and Political Sciences, here at Cambridge University. From autumn 2005 onwards, I will formally be teaching The Science of Well-Being as part of my lecture series. This opportunity first arose because, back in 2001, I was invited to be involved in the fast emerging Positive Psychology movement in the USA, and its week-long 'think tanks' hosted in Mexico's Yucatan peninsula. These lagoon-side get-togethers ran for three consecutive years, as we tried to forge a gameplan for our new field. (I eventually stumbled across the identity of the anonymous millionaire who sponsored my place at those fabulous meetings. That quiet, considerate American has yet to let me stand him a pint and a pie at The Eagle pub here in Cambridge.)

In addition to my University lecturing, I give tutorials and act as an examiner; and I've now written one hundred pieces on *The Science of Happiness* for my Saturday column in *The Times.* Before that, I wrote a weekly life-coaching piece for *The Financial Times.*

I also run a small part-time private practice in coaching and therapy for adults of all ages, and for several years have enjoyed occasional one-to-one coaching for Cambridge University students at the invitation of their colleges. I like to use a wide range of well-proven techniques, such as the combination of Cognitive-Behavioural Therapy with Clinical Hypnosis that has shown itself so effective not only for health problems but for personal development and skills training.

Throughout the year, I enjoy giving talks and training days for companies and professional bodies such as:

- The Royal College of General Practitioners, responsible for the professional development and all-round welfare of medical doctors in general practice.
- Teach First, the highly innovative charitable organisation which trains and fast-tracks top young graduates for full-time teaching at some of the most challenging and rewarding inner-city secondary schools.
- The Chartered Institute for Personnel and Development, which is the leading professional body in its field.
- St Christopher's Hospice in London, one of the flagships of the modern-day Hospice movement, which cares for terminally-ill children and adults.

In my free time, I love to go walking with friends and family, to dance and play soccer, and to catch a film at the cinema.

Some time ago
Having taught in adult education, in comprehensive schools, and in a special school for emotionally troubled teenagers, I then took a year out to study for the Master of Arts in Creative Writing from the University of East Anglia (1992); and later, in the summer of 1994, did The National Film & Television School screenwriting course.

During all of that time, I moonlighted on The Open University Postgraduate Diploma in Criminology and Prison Studies, which was an extremely well-run and intriguing correspondence program. This unusual combination of criminology and creative writing allowed me to approach the producers of *Four Weddings and a Funeral* (that summer's big box-office hit), as well as the Levi's Jeans Company and Channel 4 Television, who clubbed together so as to fund my initial foray into Feltham Young Offenders institution as a creative writing tutor. That was 1994, but when I went off to my postgraduate psychology studies at Cambridge University, I maintained a role as a part-time volunteer in Feltham gaol, and in 1998 eventually founded the initial version of the job-mentoring project called *Trail-Blazers*.

It was at Jesus College, Cambridge, that I read for my Masters and Doctorate. This ancient place not only provided me with a comforting home but, more importantly, it brought me some wonderful companions with whom I am still very close.

My eventual PhD examiners were Professor George E. Vaillant of Harvard Medical School, and Professor Donald J. West of Cambridge University. I will never be able to repay their kindness in taking on a difficult case like me, but they are selfless gentlemen who would only be embarrassed by me trying to do so.

Immediately following my PhD examination, I formed the research project *YoungLives*, asking some inspirational individuals, young and old, how each of us can best learn to '*achieve our goals and enjoy the journey*'.

More recently
My co-organisers of The Royal Society conference, and subsequent co-editors for the Oxford University Press book, *The Science of Well-Being*, were Professor Felicia A. Huppert (Fellow of Darwin College) and Professor E. Barry Keverne (Fellow of King's College), both career-long Faculty Members of Cambridge University. It was Felicia who led the Royal Society conference and was lead editor on our Oxford book, and her good-natured dynamism is an inspiration to me.

At the beginning of 2005, I was delighted of the invitation to become a Fellow of The RSA. Founded in 1754, this is the Royal Society for the encouragement of the Arts, Manufacture and Commerce. It is an entirely independent charity, and in the course of its history has brought about The Royal College of Art, The Royal College of Music, The Royal Academy, The Great Exhibition, and much more besides. Its motto is *'Inspiring the Future'*.

In that spirit, I have pledged to donate ten percent of my income from this book to The Wonderful Lives Benevolent Fund that will foster well-being in a charitable way far beyond these pages. Please visit www.NickBaylis.com to find out more.

* * *

My Previous Projects

The following projects, together with my Cambridge Masters and PhD research, all helped form my ideas about the roots of well-being.

The Trail-Blazers mentoring project

While serving as a volunteer in Feltham Young Offenders Institution, which was then Europe's largest high-security prison for young men under 21 years of age, I was incredibly fortunate to raise £150,000 so as to found the charitable mentoring project, *Trail-Blazers*. Our aim was to prepare the youngsters for personal and working life after their release, and to team them up with mentors working in professions that truly interested them. The idea was that mentors would regularly correspond with and visit the youngster so as to develop their interests and know-how.

At the project's launch in 1998, it was a real boon to have the onetime judge and former Chief Inspector of Prisons, Sir Stephen

Tumim, as our first patron. I soon handed over development of the scheme to the highly skilled and dedicated team of Lisa Taylor, Linda Patterson, and Roma Hooper (our Chair of Trustees), who together took the seeds and shape of the project from strength to strength in the following years, building a model of good practice well beyond my original horizons. One of their patrons is the former Chief Inspector of Prisons, General Sir David Ramsbotham, who did such excellent work for the welfare of young offenders. Visit www.trail-blazers.org.uk to find out more.

The YoungLives research project

Having interviewed hundreds of highly accomplished individuals in 1999 and 2000, ranging in age from 16 to 70, I was able to set-up a free mentoring website called www.YoungLivesUK.com which is all about *'How to make the most of life, and how to enjoy the journey.'*

For this face to face long-interview research, I was fortunate to be sponsored by the likes of Reuters News Agency, Nike, Channel 4 TV, Sony PlayStation, and Orange.

In search of insights about *'making the most of life'*, I enjoyed long interviews with each of a host of well-known individuals including Kate Adie (former BBC Head of News), Gary Lineker (former England soccer captain), Nick Hornby (novelist), Helen Fielding (novelist), General Sir Peter de la Billiere (former commander of the Special Air Service regiment), Bill Bryson (travel writer), Martha Lane Fox (founder of lastminute.com), Charlie Higson (founder of The Fast Show), John Madden (director of *Shakespeare in Love*), Barry Norman (film officianado), and Jamie Oliver (chef).

I was also privileged to have long interviews with top young professionals and their training directors at some of the country's leading institutions in a range of different arenas: McKinsey & Co., Dell Computers, JP Morgan, The Rambert Dance Company, The Laban Dance Centre, The Slade Art School, The Royal College of Art, The Royal Marine Commandos, The Grenadier Guards, RAF Cranwell Flight Training School, and Sandhurst Military Academy.

On top of which, I was lucky enough to be allowed long-interviews with many top A-level students and their senior teachers from Eton College, Gordonstoun, Oxford High School, The Manchester Grammar School, Rugby, Radley, Hills Road 6th Form College Cambridge, South Hampstead High School, Tonbridge Grammar School For Girls, and The William Ellis School (Kentish Town).

It is thanks to the innovative ideas so freely given by the above individuals, ideas which were deeply-rooted in their own well-grounded experience, that I was able to form the raw material for the website at www.YoungLivesUK.com which has now broadcast for over five years. I like to think the book you're holding, *Learning from Wonderful Lives*, is the natural evolution of that pilot project.

Philosophical Transactions of The Royal Society

On November 19th and 20th of 2003, The Royal Society of London hosted a Discussion Meeting that had been organised by F. A. Huppert, N.V.K. Baylis, and E. B. Keverne (all members of Cambridge University.)

Founded in 1660, The Royal Society is the independent scientific academy of the United Kingdom, dedicated to promoting excellence in science. Its journal, *Philosophical Transactions of The Royal Society of London*, is the world's longest running international science journal, and the volume that came out of the Discussion Meeting is called *The Science of Well-Being*. This was the Royal Society's first ever conference on this subject.

The specific issue is Series B, Volume 359, Number 1449, Pages 1329-1451. Edited by Huppert, Baylis and Keverne. (Published 29th September 2004; ISSN 0962-8436.)

This issue contains 10 of the 12 papers presented. The following are those who made presentations at our Discussion Meeting:

Randolph M. Nesse (Michigan)
Eric B. Keverne (Cambridge)
David J.P. Barker (Southampton)

Barbara L. Fredrickson (Michigan)
Martin E.P. Seligman (Pennsylvania)
Carol D. Ryff (Wisconsin-Madison)
Barbara Maughan (King's, London)
Richard J. Davidson (Wisconsin-Madison)
Harry Kroto (Sussex)
Sonia J. Lupien (McGill)
Robert J. Sternberg (Yale)
Robert D. Putnam (Harvard)
Johan Galtung (Transcend Network for Peace and Development, France)

Chairing the discussions that followed the formal presentations, were Richard Layard (London School of Economics), Robert Hinde (Cambridge), Lewis Wolpert (University College London), and Felicia Huppert (Cambridge).

The Royal Society two-day Discussion Meeting was open to the public, but the speakers, chairs and organisers then took part in a final day of round-table 'think tanking', courtesy of The Novartis Foundation in Portland Place, London.

Visit www.royalsoc.ac.uk to purchase copies of *Philosophical Transactions*.

The Science of Well-Being

I was delighted when Oxford University Press invited Felicia Huppert, Barry Keverne and myself to jointly produce a book on our general theme of *The Science of Well-Being*, building on the foundations of our Royal Society Discussion Meeting of November 2003. This Oxford book is intended for lecturers and researchers in a broad range of scientific and social scientific disciplines, as well as for policy-makers. It contains some outstanding ideas from leading voices in their respective fields, and is available in both paperback and hardback from Oxford University Press, 2005.

This is an itinerary of the chapters in The Science of Well-Being:

1. Evolution and Development
Randolph Nesse
Natural selection and the elusiveness of happiness
Barry Keverne
Understanding well-being in the evolutionary context of brain development
David J.P. Barker
The developmental origins of well-being
Sonia Lupien & N. Wan
Successful aging: from cell to self

2. Physiology and Neuroscience
Richard J. Davidson
Well-being and affective style
Stuart J.H. Biddle & Panteleimon Ekkekakis
Physically active lifestyle and well-being
Bernard Gesch
The potential of nutrition to promote physical and behavioural well-being

3. Psychology of Well-being
Barbara L Fredrickson
The broaden-and-build theory of positive emotions
Nick Baylis
Relationship with Reality – and its role in the well-being of young adults.
Martin E.P. Seligman, Acacia C. Parks & Tracy Steen
A balanced psychology and a full life
Daniel Kahneman & Jason Riis
Living, and thinking about it: two perspectives on life
Felicia A. Huppert
Positive mental health in individuals and populations

4. Cultural Perspectives
Susan Verducci & Howard Gardner
Good work: its nature, its nurture.

Robert J. Sternberg & Elena Grigorenko
Intelligence and culture: how culture shapes what intelligence means
and the implications for a science of well-being
Antonella Delle Fave & Fausto Massimini
The relevance of subjective well-being to social policies
George Burns
Naturally happy, naturally healthy: the role of the natural environ-
ment in well-being

5. Social and Economic Considerations
John Helliwell & Robert D. Putnam
The social context of well-being
Robert Frank
Does money buy happiness?
Johan Galtung
Meeting basic needs; peace and development
Nic Marks and Hetan Shah
A well-being manifesto for a flourishing society

From the Oxford book's back cover:

This landmark volume heralds the emergence of a new field of science that endeavours to understand how individuals and societies
thrive and flourish, and how this new knowledge can be applied to
foster happiness, health and fulfillment.

Taking a dynamic cross-disciplinary approach, it sets out to explore
the most promising routes to well-being, derived from the latest research
in psychology, biomedical science, social science, economics and the
effects of our natural environment. Contributions come from some of
the world's leading researchers, practitioners, and policy advisors.

Designed for a general readership, this volume will be of compelling interest to all those in the social, behavioural and biomedical
sciences, the caring professions and policy makers. It provides a stimulating overview for any reader with a serious interest in the latest
insights and strategies for enhancing our individual well-being and the
well-being of the communities in which we all live and work.

Chapter Notes

This book attempts to bring together some state-of-the-art research on well-being. In the following pages, I gladly pay tribute to the leading research scientists and practitioners whose many works have been the bricks and mortar of my ideas.

Bearing in mind that I've written this book to be helpful for individuals who may not have easy access to a university library, where ever possible I give a website address. This will allow my reader to keep bang-up-to-date with what a particular scientist is doing in their specialist field. If a website isn't available, I try to name a readable book. This approach seems far more practical than my naming a research paper that may be hard to get hold of, or an expensive academic textbook, neither of which would make a lot of sense if read on its own by someone rather new to the field.

Though I'd be delighted if my work is of interest to professional researchers, forgive me if I haven't provided the level of detail that you would wish for.

Science isn't certainty

Before we move on to the scientific studies, let's remind ourselves that the practice of science has its fashions, politics and pressure groups. As in every field, the accepted wisdoms very largely rely on what's of interest to whomsoever is in charge at the time. What our leading institutions set out to investigate and claim to discover will be strongly influenced by the groups in power . . . be they research, corporate, or political.

Let's not forget, either, that science tends to be interested in average effects on the majority of people, so you and I as individuals need to explore what works for us personally.

Furthermore, science is not truth nor certainty nor the final word; science is simply an approach, a particular way of going about things in search of a better understanding. And at its heart, science is exploration . . . an inquiring mind and a spirit of adventure.

It is in this sense, I think, that the esteemed spiritual and political leader, Mahatma Gandhi, called his autobiography *The Story of My Experiments with Truth*, and referred to his whole life as a series of experiments in everything from what he chose to eat, all the way through to his international doctrine of *non-violent* protest against injustice.

With this spirit of exploration, we can *all* be scientists: wanting to know more, trying out new ideas to see if we can change some outcomes, watching carefully and sharing the possibilities of improvement with those around us. I believe that film, literature, philosophy and all the other disciplines through which mankind investigates the universe, can equally serve as ways to understand life and to shape it for the better. Science has no monopoly on what it all means.

Trying to keep open-minded like this, brings us something akin to the joy of travelling: seeing how other people go about their daily lives, seeing what they hold dear above all else. It's a relief to realise that ours is not the only way, and there are other worlds beyond our present horizons. So I apologise for whenever I have come across as too sure of myself. I claim no truths, no certainties. I report only what strikes me at the present time, and from where I'm standing, as the guiding principles of some rather wonderful lives.

So it is that the following notes are intended merely as a starting point.

Apologies for the repetitions

Because the 16 chapters of this book were designed so they could be read in any order, there is some repetition in these *Chapter Notes* about researchers, websites and the like; but I'd rather have this repetition than leave the reader high and dry with no means of following up their interest in something.

* * *

Nick's Introduction

What's this book all about?

Our setting out to see . . .

The health-bringing qualities of happiness are supported by the lifetime's work of Professor Ed Diener at the University of Illinois at Champaign-Urbana (see his homepage at: www.psych.uiuc.edu/~ediener/). Despite the gentleman's winning personal modesty, I consider Professor Diener to be one of the world's leading experts on scientific research on the subject of happiness. See Professor Diener's chapter called 'Subjective Well-Being: The Science of Happiness and Life Satisfaction'. This is co-authored by Richard E. Lucas and Shigehiro Oishi, and appears in the *Handbook of Positive Psychology,* edited by C. Snyder and S. Lopez.

See also the article Professor Diener co-authored with M. E. P. Seligman 'Beyond Money. Toward an economy of well-being'. It is available at: www.psychologicalscience.org/pdf/pspi/pspi5_1_1-2.pdf

See also work of the late Professor Michael Argyle who was a pioneer in the study of social psychology in Britain.

Likewise, if we continue to develop . . .

This statement is well supported by the unparalleled research study directed for 30 years by Professor George E. Vaillant, which he writes about with great sensitivity and eloquence in *Aging well: Surprising Guideposts to a Happier Life from the Landmark Harvard Study of Adult Development.* This study tracked 824

American lives for over 60 years. From teenagers through to seventy-somethings and beyond, the majority of these men and women were regularly monitored with face to face interviews, questionnaires, and medicals, all in an attempt to better understand how lives go well. Professor Vaillant provides a useful overview of the study on this website: psychology.about.com/library/submit/blsubmit_vaillant1.htm

George's books about the Harvard Study are, each one, (*Adaptation to Life*, *Wisdom of the Ego*, and *Aging Well*), a fascinating and pleasurable read providing a fine mix of science, of artistic sensitivity, and of sheer compassion for the individual lifetimes being studied and written about. These qualities in the writing are equally characteristic of their author. I regret to say that these three books and the Harvard Study have been overlooked by some parts of the educational community and the national media, particularly in the UK, and I'm glad to give them prominence here in my own work.

This isn't just wishful thinking . . .

This study is reported in a journal article by D. Danner, D. Snowdon, and W. Friesen. Entitled 'Positive emotions in early life and longevity: Findings from the nun study', the article is available at: www.apa.org/journals/psp/psp805804.html The research was based at the Department of Preventive Medicine and Sanders-Brown Center on Aging, College of Medicine, University of Kentucky.

See also: Harker, L. and Keltner, D. (2001) Expressions of positive emotions in women's college yearbook pictures and their relationship to personality and life outcomes across adulthood. *Journal of Personality and Social Psychology, 80, 112-124.*

That's not to say . . .

See Professor Randolph M. Nesse's chapter 'Natural Selection and The Elusiveness of Happiness' in *Philosophical Transactions of The Royal Society of London*. (Huppert, Baylis and Keverne 2004). Randolph M. Nesse, M.D., is professor of psychiatry and psychology at the University of Michigan and has made the chapter available at: www-personal.umich.edu/~nesse/Articles/Nesse-EvolElusiveHappiness-ProcRoyalSoc-2004.pdf

All the evidence suggests . . .

See www.positivepsychology.org for an extensive website which gives you some idea of the range of experiments upon which this statement is based.

To this end . . .

The Princeton Psychologist, Professor Daniel Kahneman, who was the 2002 Nobel Laureate in Economics, (jointly awarded to his onetime colleague A. Tversky), was the keynote speaker at The 2003 International Positive Psychology Summit in Washington D.C. His presentation is available here:

www.gallup.hu/pps/2003_ipps_archives.htm See also his autobiographical
account at: nobelprize.org/economics/laureates/2002/kahneman-autobio.html

See Professor Daniel Kahneman's chapter, co-written with Jason Riis, called
Living, and Thinking About it: Two Perspectives on Life. This chapter appears in
The Science of Well-Being. (Huppert, Baylis and Keverne 2005).

Another example is Professor Kahneman's chapter 'Objective happiness' in
(Eds.), *Well-being: The foundations of hedonic psychology* edited by D.
Kahneman, E. Diener, & N. Schwarz.

The Royal Society

The motto of the society is *Nullius in verbia*, i.e. *nothing in words* . . . which I take
to mean that actions are what's important in life. I appreciate the point, but words
can be a great starting place for useful activity. Visit www.royalsoc.ac.uk

For more about this meeting, see *My Previous Projects*, located in these latter
pages of this book you're holding.

This new science has arrived not a moment too soon . . .

Since World War II, such a positive focus has been an extremely rare phenomenon
in medicine and psychology, largely because the newly formed NHS and its
American equivalents invested exclusively in the urgent job of healing the wound-
ed. The trouble is, this 'emergency-only' approach has dominated to the present
day, tending to obscure how studying exceptional health can shed fresh light on
the prevention and cure of suffering.

The Study of Wonderful Lives

The power of such an approach . . .

See the work of Professor Dean Keith Simonton at the University of California,
Davis: psychology.ucdavis.edu/simonton/

Who am I?

I was a volunteer . . .
I was a part-time volunteer at the prison between 1993 and 1998, first as a creative writing tutor, and then as the founder of *Trail-Blazers*, the charitable project offering job mentorship. To find out more, see www.trail-blazers.org.uk.
With support from . . .
For five years now, the conclusions from that 1999 YoungLives research project have been broadcast free-of-charge at www.YoungLivesUK.com This website has received many thousands of visitors of all ages, from young people through to educators and policy makers. Five years on, I like to think the book you're holding, *Wonderful Lives*, is the natural evolution of that pilot project.

And for whom did I write this book?

It doesn't matter what age . . .
See the work of Professor Ed Diener at: www.psych.uiuc.edu/~ediener/

How do we know it will work?

The skills, strategies, route-plans and philosophies . . .
See the work of Harvard University's George E. Vaillant (detailed in my notes above) and his overview of his study at: psychology.about.com/library/submit/blsubmit_vaillant1.htm

Making the most of this book

The guiding principles that I'm proposing here, will be supported and illustrated in detail in every chapter of this book, so I do not attempt to reference the ideas at this stage.

PART ONE

Partnering-Up with Good People

Companionship Comes First

Happiness is a game better enjoyed when . . .
Our close relationships are very likely our greatest single source of happiness, a claim supported by the extensive research synthesised by Professor Robert D. Putnam. Visit the website www.BowlingAlone.com

And Professor Putnam is not alone . . .
For 30 years the director of this study has been George E. Vaillant. His work is summarised in his book *Aging well: Surprising Guideposts to a Happier Life from the Landmark Harvard Study of Adult Development.* Professor Vaillant provides an overview of his study at: psychology.about.com/library/submit/blsubmit_vaillant1.htm

My father recently gave me . . .
All Quiet on the Western Front is the novel by German writer, Erich Maria Remarque. Published in 1928, the story was then made into a fabulous feature film in 1930, directed by Lewis Milestone, and this became the third film to win the Academy Award for Best Picture.

They know that simply acting as a sandbag . . .
See the work of Dr Daniel Goleman on the website of the Emotional Intelligence Consortium at www.eiconsortium.org

Such mums and dads . . .
See the book by Harvard psychologist Dr Edward M. Hallowell, *The Childhood Roots of Adult Happiness: Five Steps to Help Kids Create and Sustain Lifelong Joy.* I personally count this as one of the finest books I've read about childhood happiness. Visit www.DrHallowell.com

Moreover, in my own interview research . . .
'How to achieve your goals in life, and how to enjoy the journey' were the two questions at the heart of my YoungLives research when, on the brink of the new millennium, I set out to garner the experience and insights of some of the most accomplished individuals of their generation, ranging in age between 16 and 78. My team and I visited leading schools, blue chip companies, and elite organisations, from the Royal Marines to the Royal College of Art. I asked each

establishment to invite a handful of their most out-standing members to take part, in addition to which I went on to interview several dozen well-known individuals whose work offered helpful perspectives on how lives go well. These voices ranged from the authors Nick Hornby (*High Fidelity*), Helen Fielding (*Bridget Jones's Diary*) and Bill Bryson (*The Lost Continent*), through to Gary Lineker (England soccer captain in the 1990s), Kate Adie (former BBC Head of News) and General de La Billiere (formerly the Commanding Officer of The Special Air Service).

By studying the development of several hundred lives . . .
See the work of Professor Ed Diener at www.psych.uiuc.edu/~ediener
See also: www.YoungLivesUK.com

Their claims are supported by a host of studies . . .
Such studies are well summarised by Professor Diener's chapter called 'Subjective Well-Being: The Science of Happiness and Life Satisfaction'. This is co-authored by Richard E. Lucas and Shigehiro Oishi, and appears in the *Handbook of Positive Psychology*, edited by C. Snyder and S. Lopez.

In short, let's beware the 'mermaid calling' . . .
See the work of the late Professor Michael Argyle, who was a pioneer in the study of social psychology in Britain.

Let's share enjoyable journeys . . .
See the work of social psychologist Dr Helen Street at the University of Western Australia. Visit www.psychiatry.uwa.edu.au/people/staff.cfm/STID/20

The critical flaw in such thinking is . . .
See the work of Professor Diener at: www.psych.uiuc.edu/~ediener

Finding someone special . . .
See the work and website of The Gottman Institute led by John Gottman, who is Emeritus Professor of Psychology at Washington University in Seattle. Visit www.gottman.com.

A whole combination of factors has meant that . . .
See the work of Professor Robert D. Putnam at www.BowlingAlone.com and my notes above.

Successful life-partnerships are the single richest source of happiness . . .
See the work of Professor Robert D. Putnam at www.BowlingAlone.com and my notes above.

To prevent ourselves drawing apart like this . . .
See the work of Professor George E. Vaillant via my notes above.

Endeavouring to understand the makings of a successful marriage . . .
See the research findings of Dr John Gottman at www.gottman.com.

In fact, research by Shelly Gable at UCLA says . . .

See the article 'What do you do when things go right? The intrapersonal and interpersonal benefits of sharing positive events' by Dr Shelly Gable and her co-authors. It is available at: www.apa.org/journals/psp/featured_article/august_2004/psp872228.pdf

What's more . . .

See the work of Professor George E. Vaillant via my notes above.

Developing our Passions in Life

Such sentiments echo a theme . . .

For more information on my YoungLives project, see *My Previous Projects* in the latter pages of this book.

Thankfully, the psychological studies are now quite clear . . .

The lifetime's research work of Professor Ed Diener on happiness is a key source for these conclusions. (See his homepage at: www.psych.uiuc.edu/~ediener/).

Respecting our true callings . . .

See the website of Dr Harriet B. Braiker at www.diseasetoplease.com

This would explain why The Harvard Study of Adult Development . . .

See the excellent books by lifelong Harvard Psychiatrist and Research Director, Professor George E. Vaillant. For instance, *Aging well: Surprising Guideposts to a Happier Life from the Landmark Harvard Study of Adult Development.* Professor Vaillant provides an overview of his study at: psychology.about.com/library/submit/blsubmit_vaillant1.htm

The transforming role of a supportive person . . .

See the Professor George E. Vaillant via my note above.

Being happy with who we are . . .

The work of American psychotherapists Dr Jeffrey E. Young and Dr Janet S. Klosko (see www.ctcli.com/klosko.htm) is excellent for helping us understand the ruts that our thinking and behaviour can get into.

If we find ourselves under-valuing . . .

Happiness being a highly productive emotion is a theme being explored by Dr Barbara L. Fredrickson, the Director at the Positive Emotions and Psychophysiology Laboratory of The University of Michigan (www.positiveemotions.org). See her chapter called 'The Broaden-and-Build Theory of Positive Emotions' in *Philosophical Transactions of The Royal Society of London* (Huppert, Baylis and Keverne 2004).

Playing to our special strengths . . .
See the website of the Gallup Organisation at www.strengthsfinder.com
Harvard's most eminent Educational Psychologist . . .
See the work of Professor Howard Gardner at www.pz.harvard.edu/PIs/HG.htm
And it can be no coincidence . . .
The Pareto Principle was named after the Italian economist Vilfredo Pareto, who
observed in 1906 that 80% of property in Italy was owned by 20% of the Italian
population. Quality Management pioneer, Dr. Joseph Juran, working in the U.S. in
the 1930s and 40s, recognized a more universal principle behind Pareto's formula.
Our age doesn't matter . . .
See the work of Professor Ed Diener at: www.psych.uiuc.edu/~ediener
Where to look . . .
See Dr Viktor Frankl's *Man Search for Meaning* and visit www.viktorfrankl.org
See also the work of Po Bronson at www.pobronson.com
It's worth noting . . .
See the work of Professor Dean Keith Simonton at the University of California,
Davis: psychology.ucdavis.edu/Simonton
Keeping our passions flexible . . .
See the work of Professor Randolph M. Nesse at www-personal.umich.edu/~nesse/
See also the work on 'obsessive passions' that has been done by Developmental
Social Psychologists at McGill University in Canada (visit www.psych.mcgill.ca).
And now let's consider . . .
Dr Viktor Frankl's book is called *Man's Search for Meaning*.
See www.viktorfrankl.org
Such thoughts brings us back, I hope, to love . . .
Casablanca is surely one of my very favourite films.

A Special Sense of Rapport

The Gentle Partnership
Visit www.MontyRoberts.com to read about this remarkable and inspiring man
and to discover where around the world you can see him demonstrating his craft.
Sending signals . . .
Visit www.YoungLivesUK.com
But if we are off to the stores for some seasonal clothing . . .
Positive mood being a highly productive emotion is a theme being explored by

Dr Barbara L. Fredrickson, the Director at the Positive Emotions and Psycho-physiology Laboratory of The University of Michigan (www.positiveemotions.org). See her chapter called 'The Broaden-and-Build Theory of Positive Emotions' in *Philosophical Transactions of The Royal Society of London* (Huppert, Baylis and Keverne 2004).

Coming to our senses . . .

See the homepage of Dr Charles Spence at

www.psych.ox.ac.uk/xmodal/members/charles_spence.htm

This possibility may well be related to a finding . . .

See the work by Harvard Psychiatrist and Research Director, Professor George E. Vaillant. For instance, *Aging well: Surprising Guideposts to a Happier Life from the Landmark Harvard Study of Adult Development*. Professor Vaillant provides an overview of his study at:

psychology.about.com/library/submit/blsubmit_vaillant1.htm

Sensuality

The Wind in the Willows by the Scottish author Grahame Kenneth was first pub-lished in 1908. While he was serving as a secretary of the Bank of England, Kenneth wrote the book for his only son, Alastair.

This was read to me when I was a very small child, and I never forgot the insights into personalities and relationships. It was, I suspect, my first brush with psychology on the page.

So has science got anything to say . . .

Visit the website of Physics Nobel Laureate, Professor Brian Josephson, at www.tcm.phy.cam.ac.uk/~bdj10/

Visit the website of Dr Rupert Sheldrake at www.sheldrake.org

In 1995, Jessica Utts, a professor of statistics at the University of California . . .

Professor Utts prepared the report with Professor Ray Hyman from the University of Oregon. Entitled 'An Assessment Of The Evidence For Psychic Functioning', the report is available on Professor Utts' homepage at: anson.ucdavis.edu/%7Eutts/air2.html.

At Princeton University, Professor Robert Jahn . . .

The Princeton Engineering Anomalies Research (PEAR) Program was established at Princeton University in 1979 to pursue rigorous scientific study of the interaction of human consciousness with sensitive physical devices, systems, and processes common to contemporary engineering practice. Visit www.princeton.edu/~pear.

Helping Others

It's a cast iron fact . . .
Happiness being a highly productive emotion is a theme being explored by Barbara L. Fredrikson, the Director at the Positive Emotions and Psychophysiology Laboratory of The University of Michigan (www.positiveemotions.org). See her chapter called 'The Broaden-and-Build Theory of Positive Emotions' in *Philosophical Transactions of The Royal Society of London* (Huppert, Baylis, and Keverne 2004).

The Goodwork Project . . .
Visit www.goodworkproject.org.

Particularly telling are the results . . .
Visit www.YoungLivesUK.com

Columbia University's Charles Harrington and Susan Boardman . . .
A review of their study can be found at:
www.aaanet.org/cae/aeq/br/harrington.htm

From mentors to role-models
The PhD thesis of Dr Sarah L. Fitzharding is held at Cambridge University since 1999. Dr Fitzharding read for the Cambridge BA, MPhil and PhD as a member of Sidney Sussex College, and during this time spent a year as a Fox Fellow at Yale and then a year at Harvard. Her thesis was regarded by her examiners as one of the finest they had read.

Taking this thought one step further . . .
Visit www.YoungLivesUK.com

Asking helpful questions . . .
See the work of Dr Christine A. Padesky, the former President of the International Association for Cognitive Psychotherapy, at www.Padesky.com

Gentle Teaching . . .
Visit www.MontyRoberts.org

Helping children acquire a passion for life . . .
On this theme, I particularly admire the book called *The Childhood Roots of Adult Happiness* by child and adult psychiatrist, Dr Edward M. Hallowell. Visit www.DrHallowell.com

See the work of Dr Jeffrey E. Young and Dr Janet S. Klosko (see www.ctcli.com/klosko.htm), for the thinking traps that we can fall into, and that we can accidentally drag young people into while we're about it.

Children who thrive not just survive . . .
See the excellent work of Professor George E. Vaillant which has considerable

bearing on this whole section. Professor Vaillant provides an overview of The Harvard Study of Adult Development at:

psychology.about.com/library/submit/blsubmit_vaillant1.htm

Also see the joint work of Dr Robert Brooks of Harvard Medical School and Dr Sam Goldstein of the University of Utah, who are leading voices in the field of resilience in children. They have set up a foundation; visit www.raisingresilientkids.com

I am also glad to recommend the work of British Psychiatrist, Dr Kerry Bluglass, who has written about those many children who thrived in later life despite their experiences of the Nazi Holocaust.

With Eleanor's story in mind, let's keep our eyes open . . .

See the work of Dr Karen Reivich who is one of the founding members of the Penn Resiliency Project that is doing such good work to fight depression in school-age youngsters. Visit www.positivepsychology.org/prpsum.htm

A good mentor . . .

See the work of Kansas University psychology researcher and therapist, Dr Shane Lopez, who is pioneering methods to generate 'hope' as a profoundly therapeutic and energising emotion. Visit www.soe.ku.edu/faculty/LopezS.php

No matter how downhearted . . .

Feltham YOI in West London was for a long time the largest high security young offender prison in Europe, with more than 1,000 lads age between 15 and 21. I was a part-time volunteer there between 1993 and 1998, first as a creative writing tutor, and then as the founder of *Trail-Blazers*, the charitable project offering job mentorship. Visit www.Trail-Blazers.org.uk

I'm not the least bit surprised to read the studies . . .

See the work of Sociology Professor Jane Allyn Piliavin at the University of Wisconsin-Madison at www.ssc.wisc.edu/~jpiliavi/

Better still, a study led by Doug Oman . . .

See Dr Oman's homepage at: sph.berkeley.edu:7133/faculty/oman.htm

My thanks for comments on this chapter by my dear friends and very experienced schoolteachers, Sue & Jonah Dudman Jones, who are M&D to Sam & Alfie.

* * *

PART TWO

Becoming an Expert
in our Favourite Pursuits

Why become an Expert?
and Facts and Fiction about Becoming an Expert

My favourite researchers in this broad-ranging field are the following, and taken together their lifetime's work have inspired this part of my book.

First and foremost is Professor Michael J.A. Howe, formerly of Exeter University (who, a long time ago, was my tutor for one year). His seminal body of works all challenged the received wisdom on the acquisition of expertise, and I owe him a profound debt for lighting the way. His books include: *Genius Explained, IQ in Question, The Origin of Exceptional Abilities.*

Further inspiration is the lifetime's work of Professor Robert J. Sternberg of Yale University, who is Director of The Center for the Psychology of Abilities, Competencies, and Expertise (Pace Center). In 2003, he was the elected President of the American Psychological Association. Visit his homepage at: www.yale.edu/pace/teammembers/personalpages/bob.html

Excellent studies, books and theories have also been produced by:
Professor K. Anders Ericsson of Florida State University at www.psy.fsu.edu/faculty/ericsson/ericsson.hp.html
Professor Howard Gardner of Harvard Graduate School of Education, at www.pz.harvard.edu/PIs/HG.htm
Professor Ian H. Robertson of Trinity College Dublin, at: www.tcd.ie/Psychology/Ian_Robertson/
The work of Professor Dean Keith Simonton of the University of California, Davis, at: psychology.ucdavis.edu/Simonton/

7. If we don't get better and better . . .
For more on psychology's so called Matthew Effect, see the work of Dean Keith Simonton via my note above.

The Surest Routes
to Getting Really Good at Something

This proposition pays respect to the scientific observation . . .
The Pareto Principle was named after the Italian economist Vilfredo Pareto, who observed in 1906 that 80% of property in Italy was owned by 20% of the Italian population. Quality Management pioneer, Dr. Joseph Juran, working in the US in the 1930s and 40s, recognized a more universal principle behind Pareto's formula.

One of America's leading sociologists . . .
See the work of Professor Robert D. Putnam at Harvard University. Visit www.BowlingAlone.com

We need to learn with our head . . .
See the work of Professor Ian Robertson, Professor of Psychology, Trinity College Dublin, at: www.tcd.ie/Psychology/Ian_Robertson/

By contrast, my Latin classes were brought to life . . .
I have to thank two very fine teachers for such vivid memories of Ancient Rome. First, Mr Rex Thomas who dedicated his whole working life to Aldwickbury School, Harpenden; and, thenafter, Mr David Billingham of St. Albans Boys' School, who all the lads held in the very highest regard and affection on account of the passion with which he taught Latin and Ancient History.

Making mistakes is all part of the learning process . . .
Visit www.MontyRoberts.com

One classic study has shown . . .
See *Mind Sculpture* by Professor Ian Robertson, Professor of Psychology at Trinity College, Dublin. Visit his homepage at: www.tcd.ie/Psychology/Ian_Robertson/

End every session on a high note . . .
See Professor Kahneman's article 'Experienced Utility and Objective Happiness: A Moment-Based Approach', which is available at:
www.international.ucla.edu/cms/files/Kahneman.pdf

The wisdom of knowing what to learn . . .
Visit www.YoungLivesUK.com

Performing Well while Under Pressure

Perfectionism is the enemy of high performance and happiness
On the subject of perfectionism, see the homepage of anti-perfectionism special-
ists, Dr Martin M. Antony at www.martinantony.com and Dr Richard P.
Swinson, M.D. at www.fhs.mcmaster.ca/psychiatryneuroscience/faculty/swinson

Perfectionism is part and parcel of several of the thinking-traps so poignantly
studied by psychotherapists Dr Jeffrey E. Young and Dr Janet S. Klosko (see
www.ctcli.com/klosko.htm).
The antidote: . . .
See the work of Professor Dean Keith Simonton at:
psychology.ucdavis.edu/simonton/
We can guarantee our self-confidence . . .
See the work of Stanford Professor of Psychology, Albert Bandura, and particu-
larly the characteristic he calls 'Self-Efficacy'. Professor Bandura provides an
extract from an encyclopedia, explaining self-efficacy, at this internet address:
www.emory.edu/EDUCATION/mfp/BanEncy.html
Having a sense of control . . .
See *Fear and Courage* by former Professor of Psychology at British Columbia,
Stanley J. Rachman.
Combining visualisation . . .
See the work of Professor Ian H. Robertson, Professor of Psychology, Trinity
College Dublin, at: www.tcd.ie/Psychology/Ian_Robertson/
Make real-life practice highly realistic . . .
See *Looking For Trouble: SAS to Gulf Command*, the autobiography by General
Sir Peter de la Billiere who won two medals for gallantry-under-fire before he was
25. He then had a career leading the Special Air Service regiment and commanded
the British Armed forces in the Gulf War of 1990. A digest of the autobiography
is available here: www.britains-smallwars.com/gulf/Billiere.html
Performance-enhancing drugs . . .
See *The Natural History of Alcoholism Revisited* by Professor George E. Vaillant
of Harvard Medical School. This acclaimed book is based on an evaluation of
more than 600 individuals followed for over forty years.
Optimism and joy are far more productive . . .
Visit Professor Railo's homepage at: www.willirailo.com
This relationship was born out by the thousand of men and women . . .
That longitudinal study of optimism among Netherlanders can be found in

Archives of General Psychiatry of 2004. Visit the homepage of Dr Kubzansky at the Harvard School of Public Health at:
www.hsph.harvard.edu/facres/kbznsky.html

And it's just possible . . .
Kay Redfield Jamison is Professor of Psychiatry at John Hopkins University (see www.hopkinsmedicine.org).

It's important to keep our spirits up . . .
Happiness being a highly productive emotion is a theme being explored by Dr Barbara L. Fredrickson, the Director at the Positive Emotions and Psycho-physiology Laboratory of The University of Michigan (www.positiveemotions.org). See her chapter called 'The Broaden-and-Build Theory of Positive Emotions' in *Philosophical Transactions of The Royal Society of London* (Huppert, Baylis, and Keverne 2004).

Research by Shelley Gable at UCLA . . .
See the article 'What do you do when things go right? The intrapersonal and inter-personal benefits of sharing positive events' by Dr Shelly Gable and her co-authors. It is available at:
www.apa.org/journals/psp/featured_article/august_2004/psp872228.pdf

Case in point is the research by Harvard psychologist, Daniel Gilbert . . .
See the homepage of Professor Gilbert at www.wjh.harvard.edu/~dtg/gilbert.htm

What can Slow our Progress?

The trouble with too much television . . .
For the scientific evidence and theory in this chapter, I am particularly grateful to two sources of information who have marshalled great tracts of evidence:

See www.BowlingAlone.com. This is the website for the book by Professor Robert D. Putnam, onetime head of the JFK School of Government at Harvard, where he still resides as one of America's leading voices on social policy. His objective indictment of too much television is as good as I've read. He views too much tv as a 'severe social problem', getting in the way of the sort of healthy social interaction that fosters good will, trust and happiness.

Visit www.mediastudies.rutgers.edu to read more about Professor Robert Kubey's innovative views and careful observations as the Director of The Center for Media Studies at Rutgers University.

The voices of those who as part and parcel of their work have also studied the interaction between too much television and young people, would also testify to its grossly inhibiting influence. See the works of Professor Michael A.J. Howe: *The Origin of Exceptional Abilities* and *Genius Explained.* It is Professor Howe's fabulous work which illustrates how it is putting in the practice hours (i.e. hours not spent watching television) which is a crucial ingredient to us attaining high levels of performance.

The work of Professor Mihaly Csikszentmihalyi and his colleagues Kevin Rathunde and Samuel Whalen with some very talented American teenagers. An overview of their study can be found at: chronicle.uchicago.edu/940203/teens.shtml

Dr Edward M. Hallowell a leading child psychiatrist based in Boston, whose book *The Childhood Roots of Adult Happiness* is one of the best books I've read on the principles of child-raising. Visit his website at: www.DrHallowell.com

The work of Michael Medved at www.michaelmedved.com/

It doesn't help our body

See the homepage of Dr Hu at: www.hsph.harvard.edu/faculty/FrankHu.html

It may be for the reasons cited in this chapter, or for a host of other reasons, that too much tv watching has been strongly linked in medical studies with obesity, depression, eating disorders, too little sleep, teenage aggression, and early onset of Alzheimers.

Lucky for us, in the 1970s, a team of researchers . . .

The impact of television: a natural experiment in three communities, edited by the Canadian researcher, Tannith Macbeth Williams. The work was published in Orlando, Florida, by Academic Press, 1986.

And let's remember, IQ tests bear no meaningful relationship . . .

For a definitive trouncing of IQ tests as unhelpful mumbo-jumbo, see the works of the following two leading researchers in the field:

The late Professor Michael J.A. Howe, formerly of Exeter University. His most relevant book is *IQ in Question: the truth about intelligence.*

Professor Robert J. Sternberg, Director of the Center for the Psychology of Abilities, Competencies, and Expertise (Pace Center) at Yale. He is also IBM Professor of Psychology Education at Yale University. In 2003, he was the elected President of the American Psychological Association. Visit his homepage at: www.yale.edu/pace/teammembers/personalpages/bob.html

* * *

PART THREE

Helping Mind and Body to Thrive and Flourish

Nourish and Nurture Beautiful Health

One could be forgiven for thinking . . .
See the work of Professor Ed Diener at the University of Illinois at Urbana-Champaign (see his homepage at: www.psych.uiuc.edu/~ediener/).
Professor Richard Davidson at Wisconsin University . . .
Visit his homepage at: www.psychiatry.wisc.edu/Faculty/FacultyPages/Davidson.htm
This can be estimated because in 1996 . . .
The research article by emeritus professors David Lykken and Auke Tellegen is available here: www.psych.umn.edu/psylabs/happness/happy.htm
And there are other reasons to feel . . .
See again the work of Professor Ed Diener at: www.psych.uiuc.edu/~ediener/
Sleeping well supports everything . . .
See the work from 2002 of Dr Paul Martin at Wolfson College, Cambridge University. Visit www.wolfson.cam.ac.uk/fellows/fellows
The take away message is . . .
Dr Sara Mednick who trained at Harvard, is one of the world's leading young researchers in the field of sleep, and particularly the role of power naps. Dr Mednick is based at The Salk Institute for Biological Studies in La Jolla, California. She is a rising star in the world of science, whose ground-breaking work is extremely promising. Visit her homepage at www.snl.salk.edu/~smednick/
Broad daylight prevents the blues and feeds the brain . . .
Visit www.sada.org.uk, the website of the world's longest established support organisation for Seasonal Affective Disorder.
Vigorous exercise lifts our spirits . . .
See the work of Stuart Biddle, Professor of Exercise and Sport Psychology, who is Head of the School of Sport & Exercise Sciences at Loughborough University, UK. He has co-authored a particularly relevant chapter entitled 'Physically active lifestyle and well-being' in *The Science of Well-Being* (Huppert, Baylis, and Keverne, 2005).Visit his homepage at: www.lboro.ac.uk/departments/sses/institutes/iys/pages/staff/biddle.html

If we eat a vegetarian diet ...

Professor Stuart Biddle has written on the athletic prowess of vegetarians (see his chapter in 'The Science of Well-Being', edited by Huppert, Baylis, and Keverne, 2005).

J.G. Vaughan, Emeritus Professor of Food Sciences at King's College London, has written on the various plants as food, as has Pat Judd, Professor of Nutrition and Dietics at the University of Central Lancashire (see www.uclan.ac.uk/facs/health/lshpm/staff/juddp.htm).

Essential thoughts on eating ...

A leading scientist in this field is the Oxford University Senior Physiologist, Bernard Gesch, who is a fervent advocate of the importance of adequate intake of vitamins, minerals, trace elements and omega oils ... particularly for the young and for pregnant women or new mothers. He has a substantial chapter entitled 'The potential of nutrition to promote physical and behavioural well-being' in *The Science of Well-Being* (Huppert, Baylis, and Keverne, 2005). Bernard Gesch is the Director of the research charity Natural Justice, which studies the link between nutrition and antisocial behaviour. Visit www.physiol.ox.ac.uk/natural.justice/

In the study cited in my chapter, Bernard used a double-blind, placebo controlled randomised stratified design comprising 231 young adult prisoners, 18 to 21 years of age.

In the same 'Science of Well-Being' book, chapters by two Fellows of the Royal Society, Professor E. Barry Keverne ('Understanding well-being in the evolutionary context of brain development'; visit his homepage at www.zoo.cam.ac.uk/zoostaff/keverne.htm), and by Professor David J.P. Barker ('The developmental origins of well-being'; visit his homepage at www.som.soton.ac.uk/research/foad/barker.asp), are also relevant to the crucial role of nutrition for the physical, psychological and social well-being of individuals, particularly children and teenagers and young adults, if they are to be helped to lead healthy adult lives.

Physical Dynamism beats dieting, any day ...

One of the country's leading scientists on the subject of obesity, appetite and well-being, is Professor Michael E.J. Lean in the Department of Human Nutrition at the University of Glasgow. Visit www.gla.ac.uk/departments/humannutrition/staff/lean.html

There's more than one way to be beautiful ...

Dr Nancy Etcoff is a psychologist and faculty member of the Harvard Medical School and of Harvard University's Mind/Brain/Behavior Initiative. She directs the Program in Aesthetics and Well-Being at the Massachusetts General Hospital Department of

Psychiatry. Dr Etcoff has conducted research on the perception of beauty, emotion, and the brain. Visit www.researchmatters.harvard.edu/people.php?people_id=245

Yale University's Professor of Computer Science, David Gelernter, is also an exciting advocate of the importance of beauty in new technologies. Visit his homepage at www.cs.yale.edu/people/faculty/gelernter.html

Self-Control and Self-Motivation

And the younger we start the better . . .

The marshmallow study is written up in Shoda, Y., Mischel, W., & Peake, P. (1990). Predicting Adolescent Cognitive and Self-regulatory Competencies from Preschool Delay of Gratification. *Developmental Psychology, 26*(6), 978-986.

The Harvard Study of Adult Development tracked the progress . . .

The work of Professor Vaillant is summarised in his book *Aging well: Surprising Guideposts to a Happier Life from the Landmark Harvard Study of Adult Development.* Professor Vaillant provides an overview of his study at: psychology.about.com/library/submit/blsubmit_vaillant1.htm

Rearrange our routines . . .

A leading researcher in the field of self-control is Roy Baumeister, Professor of Psychology at Florida State University. Visit his homepage at: www.psy.fsu.edu/faculty/baumeist.dp.html

Second Method: Associate the negative habit . . .

One of the lessons from the work of Harvard Professor George E. Vaillant. See my note above.

Defusing our rage . . .

Emeritus Psychology Professor, Marvin Levine, of the State University of New York, has written an excellent book that has much to say on this subject: *The Positive Psychology of Buddhism and Yoga: paths to mature happiness. With a Special Application to Handling Anger.*

Liberating though these measures can be . . .

See the work of Harvard Medical School Psychiatrist, Professor George E. Vaillant, summarised in his excellent book *Ageing Well: Surprising Guideposts to a Happier Life from the Landmark Harvard Study of Adult Development.* Professor Vaillant provides an overview of his study at: psychology.about.com/library/submit/blsubmit_vaillant1.htm

Defusing our fears . . .

See *Fear and Courage* by former Professor of Psychology at British Columbia, Stanley J. Rachman.

We need to master time travel ...

Professor Philip G. Zimbardo is one of the true greats of American psychology since the Second World War. Retired now from his full-time teaching and research roles at Stanford, he is still an inspiration and a wonderful soul in whose company to spend time. He has made several articles on 'Time-Perspective' available via his homepage at www.zimbardo.com

Recuperate and Rekindle

In a recent study ...

See the recent work of Professor Lord Richard Layard, the founder-director of the Centre for Economic Performance of the London School of Economics and Political Science. Visit his homepage at cep.lse.ac.uk/layard/

By redirecting some resources like this ...

See the work on the pleasing and productive state of psychological immersion called 'Flow', that has been done by Dr Antonella Delle Fave at the university of Milan, and Professor Mihaly Csikszentmihaly.

Don't let a calling become an obsession ...

To read more about how this can happens and how it can be remedied see the compelling work of Dr Jeffrey E. Young and Dr Janet S. Klosko (visit www.ctcli.com/klosko.htm).

And also the excellent work of Dr Judith Beck, Director of the Beck Institute in Philadelphia (see www.beckinstitute.org).

This brings me yet again to a major theme ...

See the chapter called 'Natural Selection and the Elusiveness of Happiness', by Professor Randolph M. Nesse in *The Science of Well-Being* (Huppert, Baylis, and Keverne, 2005). Professor Nesse, a psychiatrist at the University of Michigan has some timely warnings for us about the danger of over-large, over-distant goals leading to depression. Professor Nesse has made the chapter available at: www-personal.umich.edu/~nesse/Articles/Nesse-EvolElusiveHappiness-ProcRoyalSoc-2004.pdf

In achieving such an admirable state of equilibrium . . .

See the work of Professor C. Richard Snyder, for many years the director of the clinical psychology program at the University of Kansas (visit www.psych.ukans.edu/faculty_Richard_Snyder.html). With Dr Shane Lopez (visit www.soe.ku.edu/faculty/LopezS.php), also at Kansas, he has pioneered work on how to build hope through generating multiple goals, and multiple routes forward to those goals.

Taking time off . . .

Dr Brendan Burchell at Cambridge University is one of the UK's leading authorities on the changing patterns of work in the 21st century and its likely effects on psychological well-being and community health. Visit his homepage at: www.sps.cam.ac.uk/stafflist/bburchell.html

In the USA, Professor Robert D. Putnam has some fascinating theories and evidence on the problems of longer working hours and commuting times. Visit www.BowlingAlone.com

It's worth noting that . . .

See the work of Harvard University's Professor George E. Vaillant, who provides an overview of his study at: psychology.about.com/library/submit/blsubmit_vaillant1.htm

Making the most of unexpected time out . . .

See the work of Drs Brendan Burchell and Colin Fraser at Cambridge University. Visit www.sps.cam.ac.uk/stafflist/bburchell.html

So, to foster relaxation . . .

See the work on the relaxation response by Professor Herbert Benson, M.D., the founding President of the Mind/Body Medical Institute of Harvard Medical School. Visit www.mbmi.org

What's good to hear is that scientists at the Goethe University . . .

Visit the homepage of Dr Gunter Kreutz at: web.uni-frankfurt.de/fb09/musikpaed/kreutz.html

Likewise, London University's Elizabeth Valentine and Claire Evans . . .

A summary of their article 'The effects of solo singing, choral singing and swimming on mood and physiological indices' is available at: www.pc.rhul.ac.uk/schools/Liz/singing.html

Professor Gene Cohen of George Washington University . . .

Professor Gene D. Cohen, M.D., is Director of the *Center on Aging, Health & Humanities* at George Washington University. Visit his homepage at: www.gwumc.edu/cahh/About/cohen.htm

Such findings will come as no surprise to Graham Welch . . .
Visit his homepage via: ioewebserver.ioe.ac.uk/ioe/

Studies suggest that hearing singing voices can . . .
See for example the article 'Music, stress reduction and medical cost savings in the neonatal intensive care unit' by Dr Fred J. Schwartz, M.D., and his colleagues at www.transitionsmusic.com/ISMM_ARTICLE.html

The remedial effect of musical sounds is also evident in a study . . .
See the work of Dr Ralph Spintge, the Director of the International Society for Music in Medicine and the Head of the Pain Clinic at Sportkrankenhaus Hellersen. Visit www.schmerzzentrum.de

Further confirmation comes from Harvard's Tom Perls and Margery Silver . . .
See the website of the The New England Centenarian Study at:
www.bumc.bu.edu/centenarian

The restorative powers of the natural environment
See the work of Professor Roger Ulrich, the Director of the Center for Health Systems and Design Texas A&M University. Visit: archone.tamu.edu/chsd/

Though these studies do not demonstrate conclusively that . . .
Visit the webpage of Professor Edward O. Wilson at the Museum of Comparative Zoology at Harvard University at: www-museum.unl.edu/research/entomology/workers/EWilson.htm

Powerful New Approaches to Common Health Problems

Keeping cheerful . . .
See the award-winning work of Dr Barbara L. Fredrickson, the Director at the Positive Emotions and Psychophysiology Laboratory of The University of Michigan (visit www.positiveemotions.org).

What therapy might involve . . .
My own method of therapeutic practice attempts to be holistic and highly eclectic, drawing on the best evidence from The Study of Well-Being and Positive Psychology. For instance, I view improved exercise, nutrition, and other physical measures as crucial to the psychotherapeutic process. But in terms of mainstream psychological approaches, at time of writing I am much guided by the work of:

• Drs Milton H. Erikson (see www.erickson-foundation.org) and Michael D.

Yapko (see www.yapko.com) in the USA, and Professor David Oakley and his co-director Val Walters (see www.ucl.ac.uk/hypnosis) in the UK, who all use hypnosis as a key tool.

- Dr Judith Beck and her approach to Cognitive Behaviour Therapy (see www.beckinstitute.org)
- Dr Christine Padesky and her use of Socractic Questioning (see www.padesky.com)
- Dr Arnold A. Lazarus and his own method called Multimodal Therapy
- Dr Francine Shapiro and her own method called EMDR (see www.emdr.com)
- Joe Griffin and Ivan Tyrrell and the techniques they are pioneering in the UK at the European Therapy Studies Institute (see www.mindfields.org.uk/etsi.html).

Taking action to prevent and lift depression . . .
All of the therapists I have named immediately above are pioneering excellent approaches to depression.

See www.positivepsychology.org/prpsum.htm for an in-school programme that is highly effective and preventing and reducing depression among teenagers.
Increase our physical activity . . .
See the chapter 'Physically active lifestyle and well-being' coauthored by Professor Stuart Biddle in *The Science of Well-Being* (Huppert, Baylis, and Keverne, 2005).

This is an extract from Professor Biddle's chapter:

"As a case in point, consider the arguably most complete study on the effects of physical activity on depression (Blumenthal et al., 1999). In this study, 156 men and women, 50 years of age or older, who had been diagnosed with major depressive disorder, were randomly assigned to one of three 16-week treatment conditions: (a) exercise (3 sessions per week, lasting for 45 minutes each, at 70% to 85% of heart rate reserve), (b) antidepressant medication (using the popular serotonin reuptake inhibitor sertraline hydrochloride or ZoloftTM), or (c) a combination of the exercise and antidepressant treatments. The dropout rates at the end of the 16-week period were not significantly different between the three groups (Herman et al., 2002; 26%, 15% and 20% for groups a, b and c, respectively). At the end of the treatment period, both clinician-rated and self-reported levels of depression were reduced compared to baseline, with no significant differences between the groups. A similar result was also found for anxiety, self-esteem, life satisfaction and dysfunctional attitudes. At the 10-month follow-up (6 months after the conclusion of treatment), self-reported depression scores were also not

different across the three groups. However, based on DSM-IV criteria and clinician ratings (a Hamilton Rating Scale score higher than 7), the participants in the
exercise group had a lower rate of depression (30%) than those in the medication
(52%) and combined-treatment groups (55%). Furthermore, of the participants
who were in remission after the initial 16-week treatment period, those who had
been assigned to the exercise group were more likely to have partly or fully recovered after 6 months than those in the medication and combined-treatment groups
(Babyak et al., 2000). The authors discussed these findings stating that exercise
helps participants develop "a sense of personal mastery and positive self-regard,"
whereas the exclusive reliance on or the inclusion of medication "may undermine
this benefit by prioritising an alternative, less self-confirming attribution for one's
improved condition" (Babyak et al., 2000, p. 636)."

Worry won't solve anything . . .

See the *New Scientist* interview with Joe Griffin about his work on sleep and
depression at www.humangivens.com/joe-griffin/dreamcatcher.html

On the subject of ruminating and its link to depression, please see the work
of Professor Susan Nolen-Hoeksema at the Department of Psychology at Yale
University. Visit www.yale.edu/psychology/FacInfo/Nolen-Hoeksema.html

Improve our social life . . .

The academic research of Professor Robert D. Putnam has shed light on this phenomenon. Visit www.BowlingAlone.com

Be optimistic . . .

Professor Martin E.P. Seligman, 1998 President of the American Psychological
Association, and co-founder of the Positive Psychology movement in the USA, is
the definitive writer on the relationship between optimism and depression. Visit
his homepage at: www.psych.upenn.edu/~seligman/

Reconsider our goals . . .

See the chapter 'Natural selection and the elusiveness of happiness' by Professor
Randolph M. Nesse in *The Science of Well-Being* (Huppert, Baylis, and Keverne,
2005). Also visit Randy's website at: personal.umich.edu/~nesse/Articles/Nesse-
EvolElusiveHappiness-ProcRoyalSoc-2004.pdf

Good Nutrition . . .

See the chapter 'The potential of nutrition to promote physical and behavioural
well-being' by Bernard Gesch in *The Science of Well-Being* (Huppert, Baylis, and
Keverne, 2005).

Herbal supplements . . .

British health writer, Patrick Holford, has gathered some interesting studies on this topic. Visit his website at www.patrickholford.com.

What seems very likely . . .

See the work by Professor Stuart Biddle at www.lboro.ac.uk/departments/sses/institutes/iys/pages/staff/biddle.html

When it comes to anxiety . . .

See the classic text book, *Abnormal Psychology,* 4th Edition 2001, authored by Martin Seligman, Elaine Walker and David Rosenhan, published by W.W Norton and Company.

The Boston University researchers, Drs Tom Perls and Margery Silver . . .

See the website of the The New England Centenarian Study at: www.bumc.bu.edu/centenarian

Overcoming shyness . . .

See the website of Professor Philip G. Zimbardo, Professor of Psychology at Stanford University, and former President of the American Psychological Association. www.Zimbardo.com

Technique No. 1 . . .

Joe Griffin and Ivan Tyrrell, as founding directors of the European Therapy Studies Institute are doing good work in trying to demystify and popularise the use of this technique. Visit www.HumanGivens.org

Technique No. 2 . . .

Dr Francine Shapiro (who practices in California) created this technique. The supervised group training in EMDR for a therapist who already has an appropriate clinical training and background, takes circa six full days. Visit www.emdr.com

Making counter-attacks on migraines . . .

See the website of the Migraine Action Association: www.migraine.org.uk

Seeking help is all the more important . . .

See the 2005 article 'Risk of ischaemic stroke in people with migraine: systematic review and meta-analysis of observational studies' by Dr Ali Samii and his co-authors, which is available via the website of the British Medical Journal at bmj.bmjjournals.com

On a far more cheerful note . . .

See the 2004 article 'Acupuncture for chronic headache in primary care: large, pragmatic, randomised trial' by Dr Andrew J. Vickers and his co-authors, which is available via the website of the *British Medical Journal* at bmj.bmjjournals.com

Controlling unhelpful yeasts . . .

Visit www.candida-uk.com as a starting place for more information.

Rediscovering an ancient remedy for PMS...

See the article 'A comprehensive evaluation of premenstrual syndrome' by Dr Michael T. Murray at:

'www.immunesolutions.net/suggested_reading_resources/health/PMS3_97DrM urray.pdf

In a recent study in Germany...

See the 2001 article 'Treatment for the premenstrual syndrome with agnus castus fruit extract: prospective, randomised, placebo controlled study' by Rüdiger Schellenberg from the Institute for Health Care and Science in Hüttenberg, Germany. It is available via the website of the *British Medical Journal* at bmj.bmjjournals.com

Hypnosis is a highly effective therapeutic technique...

My first experience of using hypnosis in therapy was being tutored by the wonderful Joe Griffin, co-founding director of the European Therapy Studies Institute and the Human Givens approach to psychotherapy (see www.HumanGivens.org). Joe's approach is strongly redolent of the work of the remarkable and pioneering Dr Milton H. Erikson who died some time ago. Visit www.erickson-foundation.org

The American psychotherapist, Dr Michael D. Yapko is also an inspiring practitioner (see www.yapko.com).

More recently, I was privileged to receive further professional training at the University College London Hypnosis Unit in the Department of Psychology. The hypnosis unit was founded in 1993 by the excellent Professor David Oakley, soon to retire from the unit, and it offers a range of thorough and enjoyable courses designed for busy health practitioners, whether psychotherapists, nurses, medics, or dentists ... individuals who are already qualified in their respective professions and who wish to incorporate hypnosis in to their work. The UCL Hypnosis Unit also offers psychotherapy for individuals whether as private or NHS clients. Visit www.ucl.ac.uk/hypnosis/

Many cutting-edge research articles concerning hypnosis can also be accessed at this same website. Also visit www.bsech.com for the British Society of Experimental & Clinical Hypnosis.

Depression

See the work of American psychotherapist, Dr Michael D. Yapko, who is a leading practitioner in this specific field . Visit www.yapko.com

Irritable Bowel Syndrome

Michael Mahoney is a psychotherapist who has specialised in the treatment of IBS using hypnosis. He is an internationally respected practitioner, and can be reached through his website at www.ibsaudioprogram.com

* * *

PART FOUR

Choosing and Changing our Journeys and Life Directions

Making a Good Living

Coping with all the choices . . .
Professor Barry Schwartz of Swarthmore College, U.S.A., is an inspiring psychologist and educator, and a very charming and considerate guy to be around. He is the leading voice on what he has sometimes called 'the tyranny of choice'. In the U.K., his recent book is called *The Paradox of Choice – why more is less*. Visit his homepage at: www.swarthmore.edu/SocSci/bschwar1/

When decisions are genuinely necessary . . .
See the page of Professor Simon on the Nobel Prize website at: nobelprize.org/economics/laureates/1978/index.html

Nobel Laureate psychology professor, Daniel Kahneman . . .
See Professor Kahneman's pages on the Nobel Prize website at: nobelprize.org/economics/laureates/2002/kahneman-autobio.html

And I'm reminded, too . . .
This quote is taken from *Ageing Well: Surprising Guideposts to a Happier Life from the Landmark Harvard Study of Adult Development*, by Professor George E. Vaillant. An overview of this study is available at: psychology.about.com/library/submit/blsubmit_vaillant1.htm

To thrive we need to feel in control . . .
The work of Professor Albert Bandura (formerly of Stanford University) on what he calls 'self-efficacy', is eloquent on this issue. Professor Bandura provides an extract from an encyclopedia, explaining self-efficacy, at this Internet address: www.emory.edu/EDUCATION/mfp/BanEncy.html

In the 1990s, psychology professors Charles Harrington
See the homepage of Professor Harrington at
www.tc.columbia.edu/faculty/?facid=cch20

A landmark study of 10,000 British civil servants . . .
The study called 'Whitehall II' was carried out by the Department of Epidemiology & Public Health and University College Medical School of University College London. A summary report on this study is available at: www.ucl.ac.uk/whitehallII/Whitehallbooklet.pdf

The positive role of self-assertion . . .
See the work of Professor George E. Vaillant via my note above.

What sort of work would suit us . . .
This section synthesises an eclectic range of Positive Psychology findings, and my own research for www.YoungLivesUK.com

Po Bronson has also written very helpfully on the subject of career choice. See www.pobronson.com

Motivation that comes from inside . . .
The leading researchers on intrinsic motivation are Edward L. Deci and Richard M. Ryan, professors in the Department of Clinical and Social Sciences in Psychology at the University of Rochester. Visit www.psych.rochester.edu/SDT

So let's be sure to keep versatile . . .
The books of technology entrepreneur, Bill Gates, are a useful catalyst to debates about what the future might hold. Visit www.microsoft.com/billgates

So if I had my time again . . .
Interestingly, Cambridge physicist Professor Stephen Hawking has not ruled out the possibility of travelling back in time.

Finding the right size pond . . .
The American economist Professor Robert Franks has written some intriguing thoughts on what size pond might suit us.

The most impressive voice on this subject . . .
Visit the homepage of Professor Diener at www.psych.uiuc.edu/~ediener/

It would seem Mother Nature . . .
See again the work of Professor Ed Diener which offers a good summary of the studies of such phenomena. Visit his homepage at:
www.psych.uiuc.edu/~ediener/

Professor Daniel Gilbert of Harvard has established . . .
See his homepage at: www.wjh.harvard.edu/~dtg/gilbert.htm

For instance, Professor John Helliwell . . .
Visit his homepage at: www.econ.ubc.ca/helliwell
And if, like me, . . .
I am referring to *The Italian Job* (1969) starring Michael Caine, either one of the
Ocean's Eleven (there was one in 1960 and one in 2001), and thank goodness
there's only been the one version of *Butch Cassidy and The Sundance Kid* (1969),
starring Paul Newman and Robert Redford in the title roles.
Such clever observations have been the pioneering work of . . .
Visit www.positiveemotions.org to find out more about the work of Professor
Fredrickson, the Director at the Positive Emotions and Psychophysiology
Laboratory of The University of Michigan. See also her chapter called 'The
Broaden-and-Build Theory of Positive Emotions' in *Philosophical Transactions of
The Royal Society of London* (Huppert, Baylis, and Keverne, 2004).
In a similar vein, her colleagues, Marcial Losada and Emily Heaphy . . .
See their article 'The Role of Positivity and Connectivity in the Performance of
Business Teams' in the 47th issue of the *American Behavioral Scientist* in 2004. See
also the homepage of Emily D. Heaphy at:
www.bus.umich.edu/Academics/Departments/OBHRM/OBHRM/Phd/Students/
heaphy.htm
Likewise, Washington University's John Gottman . . .
Visit www.gottman.com
And here's some more food for thought . . .
See Professor Kahneman's pages on the Nobel Prize website at:
nobelprize.org/economics/laureates/2002/kahneman-autobio.html
The remaining ideas in this subsection are an integration of the works of Profs.
Fredrickson and Kahneman mentioned immediately above.
Choosing *where* we live to fit *how* we live . . .
For international comparisons, see the work on happiness by Professor Ed Diener
of the University of Illinois at Champaign-Urbana. Visit
www.psych.uiuc.edu/~ediener/
Nobel Laureate Princeton Psychologist, Daniel Kahneman, is pioneering some
fascinating rethinking about how individuals of different nationalities rate them-
selves when it comes to happiness and life-satisfaction. See his *chapter Living, and
Thinking About it: two perspectives on life*, in our book *The Science of Well-Being*
(Huppert, Baylis, and Keverne, Oxford University Press, 2005).

Growing Strong in the Face of Adversity

Her insight is born out by the work of Peter Herschbach . . .
See the homepage of Professor Herschbach at:
www.psychosom.med.tum.de/data/mitarbeiter/herschbach.htm
By contrast, an ignored or inadequately resolved problem . . .
This is born out by the work of Dr Barbara L. Fredrickson, the Director at the
Positive Emotions and Psychophysiology Laboratory of The University of
Michigan (www.positiveemotions.org). See her chapter called 'The Broaden-and-
Build Theory of Positive Emotions' in *Philosophical Transactions of The Royal
Society of London* (Huppert, Baylis, and Keverne, 2004).
There is no problem that is not improved by our asking for help . . .
Read more by visiting www.YoungLivesUK.com or the autobiographical materi-
al towards the back of this book.
A sense of mission and standing strong . . .
The psychological ideas in this section are based on the work of the Holocaust
survivor and Viennese professor of neurology and psychiatry, Viktor Frankl. See
his book *Man's Search for Meaning* and visit www.viktorfrankl.org.

I believe many films are distinguished for their powerful inspirational value if
they catch us at the right time in our life and in a ready mood. My personal list of
old-time favourite classics might well include: The 39 Steps, Casablanca, Singin' in
the Rain, It's a Wonderful Life, To Kill a Mockingbird, Ice Cold in Alex, What's
Up Doc, The Producers, and The Italian Job. And, more recently, Ferris Bueller's
Day Off, Forrest Gump, Ground Hog Day, Toy Story, American Pie, American
Beauty, and Goodbye Lenin (a German language film).

Recent Oscar-winning documentaries which I have greatly admired are: Into
the Arms of Strangers: *Stories of the Kindertransport*, Bowling for Columbine,
and The Fog of War.
Can we reconsider our sadness? . . .
One of the world's leading clinician's in the field of depression is the Californian
psychologist, Dr Michael Yapko, whose works can be read about at
www.Yapko.com
Professor Martin E.P. Seligman of the University of Pennsylvania is world-
renowned for his expertise on the research on depression. Visit
www.psych.upenn.edu/~seligman/

And this, perhaps, is a good time for me to pay tribute to this pioneering scholar:
While still in his twenties, Professor Martin E.P. Seligman launched his career

with a courageous and visionary contribution to psychology when his theories and experiments irrefutably demonstrated the role of cognition to a science totally dominated by blinkered behaviourists, and thereby he initiated a quantum leap forward for the entire discipline. Half a lifetime later, by using his election as President of the American Psychological Association in 1998 to enable him to act as the initiator and figurehead for the Positive Psychology movement, Professor Seligman successfully united many previously isolated pockets of research around the world. By doing so, Professor Seligman demonstrated that he has lost none of his intellectual bravery and vigour, which is why his indelible achievements, which have so often required him to swim against the swollen current of popular scientific opinion, are an absolute inspiration.

When it comes to developing our character strengths such as resilience and optimism and love and friendship, we would do well to consider the work of one of Professor Seligman's close colleagues, Dr James Pawelski. Formally a faculty member at Vanderbilt University, Dr Pawelski is now 'Director of Education and Senior Scholar in the Positive Psychology Center at the University of Pennsylvania', where he is developing the world's first degree program in Positive Psychology (a Masters in Applied Positive Psychology). James is an outstanding philosopher and psychologist who exudes remarkable spirit and good humour, and in my eyes is a leading torch-bearer in the American vanguard for the everyday applications of Positive Psychology. Visit www.sas.upenn.edu/CGS/graduate/mapp/faculty.php

I should add, too, that there is no more gifted and effective a Personal Coach and Corporate Lecturer than Dr James Pawelski. pawelski@psych.upenn.edu

Let's focus on what's helpful . . .
See the work of Dr Michael Yapko sourced via www.Yapko.com for an excellent and detailed account of these strategies to counter unhelpful thinking styles.

Finding life in death . . .
See the work of Dr Chris G. Davis at the University of British Columbia. Visit www.carleton.ca/psychology/directory/davis_c.html

Mulling such thoughts, I went to spend a day at St Christopher's Hospice . . .
The staff of this hospice are remarkable individuals who have teamed together to do vital work. www.stchristophers.org.uk

American psychology professor Mihaly Csikszentmihalyi
See his homepage at Claremont University: www.cgu.edu/pages/1871.asp

What's most likely to promote this productive 'flow' state . . .
See the website of the Gallup Organisation at www.strengthsfinder.com

American psychology professors, Robert Emmons and . . .

Professor Michael E. McCullough provides an overview of their research on gratitude at: www.psy.miami.edu/faculty/mmccullough/Gratitude_Page.htm

It's worth noting here that Professors Fred Bryant and Joseph Veroff . . .

Professor Fred B. Bryant is Director of the Graduate Applied Social Psychology Program at Loyola University in Chicago. Visit www.luc.edu/psychology/psy-faculty/bryant.htm

See the homepage of Emeritus Professor Joseph Veroff at the University of Michigan: www.lsa.umich.edu/psych/people/directory/profiles/faculty/?unique-name=jveroff

Feeling happy about the future . . .

Professor Martin E.P. Seligman is a world authority on how the skill of optimism can prove extremely beneficial to us. See his work at
www.psych.upenn.edu/~seligman/

A team led by the longtime Director of Clinical Psychology . . .

Visit Professor Peterson's homepage at: www.lsa.umich.edu/psych/people/directory/profiles/faculty/?uniquename=chrispet

Nice to know, then, . . .

The website for the Penn programme is
www.positivepsychology.org/prpsum.htm

Giving ourselves every reason to become more hopeful

See the work of Professor C. Richard Snyder, for many years the director of the clinical psychology program at the University of Kansas (visit www.psych.ukans.edu/faculty_Richard_Snyder.html).

See also the work of a brilliant young psychotherapist and psychology researcher, Dr Shane Lopez of the University of Kansas. He has helped develop the idea of *Hope Therapy* so that clinicians can help clients acquire the skills of more hopeful thinking and behaviour. Shane's pioneering work is certainly something to keep an eye on. Visit his homepage at:
www.soe.ku.edu/faculty/LopezS.php

Squaring ourselves with a painful past . . .

On the subject of ruminating about the recent and distant past, and its link to depression, please see the work of Professor Susan Nolen-Hoeksema at the Dept of Psychology at Yale University. Visit
www.yale.edu/psychology/FacInfo/Nolen-Hoeksema.html Her area of expertise is rumination versus active problem-solving.

Well, Professor Martin Seligman at the University of Pennsylvania . . .
Visit the homepage of Professor Martin E.P. Seligman at
www.psych.upenn.edu/~seligman/
Secondly, we should allocate a particular time . . .
See an overview of Professor George E. Vaillants's work at
psychology.about.com/library/submit/blsubmit_vaillant1.htm, and his book
*Ageing Well: Surprising Guideposts to a Happier Life from the Landmark
Harvard Study of Adult Development.*
A quite different study of 700 eminent individuals . . .
See the fascinating books by the Goertzel family: Mildred, Victor and Ted. A
powerpoint presentation about their work can be viewed at:
crab.rutgers.edu/%7Egoertzel/cradles.ppt
It's good news, then, that psychology professor Neal Roese . . .
Visit Professor Roese's homepage at: www.psych.uiuc.edu/~roese/

Reinventing Ourselves and Reinvesting in Life

One key proviso is this . . .
This is one of the key tenets of Positive Psychology: to build upon our strengths,
rather than being mesmerised by our weakness. The same goes for our relation-
ship with others: foster their strengths rather than harping on about their weak-
nesses. The idea is that the strengths will grow if fed encouragement, and so, of
their own accord, push out the weaknesses.
It's encouraging to note . . .
See the work of Professor George E. Vaillant, the long-time director of that
Harvard Study of Adult Development. An overview of his study is available at:
psychology.about.com/library/submit/blsubmit_vaillant1.htm
The Study of Well-Being . . .
I'm referring here to the whole field of research and also the new textbook, *The
Science of Well-Being* (Huppert, Baylis, and Keverne. Oxford University Press
2005).
Such ingrained habits . . .
See the work of the two American psychotherapists Dr Jeffrey E. Young and Dr
Janet S. Klosko (visit www.ctcli.com/klosko.htm), who write with great insight
on the topic of ingrained negative emotional habits.

It will also help us to visualise . . .
Psychology Professor Ian H. Robertson of Trinity College Dublin has written eloquently on the power of visualisation combined with deep relaxation. Visit his homepage at: www.tcd.ie/Psychology/Ian_Robertson

For therapeutic purposes, it's hard to find better than the work of the American psychologist, Dr Michael D. Yapko who combines Cognitive-Behavioural Therapy with hypnosis. Visit www.yapko.com

Let's free up our rigid thinking . . .
In England, The Oxford Cognitive Therapy Centre have done excellent research in this field; as has the Beck Institute in Philadelphia, U.S.A. (see www.beckinstitute.org).

Changing our tune . . .
For more on this approach, I know of no better account of Cognitive Behavioural Therapy than that given by Dr Judith Beck, Director of the Beck Institute in Philadelphia. Visit www.beckinstitute.org

My story much like any other . . .
I dedicate this autobiographical account to the loving memory of my mum, Beryl Baylis, whose wonderful courage and love in both life and in death, taught me the true meaning of *death shall have no dominion.*

The theory and empirical work reported here reflect the principle tenets of my Cambridge University PhD thesis titled *Learning From Young People's Lives*, which was supervised by Richard Green, and examined by Donald J. West (Cambridge) and George E. Vaillant (Harvard). My heartfelt thanks also go to Dr Sarah Fitzharding, Dr Anja Minnich, Maria Loades, Dr Shane Lopez, Cerstin Henning, and Professor Felicia Huppert for invaluable contributions at various stages in the writing-up of these ideas.

There is a fuller, 14,000 word explanation of this thesis, that can be read in my chapter called 'Relationship with Reality – and its role in the well-being of young adults', which can be found in *The Science of Well-Being* (Huppert, Baylis, and Keverne. Oxford University Press 2005).

Cut forward several years . . .
Here begins my time as a volunteer in Feltham Young Offenders Prison.

Imprisoned Young Offenders and The Grenadier Guards . . .
It was a privilege for me to interview all of these young men, and I will always be grateful to them for their honesty, and to the people in charge who lifted the red-tape and made the project possible.

For 12 weeks that autumn . . .

Thank you to Dr Loraine Gelsthorpe, a University Lecturer and Fellow of Pembroke College Cambridge, who, with great compassion, spotted my hunger and helped make possible my place on the Masters course.

I was intrigued to read an account . . .

This beautiful account of the Harvard College graduates (one of whom, legend has it, was JFK) is to be found in Professor George E. Vaillant's book *Adaption to Life.* Professor Vaillant provides an overview of the study at:

psychology.about.com/library/submit/blsubmit_vaillant1.htm.

Even more intriguingly, the professor . . .

This account of Florence Nightingale is to be found in Professor George E. Vaillant's book, *Wisdom of The Ego: Sources of Resilience in Adult Life.*

A second group was made up for 14 'High Physical Achievers' . . .

There would have been many more Commandos to research among, but their units were rather prone to being required at an hour's notice for active service deployment in some trouble-spot somewhere around the world.

This decision to 're-engage' was helped immeasurably . . .

Thank you, dear Claudia . . .you were then, and are now, a truly wonderful woman.

How can we harness inventions . . .

See the ideas of Professor Robert D. Putnam at www.BowlingAlone.com for an eloquent and robustly academic treatise that addresses this subject.

For anyone suffering a stammer in their speech, may I suggest the possible routes forward:

- The British Stammering Association at: www.stammering.org
- Seek a weekly course of therapy from a well qualified psychotherapist who is experienced in incorporating Clinical Hypnosis into their work (and so can teach self-hypnosis). Such a therapist might be found at the University College London Hypnosis Unit. (See my chapter called *Powerful New Approaches to Common Health Problems*; as well as my book's final chapter, *Nick's Special Topics.*)
- Seek guidance from a leading-edge Speech Therapy Centre such as The Michael Palin Centre for Stammering Children
  (see www.stammeringcentre.org/MPC/home.html).
- Investigate the effects of a tiny electronic speech aid worn in the ear canal (such as a product called the SpeechEasy; see www.speecheasy.com). However, these presently cost around three thousand pounds and are still a very recent speech-enhancement innovation. However, the American distributors do offer a trial

period of a month or more, and if used in conjunction with the other techniques suggested, could form part of an investigation of what helps a particular individual to greater speech fluency.

Nick's Special Topic

My views on hypnosis and its therapeutic role within the sub-conscious are, at time of writing, based largely upon the following scientific sources:

The lifetime's work of Dr Milton H. Erikson and the subsequent foundation that bears his name: Visit www.erickson-foundation.org

The works of Dr Michael Yapko at www.Yapko.com

The works of Joe Griffin at www.HumanGivens.org

The University College London Hypnosis Unit and their research and clinical associates such as Professor David Oakley and Val Walters. The UCL Hypnosis Unit website has information on many cutting-edge research articles concerning Clinical Hypnosis, and the unit's professional diploma course is a very thorough repository of up-to-date and landmark research evidence and theory. Visit www.ucl.ac.uk/hypnosis

My thoughts on good therapeutic practice are much guided by the above, and by:

- Dr Judith Beck and her approach to Cognitive Behaviour Therapy
  (see www.beckinstitute.org)
- Dr Christine Padesky and her use of Socractic Questioning
  (see www.padesky.com)
- Dr Arnold A. Lazarus and his own method called Multimodal Therapy.

To locate a therapist well-qualified in hypnosis, contact The British Society of Experimental and Clinical Hypnosis (www.bsech.com); or visit www.ucl.ac.uk/hypnosis

For more thoughts about workplace initiatives:

Visit www.positiveemotions.org to find out more about the work of Professor Barbara L. Fredrickson, the Director at the Positive Emotions and Psychophysiology Laboratory of The University of Michigan. See also her chapter called 'The Broaden-and-Build Theory of Positive Emotions' in *Philosophical Transactions of The Royal Society of London* (Huppert, Baylis, and Keverne, 2004). See, too, the work of Professor Kahneman, on the Nobel Prize website at: nobelprize.org/economics/laureates/2002/kahneman-autobio.html

How about Western governments stop using . . .
In the UK, Cambridge University Professor Felicia A. Huppert is the scientist pioneering the creation of 'National Measures of Well-Being'. Felicia's own research interests combine psychology, epidemiology and neuroscience. She is chair of the European Network of Positive Psychology, and director of CIRCA, the Cambridge Interdisciplinary Research Centre on Ageing.
http://www.psychiatry.cam.ac.uk/pages/profiles/huppert.html

I don't mean to suggest that technology is the trouble . . .
On a personal note, I have to confess to considerable frustration when, from time to time, my computer would say things like: "Catastrophic failure of all systems has destroyed your day's work, and may have affected your sex life! Please refer to the small-print in the disclaimer that you threw out with the box that came with this computer."

Looking Forward to the Future

Bring me my bow . . .
These words by the poet, William Blake, are most often heard to the music of *Jerusalem.*

Such considerations are not just word-play . . .
See the chapter 'Successful aging: from cell to self' co-authored by Dr Sonia Lupien in *The Science of Well-Being* (Huppert, Baylis, and Keverne. Oxford University Press 2005). See her profile at
www.douglasrecherche.qc.ca/profile/details.asp?id=81&l=e

Even better, an analysis of eminent . . .
Professor of Psychology at the University of California at Davis, Dean Keith Simonton, has written some fascinating books on the life-trends and personal characteristics of many of history's most eminent individuals. Visit his homepage at: psychology.ucdavis.edu/Simonton

By contrast, if we don't learn how to progress . . .
This view is well-expressed in the remarkable book, *Ageing Well: Surprising Guideposts to a Happier Life from the Landmark Harvard Study of Adult Development,* by Professor George E. Vaillant. An overview of his study can be found at: psychology.about.com/library/submit/blsubmit_vaillant1.htm

Science isn't Certainty

When thinking of how to spend my working life, and how to regard science, I am reminded of the words of two of America's most pioneering and successful psychologists, Professors Marty Seligman (University of Pennsylvania) and Bob Sternberg (Yale), at a talk given for students in 1999.

(Marty Seligman) "Good science is, by and large, courageous science. It is unpopular science. It is science that no one did before and thought should not be done."

(Bob Sternberg) "As I have gotten older, I have spent ever more time thinking about the question and less about the answer. Namely, *is this a good question to ask in the first place?* Why should I or anyone else care what the answer is?"

* * *

A final word on the above Chapter Notes

Though their names do not appear in the research notes, I have been greatly encouraged by the excellent works of the following writers on well-being:

In Britain, Susan Clark of The Sunday Times (www.whatreallyworks.co.uk), Dr Miriam Stoppard (www.miriamstoppard.com), and Drs Gillian Butler and Melanie Fennell of the Oxford University Department of Psychiatry (www.octc.co.uk).

In the USA, there has been Dr Phillip McGraw (www.drphil.com), Dr Stephen Covey and Sean Covey (www.covey.com), Anthony Robbins (www.anthonyrobbins.com), and Dr Daniel Goleman (www.eiconsortium.org).

I'd like to apologise for the times in this book where I have omitted an important point or person, or been inconsistent, or seemed to say one thing but probably meant another. On such occasions, I'm grateful for you reading between the lines and taking my thoughts in the spirit in which I intended them.

* * *

Index of Key Words and Themes

This at-a-glance index helps locate particular themes whenever they receive substantial attention in a chapter.

Our 50 Wonderful Lives

The extraordinary research findings about the hows and whys of life going well, are illustrated in this book by the voices of some remarkable people.

A wonderful life doesn't mean a life that's trouble-free or without fault or flaw. It means it's wonderful that the person is still smiling and going strong after all they've been through. And that's not to say these ships won't see high seas and storms in the future, or appear to sink beneath the waves for a while. But for now, at time of writing, they look like ships in full sail.

It was through wanting to understand how such individuals managed to cope so well, that I embarked upon this exploration. I'm hoping these personalities represent a rich mixture of women and men in all walks of life, and I chose these particular individuals because they so memorably illustrate what the best science is beginning to discover about well-being. Their unique experiences may not *prove* a point, because one example or even 50 can't do that, but they can certainly demonstrate it.

It's their lasting happiness and accomplishments that are the focus of my attention, and their fame is only relevant because it means their lives have been recorded in biographies and interviews, and in that sense are open to study by all of us.

Some of the names you'll recognise fondly, others not; but be prepared for some surprises because their personal stories go well beyond their public faces.

It's heartening to know that if we look among the most inspiring people in our own everyday lives . . . perhaps our closest friends and family . . . we can see these very same principles at work; and we can better appreciate how and when their outstanding qualities came about. I am reminded of the words on a stained glass window in The Queen's University, Belfast:

"Their deeds are written not on stone, but on the hearts of men."

My debt of gratitude

I am very grateful to have had the opportunity to learn about the following 50 individuals from a mixture of autobiographies and interviews. The books and articles I have studied and extracts I have used, have provided a deep reservoir of insights and examples to help illustrate the Study of Well-Being. My heartfelt thanks and respect to all those who have told the story of their life so that others might benefit.

* * *

Kate Adie OBE was BBC Chief News Correspondent until 2002 and has reported memorably and courageously from some of the most troubled places around the world. Her body carries the shrapnel and bullet nicks to prove it. Born in 1945 to a young mother whose husband was away at war, Kate was raised by her adoptive parents (a pharmacist and his wife in Sunderland) and recounts a relatively sheltered childhood. Her modern languages degree at Newcastle

University meant Kate spent some time in the then divided city of
Berlin where she witnessed a family being intimated by border
guards, and her curiosity and awareness of the world grew rapidly
from there. Kate joined the BBC in 1968 as a studio technician in
local radio and became a member of the National Youth Theatre. She
still attends the theatre and visits galleries when time permits, is an
avid reader of both fiction and history, and has served as a judge for
the Orange Prize for Fiction. Kate describes herself as a shy person,
but has never let this stop her. It so happens that one of Kate's school
reports mentioned that she had a very loud voice, yet it was only 40
years later that medical tests revealed she had been partially deaf since
birth. In respect of this, Kate has since become patron to the LINK
Centre for Deafened People. Kate has always known she was adopted, and it was an official form that required her to name her Next of
Kin during the first Gulf War, that prompted Kate to trace her birth
family. They are now very happily reunited and Kate dedicated her
autobiography, *The Kindness of Strangers*, to her mother Babe.

Madeleine Albright was invited by President Clinton in 1997 to
become the first woman U.S. Secretary of State, and in doing so
became the highest ranking woman in the history of the American
Government. Born in Prague in 1937, her family had emigrated to
the U.S. when she was 11, and she went on to graduate from the
prestigious women's college of Wellesley. Whilst bringing up her
three daughters, Madeleine spent thirteen years completing her part-
time PhD, and she only entered full-time paid employment at age
39. Despite going through a traumatic divorce at age 43, she went on
to establish herself as a Professor of Foreign Policy, and served as the
U.S. Ambassador to the United Nations. During the Second World
War, her parents had brought young Madeleine up as a Catholic to
avoid persecution, and only in 1997 did she learn that her grandparents were Jewish and had died in a Nazi concentration camp. In
her autobiography, *Madam Secretary,* Madeleine recounts her own
lifetime hitherto, with humility and humour. Now retired from
front-line politics, Madeleine devotes herself to teaching and serving
on boards to promote ethical foreign investments.

Muhammad Ali is a three-time winner of the World Heavyweight Boxing Championship. Born in 1942, Muhammad grew up in Louisville in the then deeply segregated South of the United States, and in his book, *The Soul of a Butterfly*, tells how his school days were made difficult because of dyslexia. It was when Muhammad converted to Islam that he left behind what he has written about as the "slave name" under which he once boxed, Cassius Clay. Declaring himself a conscientious objector to the Vietnam war, Muhammad was stripped of his Olympic title and was not permitted to box. Years later, he had the honour to light the flame at the 1996 Olympics in Atlanta, as well as at the 1979 Special Olympics in New York. Muhammad suffers from Parkinson's disease and together with his wife of 16 years, he donates his time and resources to Parkinson's related charities. Moreover, as a United Nations 'Messenger of Peace', Muhammad travels internationally lending his support to hunger and poverty relief. He is the proud father of nine children; he is also an avid poet; and together with his wife, Muhammad is setting up a cultural and educational centre in his hometown to share his legacy and ideals: Peace, Social Responsibility, Respect, and Personal Growth.

Lance Armstrong recovered from life-threatening testicular cancer to win the extraordinary Tour de France cycling race for a record-breaking six consecutive years. Born in Texas in 1971 to a financially impoverished but highly supportive single teenage mother, it was the triathlon of swimming, cycling, and running that became his teenage means of highly positive self-expression. He now treasures his own three children and several close friendships with his cycling team mates. Lance declares that his experience of cancer has felt more important to him than any of his sporting victories because of the good things it has taught him. His journey back to life after cancer and the life-philosophies his experiences have inspired, are well charted in his autobiographies *It's Not About The Bike* and *Every Second Counts*. Lance announced his decision to retire after the 2005 Tour de France so as to spend more time with his children and to continue helping others who are fighting cancer. His endeavours through the Lance Armstrong Foundation have raised tens of millions of dollars, an achievement dwarfed only by his personal involvement as a campaigner.

David Beckham OBE is the former Manchester United and more recently Real Madrid winger known world-wide as Captain of the England soccer team. Born in 1975 to a family of modest means in London's East End, the young David would wear a skull cap and accompany his Jewish grandfather to Jewish weddings. David explains in his autobiographies, *My Side* and *My World*, how he developed his prodigious soccer skills by constantly practicing with his father, an avid football fan, and other players older and more skilled than himself. Like his father, he was a fan of Manchester United and was signed-up as a full-time professional at age 16. His wife, Victoria, and he, are the proud and loving parents of their three sons, Brooklyn, Romeo and Cruz; and as a long-time supporter of UNICEF, the England Football Captain has now become a UNICEF Goodwill Ambassador with a special focus on the Sports for Development programme. Having attended a soccer school as a child, David has recently opened his own academy in South-East London near where he grew up, and David plans to focus on this project when his own playing career ends. In regard to this, he says that the most important thing to him is "to see the happiness that football brings to kids".

Sir Peter de la Billiere spent most of his career as the Commanding Officer of Britain's famous special forces regiment, The Special Air Service, until his retirement in 1992. Peter was twice awarded the Military Cross for courage under fire before he was 25 and after a quite extraordinary career around the globe eventually led Britain's Armed Forces in the 1991 Gulf War. Born in 1934, Peter was seven when he lost his father, a Surgeon Lieutenant-Commander serving in the Second World War, whose ship was bombed; and subsequently his mother became quite disabled with depression when Peter was only in his late teens. Peter also tells in his autobiography *Looking For Trouble* that he was rejected from the Navy because he was colour-blind, and joined the army to fight in Korea with little hope of promotion. Peter is married and has three grown-up children, and now enjoys carpentry and bee-keeping.

Dame Betty Boothroyd in 1992 became the first-ever woman Speaker of the House of Commons, and in 1995 became Chancellor of the Open University. Betty was born in 1929 to a working class family in West Yorkshire, and she describes in her autobiography, *Madam Speaker,* the considerable moral support she received, particularly from her mother. A keen dancer in her teenage years, Betty went to London to become one of the celebrated Tiller Girls, but these ambitions soon ended in disappointment. Betty then worked as a secretary until she discovered her vocation at age 23 and became a full-time worker for the Labour Party. Betty went to the U.S. as a volunteer for John F. Kennedy's U.S. presidential campaign in 1959, which proved to be a deeply formative experience for her, and she went on to fight no less than five British elections as a would-be MP before finally being elected to Parliament in 1973. Devoted to public service, she has never married, and cherishes her life-long friendships. Since her retirement in 2000, Betty has sat in the House of Lords.

Sir Richard Branson is arguably Britain's best-recognised entrepreneur who has created a range of successful businesses under his Virgin brand name. Born in 1950, Richard grew up with two loving parents who instilled in him a confident self-reliance and a cavalier disregard for petty or unnecessary rules. His mother provided a role-model for Richard's teenage money-making ventures at a time when his enthusiasm for schoolwork was dampened by dyslexia. At age 15, Richard and his best friend started a student magazine, and though this eventually folded, the experiences gained here fed into their Virgin Records mail-order business which several years later earned them their first millions. Richard is married with two children and since the mid-eighties has personally pioneered a range of record-breaking air balloon adventures, and is also the trustee of several charities. His autobiography, *Losing My Virginity,* frankly recounts his remarkable life.

Bill Bryson is one of the world's best-selling travel writers, much loved for his irreverent humour and fond recollections in *The Lost Continent* and *Tales of a Small Island*, about the USA and UK respectively. Bill was born in 1951 in Desmoines, Iowa, but a back-packing expedition in 1973 brought him to England where he met his wife-to-be and decided to settle. For many years, he was happily employed as a financial journalist on British papers, but eventually supplemented his income by writing travel articles. Having lived for a longtime with his wife and four children in North Yorkshire, they have since lived for some years in New Hampshire, USA, before returning once again to England. Bill continues to write extremely popular books about history and the world around him.

Sir Winston Churchill was Britain's Prime Minister during the Second World War. What this means is, that at age 65, by the sheer inspirational gravitas of his own extraordinary personality and life-experience, Winston Churchill led the British people and their armed forces from the very brink of defeat in 1939, to eventual peace in 1945. Knighted for his services to his country, Winston also received a Nobel Prize in Literature for his historical and bio-graphical works concerning the war.

Born into the wealthy 'landed gentry' of the Victorian England of 1874, Winston recounts in his autobiography *My Early Life* that he was educated at first Harrow School and then The Royal Military College Sandhurst, and while serving as a young subaltern took part in the British Army's last ever sword-drawn cavalry charge. This was not to be the least of his adventures, because in his mid-twenties and serving as a newspaper correspondent covering the Boer War in South Africa, Winston was captured and imprisoned. He eventually made a daring escape across enemy territory, and despite a price on his head, 'dead or alive', he made it back to friendly forces. His escapade catapulted him to fame and the beginning of an extraordi-nary career of public service. In all of this, he was very happily married to Clementine Hozier and together they had two children, Randolph and Mary. It is oft forgotten that it was Winston Churchill who long-anticipated the decisive role of aircraft in theatres of war, and years later it was he who coined the term 'iron curtain' to describe the cold war front that he foresaw arising between the USSR and western nations. Though Winston had to cope with a stammer throughout his life, he was nonetheless famous for his stirring oratory in Parliament, in his radio broadcasts to the British people at war, and in his addresses to the troops. Winston also suffered bouts of depression, yet very fittingly he is remembered today for his indomitable energy, optimism, and humour.

Eileen Collins treasured her childhood fascination for aircraft and the thought of flying and went on to become the first woman to pilot and command a NASA space shuttle mission. To date, barely 500 humans have traveled in the space beyond our Earth's atmosphere, and only 50 of them have been female; so it's a rather special club of which Eileen Collins has made herself a member through her skill and courage and determination. Born in 1956 to a loving family of modest means, Eileen says she did not like playing with dolls as a child and, at High School, took her inspiration from reading about women pilots who played an important role during the Second World War. Eileen enjoyed studying mathematics and science and saved her money to earn her light-aircraft pilot's license when she was 19. She married another pilot she met in the military, and they're raising two children. She still enjoys running, golf, hiking, camping, reading, photography, and astronomy. Eileen hopes that her space shuttle missions will inspire all children, girls and boys alike, to reach out with determination to develop their heart-felt passions.

Tom Cruise is a twice Oscar-nominated actor and producer who has spent more than 20 years on the A-List of the Hollywood film industry. Born in 1962, his parents moved house many times and by the age of just 14, he'd been to 15 different schools. This difficult situation was compounded by his having to deal with severe dyslexia. His father left home when Tom was 12, and he grew up with his loving mother and his three cherished sisters in a household that he describes as being short of money but rich in affection. Tom put his newspaper delivery earnings into the family housekeeping and by doing so acquired a confidence in his ability to make ends meet. Compensating for his academic difficulties by being a keen soccer player and wrestler at school, he recalls a happy home life and a mother who inspired in her four youngsters a love of helping others. Tom has been a Scientologist since his early 20s, is the devoted father of two adopted children with the actress Nicole Kidman, and is very actively involved in literacy projects.

Marie Curie won her first Nobel Prize for Physics in 1903 for discovering Radium, and her second Nobel Prize for Chemistry, just eight years later. Born in Poland in 1867, the daughter of and impoverished High School teacher, Marie passed her degree at the Sorbonne University in Paris with flying colours, where she would later become that university's first woman lecturer. She married her husband Pierre when she was 29 and they had two daughters. Marie and Pierre worked closely together until his tragic death from a car accident in 1906. Marie continued her lifesaving work for another quarter of century and pioneered the use of mobile x-ray vans in World War I. She died in France in 1934. Marie had said of herself that her real passion was to ease human suffering.

Ellen Degeneres is one of America's leading stand-up comedians with an award-winning television show and emerging movie career. Ellen was born in Los Angeles in 1958 to a devout Christian Scientist father. Her parents split up when she was 13 and it was by trying to ease her mother's subsequent depression that Ellen developed her comedy skills. Ellen had a range of low-paying jobs after High School and then dropped out of university to concentrate on her comedy act. At age 19, she explained to her family that she was gay, at which point she was asked to leave home by her father and step-mother. The death of her girlfriend in a car accident a few years later, was to prove a profound catalyst to Ellen's writing and led to her acclaimed monologue, *Phonecall to God.* Twenty years on, Ellen once again braved considerable adversity when, in 1997, she 'came out' publicly and incorporated this revelation into the sitcom character she was playing. An unhelpful media response and the canceling of her tv show meant some hard years for Ellen, but she eventually relaunched her career with an award-winning tv chat show and then her charming comic performance in the box-office hit movie, *Finding Nemo*, as the lovable fish with instant amnesia.

Céline Dion has been named the biggest selling female artist in recording history, with more than 175 million albums sold world-wide. The chanteuse was born in a rural French-Canadian town in 1968, the youngest of 14 children in a highly musical working-class family. Having performed from the tender age of five, Céline helped compose a song at age 12, which brought her to the attention of her future manager René Angélil. Céline would eventually marry René, "the first and only love of her life", when she was 20. Her husband's battle with skin cancer in 1999 brought about a deep change of priorities and Céline embarked on an extended sabbatical. Having tried for a baby for six years, Céline and René turned to IVF treatment and in 2001 became the proud parents of baby René-Charles. Céline has been a long-time supporter of cystic fibrosis charities, as her niece was born with the disease, and at age 16, died in Céline's arms. Upon her return to public life in 2002, Céline accepted a longterm engagement in Las Vegas, which allowed her to balance her performing life with her private passions. Her autobiography is aptly called, *My Story, My Dream.*

Waris Dirie is now a United Nations Special Ambassador for Women's Rights, having previously spent ten years as a leading international fashion model. One of 12 children born to desert nomads in Somalia, Waris escaped being sold into marriage for five camels at the age of 13, by running away to London where she worked as her uncle's maid. There, she taught herself to read and write, and five years later a fashion photographer spotted her working in a fast-food restaurant. Soon, she was gracing catwalks and magazine covers and even appeared in a Bond film. A decade on, Waris left modelling to campaign for the U.N. against female circumcision, having been a victim of the process herself aged five. She has recorded her extraordinary life-journey in her autobiography,

Desert Flower, along with its sequel *Desert Dawn* in which she recounts her return to her native Somalia so as to be reunited with her mother. Waris now lives in Wales with her son.

Albert Einstein received the Nobel Prize for Physics in 1921. Born in Germany in 1879 to a highly supportive Jewish family, he renounced his German citizenship and in 1901 became a Swiss citizen. Age 22, he submitted his doctoral thesis to the University of Zurich, but withdrew it some while later when his girlfriend and soon-to-be wife, Mileva, became pregnant. It was now that Albert accepted a modest post in the Patent Office in Bern issuing patents on scientific inventions and, in his spare time, produced much of his remarkable work. Indeed, it was in 1905, age just 26, that he wrote the physics papers which contained his special theory of relativity and the equation $E=mc2$ which were eventually to win him international acclaim. The following year, the University of Zurich awarded him his PhD. As the Nazi's rose to power in the Germany of the 1920s where Albert had been working for some years, he once again renounced his German citizenship and finally emigrated to the USA in 1933, settling in Princeton in 1935. With his first wife, Mileva, Albert had had a daughter and two sons. In 1919, he divorced so as to marry his cousin, Elsa, who died in 1934. Albert himself died in Princeton in 1995, at the age of 76, having spent his working life at The Institute for Advanced Study. Playing the violin had always proven an important source of relaxation for Albert, and he was an ardent pacifist and denouncer of the use of nuclear weapons.

Gertrude Elion is the American scientist awarded the Nobel Prize for Medicine in 1988 for pioneering the use of chemotherapy in childhood leukaemia. Gertrude was born in 1918, and at the age of just 15 felt a vocation to become a medical researcher after seeing her grandfather die from cancer. Losing her fiancé to disease a few years later further strengthened her resolve. Despite her excellent academic credentials, Gertrude had to fight considerable prejudice against women scientists, but took great encouragement from reading the autobiographical accounts of Marie Curie who herself won two

Nobel Prizes in science. Gertrude developed a passion for opera and for travel throughout her life. She died in 1999, but had long been renowned as an inspirational mentor to the young students who knew her.

Richard Feynman was one of America's best-loved scientists of the post-war generation, and was awarded the Nobel Prize for Physics in 1965. Born in 1918, Richard made major contributions to theoretical physics and came to public attention when he led the inquiry team that helped unravel the cause of the Challenger space shuttle disaster. Richard lost his first wife to tuberculosis when he was in his twenties, was only very briefly married a second time, but he found lasting happiness in his third marriage to an English woman with whom he had two children. Richard was famed for his exceptional ability as a teacher and he continued to lecture until two weeks before his death in 1988, after a decade of fighting cancer. To this date, he is fondly remembered for his inspirational sense of joy in life, his directness and his never-ending curiosity, which all shine through in his autobiography, *Surely You're Joking Mr Feynman*.

Cathy Freeman is the indigenous Australian who lit the cauldron and went on to win the 400 metres gold medal at the 2000 Olympic Games in Sydney. She is widely regarded as an inspiration to her people, and a model for reconciliation in Australia. Born 1973, her beloved biological father left the family on account of his alcoholism, and it was her white stepfather who became her first running coach. In her autobiography, *Cathy*, she describes how her running represented a sense of freedom from the divisions among Australians. She also writes candidly about the long-term romance with her sports manager and her struggle to free herself from what she eventually came to regard as an unhealthy dependency upon this relationship. Since her retirement from running in 2003, Cathy has invested herself in a range of social causes, from suicide prevention among young people, through to Aboriginal Rights. Cathy started suffering from exercise-induced asthma shortly after launching her professional running career and was deeply affected by the death from a sudden asthma attack of her elder sister, who suffered from cerebral palsy. One of Cathy's many benevolent roles now, is as an ambassador for asthma research and awareness.

Dawn French has become one of Britains' most popular comedians thanks to her performances in the tv hits, *The Vicar of Dibley*, and *French & Saunders*. Born in Wales in 1957, Dawn speaks fondly of her family and childhood. With her father in the RAF, her family moved on average every 18 months and Dawn found it difficult to fit in when she went to boarding school at age 11. Far worse, Dawn was deeply hurt when her much beloved father died when she was just 19. Nonetheless, she has told how his kindness as a father left her with the most profound sense that she was loved and lovable. Dawn now lives with her husband, the Jamaican-born comedian and actor Lenny Henry, and their adopted daughter, in Berkshire. She is an outspoken supporter of the philosophy that 'big can be beautiful' when it comes to a woman's body, and she is investing considerable time and money in her fashion business for larger-size clothing for women. Dawn has also been actively involved with the charity, *Comic Relief*, since 1986.

Bill Gates is the co-founder and former CEO of Microsoft and is an entrepreneurial pioneer in the business and technology of personal computers. Born in Seattle in 1955 to very encouraging parents, Bill developed his passion for computing software at age 13. While still a teenager, he left Harvard University after only a year so he could realise his vision for a readily usable personal computer, and formed Microsoft in 1975 with the help of his childhood friend. Bill and his wife Melinda now have three children, and in 2000 set up a foundation to invest considerable amounts of their time and money to help combat HIV, tuberculosis and malaria, which kill 90% of the people in the world's poorest countries. Bill counts Leonardo de Vinci, Nelson Mandela, Henry Ford, and Nobel Physicist Richard Feynman, among his life's role models.

Mahatma Gandhi was the spiritual and political leader who, through non-violent resistance, helped free the people of India from British rule, and is regarded by many as 'the father of the Indian Nation'. Born in India in 1869, Gandhi tells in his autobiography, *The Story Of My Experiments With Truth*, that he was obliged by custom to marry at the age of just 13. He and his wife raised four children. Gandhi studied law in London, but found it difficult to find work upon his return to India. He decided to accept legal work in South Africa, where he then spent 21 years struggling to secure rights for Indian people. He has written how the adversities of this experience helped him cope with his debilitating shyness. It was not until 1915, at the age of 45, that Gandhi returned to India to take up the campaign for Indian Independence. Altogether, Gandhi spent seven years in prison for his political activities, and in 1948, was assassinated. His benevolent legacy lives on.

Stefanie Graf is one of the world's most successful women's tennis champions. Born in Germany, 1969, Steffi began playing tennis at age four, but it was persistent problems with her knees that eventually forced her out of the game at the age of 30. Since her retirement from tennis in 1999, Steffi has found happiness in motherhood and married-life with fellow tennis star Andre Agassi. Alongside working for her sports management company, Steffi has established the charitable foundation 'Children for Tomorrow' to support mentally and emotionally traumatised children.

Mia Hamm captained the U.S. women's soccer team in winning two consecutive Olympic golds. Born in 1972, Mia's family moved home frequently as her father was a fighter pilot with the U.S. forces, and Mia discovered soccer as a toddler when they were stationed in Italy. Despite Mia having worn casts as a young child to help correct a foot problem, at age 15 she played her first international soccer game and became the youngest player on the women's U.S. national team. The death from a rare blood disorder of her adoptive brother inspired her to set up the Mia Hamm Foundation, which helps leukaemia sufferers and empowers young female athletes.

Emmylou Harris became one of the most popular country and folk musicians in the USA, winning 11 Grammy awards. Born in 1947, Emmylou grew up in Washington, DC, and her career took-off when she started collaborating with her friend and mentor, Gram Parsons. Emmylou has been married three times and is now a single mother. Since 1997, she has also been one of the most visible spokespersons for the Campaign for a Landmine Free World, organizing concerts with well-known singer-songwriters to raise awareness of the issue.

Dame Kelly Holmes won Olympic Gold Medals for both the women's 800 and 1500 metres in Athens 2004, at the age of 34. Her mother was just 18 when she gave birth to Kelly in 1970, and she grew up one of the few non-white children on her council estate, and the only mixed-race pupil in her school. Despite being a sickly child, Kelly took up athletics seriously at age 12, only to put that passion on hold so as to join the British Army at age 18. She thoroughly enjoyed this life, and rose to the rank of sergeant as a Physical Training Instructor; but seeing a former competitor from her teenage years appearing in the 1992 Olympics, Kelly felt motivated to return to running as a full-time athlete. A petite five feet and four inches tall, she overcame serious injuries, chronic fatigue syndrome and depression so as to achieve her twin Athens victories. Kelly Holmes was made a Dame for her outstanding contribution to British sport, and retired in 2005, the most successful female British middle-distance runner of all time. Her autobiography is called *Black, White & Gold*.

Helen Keller was an inspiring writer and campaigner for the disabled. Born in Alabama in 1880, Helen was rendered both deaf and blind by illness when aged only nineteen months and before she had learned to speak. She tells how she was frustrated for much of her early childhood until, at age 7, she met an extraordinary teacher who taught her to read and write. From then on, her progress was so prodigious that at the age of 24 she went on to Radcliffe College of Harvard University, and thus became the first deaf and blind person to graduate from an American university. She wrote thirteen books, including her famous, *The Story of My Life*, gave hundreds of lectures, and formed countless committees to help other people in situations similar to hers. She also helped standardise Braille for blind or partially-sighted readers. She died in her sleep in 1968 and is fondly remembered as a beacon of human courage and kindness.

Nelson Mandela is the Nobel Peace Laureate who led the struggle to replace the apartheid regime of South Africa with a multi-racial democracy. After his release in 1990, at the age of 71, from 27 years of imprisonment, almost twenty years of that spent on the prison colony of Robben Island off the coast of Cape Town, Nelson went on to become the first democratically elected President of South Africa, in 1994. Born in 1918, and known affectionately to his family and countrymen as Madiba, Nelson lost his father at the age of nine and was placed in the care of the acting tribal regent. He went on to qualify as a lawyer and in 1952 opened the very first black law practice in Johannesburg. Eventually, he went underground to launch a campaign of sabotage against the white government, which led to his receiving a sentence of life-imprisonment in 1964. In his autobiography, *The Long Walk To Freedom*, Nelson reveals how he kept up his spirits and health while in prison. He has given his working life to the dignity and freedom of individuals, and to the reconciliation of his homeland. Since stepping down from the Presidency in 1999, Nelson continues to campaign against the spread of HIV Aids, and has been actively involved in peace negotiations in other areas of the world.

Jamie Oliver MBE was born in 1980, and raised in a loving family running a village pub in Essex. This is where he developed his passion for both cooking and people. At age sixteen, he left school to train as a chef and spent some time working in France, and then honing his fresh, no-nonsense cooking style under some of the best chefs in London. In his early twenties, Jamie became Britain's youngest and best known cookbook author and tv chef, whose shows like *The Naked Chef* are shown in over 40 countries around the world. Having himself been an undistinguished pupil struggling with dyslexia, in 2002 Jamie set up the charity-restaurant *Fifteen*, where 15 disadvantaged young people are trained to work in the catering industry. More recently, Jamie has led the 'Feed Me Better' campaign to improve the quality of children's diets, and he has rightly received much credit for encouraging the government to increase funding and regulations for school dinners. In 1999, Jamie married his sweetheart from his teenage years, Juliette, with whom he is raising two daughters, Poppy and Daisy. In his private time, Jamie spends many evenings rehearsing on the drums for his UK band, *Scarlet Division*.

Claire Rayner was born in 1931, and has been awarded an OBE for her life's work as a health writer, novelist, media broadcaster, social campaigner, and patron of more than 60 social and charitable organisations. In her autobiography, *How Did I Get Here From There*, she writes of a cold and cruel mother and a fraudster father who was always on the run. When she was fourteen, to escape her miserable home life, Claire pretended to be seventeen so she could start training as a nurse. Happily this led her to discover her vocation: caring for and helping others. Even though her childhood experiences had made her deeply skeptical about family life, she married at age 27 and has enjoyed a very happy relationship ever since. She turned to professional writing in 1960 with the birth of her first of three children, and ever since has worked wonders through her books and columns.

Ronald Reagan was America's 40th President, governing for two terms and surviving an assassin's bullet that missed his heart by only a couple of inches and punctured a lung. Born in 1911 to an impoverished family and an alcoholic shoe-salesman father, Ronald took a summer job at age 15 as a lifeguard on the Rock River and continued this to pay his way through college, reportedly saving many folks from drowning. Ronald developed an early skill in storytelling and drama and he went on to become a radio sports announcer upon his graduation. Ronald recalls in his autobiographies, *An American Life* and *Where's The Rest Of Me?* that a screen-test in 1937 led him to Hollywood, and that he appeared in 53 movies over the next two decades. It was through being elected president of the Screen Actors Guild that Ronald became involved in U.S. politics and the rest is, literally, history. Ronald died in 2004 after a ten-year battle with Alzheimer's, leaving behind his second wife Nancy and four children. It is testimony to his spirit that even the most tenacious interviewers have said of Ronald Reagan that he was one of the nicest guys they ever interviewed, whether on or off the record.

Sir Steve Redgrave is Britain's most successful Olympic medallist with an unparalleled five consecutive wins in rowing events. Born in 1962, the son of a builder, Steve has suffered from lifelong dyslexia and left comprehensive school with one CSE in woodwork. It's interesting to note that he was recruited to the school rowing team at age 14, because of his unusually big hands and feet. In his autobiography, *A Golden Age,* Steve talks frankly about his battle with colitis and about being diagnosed with diabetes in 1997, requiring him to balance his training and diabetes regimes by giving himself up to seven insulin injections a day. Steve has a wife, who is a medical doctor, and three children. Since his retirement from Olympic rowing in 2000, Steve has busied himself helping with London's Olympic bid for 2012, mentoring six budding Olympians, commentating on rowing for the BBC, being patron for 20 charities, and running marathons. He devotes more than half his time to his own charity, the Steve Redgrave Trust, helping improve the opportunities for children and young people in their local communities.

Julia Roberts is an Oscar-winning Hollywood actress. Born in 1967, Julia grew up without television and her parents ran an actors and writers workshop in their home. Her parents divorced when Julia was four years old and six years later, Julia lost her father to cancer. Julia married to cameraman Danny Moder in 2002 and they have now become the parents of twins. For many years, Julia has given of her time and resources to UNICEF as well as many other charitable causes.

Monty Roberts is the American horseman who developed a wholly non-aggressive and benign method of training horses and thus inspired the novel and Hollywood movie, *The Horse Whisperer*. Monty was born on a ranch in California in 1935 and worked as a stunt double for riding scenes since he was a young boy. Monty has written how he had 71 bones broken by the age of 12, not one from accidents with horses, but all of them at the hands of his dangerously violent father. In his autobiography, *The Man Who Listens To Horses*, Monty reveals how as a young teenager he learned the nonverbal communication he calls Equus, by observing a wild mustang herd. Together with his wife Pam, Monty has raised three children and 47 foster children. He continues to work on his ambition to leave the world a better place for horses, and for people, too. His most recent book is *'The Horses in my Life'*.

Dame Anita Roddick is the CEO of The Body Shop, and an activist on environmental and human rights issues. Born in 1942, she describes in her autobiographies, *Body and Soul* and *Business as Unusual,* how she grew up as the child of an Italian immigrant couple in an English seaside town. This experience left her feeling something of an outsider, which drew her to other outsiders and rebels. Anita formally trained as a teacher but an educational opportunity on a kibbutz in Israel eventually evolved into an extended working trip around the world. Inspired by these experiences of other cultures, Anita started The Body Shop in 1976 without any formal business training, but strongly motivated to help earn a living for herself and her family of two daughters and a husband.

Hillary Rodham Clinton became a U.S. First Lady and then the first woman to be elected a Senator for New York. Born in 1947, Hillary recounts in her autobiography, *Living History*, that she grew up happy with the support and discipline of her parents. Hillary met her husband, Bill, at university where she was qualifying as a lawyer, and after graduation joined him in Arkansas. Together they have one daughter, Chelsea, and throughout her career she has campaigned tirelessly for the welfare of children.

Eleanor Roosevelt is remembered as one of America's most influential and fondly thought of First Ladies. Eleanor was also the single person most responsible for bringing about The Universal Declaration of Human Rights in 1948, that protects the rights of individuals irrespective of nationality, gender, race or religious belief. Eleanor was born in 1889, had lost both parents before the age of 10, and grew up with her grandmother. She said her emotionally harsh upbringing left her feeling fearful of everything and like an "ugly duckling" who might never become a swan. Married to the future President Franklin Roosevelt and bearing six children, Eleanor felt she lived a duty-bound existence of rigid conformity until her mid-life. It was only then, she feels, that she developed her own sense of individuality and a self-made career as a social campaigner.

Joanne Rowling OBE is the international best-selling author of the Harry Potter novels. Born in 1965, Joanne was brought up by committed and hard-working parents, and it was from her mother that she acquired her passion for reading and telling stories, since her mum was herself a voracious reader. After being head girl of her school and reading French literature at university, Joanne took simple temp jobs to give herself time for the attempt at two novels that would never see the light of day. Age 25, she met and was married for a short time to a native of Portugal. She'd moved there to teach English as a foreign language not long after her mother died of her ten year battle with Multiple Sclerosis. When her daughter Jessica was born in 1993, Joanne returned from Portugal to England to escape her physically abusive husband, and for two years she lived in financial poverty in Scotland. It was during this time that she suffered a bout of depression, but with the help of counselling she overcame this and went on the following year to train as a school teacher. Barely had this career begun to blossom, than she completed and eventually sold her first Harry Potter novel, and a year later was a full-time writer. Joanne now invests part of her fortune from her extraordinary literary success to help other single mothers in need.

Lady Diana Spencer was loved and respected the world-over as The Princess of Wales. Born 1961, Diana was six when her parents separated, and she grew up to become a nursery school teacher before marrying Prince Charles in 1981. Diana was a devoted mother to their two sons, the Princes William and Harry, and she was known for talking candidly and openly in public about her suicidal feelings, self-harming, her struggle with bulimia, and her eventual divorce. Before her tragic death in 1997, she was deeply involved with charities working to help children, homeless people, and AIDS sufferers, as well as with the campaign to ban land-mines.

Steven Spielberg is one of the most influential and successful figures in Hollywood film-making, with three Academy Awards among his many accolades. Born in small-town America in 1946, Steven grew up Jewish in a series of Christian suburbs, which has given him an affinity with the outcast and the isolated, a theme that Steven says binds all his movies. An amateur film-maker even before he entered high school, Steven had landed, by age 21, a seven-year contract as a television director with Universal Studios. Steven went on to make such modern movie classics as *Jaws, E.T., The Color Purple, Jurassic Park,* and *Saving Private Ryan,* and was able to fulfil his ambition to form a new production studio and music company, DreamWorks SKG. His experience making an epic account of the Holocaust, *Schindler's List,* led Steven to embrace his Jewish heritage and he subsequently established the *Righteous Persons Foundation* to further Jewish life in the USA, as well as the *Survivors of the Shoah Visual History Foundation*, which has recorded more than 50,000 Holocaust survivor testimonies. Steven remarried in 1991 to the actress, Kate Capshaw, with whom he makes a home for their seven children.

Bruce Springsteen, known by his millions of fans worldwide as 'The Boss', is an American rock singer and composer whose career has to date spanned some 40 years. Born to a blue-collar working-class family in 1949, Bruce was inspired to start a career in music when he saw Elvis on tv one night. He joined his first band in 1965, and pursued his dream against the wishes of his father. For many years, music provided an escape from the real world, and Bruce has spoken candidly about his difficulty with emotional intimacy. He has told how his wife helped him overcome such problems, and he is now the proud father of a son.

Dame Cicely Saunders founded St. Christopher's Hospice in London in 1967 and was made a Dame of the British Empire for pioneering the modern hospice movement. Born in 1918, Cicely abandoned a degree course at Oxford to go into wartime nursing. A back operation forced her to give that up, so she finished her degree and became a medical social worker. She has written that after being an unhappy child, she felt a calling to serve and help others who didn't fit in easily. Initially inspired to found a hospice movement by the death and bequest of a young Polish gentleman who she'd been nursing, it was the advice and support of a trusted mentor that persuaded Cicely to do a medical degree despite already being in her 30s. This she completed in 1957 at the unusually mature age of 39. The qualification and status this afforded her, allowed Cicely's innovative ideas to be better recognized within the medical establishment. In the half-century that has followed, 250 hospices in and around the UK, as well as many hospices world-wide, have all adopted her techniques and wholistic approach to the care of the dying and their loved-ones.

James Stewart was an Oscar-winning Hollywood actor (an Oscar won for his role in *The Philadelphia Story* playing opposite Katherine Hepburn and Cary Grant), and was widely revered as one of the golden-era greats. He went straight on from Hollywood in his mid-30s to become a highly decorated Commanding Officer of a U.S. bomber squadron based in Norfolk, England, throughout the Second World War, during which time he personally led many missions over enemy territory. Born in 1908 to the owner of a hardware store in Indiana, James first studied engineering at Princeton, changing to architecture, before falling care-freely into the film industry some time after graduation. Quite a man about town, James only married when he was age 41, and then went on to spend 45 years together with his wife, raising their twin daughters. James told how it also took him until his forties to accept his unusually slim, six foot two inch physique that weighed only nine stone. He was a fine accordian player from his early youth, and also became an extremely keen pilot of light aircraft in his time off from the studios in the 1930s. He spent much time in his final years writing poetry, and died in 1997.

Dame Kiri Te Kanawa was awarded the Order of New Zealand and made a Dame of the British Empire after her soprano performance at the wedding of Prince Charles and Lady Diana. Born as an illegitimate child in New Zealand in 1944, Kiri was adopted, and has said that knowing about her adoption from an early age helped develop her tenacious spirit. Kiri won a grant to train as a singer in London and has now set-up a charitable foundation to help struggling New Zealand singers and musicians have similar opportunities. Kiri met her Australian husband at a 'blind date' in 1967, and they adopted two children. Kiri says she was devastated when her marriage ended after 30 years, but setting up the charitable foundation has given her renewed confidence.

Alan Titchmarsh OBE is best known for presenting popular gardening programmes for BBC television, and is author of over 30 gardening books as well as best-selling novels. He counts as one of his greatest honours the privilege of designing the garden for former South African President Nelson Mandela. Born in Yorkshire in 1949, Alan has described his humble roots and a childhood of fun and innocence in his autobiography, *Trowel and Error*. He has been passionate about gardening for as long as he can remember, and when school proved a struggle, he happily started at age 15 to work his way up through plant nurseries and college right up to the Royal Botanic Gardens at Kew. Alan joined an amateur operatic society as a young man and through that interest met his wife, Alison. They live in Hampshire with their two daughters and plenty of pets.

Oprah Winfrey is probably the world's best known talk-show host, and a pioneering U.S. media executive, as well being an Oscar-nominated actress for her supporting role in Steven Spielberg's acclaimed movie, *The Color Purple*. Born in Mississippi in 1954, Oprah was at first raised by her grandmother on a farm in the southern states, where she began her performance career by reciting speeches at church at the age of three. From age six to thirteen, she lived with her mother and has spoken about how she suffered abuse and molestation at the hands of men during that desperately unhappy time. (As an adult, Oprah initiated a campaign to establish a national database of convicted child abusers, which came into law in 1993 as The Oprah Bill.) In her teenage years, young Oprah was finally sent to live across the other side of the country with her father, and she has attributed his supportive discipline to helping her achieve a place at university and her emerging career as a professional broadcaster. Oprah has always spoken frankly about her childhood traumas, her adult weight problems, and the pressures of media life, as well as her love, her faith and her friendships, and she is a major founder and contributor for many charitable causes.

Sir Terry Wogan is a BBC radio & television broadcaster. Born 1938 to a grocer father, Terry grew up in Limerick, Ireland, and remembers his childhood fondly. Terry recounts in his autobiography, *Is It Me?* that he went into banking after leaving college. Five years later, he answered a job advert and joined the Irish National Radio and TV Service as a newsreader and announcer. Terry puts his success down to good luck and he says he doesn't take himself nor his work too seriously. He has been happily married since 1967 and has two sons and a daughter. Knighted in 2005, Terry has been involved with the BBC charity, *Children in Need*, since its inception in 1979.

Tiger Woods has enjoyed exceptional success in golfing as an amateur and as a professional. Tiger was born in 1975, the son of a Thai mother and a retired Lieutenant Colonel in the U.S. Army. When he was just a toddler, Tiger started imitating his father playing golf, and feels that he has learned discipline, integrity and sportsmanship through the game, qualities he has tried to apply to the rest of his life. It is noteworthy that Tiger suffered from a stammer as a boy and attended a special school to overcome it. In 1996, Tiger set up a foundation to promote golf and non-sports related activities among disadvantaged youngsters, and says he finds that more gratifying than winning golf tournaments. Tiger married his Swedish fiancée in 2004 and is planning to start a family.

Zinedine Zidane is widely regarded by fans, players and managers alike as the world's finest footballer. The French captain until 2004, Zinedine, who is affectionately known as Zizou, led France to the world cup victory in 1998. Born in 1972 to Algerian parents, Zinedine grew up among other second generation immigrant families in a notoriously impoverished and tough estate in the suburbs of Marseilles. Zinedine takes great pride in his roots and is the life-president of the local football club. He is said to be extravert while on the soccer field, and introvert when off it. He and his wife, Veronique, who is a Spanish dancer, were married in 1992 and have two sons, Luca and Enzo. Zinedine takes an active part in their life, having breakfast with them in the morning, picking them up from school and helping with the homework. In addition to football, Zinedine has a passion for tennis and Formula-1 motor racing. Among his many personal and professional achievements, Zinedine has become the greatly admired face of young immigrant France and has campaigned boldly against racism.

* * *

**Respecting our planet's woodlands and forests,
and the fauna, flora and indigenous peoples
that rely upon them**

The first edition of 5,000 copies of 'Learning from Wonderful Lives' required about five tonnes of paper; which is the product of circa 120 trees. Good job, then, that it's printed on paper from sustainable forests. By using paper that comes from well-managed and sustainable forests, the paper industry can ensure a renewable supply of raw material as well as preservation of bio-diversity. Sustainable forestry is supported by the World Wildlife Fund, Greenpeace, Friends of the Earth and the Woodland Trust. Visit www.fsc-uk.org for advice on finding ethically responsible sources of wood, and sources of recycled and FSC-certified paper. Also visit www.saveordelete.com which is the Greenpeace website promoting better solutions for the wood, paper and publishing industries, solutions that do not endanger the world's ancient forests and the fauna, flora and indigenous peoples that rely upon them. Urgent measures are needed because as recently as May 2005, the BBC and the World Bank reported that an area the size of Belgium had been lost from Brazil's Amazon rain forest in just one single year of illegal logging.

* * *

St Christopher's Hospice

St Christopher's is a world leader in caring for the dying and those close to them. It is at the forefront of palliative care in the UK and worldwide.

Founded by Dame Cicely Saunders, OM, in 1967 St Christopher's continues to lead and inspire. Her philosophy remains at the heart of its care and outreach: "You matter because you are you".

St Christopher's mission 'to promote and provide skilled and compassionate palliative care of the highest quality' is implemented through an extensive education and training programme of courses for health and social care professionals involved in hospice care, both nationally and internationally.

St Christopher's is the largest provider of specialist palliative care education in the world. Over the last 37 years more than 50,000 students have trained at St Christopher's. Currently around 5,000 visitors come every year including health care professionals, officials and ministers from many governments.

We are a centre of excellence helping build networks which enable health professionals to share experience, skills and good practice and to support and learn from each other.

St Christopher's Hospice

St Christopher's Hospice
51-59 Lawrie Park Road
London SE26 6DZ
Te: 020 8768 4500
www.stchristophers.org.uk
info@stchristophers.org.uk

"When I decided to broaden my horizons and opportunities, I took what seemed at first a rather daunting step: I began a course with the Open University. This turned out to suit me very well because there were no entrance requirements and I could study in my spare time with their distance-learning methods. Pretty soon, I gained a diploma that helped earn me a postgraduate place at Cambridge University. The OU isn't free, but many of its students are in full-time work, and some are sponsored by their employer. Many also live outside the UK, which presents no problem at all. Based on my personal experience, and the reputation for excellence of its teaching standards and course materials, I can thoroughly recommend the Open University." (Nick Baylis)

Visit www.open.ac.uk or telephone
General Enquiries on 01908-653-231

Making Connections

When Research Psychiatrist, Professor George Vaillant of Harvard Medical School, asked a host of men and women well in to their eighties "What characterises wisdom or maturity?" they described it as ... *"The ability to step back and see a more helpful perspective, and in doing so, see the connectedness of things."*

With this in mind, where in our everyday lives beyond our own home might some of the ideas in this book prove helpful? Perhaps the local school, a neighbourhood group, or our place of work?

With whom could we discuss the possibilities over a cup of tea? And can I help?

To order another copy of *Wonderful Lives*
or send one as a gift, please go to:

www.nickbaylis.com

or

www.nicksbook.com

Alternatively, please telephone:

07890-680-925

Please note
Wonderful Lives is *not* available through high street shops
nor amazon.

To hear about my training workshops, lectures, and seminars
offered throughout the UK and overseas,
please visit www.nickbaylis.com

Thank you for reading

* * *